KU-636-646

PREFACE

This book originates from the NATO Advanced Study Institute
on Synthesis and Analysis Methods for Safety and Reliability
Studies held at Sogesta Conference Centre, Urbino, Italy, 3-14 July
1978. The Institute, co-directed by Prof. E.J. Henley and
Dr. G. Volta, was attended by 67 persons from twelve countries.
The focus of the Institute was on theoretical and applied aspects
of reliability and risk analysis methodologies.

The Institute was composed of lectures, workshops and guided
discussions. From the large quantity of written material that
was used and produced during the Institute, a number of papers
introducing the most relevant research results and trends in the
field have been selected. The papers have been edited, partly
rewritten and rearranged in order to obtain in the end an integrated exposition of methods and techniques for reliability analysis
and computation of complex systems.

The book is divided into four sections which correspond to
fairly homogeneous areas from a methodological point of view. Each
section is preceded by an introduction prepared by the Editors
which aims at helping the readers to put in perspective and appre-
ciate the contribution of each paper to the subject of the section.

ACKNOWLEDGMENTS

The Editors thank the authors for their cooperation in revising their papers to achieve a better integration of the text. They would also like to recognize the contribution made to this book by all the participants. In fact, their active participation in discussions is reflected in the content of many papers here published.

Finally the Editors take this opportunity to thank, also on behalf of all the participants in the Institute, the Scientific Affairs Division of NATO for the award of Institute funds to the Organizing Committee, and Sogesta for the facilities which have been provided.

STRATHCLYDE UNIVERSITY LIBRARY

30125 00115252 8

£31·18

ML

for ... ret... on or before

ANDERSONIAN LIBRARY
★
WITHDRAWN
FROM
LIBRARY
STOCK
★
UNIVERSITY OF STRATHCLYDE

Synthesis and Analysis
Methods for Safety
and Reliability Studies

Synthesis and Analysis Methods for Safety and Reliability Studies

Edited by

G. Apostolakis

University of California
Los Angeles, California

S. Garribba

Politecnico di Milano
Milan, Italy

and

G. Volta

C. E. C. Joint Research Centre
Ispra, Italy

PLENUM PRESS • NEW YORK AND LONDON
Published in cooperation with NATO Scientific Affairs Division

Library of Congress Cataloging in Publication Data

Nato Advanced Study Institute on Synthesis and Analysis Methods for Safety and Reliability
Studies, Urbino, 1978.
Synthesis and analysis methods for safety and reliability studies.

"Proceedings of the NATO Advanced Study Institute on Synthesis and Analysis Methods
for Safety and Reliability Studies, held . . . Urbino, Italy, July 3–14, 1978."
Includes index.
1. Reliability (Engineering)–Congresses. I. Apostolakis, G. II. Garribba, S. III. Volta, G.
IV. Title.
TS173.N366 1978   620'.004'5   79-21315
ISBN 0-306-40316-1

Proceedings of the NATO Advanced Study Institute on Synthesis and
Analysis Methods for Safety and Reliability Studies, held at SOGESTA Conference Centre,
Urbino, Italy, July 3–14, 1978

© 1980 Plenum Press, New York
A Division of Plenum Publishing Corporation
227 West 17th Street, New York, N.Y. 10011

All rights reserved

No part of this book may be reproduced, stored in a retrieval system, or transmitted,
in any form or by any means, electronic, mechanical, photocopying, microfilming,
recording, or otherwise, without written permission from the Publisher

Printed in the United States of America

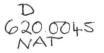

CONTENTS

SECTION 1 — BINARY SYSTEMS

SECTION 2 - MULTISTATE SYSTEMS. LOGIC DIAGRAMS

SECTION 3 - MULTISTATE SYSTEMS. OTHER METHODS

SECTION 1

BINARY SYSTEMS

Introduction by the Editors

In this section we have collected papers referring to the technique for reliability computation of systems which is usually called, mainly since the Reactor Safety Study [1]: "Fault-tree analysis". Essentially, this technique consists in a problem reduction based on the assumption that the behaviour of systems can be represented by an AND-OR graph linking the behaviour of a system with the behaviours of its subsystems.

AND-OR fault-trees came into use in the aerospace industry in the 1960's. Since then the technique has been progressively developed under many aspects. Two milestones in the development of this technique and concerning respectively the "logical" and the "numerical" analysis of the AND-OR graph merit to be mentioned. First was the non combinatorial algorithm, developed by Fussell [2] allowing the identification of minimal cut sets of the tree. Second was the finding of Vesely [3] that the failure intensity of a system can give an approximation for the failure rate, at least for highly reliable systems with repair times much shorter than the times to failure. This result opened the way for computing the reliability (probability of the first failure) of a system through the reliability of minimal cut sets.

In the most recent developments one can recognize various trends corresponding to different aims.

A first trend is towards the development of algorithms and better use of the computers in order to:

a)   save time in fault-tree analysis;
b)   assist the analyst for instance with interactive possibilities to make the technique more "reliable";
c)   introduce in the analysis heuristic approaches to use qualitative and quantitative information and to exploit the hierarchical structure of this information;
d)   allow fault-tree analysis by minicomputers.

A second trend is towards the extension of the modelling capability of the binary representation in order to deal with:

a)   non-coherent systems;
b)   multiphase systems;

1

c)   common cause failures.

A third trend is towards the refinement of the numerical analysis in order to estimate:

a)   effect of uncertainties on the overall results;
b)   error introduced by various approximations.

Broadly speaking we can say that a part of these improvements aims to refine the capability of the technique and another part is aiming to give an answer to one of the most serious objections in its use in risk analysis: i.e. the difficulty in appreciating what is wrong or what has been left out in the representation of a complex system [4].

The papers included in this section touch upon most of the development areas we have listed.

The paper by Astolfi et al., "Fault Tree Analysis by List Processing Techniques", describes a set of algorithms, based on direct manipulation of graphs by list-processing techniques, which allow to extend the modelling capability of the binary representation. The algorithms introduce the NOT operator and qualitative (marks) information at the level of gates and primary events. This procedure allows to tackle in an efficient way the analysis of large fault-trees. The algorithms have been implemented in various computer codes used currently in the batch mode, but they could be particularly suitable for interactive analysis also on minicomputers.

The paper of Blin et al., "PATREC a Computer Code for Fault-Tree Calculation" views the most recent developments of a computer code for fault-tree analysis also based on list-processing technique. The code is oriented towards direct computation of the top event availability without the use of minimal cut sets.

The critical problem of multiphase repairable systems is dealt with in an exhaustive way in the paper by Clarotti et al., "Repairable Multiphase Systems". The problem is approached by the Markov graph technique which gives the exact solution and by the fault-tree technique which can give an approximated solution.

The paper by Henley and Ong, "Reliability Parameters for Chemical Process Systems", shows a modification of the KITT (Kinetic Tree Theory) computer program which allows the analysis components, e.g. storage tanks and components in cold or hot standby, having particular time-dependent behaviour.

The following three papers of this section are short papers aiming to clarify the meaning and the implications of some basic concepts and models used in fault-tree analysis. The first short paper by Amendola et al., "About the definition of Coherency in Binary System Representation", attempts to clarify with examples the concept of non-coherent systems and proposes an operational classification based on the characteristics of the corresponding boolean function.

The paper by Parry, "Regeneration Diagrams", introduces and discusses the implications of the important concepts of the time-structure of failure and repair processes for components and systems. As an application the limitation of Vesely's approach to the system reliability is definitely clarified. It is interesting to remark the adaptation of the Faynman diagrams to reliability analysis as proposed by Parry. This technique is actually fairly exotic for reliability analysts.

Finally, the paper by Colombo, "Uncertainty Propagation in Fault Tree Analysis", shows how the structure of a fault-tree and the types of distribution can affect the uncertainty propagation in a fault-tree and gives some practical suggestions.

The papers in this section report achievements and they also show many directions in which we can expect significant developments in the near future, e.e.g non-coherent systems, computer aided fault-tree handling techniques.

REFERENCES

[1] U.S. Nuclear Regulatory Commission, "Reactor Safety Study", WASH-1400 (NUREG-75/014), NTIS, Springfield, Va. (Oct. 1975).

[2] J.B. Fussell, W.E. Vesely, "A new methodology for obtaining cut sets for fault-trees". Trans. ANS Nucl. Soc., 15:   (1972).

[3] W.E. Vesely, "A time-dependent methodology for fault-tree evaluation", Nuclear Engineering and Design, 13: 337 (1970).

[4] Fischhoff, Baruch, P. Slovic, S. Lichtenstein, "Fault-trees: Sensitivity of estimated failure probabilities to problem representation", J. of Experimental Psychology: Human perception and performance, 4: 342 (1978).

FAULT TREE ANALYSIS BY LIST-PROCESSING TECHNIQUES

M. Astolfi[1], S. Contini[2], C.L. Van den Muyzenberg[1], G. Volta[1]

[1] Commission of the European Communities, Joint Research Centre,
Ispra Establishment, 21020 Ispra (Va), Italy
[2] Sigen S.p.A., Via S. Caboto 5, Corsico, Milano, Italy

ABSTRACT

The paper outlines an approach for AND-OR-NOT fault-tree analysis which uses simultaneously logical or qualitative and numerical or quantitative information structured in the tree. The analysis is carried out in two steps: search of the most important minimal cut-sets (MCS), computation of the availability and reliability for the cut-sets and for top events. The paper describes in detail the algorithms applied in the first phase: for the simplification of the tree, for the use of the cut-off, for the evaluation of the error introduced by the cut-off, for the search of the cut-sets in order of importance taking into account quantitative (probability) and qualitative (dependencies between events or gates) information, for the optimization of the process of analysis in order to reduce the number of cut-sets to be minimized, for the analysis of the NOT operators. These algorithms are based on the use of list processing techniques for the direct manipulation of graphs. The algorithms have been implemented in computer codes SALP-3 and SALP-4 for which examples of application are given.

1. INTRODUCTION

This paper outlines the main characteristics and describes the main algorithms of a method for binary systems representation and analysis, which offers - to our opinion and experience - many practical advantages. The method is based on the use of list processing techniques for the direct manipulation of graphs. Various computer codes for fault-tree analysis have been implemented using this method. Early developments were obtained by the use of LISP programming language [1]. Later, PL/1 was considered for the implementation of the computer codes SALP-3 [2] and SALP-4 [5], this latter now under test.

Most parts of computer programmes for fault-tree analysis determine the whole set of MCS having an order not greater than a fixed value (logical cut-off). Then, on this set of MCS, they perform a sensitivity analysis which consists in determining the most important MCS through the assessment of certain parameters. This type of sensitivity analysis is called the "posterior sensitivity analysis".

However, practical cases exist for which this approach is not suitable; more precisely, when:
1)   the number of MCS is high;
2)   because MCS of an order greater than the maximum are discarded without verifying their importance.

Point 2) is important for the common mode failure analysis and when the tree contains the NOT gate, while for random failures analysis the problem does not exist. Nevertheless, non significant MCS of an order less than the maximum exist and they are always determined increasing the computer time. Therefore, a new approach has been made at the JRC, Ispra, to implement a computer programme which is able to analyse fault-trees and event-trees or whichever complexity.

The approach is called the "prior sensitivity analysis" in the sense that significant MCS of whichever order are searched without determining all the others (numerical cut-off). The description of the problems faced and the main characteristics of the algorithms implemented represent the subject of this contribution.

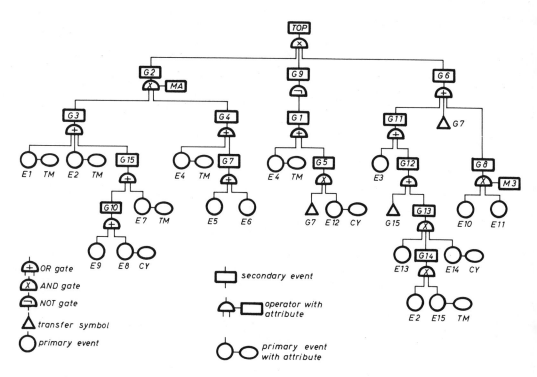

Fig. 1.   Example of a logical fault tree representation.

Assuming as a reference representation of the system the fault-tree model, i.e. a tree with the root corresponding to the top event, four types of information can be structured in it, as illustrated by Fig. 1.:

1) logical information, concerning the connection between the events, by the use of AND-OR-NOT operators;
2) numerical information: events probabilities;
3) generic non-numerical information associated both to the events and to the operators;
4) an order information concerning the operators (e.g. sequentiality).

The list processing is a technique by which it is possible to store and to easy handle data structures of whichever complexity, for example, trees and graphs. With the list processing, we have to use both the elementary structures and pointers. A pointer is the address of another word memory. An elementary structure is used to store the characteristics of the gates and the primary events. The pointer is needed to join the elementary structures to each other.

It is interesting to remark that by the list processing technique, the internal representation of the tree corresponds to the logical one. This way of storing the tree gives a great flexibility in setting-up efficient algorithms for the problem of minimal cut-sets determination. Moreover, the memory space required for the analysis of a fault-tree is proportional to the complexity of the fault-tree itself. This means that there is not any limitation in the complexity of the tree to be analyzed; the only limitation is, of course, the dimension of the computer memory.

The non-numerical information (attributes) is easily handled and offers a solution to all the problems that involve the consideration of multiple attributes for the same event, e.g. problems of location analysis, common mode failure, etc.

The analysis of the fault-tree, structured with the above mentioned quantitative and qualitative information, is carried out in two steps:
- search of the most important minimal cut-sets (MCS);
- computation of the reliability parameters for the cut-sets and for the top event.

The first step involves the application of various algorithms:
- for the simplification of the tree;
- for the use of the cut-off;
- for the evaluation of the error introduced by the cut-off;
- for the search of the cut-sets in order of importance;
- for the optimization of the process of analysis in order to reduce the number of cut-sets to be minimized;
- for the analysis of the NOT operators.

The second step involves problems of numerical computation.

In this paper we will consider in detail only the first step. As a conclusion we will just mention some examples of application of the computer codes implemented with this method.

2. SIMPLIFICATION OF THE TREE

Given a tree as it is drawn by an analyst, it is convenient first to transform it into an equivalent and much simpler one. This transformation can dramatically reduce time and effort for further elaborations. The fundamental steps are as follows:

1) A cascade of gates of the same type is replaced by a single gate. The pairing does not take place if the descendant gate is repeated. This step is also applied to each repeated subtree;

2) A further reduction is performed considering the various repeated subtrees (a subtree is a tree having as root a secondary event). In the original tree, various types of repeated subtrees are present:

   a) subtrees in which the leaves are primary events that are not repeated in any other place outside the tree;
   b) subtrees in which the leaves are primary events or transfer symbols (i.e. a reference to another repeated subtree) and at least one is repeated in the subtree, but does not appear outside it;
   c) subtrees in which the leaves are primary events or transfer symbols and at least one appears in some other place in the tree (outside the subtree).

   The distinction among the different types of subtrees above quoted is useful in order to perform a simple reduction.
   These different cases are treated as follows. For case a), the subtree can be substituted by a unique compound event whose name is the name of the top of the subtree itself, whereas in the cases b) and c), the subtree remains connected to the tree.

3) The unrepeated primary events that descend directly from the same gate are grouped into a single compound event. This step is also applied to each repeated subtree. Each of these compound events, in order to apply later the cut-off procedure, is labelled with the probability value P, corresponding to the most important cut-set contained. This value is easily obtained by sum and product of numerical operations due to the absence of repeated events.

3. ANALYSIS OF AND-OR TREES WITHOUT REPEATED EVENTS

We prefer to illustrate our methodology at first on trees without repeated events in order to point out its main characteristics.

3.1. Search of MCS in order of importance - SALP 1 algorithm

The absence of repeated events makes the problem very simple because of the absence of non-minimal cut-sets. Given in input a threshold probability L_{lim}, we can assess very simply more restrictive thresholds for the subtrees in order to decrease

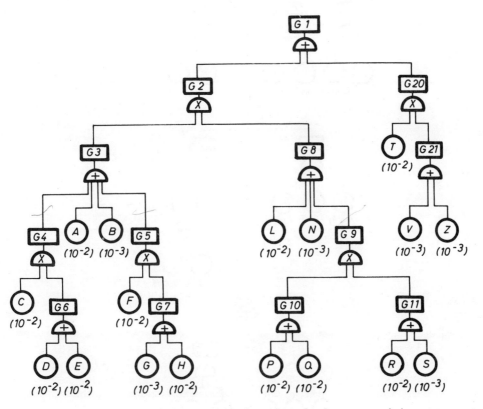

Fig. 2. SALP-1 algorithm. Example of a fault tree without repeated events.

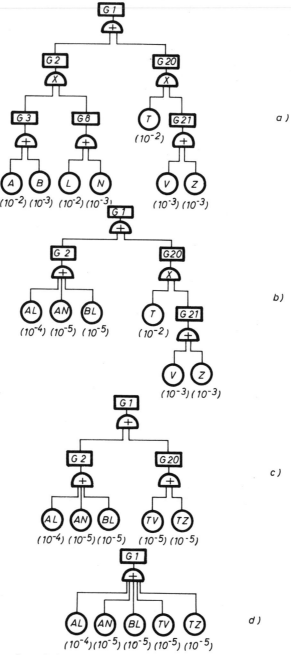

Fig. 3. SALP-1 algorithm. Tree reduction and MCS determination.

TABLE 1 : FAULT TREE INFORMATION

→ i

Gate Gx	G6	G4	G7	G5	G3	G10	G11	G9	G8	G2	G21	G20	G1
P (Gx)	10^{-2}	10^{-4}	10^{-2}	10^{-4}	10^{-2}	10^{-2}	10^{-2}	10^{-4}	10^{-2}	10^{-4}	10^{-3}	10^{-5}	10^{-4}

Gx indicates the generic gate of the tree. P (Gx) means the probability of the most important cut-set descending from Gx.

TABLE 2 : DETERMINATION OF THE GATE DEPENDENT THRESHOLDS

Gate	Type	Threshold probability	Notes
G1	OR	$L_{(G1)} = L_{lim} = 3.10^{-6}$	L_{lim} is assigned to G1.
G20	AND	$L_{(G20)} = L_{(G1)} = 3.10^{-6}$	Since G1 is an OR gate, its threshold is assigned to its descendants subtrees.
G2	AND	$L_{(G2)} = L_{(G1)} = 3.10^{-6}$	
G3	OR	$L_{(G3)} = L_{(G2)}/P_{(G8)} =$ $3.10^{-6}/10^{-2} = 3.10^{-4}$	Since $P_{G3} > L_{G3}$, subtree G3 is retained. The same value is associated to its descendant.
G4	AND	$L_{(G4)} = L_{(G3)} = 3.10^{-4}$	Since $P_{(G4)} < L_{(G4)}$, subtree G4 is deleted.
G5	AND	$L_{(G5)} = L_{(G3)} = 3.10^{-4}$	$P_{(G5)} < L_{(G5)}$; The subtree G5 is deleted.
G8	OR	$L_{(G8)} = L_{(G2)}/P_{(G3)} =$ $3.10^{-6}/10^{-2} = 3.10^{-4}$	$P_{(G8)} > L_{(G8)}$. Subtree G8 is retained.
G9	AND	$L_{(G9)} = L_{(G8)} = 3.10^{-4}$	$P_{(G9)} < L_{(G9)}$. Subtree G9 is deleted.
G21	AND	$L_{(G21)} = L_{(G20)}/P_{(T)} =$ $3.10^{-6}/10^{-2} = 3.10^{-4}$	$P_{(G21)} > L_{(G21)}$. Subtree G21 is retained.

the number of operations necessary for the determination of the cut-sets. (Gate dependent cut-off).

The fundamental steps of the algorithm are the following:
- fault-tree information;
- determination of the most restrictive threshold values;
- determination of the important MCS of whichever order.

To explain the algorithm by means of an example, let us consider the fault-tree
given in Fig. 2, where A, B, C, ... represent the primary events and the number under
parenthesis the corresponding probabilities. The visiting order of the tree, for each
step, is given by the sequence of its gates represented in various tables.

First step:
The tree is visited from the bottom to the top (see Table 1). The generic gate AND
is labelled with the product of the probabilities of its descendants, while for the generic gate OR the maximum value is taken. It is important to remark that, after the
information process of the tree, the last column of Table 1 gives $P(G1)$ which represents the probability of the most important cut-set of the tree. In the following this
probability will be indicated as P_{max}.

Second step:
The tree is visited from the top to the bottom in order to compute more restrictive
thresholds for those subtrees that can give cut-sets whose probabilities are greater
than or equal to L_{lim}. We consider Table 2 and Fig. 2. L_{lim} is first assigned to the top
gate G1. Since G1 is an OR gate, L_{lim} is also assigned to G20 and G2. Then, the
analysis proceeds with the left descendant G2. G2 is of type AND, and it can contribute to produce significant cut-sets if

$$L(G3) \equiv \frac{L(G2)}{P(G8)} \quad \text{is less than } P(G3).$$

Successively, the probability of the descendants AND gates and primary events of
G3 are compared with $L(G3)$. The analysis of subtree G3 leads to the cancellation
of subtrees G4 and G5 because they cannot significantly contribute to the top event
probability. The same procedure is applied for the assessment of $L(G8)$, $L(G9)$ and
$L(G21)$. From Table 2 it can be seen that subtree G9 is deleted.

Third step:
At this point the tree can be reduced from the bottom to the top by replacing the
subtrees by the cut-sets (Figs. 3 a - d). It can be noticed that, during the reduction,
the cut-set BN is neglected since its probability is less than $L(G2)$. In practice, the
second and third steps are performed together visiting the tree only once.

3.2. Bounds for the relative error introduced by the cut-off and choice of the cut-off limit

The algorithm described in the previous paragraph finds the MCS in order of
importance applying the cut-off procedure. This procedure allows to search and to
compute only the significant MCS without computing the others. This "a priori"

cut-off process has the advantage of saving both computer time and memory space. But it raises the problem of assessing the error introduced in the top-event probability estimation. This error is due to the fact that MCSs having probabilities less than L_{lim} are neglected. In the following, we will consider for the TOP probability the upper approximation given by:

$$P_{NTOP} = \Sigma \; P(MCS)$$
$$\text{over all MCS}$$

Therefore the error will consist of:

$$E = \Sigma \; P(MCS)$$
$$\text{over all MCS with } P < L_{lim}$$

A first bound for this error can be found in the following way.
Let us define:

N = the total number of MCS of a tree
n = the number of MCS having a probability greater than L_{lim}
P_{NTOP} = the probability of the top event, first bound approximation, obtained by the summation of the probabilities of the N MCS
P_{TOP} = the probability of the top event obtained by the summation of the probabilities of the n MCS.

Obviously,

$$E = P_{NTOP} - P_{TOP} \tag{1}$$

We can find a bound of the relative error E due to cut-off in two ways. The first way assumes that we do not know P_{NTOP} but we can know N.   As:

$$P_{NTOP} < L_{lim} \; (N-n) + P_{TOP} \tag{2}$$

we get:

$$E_1 < L_{lim} \; (N-n) \tag{3}$$

The (3) gives an upper bound of the error provided that N is computed. N can be easily determined by simple operations of sum and product visiting the tree from the bottom to the top.

The second way assumes a bound $P_{NTOPmax}$ for P_{NTOP} which is different from that given by (2). The error E_2 can be found by applying the ERROR algorithm. According to this algorithm the tree is visited from the bottom to the top. The generic AND gate is labelled with the product of the probabilities of its descendants, while for the generic OR gate we take the sum of the values of the descendants (instead of the maximum value as in the case of P_{max}).

TABLE 3 : SALP-1 ALGORITHM - Automatic determination of L_{lim} for the fault-tree of Fig. 2 - Determination of E_r.

Gate	Type	P_{max}	P_{NTOP}	N
G6	OR	10^{-2}	2.10^{-2}	2
G4	AND	10^{-4}	2.10^{-4}	2
G7	OR	10^{-2}	$1,1.10^{-2}$	2
G5	AND	10^{-4}	$1,1.10^{-4}$	2
G3	OR	10^{-2}	$1,131.10^{-2}$	6
G10	OR	10^{-2}	2.10^{-2}	2
G11	OR	10^{-2}	$1,1.10^{-2}$	2
G9	AND	10^{-4}	$2,2.10^{-4}$	4
G8	OR	10^{-2}	$1,122.10^{-2}$	6
G2	AND	10^{-4}	$1,27.10^{-4}$	36
G21	OR	10^{-3}	2.10^{-3}	2
G20	AND	10^{-5}	2.10^{-5}	2
G1	OR	10^{-4}	$1,47.10^{-4}$	38

$\uparrow$ P_{max} $\uparrow$ P_{NTOP} $\uparrow$ N

In the case of trees without repeated events, $P_{NTOPmax}$ coincides with P_{NTOP} ; therefore, being

$$E_2 \equiv E$$

the probability assessment of the set of neglected cut-sets is always possible.

The importance of balancing the need of reducing the error with the convenience of assuming an L_{lim} as high as possible in order to reduce the analysis time is evident.

An "a priori" determination of L_{lim} can be done assuming, from (3), $E_1 = P_{max}$. Then, conservatively, we can write:

$$L_{lim\ 1} = \frac{P_{max}}{N-n} \leqslant \frac{P_{max}}{N-1} \tag{4}$$

Assuming $L_{lim\ 1} = \frac{P_{max}}{N-1}$, it is sure that E_1 will always be less than P_{max} .

Another way for determining L_{lim} can be derived directly from

$$E_r = \frac{P_{NTOP} - P_{TOP}}{P_{NTOP}} \tag{5}$$

From (2) we get:

$$E_r = L_{lim} (N - n) / P_{NTOP} \tag{6}$$

This way implies the knowledge of the exact value of P_{NTOP}. We remember that exact knowledge of P_{NTOP} is possible only in the case of tree without repeated events. Assuming from (6) a certain value of E_r we get:

$$L_{lim\ 2} = \frac{E_r\ P_{NTOP}}{(N-n)} \leqslant \frac{E_r\ P_{NTOP}}{(N-1)} \tag{7}$$

Table 3 explains, on the sample tree of Fig. 2, the application of the assessment of E and L_{lim} .

Once P_{max}, P_{NTOP} and N have been determined during the first step, the significant MCS are searched using a top-event threshold value equal to:

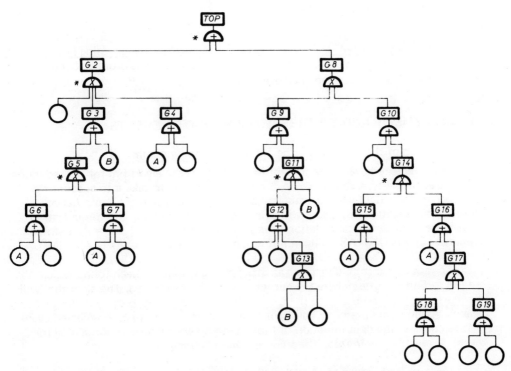

Fig. 4. Fault tree illustrating those gates on which the minimization must be performed.

$$L_{lim} = \frac{P_{max}}{N-1} = \frac{10^{-4}}{37} = 2.7 \cdot 10^{-6}$$

The first bound of the top-event probability is given by:

$$P_{TOP} = P(AL) + P(AW) + P(BL) + P(TV) + P(BZ) = 1.4 \cdot 10^{-4}$$

Now,

$$E = P_{NTOP} - P_{TOP} = 7 \cdot 10^{-6} \rightarrow E_{r\%} = \frac{7 \cdot 10^{-6}}{1.4 \cdot 10^{-4}} \cdot 100 = 5\%$$

From what has been said it is obvious that the problem of assessing both E and L_{lim} is trivial in the case of trees without repeated events. This problem becomes much more difficult when repeated events are present.

4. ANALYSIS OF AND-OR TREES WITH REPEATED EVENTS

4.1. Location of the gates where the cut-sets have to be minimized

When repeated events are present in a fault-tree, the algorithm for the reduction of the tree of the type shown in Fig. 3 must be modified to take into account the presence of redundant and non-minimal cut-sets. At each step the computer must apply a minimization procedure which is very time-consuming. This minimization procedure involves the cancellation of redundant cut-sets $(AB + AB = AB)$ of non-minimal cut-sets $(A + AB = A)$, and of redundant events in cut-sets $(AAB = AB)$.

To reduce the computer time, an efficient algorithm has been found which allows to find the gates where the cut-sets have to be minimized. The algorithm will be illustrated with reference to the tree of Fig. 4. In this tree, only two repeated events A and B are present. The algorithm must be applied to each repeated event. Let us consider the determination of those gates on which cut-sets containing the event A must be minimized. The steps are the following:

- For each occurrence of A the path, i.e. the sequence of gates, from A towards TOP, are listed;
- The number of times k that a gate is crossed by the successive paths considered is determined;
- The gates with $k = 1$ are deleted. When gates have the same k, they are also deleted, except the first one. (In fact, the same k means that between the two gates there are no repetitions of A).

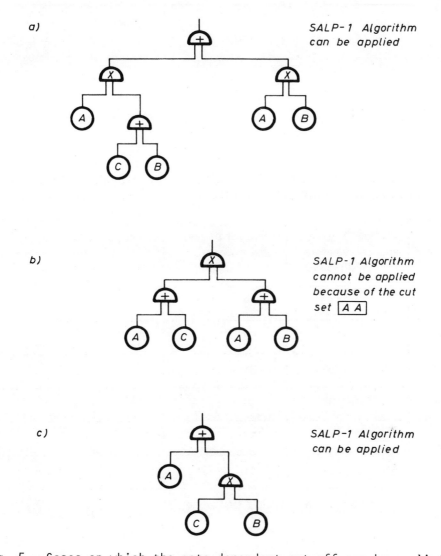

Fig. 5.   Cases on which the gate dependent cut off can be applied or not.

TABLE 4 : NUMBER OF GATES ON WHICH THE MINIMIZATION
PROCEDURE MUST BE APPLIED

Tree	Number of gates and leaves before the simplification		Number of gates and leaves after simplification		Number of gates on which the minimization must be performed
1	125	113	68	57	20
2	94	108	57	51	17
3	37	69	21	21	5
4	45	34	30	22	9
5	122	116	37	43	5
6*	45	31	41	27	5

* This tree is the one given in Table 7 (see section 7).

Example:

1st path	G6	G5	G3	G2	TOP
2nd path	G7	G5	G3	G2	TOP
3rd path	G4	G2	TOP		
4th path	G15	G14	G10	G8	TOP
5th path	G16	G14	G10	G8	TOP

Combination of various paths:

Gate	G6,	G5,	G3,	G2,	TOP,	G7,	G4,	G15,	G14,	G10,	G8,	G16
	1	2	2	3	5	1	1	1	2	2	2	1

Gates where the minimization of cut-sets containing event A must be performed, are: G5, G2, TOP, G14.

In practice, the procedure which locates those gates on which the minimization must be performed, visits the tree only once and operates on a vector in which the gates are stored. Obviously, when repeated events are not contained in the tree, the minimization must not be applied. In order to demonstrate the usefulness of this algorithm, we have analyzed some trees without the algorithm and the same trees with it: table 4 summarizes the results.

4.2. Search of MCS in order of importance

The efficiency of the SALP-1 algorithm described in the former section, resides essentially on the fact that the cut-off limit for gates (subtrees) depends on their position in the tree. The question arises if and how the same algorithm could be used in fault-trees with repeated events. We have at this point to distinguish two types of subtrees. In one type we have no repetitions of the same event in the same subtree having root in an AND gate (Fig. 5a). In other words, cut-sets with a redundant event do not exist. In the other type we have repetitions of the same event in the subtree, so that cut-sets with redundant event do exist (Fig. 5b).

For the first type of subtree the SALP-1 algorithm can be still applied, with the addition of a minimization procedure applied to the gates identified by the algorithm described in 4.1.

For the second type of subtree SALP-1 can be still applied provided that some transformations are performed. These transformations can be applied to the logical information (structure of the tree) or to the numerical information (input probabilities).

The logical transformation should modify the tree in order to obtain a tree of the type of Fig. 5c, that is, in order to eliminate redundant events in cut-sets. This transformation is shown in detail in [3].

The numerical transformation is performed associating to each occurrence of a repeated event a fictitious probability determined as follows. In general, if to the generic event with probability Q repeated n times is associated a fictitious value $Q^* = (Q)^{1/n}$, the algorithm of section 3 is still applicable. Referring to Fig. 4, to the events A and B we would associate respectively $(Q_A)^{1/5}$ and $(Q_B)^{1/3}$. But, when n increases, the fictitious values become too high and the number of cut-sets - which is not excluded from the cut-off - is also too high.

A more specific fictitious probability "topological dependent" can be then associated to the occurrence of each repeated event. For this, the algorithm described in section 4.1. can be easily modified. Using this new algorithm we can de-termine the effective number of repetition k, that is the number of times that the event can be repeated in a cut-set. So, with reference to the example of Fig. 4, we will associate to the occurrence of A :

$$Q^*_{A_1} = \sqrt[3]{Q_A} \quad \text{to the occurrence of A descending from G2,}$$

$$Q^*_{A_2} = \sqrt[2]{Q_A}, \quad \text{to the occurrence of A descending from G14}$$

Therefore, once we have labelled the events with the fictitious probabilities, we can apply the SALP-1 algorithm with the addition of a minimization procedure applied at the gates identified with the algorithm described in section 4.1.

In the next section it will be shown that also the possibility of assessing the error introduced by the cut-off requires the numerical modification described.

4.3. Bounds of the relative error introduced by the cut-off

The methods for the computation of the error shown in section 3.2. are still applicable to fault-trees in which the "numerical transformation" has been performed. But the bounds obtained, when events with many repetitions are present, could be too conservative depending on the number and probability of non-minimal cut-sets. In fact, let us consider the formulas of section 3.2. and comment the various quanti-ties when repeated events are present. Let us consider the first formula:

$$E_1 = L_{\lim} (N - n).$$

Applying the simple computation approach mentioned in 3.2., N will include minimal and non-minimal cut-sets, so it will be higher than the number of MCS. Therefore E_1 will give always a bound, which could be too conservative. Let us then consider the second formula:

$$E = P_{NTOP} - P_{TOP} < P_{NTOPmax} - P_{TOP} = E_2$$

The error algorithm which finds $P_{NTOPmax}$, when events with many repetitions are present, gives a result that could be still more conservative than that obtained by the first formula, according to the relative weight of non-minimal cut-sets with $P > L_{\lim}$. Therefore, a more efficient algorithm has been implemented. In this case, the error is given by the sum of those MCS (and a certain number of non-minimal

TABLE 5 : OUTPUT DATA FOR VARIOUS TREES ALREADY MENTIONED IN TABLE 4

Tree	Number of gates	Number of leaves	Number of re-peated events	Maximum repetition factor k_M	L_{lim}	P_{TOP}	n_R	E	Time sec
2	57	51	36	30	10^{-9}	$2,02.10^{-5}$	66	$9,37.10^{-6}$	32
3	21	21	16	5	10^{-8}	$1,02.10^{-3}$	41	$1,92.10^{-4}$	10.8
4	30	22	12	8	10^{-6}	$3,48.10^{-3}$	12	$1,3.10^{-4}$	7
5	37	43	23	4	10^{-7}	$1,4.10^{-5}$	6	$2,42.10^{-6}$	18.2
6	41	27	7	2	10^{-7}	$1,67.10^{-5}$	18	$1,64.10^{-8}$	6.75

cut-sets) having probability less than L_{lim}. This new upper bound is less conservative than the others [5].

Table 5 shows the estimation of the top-event probability and of the residual error for various trees after the simplification phase. The n_R MCS obtained, are those of the simplified tree.

5. ANALYSIS OF AND-OR-NOT TREES

The problem of the analysis of fault-trees in which NOT gates are present merits some preliminary clarifications. In fact, this problem offers various degrees of difficulties according to the various types of boolean functions that correspond to the given fault-tree. In many practical cases, fault-trees with NOT gates are used to analyze the OR of mutually exclusive non primary events, or the AND between a fault-tree and the complement of another fault-tree. In these cases the corresponding boolean function admits only one minimal disjunctive normal form which is at the same time complete and irredundant. The algorithms shown in the previous sections are still applicable. The only new problems that have to be tackled correspond to:

1) the need of cancelling cut-sets which are impossible because they contain an event and its complement;
2) the need of enlarging the cut-off criteria in order to handle cut-sets of very high order containing many complement events.

Simple approaches to these problems and particularly to the second one have been implemented. In practice, it is assumed that the probability of the complements of primary events is approximately equal to one. In the most general case, however, the boolean function can admit only one minimal disjunctive form which is not complete or can admit more than one minimal form. This more general case can be approached in two ways.
A first approach through the following phases:
-    determination of all prime implicants;
-    search of irredundant forms;
-    search of the minimal irredundant form.

Another way, which is faster than the previous one, avoids the determination of all the prime implicants but is addressed to the determination of an irredundant form which is not necessarily minimal, but it can be considered near-minimal as it contains all the "essential prime implicants" common to all the irredundant forms. We outline the algorithm for the search of this near-minimal INF. Detailed information is given in [4].

The algorithm consists in the transformation of a disjunctive normal form (DNF) into an irredundant normal form (INF) by deleting both superfluous literals and superfluous prime implicants [6]. This transformation does not need the determination of the complete set of prime implicants (PIF). However, with some modification of the algorithm, the PIF can also be obtained.

   Before describing the main characteristics of the algorithm, we give some definitions. A literal is called biform if, in the boolean function, it appears in two forms: negative and affirmative; monoform if it appears in one form only. A fundamental conjunction ψ is defined as a sequence of literals joined by the logic operator AND. E.g., $A\overline{B}C$, $BC\overline{D}E$ are fundamental conjunctions. One defines as disjunctive normal form V the disjunction of fundamental conjunctions, i.e. a sequence of fundamental conjunctions joined by the OR operator. An example of DNF is the following:

$$V = AB + \overline{B}CD + \overline{D}BE + HFG + \overline{A}D\overline{B}$$

   A fundamental conjunction ψ is called a prime implicant of V if and only if ψ implies V (i.e. if ψ is true, V is also true), but V is not logically implied by any other fundamental conjunction contained in ψ. That is, any fundamental conjunction obtained by eliminating one or more literals of ψ does not logically imply V. If ψ is an implicant and ϕ a DNF, one says that ψ is superfluous in $\phi + \psi$ when ϕ is logically equivalent to $\phi + \psi$. If α is a literal, $\overline{\psi}$ a fundamental conjunction and ϕ a DNF, one says that α is superfluous in $\alpha\psi + \phi$ if $\psi + \phi$ is logically equivalent to $\alpha\psi + \phi$.

   The expansion theorem (Shannon theorem) can be stated as follows:
A boolean function $f(x_1, x_2, x_3, ..., x_n)$ can be written as $x_i \cdot R_1 + x_i R_0$, where
$R_1 = f(x_1, ..., x_{i-1}, 1, x_{i+1}, ..., x_n)$
$R_0 = f(x_1, ..., x_{i-1}, 0, x_{i+1}, ..., x_n)$

R_1 and R_0 are called residues of $f(x_1, ..., x_n)$ with respect to x_i.
The method is articulated in two steps: expansion and reduction.

Step 1 : Expansion
This step makes use of the Shannon theorem and of another function which we call min (x). This function, applied to the boolean expression x, minimizes it deleting prime implicants, which contain other implicants, and applying the identity:

$$xy + \overline{x}yz = xy + yz. \quad \text{(If } z = 1, \text{ we have } \overline{x}y + xy = y\text{).}$$

The DNF is first expanded with respect to the most repeated variable. Then the function min is applied to the residues. If the generic residue contains at least a biform variable, it is further expanded and minimized. These operations must be applied until there is not any residue containing biform events. The recursive application of expansion + minimization allows to transform a DNF into an equivalent boolean expression containing residues in which biform events do not appear. It follows that these latter are minimal.

   Let us consider, as an example, the following DNF:

$$V = ABC + \overline{A}CD + B\overline{E}G + EFG + \overline{D}E\overline{G} + AE\overline{G} + CDE + \overline{C}EF +$$
$$\overline{A}D\overline{G} + B\overline{E}\overline{G} \tag{1}$$

Now,

$$\underline{\min} (V) = ABC + \overline{A}CD + EFG + \overline{D}E\overline{G} + AE\overline{G} + CDE +$$
$$\overline{C}EF + \overline{A}D\overline{G} + B\overline{E}$$

Expanding with respect to the variable E and minimizing the residues, we obtain:

$$V = E \, [ABC + FG + \overline{D}\overline{G} + A\overline{G} + CD + \overline{C}F] \, + \, \overline{E} \, [\overline{A}CD + \overline{A}D\overline{G} + B]$$

The first residue is then expanded with respect to C and the second one with respect to D. After the minimization, we obtain a boolean function equivalent to (1)

$$V = E \, [C \, (AB + F + \overline{G} + D) \, + \, \overline{C} \, (\overline{D}\overline{G} + A\overline{G} + F)] \, +$$

$$\underbrace{\qquad R_{11} \qquad}_{} \underbrace{\qquad}_{R_1} \qquad R_{10}$$

$$\overline{E} \, [D \, (\overline{A}C + B) \, + \, \overline{D} \, (\overline{A}\overline{G} + B)]$$

$$\underbrace{R_{01}}_{} \underbrace{\quad}_{R_0} \underbrace{R_{00}}_{} \qquad\qquad\qquad (2)$$

Expression (2) is no more expansible because residues R_{11}, R_{10}, R_{01} and R_{00} do not contain biform variables.

Step 2 : Reduction

The reduction procedure allows to obtain one of the irredundant normal forms analyzing expression (2) starting from the innermost terms. The typical subexpression can be represented in the following way:

$$yR_1 + \overline{y}R_0 \qquad\qquad\qquad (3)$$

where R_1 and R_0 are the residues, and y, $\overline{y}$ the variables with respect to which the expansion theorem was previously applied.

To obtain the irredundant form, a precedure by which it is possible, starting from (3) with R_1 and R_0 irredundant to obtain a new irredundant form, must be found. This in its turn represents the residue of another variable. The repeated application of this operation results in a final irredundant form.

We define the function reduce [x] that, applied to (3), deletes both superfluous literals and superfluous prime implicants. Referring to expression (2) we have:

$$\underline{\text{reduce}} \, [R_1] \, = \, ABC + CD + F + \overline{D}\overline{G} + A\overline{G}$$

$$\underline{\text{reduce}} \, [R_0] \, = \, \overline{A}CD + \overline{A}D\overline{G} + B$$

The equivalent boolean expression is now the following:

$$V = E[ABC + CD + F + \overline{D}\overline{G} + A\overline{G}] + \overline{E}[\overline{A}CD + \overline{A}\overline{D}\overline{G} + B]$$

Now,

$$\underline{reduce}[V] = CDE + EF + AE\overline{G} + B\overline{E} + ABC + \overline{A}CD + \overline{A}\overline{D}\overline{G} \qquad (4)$$

Expression (4) represents one of the irredundant forms of (1). If the irredundant form is unique, then it is also minimal, and constitutes the outcome of our algorithm.

We have already seen that, by the list processing approach, the location of those gates on which the minimization must be performed becomes very easy. In a similar way we can locate those gates on which the algorithm for assessing the INF must be applied.

It is also possible to use the cut-off rule to obtain the most important prime implicants of the INF assigning a probability value equal to 1 to the biform events. This is useful when in the fault-tree there are both biform and monoform events.

In order to have an idea about the efficiency of the algorithm, we have applied it to a certain number of DNFs taken from [7] and also analyzed by Caldarola in [8]. The difference in the number of prime implicants of the irredundant form obtained, and the number of prime implicants of the minimal (smallest) irredundant form is given in Table 6.

TABLE 6

DNF	minimal irredundant form	near-minimal irredundant form
1	3	3
2	3	3
3	7	7
4	8	8
5	12	12
6	17	18

6. ANALYSIS OF FAULT-TREES WITH DEPENDENCY BETWEEN EVENTS

The list processing technique is a powerful tool for dealing with "qualitative" information to be linked to primary events or gates. Specific "marks" or "attributes" inserted at gate level or at primary event level can represent all types of dependency between gates or between events: statistical dependence, sequentiality, common failure susceptibility, etc.

When the fault-tree contains one or more attributes, they are treated as follows. First of all, the attribute associated to the generic gate is inserted to all the primary events contained in the subtree. Then, for the cut-off rule, the probability of these primary events could be considered equal to the unity or to some value given by the analyst, according to the meaning he wants to associate.

The attributes associated with the primary events and gates are given, in output, in the list of minimal cut-sets.

In order to better explain how the non-numerical information is dealt with, let us consider two simple examples concerning two partial cut-sets descending from an AND gate.

The first example shows an application of the attributes for the common cause analysis. Let us consider the following situation which arises during the MCS deter- mination.

$$
\left(
\begin{array}{cc}
\text{PUMP} & \text{SWITCH} \\
\text{*UM} & \\
 & \text{*VB} \\
\text{*FR} & \text{*FR}
\end{array}
\right)
\quad \underline{\text{AND}} \quad
\left(
\begin{array}{cc}
\text{PUMP} & \text{VALVE} \\
\text{*UM} & \\
 & \text{*VB} \\
\text{*FR} & \text{*FR}
\end{array}
\right)
$$

Here, we suppose that the primary event PUMP is subjected to the hymidity (UM) and to the fire (FR), whereas events SWITCH and VALVE are both subjected to the vibration (VB) and to the fire.

The resulting combination, which is supposed to be a MCS is the following:

PUMP	SWITCH	VALVE
*UM		
	*VB	*VB
*FR	*FR	*FR

It can be seen that the most important external event is the fire. It can, when occurs, lead to the failure of the system and, consequently, the analyst must take the proper action to eliminate this situation.

Another external event of interest is the vibration which affects two components. Finally, the event UM is not important because it affects only one element.

The application of the attributes to the common cause failure analysis is the most intuitive but not the only one. In fact, other problems could be solved; for example, one or more attributes could be used to identify those cut-sets in which the sequence of failure does exist, or in which the delay plays a significant role.

The following example illustrates a trivial case of sequential events:

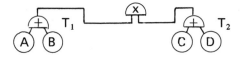

TABLE 7 : SIMPLE FAULT TREE OF A SIMPLIFIED
SCRAM SYSTEM

TOP	AND	G2	G3		
G2	OR	G4	E28		
G4	AND	G6	G7		
G6	OR	E30	E31	G10	
G10	2/3	G14	G15	G16	
G14	OR	E38	E52		
G15	OR	E39	E53		
G16	OR	E40	E54		
G12	2/4	G20	G21	G22	G23
G3	OR	G5	E29		
G5	AND	G8	G9		
G8	OR	E34	E35	G11	
G9	OR	E36	E37	G13	
G11	2/3	G17	G18	G19	
G17	OR	E45	E52		
G18	OR	E46	E53		
G19	OR	E47	E54		
G13	2/4	G24	G25	G26	G27
G24	OR	E48	E58		
G25	OR	E49	E59		
G26	OR	E50	E60		
G27	OR	E51	E61		
G7	OR	E32	E33	G12	
G20	OR	E41	E58		
G21	OR	E42	E59		
G22	OR	E43	E60		
G23	OR	E44	E61		

TABLE 8 : PRIMARY EVENTS DATA FOR THE SAMPLE TREE
OF TABLE 7

Events	Unavailable on demand	λ
E28, E29	3.10^{-5}	
From E30 to E51		$1{,}4.10^{-7}$
From E52 to E54		4.10^{-5}
From E58 to E61		$4{,}8.10^{-5}$

TABLE 9 :   LIST OF THE SIGNIFICANT CUT - SETS

Nr.	MINIMAL CUT - SETS			
1	E52	E53	E58	E59
2	E52	E53	E58	E60
3	E52	E53	E58	E61
4	E52	E53	E59	E60
5	E52	E53	E59	E61
6	E52	E53	E60	E61
7	E52	E54	E58	E59
8	E52	E54	E58	E60
9	E52	E54	E58	E61
10	E52	E54	E59	E60
11	E52	E54	E59	E61
12	E52	E54	E60	E61
13	E53	E54	E58	E59
14	E53	E54	E58	E60
15	E53	E54	E58	E61
16	E53	E54	E59	E60
17	E53	E54	E59	E61
18	E53	E54	E60	E61
19	E28	E29		

TABLE 10 :   MAIN RESULTS FOR THE TREE OF FIG. 7
COMPARISON BETWEEN SALP-3 AND SALP-4

L_{lim}	n	P_{TOP}	E (SALP-4)	Time (sec) SALP-3	Time (sec) SALP-4
10^{-7}	18	$1,67.10^{-5}$	$1,64.10^{-8}$	4.44	7.46
10^{-8}	18	$1,67.10^{-5}$	$1,64.10^{-8}$	4.56	7.58
10^{-9}	18	$1,67.10^{-5}$	$1,64.10^{-8}$	24.96	7.74
10^{-10}	19	$1,67.10^{-5}$	$1,31.10^{-8}$	28.83	14.30
10^{-11}	43	$1,67.10^{-5}$	$8,07.10^{-9}$	38.89	18.84

The MCS are:

A	C	B	C
*T1	*T2	*T1	*T2
A	D	B	D
*T1	*T2	*T1	*T2

The attributes associated in output with the MCS indicate that the component A (B) must <u>fail</u> before C or D.

7. EXAMPLE OF APPLICATION - THE SALP-3 AND SALP-4 COMPUTER CODES

The various algorithms described in the preceding sections have been implemented in various computer codes. One of these, the SALP-3, is already used for routine analysis of AND/OR fault-trees at JRC, Ispra, and in various European industries and organisations.

SALP-4, which deals with AND-OR-NOT trees, is now under test at the JRC, Ispra. For a detailed description of the codes we refer to [2] and [5]. Being SALP-3 a first version, it does not contain neither the algorithm described in section 3 nor the determination of the residual error.

To give an example of the performance of the codes, let us consider the simple fault-tree described by Table 7. The input data set is given in Table 8. The most important MCS in order of importance are given in Table 9. (Cut-off limit of 10^{-10}).

The fault-tree has been analyzed assuming various cut-off limits. Table 10 resumes the results for the various cases and gives also the CPU time of both SALP-3 and SALP-4 (IBM 370/165).

It can be seen that the reduction in computer time for SALP-4 is due to the algorithm which locates the set of gates on which the minimization procedure must be applied.

8. CONCLUSIONS

List-processing technique is a powerful technique for developing algorithms suitable for heuristic AND-OR NOT tree analysis. These algorithms allow the most efficient use of computer capabilities and can assist the analyst in interactive way at various stages of the logical and numerical analysis of a system.

REFERENCES

[1] M. Astolfi, S. Contini, G. Volta, "Analysi di alberi logici AND/OR mediante tecniche non numeriche: Il codice SALP", Report EUR 5641, 1975.
[2] M. Astolfi, S. Contini, C.L. Van den Muyzenberg, G. Volta, "SALP-3 (Sensitivity Analysis by List Processing), A computer program for fault-tree analysis, des-

cription and how-to-use'', Report EUR 6183 EN, 1978.

[3] S. Contini, S. Garribba, G. Volta, ''Prior built-in sensitivity analysis for fault-trees with special concern for reliability calculation in nuclear power plant'', CESNEF/IAEA 02, Politecnico di Milano, Milano, Italy, 1979.

[4] S. Contini, ''Descrizione di un algoritmo per la determinazione di una forma disgiuntiva normale irriducibile'', Technical Note Nr. 1.06.01.79.55, April 1979, J.R.C. Ispra Establishment, Italy.

[5] M. Astolfi and al., ''SALP-4, A computer code for fault-tree analysis'', to be published as EUR report.

[6] E. Mendelson, ''Theory and problems of boolean algebra and switching limits'', McGraw Hill, 1970.

[7] B.L. Hulme, R.B. Warrell, ''A prime implicant algorithm with factoning'', IEEE Trans. on Computers, November 1975.

[8] L. Caldarola, ''Fault-tree analysis with multistate components'', Probabilistic Analysis of nuclear reactor safety, Topical Meeting, May 8 - 10, 1978, Los Angeles, California.

PATREC, A COMPUTER CODE FOR FAULT—TREE CALCULATIONS

A. Blin, A. Carnino, J.P. Signoret, F. Bouscatie[1]
B. Duchemin, J.M. Landré, H. Kalli, M.J. De Villeneuve[2]
[1] CEA.CEN.FAR, France, [2] CEA.CEN. Saclay, France

ABSTRACT

A computer code for evaluating the unreliability/unavailability of complex systems defined in the fault-tree representation is described. It uses a successive reductions approach with pattern recognition; the realization is based on various programming techniques from IBM PL/1 language. The code can take into account several present-day problems: multi-dependencies treatment, uncertainties in the reliability data parameters, influence of common mode failures ... The code has been running steadily for two years.

INTRODUCTION

Three methods are classically used for complex system reliability assessment:
1)   Cut and tie sets [1,2,3,4,5,6];
2)   Truth tables [7,8];
3)   Monte Carlo [9,10,11].

A method proceeding in a totally different way has recently been developed [12,13]. This new method is based on the "successive reductions" of the fault-tree. In the computer code PATREC the reduction of the fault-tree is realized by recognizing and replacing known subtrees or patterns by equivalent leaves with the corresponding unreliability/unavailability. By repeatedly pruning the fault-tree, it is finally reduced to a single leaf which represents the system unreliability for unrepairable systems and unavailability for repairable systems.

This paper intends to explain the theory of the PATREC code, to indicate the main options presently available and to discuss the improvements in progress.

33

PATTERN RECOGNITION

   The basic principle upon which the code functions is a so-called "pattern recognition". A library of patterns, i.e., subtrees corresponding to different simplest combinations of logical gates AND and OR, is stored into the memory of the computer along with the expressions which give the corresponding unreliability/unavailability of the patterns.

   PATREC is written in the computer language PL/1. The input tree is linked using list processing techniques and "pointers"; it is then represented in "End Order" [14]. This is realized by a recursive algorithm which creates the end order traverse, i.e., a linear list where each node of the tree appears only once. Along this list the program locates the known subtrees of the library.

   A subtree found in the list is always replaced by a leaf which has the corresponding unreliability/unavailability of the subtree. Hence, the fault-tree is successively reduced to a fault-tree of increasing simplicity and, finally, to a single leaf. The corresponding expression of this single leaf gives the unreliability/unavailability of the system. The reduction procedure is illustrated by an example in Fig.1.

CURRENT VERSION OF THE PATREC CODE: PATREC—RCM

   The PATREC code was developed at Saclay (France) in its first version in 1972 [12,15]. Since that time the code has been gradually improved by introduction of:
- multientry gates;
- various optional probability laws for the leaves of the fault-tree;
- treatment of dependencies;
- r/m logics;
- complementary events (X and $\overline{X}$);
- identification of minimal cut-sets.

1. Probability laws of the leaves

   To describe the realization of each elementary failure event - that is, each leaf of the fault-tree - it is possible to use one of the following six time-dependent probability laws:
1)   Exponential law with a constant failure rate λ :

$$P(t) = 1 - e^{-\lambda t}$$

2)   Exponential law with a constant failure rate λ and a constant repair rate μ :

$$P(t) = \frac{\lambda}{\lambda + \mu} [1 - e^{-(\lambda + \mu)t}]$$

This law is used to assess the unavailability of a repairable component.

3)   Weibull law.
4)   Gaussian law.
5)   Log-normal law.
6)   "Point by point" law. In this case, an unreliability/unavailability value is given

to the leaf at each time point t of the calculation.

In connection with the probability laws it is possible to introduce a constant probability of failure upon demand. Let us suppose a component which has a probability k to fail upon demand (refusing to start for example), and a probability law $P(t)$ if it has not failed upon demand at the time $t = 0$. The probability law (including start) is :

$$P^*(t) = k + (1 - k) P(t)$$

These probability laws contain at most three parameters; e.g. for the second law the parameters are λ, μ and k. In what follows, these parameters are called the reliability parameters of the leaves.

The calculation is performed for a given set of time values t. Along with the logical structure of the fault-tree and with the time values, the reliability parameters of the leaves form the main body of the input data of the program.

2. Dependencies processing

When the same event appears several times in the tree, it is called a "dependency", [16]. When the tree contains one or more dependencies, it is not possible to carry out the computation by using only pattern recognition. Some auxiliary steps are needed.

2.1. Principle of the method.   Let us assume a tree containing one dependency X and let $\overline{TE}$ be the top event of the tree. We can use the well known "Bayes theorem" to write :

$$P(TE) = P(X) \cdot P(TE/X) + P(\overline{X}) \cdot P(TE/\overline{X})$$

To compute the conditional probability $P(TE/X)$ we have to assume that X has occurred. Hence, by replacing $P(X)$ by the value 1 in each leaf corresponding to the dependency and computing the tree without any change for the other events, we find $P(TE/X)$. In the same way, replacing $P(X)$ by zero, we find $P(TE/\overline{X})$.

Combining these two conditional probabilities with $P(X)$ and $P(\overline{X}) = 1 - P(X)$, we find the probability of the top event, that is the system unreliability/unavailability.

When there are several dependencies, a dependencies truth table can be used; for example with 2 dependencies :

X	Y			
1	1		$P(X) P(Y)$	$PTE/X, Y)$
1	0	+	$P(X)[1-P(Y)] P(TE)/X, \overline{Y})$	
0	1	+	$[1-P(X)] P(Y) P(TE/\overline{X}, Y)$	
0	0	+	$[1-P(X)][1-P(Y)]P(TE/\overline{X}, \overline{Y})$	
		=	$P(TE)$	

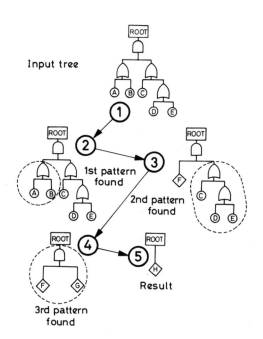

Figure 1

For 1 dependency 2 computations are needed.
For 2 dependencies 4 computations are needed.
More generally, for N dependencies 2^N computations are needed.

2.2. Dependencies elimination using Boolean algebra. The fault-tree of a system can have several logically equivalent representations which differ, however, in the number of dependencies. Because the computing time of PATREC varies roughly as $\sim 2^N$ (N is the number of dependencies), it is important to find the representation where N is minimized.

This minimization of N is performed before the actual calculation by a special module of the program. The rules of dependency elimination are derived by using Boolean algebra; they are described in detail in reference [17]. By eliminating some of the dependencies, the module can give a considerable improvement in running time for a large class of problems.

When N still remains large, even after the minimization, it is necessary to use approximations.

2.3. Approximation for a large number of dependencies. Among the lines of the dependencies truth table, there are a large number, which do not contribute significantly to the final result. In an approximation it is possible to keep only the significant terms.

Each line of the dependencies truth table is a chain of N bits. Then, only the lines which have a maximum of ν bits equal to 1 are kept. A bit in a given position is equal to 1 if the corresponding failure has occurred.

In this way, $\sum_{i=0}^{\nu} C_N^i$ computations are needed instead of 2^N .

In the present implementation, ν is taken equal to 3; in this case, the running time is improved by a factor of 700 for 20 dependencies.

The lower the probability of the dependent failure events, the more accurate the approximation.

This approximation is one option of PATREC-RCM (and PATREC-MC).

3.   r/m Logics

The program can handle the logical gates 2/3 and 2/4 in a given fault-tree directly in the same manner as the gates AND and OR.

4.   Complementary events

The program can also handle a given event and its complementary event (X and $\overline{X}$) simultaneously in a fault-tree. This case is treated as a special type of dependency; in the calculation of the conditional probabilities $P(TE/X)$ and $P(TE/\overline{X})$ of "Bayes theorem", $P(\overline{X})$ is replaced by the values 0 and 1 whenever $P(X)$ is replaced by the values 1 and 0, respectively.

5.   Identification of minimal cut-sets

The knowledge of minimal cut-sets is interesting for a qualitative system analysis. Although they are not used for the probability computation, an option of the
code using an algorithm developed by J.B. Fussel [3] permits to identify these minimal cut-sets.

DISPERSION OF THE RESULT : PATREC—MC

In practice, the reliability parameters of the fault-tree leaves (defined in the
previous paragraph "Probability laws of the leaves") are known only with a confidence interval which in certain cases may be rather wide. It is useful to know how
these uncertainties propagate across the fault-tree , i.e. what is the dispersion of the
system unreliability/unavailability.

In this case, the reliability parameters of the leaves are considered as random
variables with known distributions; the system unreliability/unavailability is a
function of these variables. Hence, the problem is to construct the distribution of a
function of several random variables.

1.   Principle of the version PATREC—MC

In the version PATREC—MC [18] the problem is solved by using the Monte
Carlo method. In the beginning of the calculation the program reads the necessary
information on the structure of the fault-tree as well as on the dependencies, similar-
ities and common mode failures between the leaves; then the reliability parameters
of the leaves are introduced by giving the value of the median and the error factor
for each parameter. As in reference [19], we have supposed that the distributions of
the reliability parameters is log-normal.

A preliminary PATREC—RCM calculation is performed using the median values
of the reliability parameters. During this very first calculation, the patterns of the
tree are identified; we can say that the expression of the system unreliability/
unavailability is stored in the computer memory. Now the program is ready to
enter the Monte Carlo part. In the beginning of each Monte Carlo history, the individual reliability parameters of the leaves are randomly sampled from their log-normal
distributions. Then the expression found during the preliminary calculation is utilized
to evaluate the corresponding system result. This trial value is stored and the calculation is repeatedly started again from the sampling of the reliability parameters.
Using these trial values, the program finally constructs the distribution of the system
unreliability/unavailability.

The Monte Carlo method has been used in similar cases earlier, e.g. in the program SAMPLE of reference [19]. The main difference here is in the level of
sophistication; PATREC—MC starts from relatively raw information about the system (such as fault-tree, reliability parameters of the leaves) and constructs the expression of the system unreliability/unavailability. The evaluation of this expression
is then rapidly repeated in the Monte Carlo part.

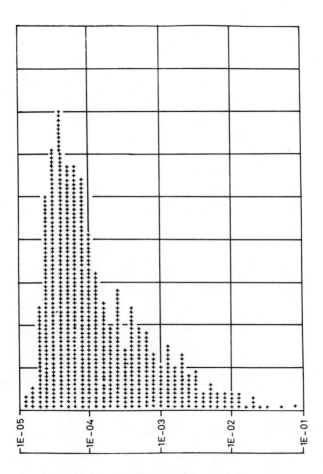

Figure 2.   PATREC output histogram.

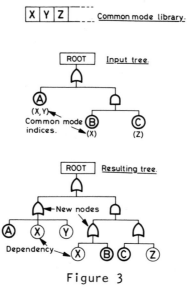

Figure 3

2.   Output of PATREC—MC

In the output of the program the distribution of the system unreliability/ unavailability is achieved in the form of tables and a histogram. Its most important statistical characteristics (such as mean, median, standard deviation, 90% confidence interval, parameters of the best-fitting log-normal distribution) are also evaluated.

In Fig.2 a sample distribution is given in the case of a simplified containment spray system of reference [18]. The main structure of the fault-tree is an OR gate with several entries. We can see that the distribution is not log-normal; the abnormally long tail is due to the large error factor given to the failure rate of the tank in the system.

COMMON MODE FAILURES

The reliability of nuclear systems has been improved in particular by using redundancy. In such cases, the influence of common mode failures can, however, be very important. This problem has been studied by several authors [20,21,22,23]; also the versions PATREC—RCM andPATREC—MC have been modified to deal with this problem.

1.   Principle of the method (Fig.3)

For each leaf of the fault-tree, a list of common mode failures to which this leaf is sensitive, is given as input. New leaves (X, Y and Z in Fig.3) describing the common mode failures, are automatically added and linked with the original leaves by OR gates. At the same time a corresponding dependency is created for each common mode. The dependencies processing program module is then utilized to modify the tree in order to minimize the number of dependencies. The reliability parameters of the new leaves are taken from a so-called common mode library.

2.   Results

This new version has been used, for instance, in a study of the failure probability of the Fessenheim protective system. With the failure rate taken from reference [21] and the General Atomic Method [20], using $\beta = 0.1$ to get the common mode failure rates of the components, the failure probability of the system is $3.24 \ 10^{-5}$ /demand.

A dispersion study has also been made and gives, (/d.) :

With common cause failure	Without common cause failure
Lower limit 5% : $1.2 \ 10^{-5}$	$2.00 \ 10^{-8}$
Upper limit 95% : $5.4 \ 10^{-4}$	$1.06 \ 10^{-5}$
Median value 50% : $4.3 \ 10^{-5}$	$3.72 \ 10^{-7}$

In this example the original fault-tree contains 38 leaves, 27 gates (two of the type 2/3 and two 2/4), and 7 dependencies. After the linking of the new leaves describing the common mode failures, the dimensions of the tree are increased to 76 leaves, 65 gates and 11 dependencies. The program module processing the dependencies simplifies then the situation to some extent; the final tree contains 44 leaves, 37 gates and 9 dependencies. The computing time with the version PATREC—MC is about 4 minutes for a run of 500 histories on the IBM 370/168 (System MVS).

CURRENT DEVELOPMENTS IN PROGRESS

1.   Optimization of existing versions

PATREC—RCM and PATREC—MC are presently in the course of optimization in order to reduce the required computer memory and execution time. In particular, a study of a new and reliable approximation in the computation of cases with many dependencies is in progress.

2.   Dynamic management of pattern library

The efficiency of the pattern recognition algorithm is a function of the pattern library which is stored in the computer memory. Work is in progress to permit this library to vary, according to the needs of a particular problem [24].

3.   Automatic construction of fault-trees from logical diagrams

It is often more simple to determine the functioning diagram than the fault-tree for a system to be studied. A project is in progress to develop an algorithm which would permit a given logic diagram to be mapped into an equivalent fault-tree [25].

CONCLUSION

The PATREC code which is presently operational in two versions offers a wide number of possibilities and is very efficient. These two versions are planned to be merged into a single version having all the possibilities of the two separate ones. PATREC uses to the maximum the advantages of the computer language PL/1 and there are no limits a priori to the size of the fault-tree to be computed. With respect to the computer time, the limiting factor is the number of dependencies.

Improvements in progress would lead to an advanced version of PATREC code with more possibilities and more efficiency.

REFERENCES

[1]   Vesely W.E., Narum E.E., PREP & KITT - Computer Codes for Evaluation of a
            Fault-tree. Idaho Nuclear Corporation - Report IN 1349 (1970).
[2]   Colombo A.G., Cadi. A Computer Code for System Availability and Reliability
            Evaluation. EUR 4940 E (1973).
[3]   Fussel J.B., Vesely W.E., A New Methodology for Obtaining Cut-sets for
            Fault-trees. Transactions of the A.N.S., June 1972.
[4]   Lacotte D., PREP-TRI: Un Programme de Calcul pour la Recherche des Coupes
            Minimales des Arbres de Défaillances. Report SETSSR n.49 (1976).

[5] Lacotte D., KITT-7. Un Programme de Calcul de la Fiabilité des Grands Systèmes Complexes. Report SETSSR n.50 (1976).

[6] Kalli H., Duchemin B., CM-MC Programme de Coupes Minimales pour Calcul de l'Incertitude de la Fiabilité par la Méthode de Monte Carlo. Report SERMA/S N.338 (1978).

[7] Garrick J.B., Reliability Analysis of Nuclear Power Plant Protective Systems. Report Holmes and Narver 190 (1967).

[8] Anonymous, Generalized Fault-tree Analysis for Reactor Safety. EPRI 217-2-2 (1975).

[9] Garrick et al., System Analysis by Fault-tree Evaluation, SAFTE-1, in Reliability Analysis of Nuclear Power Plant Protective Systems. Holmes and Narver, Report HN.190 (1967).

[10] Kongso H.E., RELY-4. A Monte Carlo Computer Program for System Reliability Analysis. Danish Atomic Energy Commission Research Establishment RISO, Report RISO-M 1500.

[11] Lanore J.M., Kalli H., Usefulness of the Monte Carlo Method in Reliability Calculation. Transactions of the A.N.S., Vol.27, p.374 (1977).

[12] Koen B.V., Application de la Reconnaissance des Formes aux Calculs de la Fiabilité des Systèmes. Report CEA - R.4368 (1972).

[13] Olmos J., Wolf L., A Modular Approach to Fault-tree and Reliability Analysis. Dt. of Nuclear Engineering - MIT 1977.

[14] Katzan H., Advanced Programming - Computer Science Series, Van Norstand Reinhold Company, 1970.

[15] Koen B.V., Carnino A., Reliability Calculations with a List Processing Technique, I.E.E.E. Trans. on Reliability, Vol.23, N.1 (April 1974).

[16] Blin A., Carnino A., Jubault G., Jegu J., Programme de Calcul de Fiabilité de Systèmes Complexes par la Reconnaissance des Formes: PATREC-DE. Congrès de Fiabilité, PERROS-GUIREC (1974).

[17] Kalli H., FEUIDEP - Module du Programme PATREC pour la Simplification des Arbres de Défaillance, Report CEA/SERMA/S, N.352 (1978).

[18] Kalli H., Lanore J.M., PATREC-MC - Programme de Calcul de l'Incertitude de la Probabilité de Défaillance d'un Système Complexe par la Méthode de Monte Carlo. Report CEA/SERMA/S, N.263 (1976).

[19] Reactor Safety Study. An Assessment of Accident Risks in U.S. Commercial Nuclear Power Plants. Report WASH-1400.

[20] H.T.G.R. Accident Initiation and Progression Analysis Status Report GA-A 13617, Vol.II (1975).

[21] Bourne A.J., Task Forces on Problems of Rare Events in the Reliability Analysis of Nuclear Power Plants. OECD/NEA CSNI report n.23 (1977).

[22] Wagner D.P., Cate C.L., Fussel J.B., Common Cause Failure Analysis Methodology for Complex Systems. Gatlinburg (Tennessee), June 20-24 (1977).

[23] Mankamo T., Common Mode Failures. IAEA International Symposium on Application of Reliability Technology to Nuclear Power Plants, Vienna October 1977.

[24] Lorigeon M., Koen B.V., Creation de Bibliothèques de Composants en Vue de l'Evaluation de la Fiabilité. Report SETSSR n.69 (1977).

[25] Koen B.V., Automatic Fault-tree Construction. Report DSN to be published.

REPAIRABLE MULTIPHASE SYSTEMS - MARKOV AND FAULT-TREE APPROACHES FOR RELIABILITY EVALUATION

C.A. Clarotti[1] , S. Contini[2] , R. Somma[3]

[1] CNEN-Casaccia, Italy; [2] SIGEN-Milano, Italy; [3] SELENIA-Roma, Italy

ABSTRACT

The reliability evaluation of a multiphase system has been described in a number of papers, if components were assumed to be non repairable. If a system is composed of repairable components, only an upper bound can be found using the fault-tree approach. In order to find an exact solution to the problem, the Markov approach can successfully be used. The purpose of this paper is to present both above-mentioned approaches.

INTRODUCTION

When considering spacecraft, complex electronic and nuclear systems, we observe that some of them have to perform a number of different tasks during their operational life. This fact has introduced the concept of phased mission systems. People involved in electronic and nuclear fields use different approaches to face the reliability analysis of such systems, namely: in the electronic field, the solution is found via the application of the Markov analytical methods; in the nuclear field, extensive use is made of the fault-tree techniques.

Use of the fault-tree technique in the nuclear field derives from the fact that the considered systems are much more complex than the systems usually taken into consideration in electronics; this fact reflects on the number of differential equations to be solved if a Markov approach were to be used.

Of course, a price is paid in order to be able to treat large systems, i.e. fault-tree technique gives an exact result only if a complete independence among system com-

Part of this work has been performed at the Engineering Division of the J.R.C. of Ispra, as a part of the collaboration agreement between CEC Joint Research Centre, SIGEN S.p.A. and CNEN.

ponents can be assumed. The present NATO-ASI has offered to people working with the above two techniques, the opportunity to meet. The present paper is a result of the meeting of people involved in two different areas.

The purpose is to consider phased mission systems when the independence does not hold.

THE PROBLEM STATEMENT

According to [1], a phased mission system is defined as a system whose "...relevant configuration (block diagram or fault-tree) changes during consecutive time periods (phases)". During various phases, different features (reliability, availability, etc.) m ay be of interest, according to the specific task being performed in that phase and to the particular need of the user.

Each phase is identified by: phase number, time interval, system configuration, task to be performed, parameter of interest and maintenance policy.

The whole mission, detailed in its phases, may be described with a mission profile table as the example in Table 1, where, specifying maintenance, the terms: single, double, ..., multiple, mean that respectively one repairman, two repairmen, ..., one repairman per item have been foreseen; none means no maintenance at all.

The success probability of a phased mission is given by the probability that the mission is successful in each single phase, where the phase success is measured in terms of the related parameter of interest.

Among the various possible cases, the most interesting is the one in which:
-      the system changes its configuration in each phase,
-      the parameter of interest is the reliability in any phase.
In this case, maintenance (single, ..., multiple) may or may not be planned. If no-maintenance is provided, and common mode failures are not considered, complete independence holds in each phase and the approach based on fault-tree technique leads to the exact problem solution. This case has been extensively treated in [1].

As has been pointed out in [2], the problem exists of "Extending the methods to handle repairable systems". It is well known that, if reliability with maintenance (single, ..., multiple) is of interest, independence cannot be assumed, in the sense that any component may be repaired or not depending upon the system state. In such cases, methods based on combinatorial reliability cannot be used to find an exact solution; this is the case of the fault-tree analysis.

In order to find an exact solution, one needs a method which is not constrained by the independence assumption such as the analytical Markov approach.

The purpose of this paper is to present for the case in consideration, the analytical Markov approach and a first bound approximated solution via fault-tree analysis. Finally, in the last section, some ideas on how to implement the fault-tree methodology are given.

TABLE 1 : MISSION PROFILE

Phase No.	TIME interval	System Configuration	System task	Parameter of interest	Maintenance policy
1	(t_0, t_1)	A, B, C configuration	x	Reliability	Single
2	(t_1, t_2)	C, B, C configuration	y	Availability	Multiple
3	(t_2, t_3)	A–B–C configuration	z	Reliability	None
⋮	⋮	⋮	⋮	⋮	

THE MARKOV APPROACH

For tutorial purpose, let us consider a 3-phase mission, whole profile is shown in Table 2. The mission reliability cannot be obtained by simply multiplying the system reliabilities of the various phases; this is due to the fact that at the times at which the system changes its configuration (phase change times), it must occupy a state which is successful for both the phases involved. So, the system evolution must be such that: during each phase the system can evolve through all the states allowed for that phase, (i.e., if reliability is involved, through the states that are good for the phase); at any phase change time the system must occupy one of the states that are good for both phases, starting from which it begins the evolution in the following phase with the same constraints.

As has been shown in [3], the whole information about the system condition is contained in the structure vector associated with the states tables.

In a k-phase system, of course, k structure vectors can be associated with the states table, i.e. one for each configuration.

In order to show how the Markov approach works, let us focus on the considered example. First of all, let us depict the system in terms of its states table, and the three

TABLE 2 : MISSION PROFILE (3 phases)

Phase No.	Time interval	System Configuration (Block Diagram)	System task	Parameter of interest	Maintenance policy
1	$(0, t_1)$	A / B / C (parallel)	x	Reliability	Multiple
2	(t_1, t_2)	A — (B / C parallel)	y	Reliability	Multiple
3	(t_2, t_3)	A — B — C	z	Reliability	Multiple

TABLE 3 : PHASES STATES DESCRIPTION

St.	C	B	A	$\underline{C}_1$	$\underline{C}_2$	$\underline{C}_3$
s_1	1	1	1	1	1	1
s_2	1	1	0	1	0	0
s_3	1	0	1	1	1	0
s_4	1	0	0	1	0	0
s_5	0	1	1	1	1	0
s_6	0	1	0	1	0	0
s_7	0	0	1	1	0	0
s_8	0	0	0	0	0	0

structure vectors for the phases described in Table 2; this is shown in Table 3.
    Let us now consider the three phases:

a)   First phase: from 0 to t_1.
In order to have success during the 1st phase, the system has not to pass through state s_8; in addition, at the phase change time t_1, it has to occupy one of the states s_1, s_3, s_5 good for phases 1 and 2.

    As the system is not allowed to pass through state s_8, one has to consider the basic equation for the multiple repair reliability evaluation [3], with structure vector $\underline{C}_1$ and with initial condition given by:

$$\underline{p}(0) = \underline{u}_1 = \begin{bmatrix} 1 \\ 0 \\ 0 \\ 0 \\ 0 \\ 0 \\ 0 \\ 0 \end{bmatrix} \tag{1}$$

The equation to be considered for the evolution in phase 1 is then:

$$
\begin{bmatrix}
\dot{p}_1(t) \\
\dot{p}_2(t) \\
\dot{p}_3(t) \\
\dot{p}_4(t) \\
\dot{p}_5(t) \\
\dot{p}_6(t) \\
\dot{p}_7(t) \\
\dot{p}_8(t)
\end{bmatrix}
=
\begin{bmatrix}
-\Sigma_1 & \mu_A & \mu_B & & \mu_C & & & \\
\lambda_A & -\Sigma_2 & & \mu_B & & \mu_C & & \\
\lambda_B & & -\Sigma_3 & \mu_A & & & \mu_C & \\
& \lambda_B & \lambda_A & -\Sigma_4 & & & & 0 \\
\lambda_C & & & & -\Sigma_5 & \mu_A & \mu_B & \\
& \lambda_C & & & \lambda_A & -\Sigma_6 & & 0 \\
& & \lambda_C & & \lambda_B & & -\Sigma_7 & 0 \\
& & & \lambda_C & & \lambda_B & \lambda_A & 0
\end{bmatrix}
\begin{bmatrix}
p_1(t) \\
p_2(t) \\
p_3(t) \\
p_4(t) \\
p_5(t) \\
p_6(t) \\
p_7(t) \\
p_8(t)
\end{bmatrix}
\tag{2}
$$

where Σ_i is the sum of the entries of the i-th column.

It is to be stressed that, if a coefficient is zero due to the impossibility of the corresponding instantaneous states transition, it does not appear in the matrix (structure zeroes); if an entry is zero due to the particular parameter of concern, it appears explicitly in the matrix (feature zeroes). In the considered example the feature zeroes are those derived from the fact that the state s_8 is an absorbing one.

Solving system (2) with initial condition (1), one obtains the solution vector:

$$
\underline{p}(t_1) =
\begin{bmatrix}
p_1(t_1) \\
p_2(t_1) \\
\vdots \\
p_8(t_1)
\end{bmatrix}
\tag{3}
$$

The system is ready to start for the second phase only if at t_1 it is in one of the states s_1, s_3, s_5; these events have probability $p_1(t_1)$, $p_3(t_1)$, $p_5(t_1)$ respectively, then the probability that the system has success in the first phase and it is able to start the second one is:

$$
R(t_1) = p_1(t_1) + p_3(t_1) + p_5(t_1)
\tag{4}
$$

b) Second phase: from t_1 to t_2.
The system is successful during the second phase if it starts the phase in one of the states s_1, s_3, s_5 and evolves only through these states; in order to consider the whole mission as a success, the system at t_2 has to occupy state s_1, i.e. the only state suitable for both the second and the third phase.

Also in this case, in the first phase, one has to consider the fundamental equation for multiple repair reliability evaluation, with structure vector C_2, but this time, in order to consider that the present phase is successive to a first one, the initial condition has to take into account the first phase. Then, denoting with $G(1,2)$, the set of states good for phases 1 and 2:

p {1st phase success AND 2nd phase success} =

= p {2nd phase success | 1st phase success} p {1st phase success} =

= $\sum\limits_{\underline{s}_i \in G(1,2)}$ p {2nd phase success | system in $\underline{s}_i$ at t_1} × p {system in $\underline{s}_i$ at t_1}

The structure vector for matrix construction is C_2.
So now the system to solve is:

$$\underline{p}(t) = \underline{\wedge}\,\underline{p}(t) \qquad (5)$$

with initial condition given by a vector whose components 1, 3 and 5 correspond to $p_1(t_1)$, $p_3(t_1)$ of vector $\underline{p}(t_1)$ in eq.(3), while the other components are zero.
The $\underline{\wedge}$ matrix for the second phase is:

$-\Sigma_1$	0	μ_B		μ_C			
λ_A	$-\Sigma_2$		0		0		
λ_B		$-\Sigma_3$	0			0	
	λ_B	λ_A	$-\Sigma_4$				0
λ_C				$-\Sigma_5$	0	0	
	λ_C			λ_A	$-\Sigma_6$		0
		λ_C		λ_B		$-\Sigma_7$	0
			λ_C		λ_B	λ_A	0

$$(6)$$

The system is now able to start the third phase, having successfully completed the first two phases with a probability:

$$R(t_2) = p_1(t_2) \qquad (7)$$

first component of the vector $p(t_2)$ solution of eq.(5) for the described initial condition.

c)   Third phase: from t_2 to t_3.
The previous considerations can be applied to this phase; so now the problem is to solve a system such as (5) with the initial condition given by a vector having only the first component different from zero and equal to $p_1(t_2)$, first entry of the solution of the previous phase equation. The $\underline{\wedge}$ matrix for the 3rd phase is:

$$\begin{bmatrix}
-\Sigma_1 & 0 & 0 & & 0 & & & \\
\lambda_A & -\Sigma_2 & & 0 & & 0 & & \\
\lambda_B & & -\Sigma_3 & 0 & & & 0 & \\
 & \lambda_B & \lambda_A & -\Sigma_4 & & & & 0 \\
\lambda_C & & & & -\Sigma_5 & 0 & 0 & \\
 & \lambda_C & & & \lambda_A & -\Sigma_6 & & 0 \\
 & & \lambda_C & & \lambda_B & & -\Sigma_7 & 0 \\
 & & & \lambda_C & & \lambda_B & \lambda_A & 0 \\
\end{bmatrix} \tag{8}$$

The result of the last phase, $R(t_3)$, in the present case gives the success probability of a phased mission system; the system unreliability is, of course, the complement to one of the above results.

THE FAULT-TREE APPROACH TO A PHASED MISSION SYSTEM

A repairable multiphase system cannot be reduced to an equivalent single phase one, i.e. to a single phase system having the same minimal cut set (MCS). This is due to the fact that logical operations used for non repairable systems cannot be carried out if repair is foreseen.

Let us again consider the three phase system of the previous paragraph. In the fault-tree notation, the mission profile can be described as in Table 4. The solution of the problem of evaluating the unreliability of the system represented in Table 4 is straight forward if Monte Carlo simulation technique is employed.

When using asincronous simulation technique [4], the fault-tree of the system whose unreliability has to be calculated, is checked every time a failure occurs. Let t_i be the phase change time between phases i and (i + 1). Let us suppose that, when generating the failure times t_A, t_B and t_C of components A, B and C, the following situation is found:

$$t_A < t_1$$
$$t_2 < t_B < t_3$$
$$t_C > t_3$$

The fault-tree of the system in the first phase is checked and the system is found to be functioning. The restoration time τ_A of component A is then generated and let us admit that is $t_1 < t_A + \tau_A < t_B$.

This situation corresponds to a system failure at t_1, due to a permanence of A in a failed condition at the phase change. A normal Monte Carlo code, based on asincronous simulation, would ignore this failure for the system is checked only when a failure occurs. In order to avoid this situation, a check of the system state is performed at the beginning of each phase, in order to verify if a system failure occurs

TABLE 4 : MISSION PROFILE (3 phases)

Phase No.	Time interval	System Configuration (Fault tree)	System task	Parameter of interest	Maintenance policy
1	$(0, t_1)$		x	Reliability	Multiple
2	(t_1, t_2)		y	Reliability	Multiple
3	(t_2, t_3)		z	Reliability	Multiple

at that time due to the change in configuration. Fault-tree technique can be used to find, in general, an analytical upper bound system unreliability.

As demonstrated in [5,6,7] the exclusion inclusion principle, (in the hypothesis of complete independent performance processes of the components) can be applied to calculate via MCSs method the expected number of failures (ENF) of a system, even though it cannot be used to compute its unreliability with such method.

On the other hand, for highly reliable systems, as is the case of systems of interest in the nuclear field, the expected number of system failures is a close approximation for the unreliability.

For this reason, in all the equations which will follow, we shall use probabilities instead of expected number of occurrences as it should be theoretically required.

The assumed hypotheses are:
- a multiple repair policy is assumed in any case; this fact does not appreciably affect the results due to the large difference between times to failure and to repair;
- the upper bound is found by stopping the ENF expansion to the first order terms.

Let k be the number of system phases and n the number of all different minimal cut-sets (MCS) considering all phases together; let $x(i, j)$ indicate the event: the minimal cut-set i, $1 \leqslant i \leqslant n$, occurs for the first time in phase j, $1 \leqslant j \leqslant k$; of course $x(i, j)$ is the null event, i.e. the impossible event, if the ith MCS does not appear in the jth phase.

The system unreliability at the mission time T is given by:

$$\overline{R}_s(T) = p\{ \bigcup_{i=1}^{n} [\bigcup_{j=1}^{k} x(i, j)] \} \tag{9}$$

then, according to the above assumption:

$$\overline{R}_s(T) \leqslant \sum_{i=1}^{n} p\{ \bigcup_{j=1}^{k} x(i, j)\} \tag{10}$$

As the $x(i, j)$ are mutually exclusive with respect to j, whatever is i, one has:

$$p\{ \bigcup_{j=1}^{k} x(i, j)\} = p\{ x(i, j_1)\} +$$

$$+ p\{ x(i, j_2) \mid \overline{x}(i, j_1)\} \, p\{\overline{x}(i, j_1)\} +$$

$$+ p\{ x(i, j_3) \mid \overline{x}(i, j_1), \quad \overline{x}(i, j_2)\} \, p\{\overline{x}(i, j_1), \overline{x}(i, j_2)\} +$$

$$+ \ldots\ldots \tag{11}$$

where: $p\{ x(i, j_r)\}$ is the probability that the i_{th} MCS first occurs in phase j_r;
j_r is the rth phase in which the considered MCS appears;
$p\{ x(i, j_r) \mid \overline{x}(i, j_1), ..., \overline{x}(i, j_{r-1})\}$ is the conditional probability of the ith MCS that first occurs in its rth possible phase, given that it did not occur in the previous (r−1) possible phases;
$p\{ x(i, j_1), ..., x(i, j_{r-1})\}$ is the probability that the ith MCS never occurred in its first r−1 possible phases.

When evaluating the terms of eq.(11), the following three cases are considered:

a) none of the components of the ith MCS appears in the phases in which that MCS does not appear, i.e. those components work only in the phases in which all of them give rise to the ith MCS;

b)   all components of the ith MCS appear, i.e. are working, in some other MCS in the phases in which ith MCS does not appear;

c)   some of the components of the ith MCS appear in some other MCS in the phases in which ith MCS does not appear; it is the intermediate case.

Let us indicate with $R_{x(i,j_r)}$ the reliability of ith MCS in its rth possible phase, and with $\bar{R}_{x(i,j_r)}$ its unreliability.
Let us now examine the above stated cases.

a)   In this case it is impossible that the ith MCS occurs at a phase change time due to a change in configuration; then eq.(11) reduces to:

$$p\{ \bigcup_{j=1}^{k} x(i,j)\} = \bar{R}_{x(i,j_1)} + \bar{R}_{x(i,j_2)} \ R_{x(i,j_1)} +$$

$$+ \ \bar{R}_{x(i,j_3)} \ R_{x(i,j_2)} \ R_{x(i,j_1)} + \ ... \tag{12}$$

b)   In this case let the j_rth phase be the first one in which the MCS appears again after a certain number of phases in which it did not appear, but its components all worked belonging to other MCS. That is: phases $j_1, j_2, ..., j_{r-1}$ are adjacent but phases j_{r-1} and j_r are not, as is shown below:

| phase j_1 | phase j_2 | .... | phase j_{r-1} | generic intermediate | phase j_r |
                                                      phase in which the
                                                      MCS considered is
                                                      not present

In this situation the term $p\{x(i,j_r), \bar{x}(i,j_{r-1}), ..., \bar{x}(i,j_1)\}$ may be split into the sum of two mutually exclusive events, such as:

$$p\{x(i,j_r), \bar{x}(i,j_{r-1}), ..., \bar{x}(i,j_1)\} =$$

$$= p\{x_b(i,j_r), ..., \bar{x}(i,j_1)\} +$$

$$+ p\{x_d(i,j_r), \bar{x}_b(i,j_r), \bar{x}(i,j_{r-1}), ..., \bar{x}(i,j_1)\} \tag{13}$$

where the subscripts b and d mean respectively at the beginning and during the possible j_rth phase of ith MCS. The cut-set, in fact, may occur at the beginning of the phase due to the change of configuration. Now:

$$p\{x_b(i,j_r), \bar{x}(i,j_{r-1}), ..., \bar{x}(i,j_1)\} =$$

$$= p\{x_b(i,j_r) \mid \bar{x}(i,j_{r-1}), ..., \bar{x}(i,j_1)\} \cdot p\{\bar{x}(i,j_{r-1}), ..., \bar{x}(i,j_1)\} \tag{14}$$

It can be easily shown (see Appendix) that the conditional probability in eq.(14) is upper bounded by the unavailability of the ith MCS at the beginning of the possible j_rth phase, taking into account the previous evolution of the components.

Furthermore:

$$p\{\overline{x}(i, j_{r-1}), ..., \overline{x}(i, j_1)\} = \prod_{h=j_1}^{j_{r-1}} R_{x(i,h)} \qquad (15)$$

Analogously:

$$p\{x_d(i, j_r), \overline{x}_b(i, j_r), \overline{x}(i, j_{r-1}), ..., \overline{x}(i, j_1)\} =$$

$$= p\{x_d(i, j_r) \mid \overline{x}_b(i, j_r), \overline{x}(i, j_{r-1}), ..., \overline{x}(i, j_1)\} \cdot$$

$$\cdot p\{\overline{x}_b(i, j_r) \mid \overline{x}(i, j_{r-1}), ..., \overline{x}(i, j_1)\} \cdot$$

$$\cdot p\{\overline{x}(i, j_{r-1}), ..., \overline{x}(i, j_1)\} \qquad (16)$$

The first factor in eq.(16) is obviously the unreliability of the ith MCS during its j_rth phase, i.e. $\overline{R}_{x(i,j_r)}$; the second factor is upper bounded by 1; the third is given by eq.(15).

c)   If, among the components which do not work in phases between the j_{r-1}th and the j_rth, at least one has a mean time to repair much shorter than the time interval between the end of the former and the beginning of the latter, the probability of failure at the j_rth phase change time is zero. This can be easily understood thinking that, if a component of the MCS, say A, does not work between times $t_{j_{r-1}}$ and t_{j_r} but can be repaired in that time interval, the set of states having that component functioning becomes ergodic, i.e. has probability 1 for $(t_{j_r} - t_{j_{r-1}}) \to \infty$.

Now, if one of the components of the MCS is functioning, that MCS does not occur. It is clear that time $(t_{j_r} - t_{j_{r-1}})$ can be considered to be infinite if it is much longer than the mean time to repair component A.

It is to be stressed that the hypothesis of mean time to repair much shorter than the time interval between the two phases, is not a heavy (restrictive) one. Indeed, that hypothesis simply means that one has sufficient time for the repair.

From what has been said, case c) can be handled like case a).

We have now simply to calculate the unreliability $\overline{R}_{x(i,j)}$ of the ith phase. With the hypothesis of exponentially distributed time to failure and time to repair, as shown in [5], one has

$$\overline{R}_{x(i,j)} \leqslant \sum_{h=1}^{c} \lambda_h \int_{t_{j-1}}^{t_j} [1 - q_h(t)] \prod_{s=h}^{c} q_s(t)\, dt \qquad (17)$$

where h and s indicate the generic component of the ith MCS and $q_r(t)$ is the unavailability of the rth component calculated taking into account the fact that, if the component worked previously in some other phase, its initial unavailability q_s is different from zero.

HOW TO IMPLEMENT THE FAULT-TREE METHODOLOGY

The methodology described in the previous section can be easily implemented by modifying the computer programs for fault-tree analysis. In order to correctly apply the methodology, the logical analysis must produce, for each MCS, the information regarding the phases in which it appears. The same type of information for the primary events is easily obtained from the input data (fault-trees and primary events parameters).

In this section, we are going to supply the basic operations of the algorithm for the logical analysis. This information concerns:

-       the representation of the MCS for the generic phase;
-       the matching of each phase with the previous ones.

A progressive prime number (except 1) is associated to each phase, i.e. 2 means first phase, 3 second phase, and so on. A progressive integer number is associated to each primary event. This is necessary in order to reduce the computer time when searching either the generic primary event or a minimal cut-set in their respective files.

The analysis of the generic phase gives a list of important MCS which are stored in an array whose generic row contains the following information:

$$| \alpha | \leftarrow MCS \rightarrow | \beta |$$

where: α is the prime number for that phase, and β the sum of the integer numbers corresponding to the components of the MCS.

For example, the cut-set composed of events PUMP $= 2$, SWITCH $= 4$, POWER $= 7$ of the second phase is represented by: $| 3 | 2 \ 4 \ 7 | 13 |$.

Now, given the set of MCS of a certain phase (say $\{x\}$) and the ones of the previous phases (say $\{y\}$), the operations that must be carried out are the following. Indicating with x_i the ith MCS of $\{x\}$, we must search if it is contained in $\{y\}$. To do this, each MCS belonging to $\{x\}$ is to be compared only with those MCSs of $\{y\}$ which are characterized by the same β. If it is found that x_i is equal to y_k, then the parameter α_k of y_k is multiplied by α_i of x_i and x_i is deleted from $\{x\}$. At the end of these tests, the set of MCSs of the phases examined is given by $\{y\} \cup \{x\}$ (where obviously $\{x\}$ does not contain the MCSs previously deleted).

Finally, when all the phases have been logically examined, the numerical analysis must be performed. The parameter α_i gives the information about the phases in which the ith MCS appears, i.e. $\alpha = 30 = 2 \times 3 \times 5$ means first, second and third phase; $\alpha = 10 = 2 \times 5$ means first and third phase, etc. Moreover, the codification used for the primary events allows a direct access to the parameters characterizing each of them.

It is to be noticed that the data structure described above can be used for the implementation of the cut cancellation [1] needed for cut-sets composed of non-repairable components.

CONCLUSIONS

As has been shown in the previous sections, fault-tree technique leads to an approximate solution to phased mission problems, while the Markov approach gives the exact analytical solution. The reason which compelled a search for a solution via fault-tree is that up to now the Markov approach has limitations in dimention of tractable systems. Of course, studies are in progress to overcome those limitations, and, in addition, the Markov approach demonstrates the existence of an exact solution to such a problem.

APPENDIX

The availability $p_0(t)$ of a generic MCS at j_r th phase change time is obtained by solving the following Markovian equation (see ref.6):

$$p_0(t) + [\wedge_0(t) + \mu_0(t)] p_0(t) = \mu_0(t) \qquad (1.A)$$

with the initial condition $p_0(t_{j_{r-1}}) < 1$. The conditional probability $\hat{p}_0(t)$ that the MCS does not occur at the j_r phase change time given that the MCS never occurred up to $t_{j_{r-1}}$, is obtained by solving the same equation (1.A) but with the boundary condition $\hat{p}_0(t_{j_{r-1}}) = 1$; it is then evident that in a time interval on the right of $t_{j_{r-1}}$, the following condition holds:

$$\hat{p}_0(t) > p_0(t)$$

and, being equation (1.A) of the first order, if at a certain time point t^* results

$$\hat{p}_0(t^*) = p_0(t^*)$$

from that time on we have identically:

$$\hat{p}_0(t) = p_0(t)$$

REFERENCES

[1] Esary J.D., Ziehms H., "Reliability Analysis of Phased Missions", Reliability
        and Fault-tree Analysis, SIAM, 1975.
[2] Burdick G.R., Fussell J.B., Rasmuson D.M., Wilson J.R., "Phased Mission
        Analysis: A Review of New Developments and an Application",
        IEEE Trans. on Reliability, Vol.R-26, No.1, April 1977
[3] Amoia V., Carrada E., Somma R., "System Reliability: The Basic Equation",
        Rivista Tecnica Selenia, Vol.4, No.3, 1977. Special Issue on "System
        Reliability: The Markov Approach".
[4] Ricchena R., "Modified Version of Code REMO for Reliability Calculation
        Via Monte Carlo Technique", (EUR report to be published).
[5] Vesely W.E., "A Time Dependent Methodology for Fault-tree Evaluation",
        Nuclear Eng. and Design, 13 (1970).
[6] Vesely W.E., "Reply to J.D. Murchland's Comment on a Time Dependent
        Methodology for Fault-tree Evaluation", Nuclear Engineering and
        Design, 22 (1972), 170–172.
[7] Caldarola L., "A Method for the Calculation of the Cumulative Failure
        Probability Distribution of Complex Repairable Systems", Nuclear
        Engineering and Design, 36 (1976), 109–122.

LIST OF MAIN SYMBOLS USED

K number of system phases

n total number of MCS (minimal cut-sets) of the system

$x(i,j)$ the event "the ith MCS occurs for the first time in phase j"

$\bar{x}(i,j)$ the complement of $x(i,j)$

T mission time

Λ transition matrix

$R_{x(i,j)}$ reliability of ith MCS in phase j

$\bar{R}_{x(i,j)}$ the complement to one of $R_{x(i,j)}$

$\bar{R}_s(T)$ unreliability of the system at the mission time

RELIABILITY PARAMETERS FOR CHEMICAL PROCESS SYSTEMS

Ernest J. Henley and James O. Y. Ong

Chemical Engineering Department
University of Houston
Houston, TX   77004

ABSTRACT

The KITT (Kinetic Tree Theory) computer program for calculating system reliability parameters was modified to include time delays (storage tanks) and component (standby) redudancy. The modified program was applied to the material handling subsection of an oil shale process to obtain system availability.

INTRODUCTION

The objective of this paper is to illustrate how a computer algorithm, developed primarily for nuclear and aerospace applications, can be modified to calculate process system reliability parameters. The computer program selected was the KITT program, which is based on the Kinetic Tree Theory[7],[8]. The original KITT code cannot be applied directly to a process scheme such as the material handling subsection of the shale oil plant shown in Fig. 1 because it does not account for:

(a) the time delay provided by the storage area, and
(b) the presence of redundant components, in cold or hot standby.

BACKGROUND AND DEVELOPMENT

KITT-1 Computer Code

The following assumptions are made in the KITT code:

(a) Components of the system may be nonrepairable or

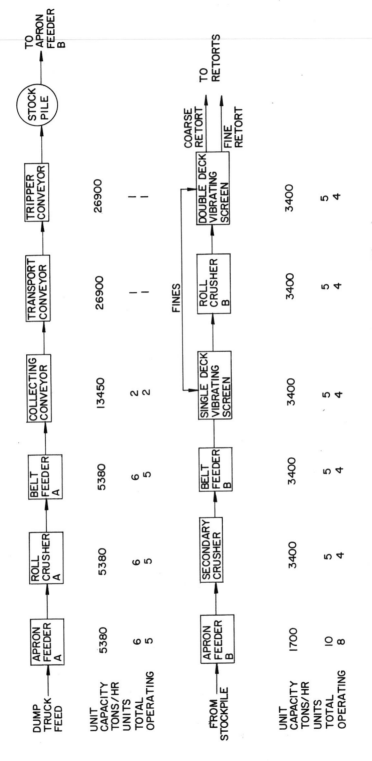

Figure 1.   White River Shale Oil Project Flowsheet

> repairable (replaceable) with a constant repair time τ.
> (b) Failure rate, λ, of a component is assumed to be constant with time (e.g., failure distribution is exponential).
> (c) All components are assumed to be operating at time $t = 0$.

Since most components in a process are either repairable or replaceable, assumption (a) is generally applicable. Assumption (b) is not strictly applicable to mechanical process systems. However, it serves as a very useful simplification and often the data may be so limited or the system so complicated as to make a more sophisticated treatment impractical. Assumption (c) is not valid for (cold) stand-by components which are brought on line only in case of failure.

Besides requiring inputs of λ and τ, the code requires input of all minimal cut sets, a minimal cut set being a set of the least number of components such that the system will fail only if all components in that set are failed.

Given component reliability data and the cut sets, KITT calculates system reliability parameters. For many process systems, the system availability, A, is the reliability parameter of primary concern.

$$A = \frac{Uptime}{Uptime \ + \ Downtime} \tag{1}$$

$$A = \frac{Mean \ Time \ to \ Failure}{Mean \ Time \ to \ Failure \ + \ Mean \ Time \ to \ Repair} \tag{2}$$

The KITT program calculates the pointwise unavailability, Q, from which all other availability parameters are derived. Proceeding on the assumptions of exponential failure, constant repair time, and immediate repair, repairable component unreliability and rate of failure, are calculated by:

$$q_i = 1 - \sum_{j=0}^{[t/\tau_i]} \frac{\lambda^j (t-\tau_i)^j \ e^{-\lambda(t-\tau_j)}}{j} \ ; \tag{3}$$

$$[t/\tau_i] = even \ integer \tag{4}$$

$$w_i = (1 - q_i)$$

Equations (3) and (4) are utilized only for $t \leq 3\tau$ in the KITT program. For $t > 3\tau$, q is assumed at steady state at a value slightly less than q at $t = 3\tau$. Figure 2 shows the general shape of the curves for unavailability, q_i, of a repairable component.

Nonrepairable components, although normally less important than repairable components for industrial processes, can also be handled in the KITT program simultaneously with repairable components. Reliability characteristics are calculated using the following equations:

$$q_i = 1 - e^{-\lambda_i t} \tag{5}$$

$$w_i = \lambda_i \, e^{-\lambda_i t} \tag{6}$$

The unreliability and rate of failure for minimal cut sets are calculated by the following equations:

$$Q_j = \prod_{i=1}^{v} q_i \tag{7}$$

$$W_j = \sum_{i=1}^{v} w_i \prod_{\substack{\ell=1 \\ \ell \neq j}}^{n} q_\ell \tag{8}$$

System unreliability and rates of failure are approximated by the following inequalities:

$$Q_o \leq 1 - \prod_{j=1}^{N_c} (1 - Q_j) \tag{9}$$

$$W_o \leq \sum_{j=1}^{N_c} W_j \tag{10}$$

Equations (9) and (10) represent an upper bound approximation to the exact values since the effect of the failure of two or more minimal cut sets occurring at the same time is not accounted for[1]. These approximations are conservative and are extremely close to the exact number for large systems[3]. Because of this and the desire to minimize the computational time required, these approximations were judged adequate for the purpose of this study. Integrated forms of Q, W, and Λ are calculated numerically using linear interpolation.

Incorporating a Time Delay

The stockpile in Fig. 1 is analogous to a storage tank in a process scheme and represents a simple time delay for processed material. To modify the KITT-1 code to handle time delays, the following relationships, derived by Henley and Hosino[5], were incorporated:

$$Q_o(t) = [e^{-T/\tau}u] \ Q_u(t-T) \tag{11}$$

$$\dot{W}_o(t) = [e^{-T/\tau}u] \ W_u(t-T) \tag{12}$$

where the subscript u denotes application to the system of units upstream of the time delay.

All the upstream units can be treated as a subsystem before applying the correction for a time delay (storage tank). Accordingly, if a time delay exists in the subsystem, all units upstream of the time delay in the subsystem must be treated as another separate subsystem to be calculated first.

To illustrate, consider the schematic flow system of Fig. 3. Units 1, 2, 3, and 4 are calculated as subsystem, S_1 before the effect of T_1 is applied, yielding a subsystem S_1. Similarly, units 5 and 6 are calculated as subsystem S_2 before the effect of time delay T_2 is applied to yield S_2'. Mathematically for S_1,

$$Q_{S_1'}(t) = [e^{-T_1/\tau}S_1] \ Q_{S_1}(t-T_1)$$

and

$$W_{S_1'}(t) = [e^{-T_1/\tau}S_1] \ W_{S_1}(t-T_1).$$

Subsystem S_2' is treated similarly.

By this "blocking" procedure[9], the process topology is reduced to that of Fig. 4 where S_1' and S_2' are subsystems with respective time delays T_1 and T_2. At this point it is unimportant whether S_1' or S_2' are calculated first. Both must be calculated by the time subsystem S_3 is reduced and the effect of T_3 applied. Further blocking reduces the process to that shown in Fig. 5A and finally to Fig. 5B.

The time delay is also assumed to be a constant. If there is to be an increase in overall system availability, reference[5] points out that the capacity of the upstream units must be greater than the capacity of the downstream units. The amount of excess capacity of the upstream units compared to that of the downstream units is relatively thusly[10].

$$c_u A_u \geq c_d A_d = \text{Total System Throughout} \tag{13}$$

If this inequality is not true, then the time delay is not always

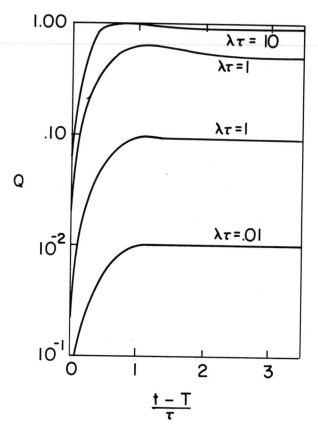

Fig. 2.   General Unavailability

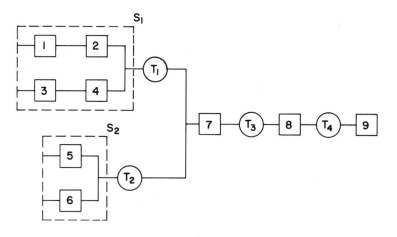

Fig. 3.   Blocking, 1st step

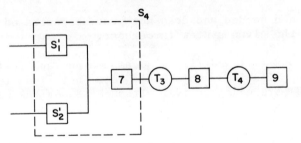

Fig. 4.   Blocking, 2nd step

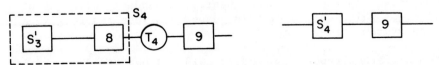

Fig. 5A.   Blocking, 3rd step   Fig 5B.   Blocking, Final Flowsheet

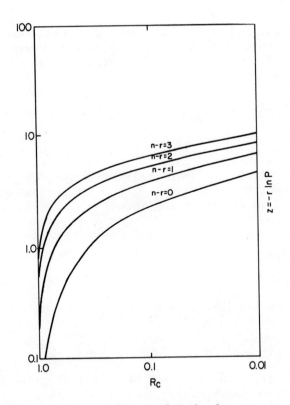

Fig. 6.   Effect of Redundancy

available when needed and does not provide increased process availability at the given system throughput.

Equations (11) and (12) also assume no tank failure. For most
practical applications, this would seem justified since equations
(9) and (10) are conservative. If such is not the case, however,
overall system reliability can be suitably adjusted.

Incorporating Redundant Units

The flowsheet, Fig. 1, incorporates redundant units to improve
availability. This is reasonable, since the state of the art in
equipment design may limit the maximum size that an equipment vendor
will guarantee and supply. Subsequently, redundant units may be
installed, of which only a certain number are required to give a
specified system throughput.

Two different types of standby, cold and hot standby, are included into the modified KITT-1 code. Cold standby assumes that
non-operating (redundant) units have zero probability of failure
while hot standby assumes that non-operating units have a probability
of failure equal to that of an active (onstream) unit[6]. If r = number of units required to be operating, n = total number of units
available and a = probability that one unit is operational, the equation for the reliability of (n-r) identical, parallel, and redundant
units in cold standby is

$$A_c = \sum_{j=0}^{n-r} \frac{a^r}{j!} (-r \ln a)^j \tag{14}$$

Equation (14) is shown graphically in Figs. 6 and 6A for rapid "hand"
estimates. For inclusion into the KITT-1 code, the reliability of
the redundant units can be treated as a cut set and equation (14)
can be modified to the following forms:

$$\overset{v}{Q} = 1 - A_c = k = \sum_{j=0}^{n-4} \frac{(1-q)^r}{j!} [-r \ln (1-q)]^j \tag{15}$$

$$\overset{v}{Q} = 1 - \exp \left\{ \ln \left[\sum_{j=0}^{n-r} \frac{z^j}{j!} \right] - z \right\} \tag{16}$$

where $z = -r \ln (1-q)$

Similarly, the equation for a set of identical, parallel, and redundant units in hot standby is:

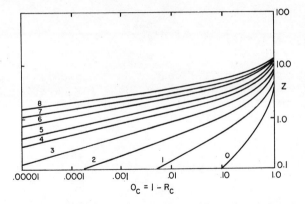

Fig. 6A.   Alternative Display of Effect of Redundancy

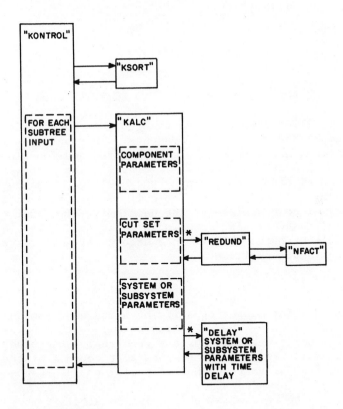

* IF REQUIRED

Fig. 7.   Subroutine Organization

$$A_H = \sum_{k=r}^{n} \frac{n!}{k!(n-k)!} \, a^k (1-a)^{n-k} \tag{17}$$

Unfortunately, equation (17) cannot be graphically displayed for all combinations of r and n such as was done for equation (14) in Fig. 6. This poses no problem for inclusion into the KITT-1 code. Equation (17) can be modified to the following form:

$$\overset{v}{Q} = 1 - A_H = 1 - \sum_{k=r}^{n} \frac{n!}{k!(n-k)!} \, (1-q)^k \, q^{n-k} \tag{18}$$

To complete the calculations made by the KITT code, $\overset{v}{W}$ or $\overset{v}{Q}$ for a redundant cut set must be calculated. For either hot or cold standby, the following equation was derived[10].

$$\overset{v}{W} = [-\sum_{k=1}^{r} (-1)^k \binom{r}{k} w^k][\binom{n}{r} q^{n-r}] \tag{19}$$

The information required to modify the KITT-1 code for time delays and redundant units is now complete.

EXPLANATION AND USE OF THE MODIFIED COMPUTER CODE

The KITT-1 computer code was reorganized for the inclusion of time delays and redundant components. This was done to subdivide the numerous algorithms into more limited and functional subprograms. The new organization is shown in Fig. 7. The primary calculations performed by each subprogram as they relate to the equations presented earlier are noted in Table I. Future reference to the modified KITT-1 code will be by the name "KITT-IT" code. It should be mentioned that existing coded data decks for KITT-1 input are fully compatible with the KITT-IT code except for some restrictions on component data specification.

Using the KITT-IT code, system reliability of the solids processing section of the oil shale project in Fig. 1 can be readily programmed. Throughput capacity of units upstream and downstream of time delays must be checked using equation (13) to insure that availabilities not exceeding 100% are required. Otherwise, the calculated process availability would be incorrect because of the absence of sufficient upstream throughput capacity to insure a non-empty tank.

It may be helpful at this point to simplify the process to a form such as illustrated in Fig. 9. This aids in generation of the fault tree. From the fault tree or the block diagram, minimal cut sets may be obtained.

Since the proposed example is primarily a series arrangement (which is the case in many processes), the minimal cut sets can easily be determined by inspection. The minimal cut sets are:

1.   (Primary Crusher Train Cut Set Failure
2.   (4), Collecting Conveyor Failure
3.   (4), Collecting Conveyor Failure (Either Conveyor failure results in system failure with respect to the rated throughput).
4.   (5), Transport Conveyor Failure
5.   (6), Tripper Conveyor Failure
6.   (Secondary Crusher Train Cut Set Failure)

Note that the redundant units are actually a "train" or a series of units in parallel and that these trains must be treated as a separate subsystem to make the problem manageable.

The sketch in Fig. 10 shows the same process modified for input to the KITT-IT program. Additional "dummy" time delays have been added to facilitate the storage of intermediate calculated values. The addition of a time delay unit requires that all upstream units be treated as a subsystem. Reliability calculations are executed for the subsystem and the results for the subsystem are then adjusted to reflect the time delay.

The KITT-IT code then stores the final overall reliability parameters for a subsystem with a time delay for future reference. The results are recalled as if the subsystem and time delay combined were a single component. Thus addition of a "dummy" time delay, unit 14, groups units 1, 2, and 3 together as a subsystem with a time delay specified by component 14 input data. The subsystem, adjusted for the presence of a time delay, can then be treated as a single unit, unit 14, in future calculations.

The order of calculating subsystem reliability parameters is left to the process designer. In general, subsystems will normally be treated in a left to right sequence where system flow is from left to right. The subsystems considered for Fig. 8 are shown by the dashed lines in Fig. 9.

A tabulation of the assumed reliability characteristics of the individual units for the shale material handling process is given in Table II. The unavailability, Q, of various portions of the process is graphed in Fig. 11. Steady state unavailability, can be considered as existing at t = 100 hours for all the subsystems shown. Curve E indicates that an onstream factor of 0.62 can be regarded as the best estimate of the average availability of the overall process. This availability exists for the capacity of (3400) x (14) = 13,600 tons/hr (with four secondary crusher trains in operation).

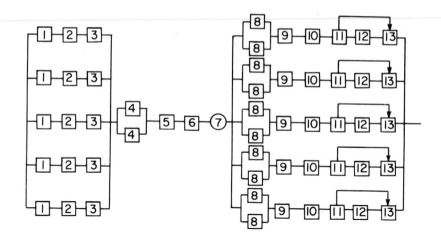

Fig. 8.   Block Diagram

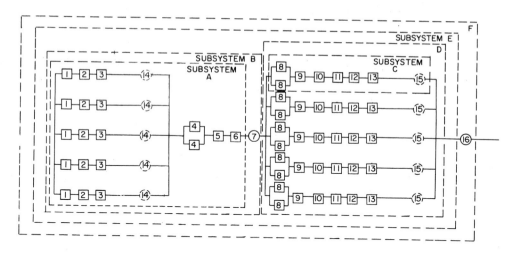

Fig. 9.   Blocking for Fig. 8

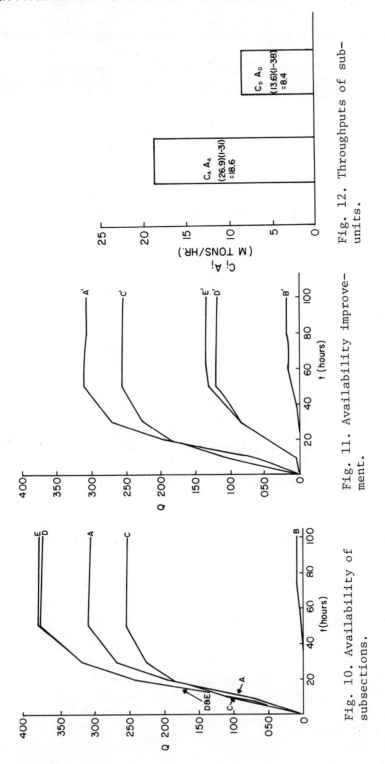

Fig. 10. Availability of subsections.

Fig. 11. Availability improvement.

Fig. 12. Throughputs of sub-units.

To illustrate where process changes can be made to improve over-all system availability, the bar graph representation of subsystem throughput around each time delay of the process in Fig. 12 may be instructive. According to equation (13), $c_A A_A$ must be greater than or equal to $c_D A_D$, which is true. However, $c_D A_D$ is less than half of $c_A A_A$. This indicates that subsystem D must be increased in capacity if it is necessary to increase availability through the use of a storage tank.

Assuming that an overall system availability of 0.95 is desired at a capacity rating of 13,600 tons/hr, implies that an average throughput of (13,100) x (0.95) = 12,920 tons/hr. is required. Keep-ing subsystem A the same, the availability of subsystem D can be estimated using equation (9).

$$0.05 \geq Q_E \cong 1 - (1 - Q_B)(1 - Q_D)$$

$$(1 - Q_D) \geq 0.95/(1 - .009)$$

$$Q_D \leq 0.0414$$

If only additional secondary crusher trains were added to increase the availability of subsystem D, three standby trains would provide (see equation (18))

$$Q_D^v = 1 - \sum_{k=4}^{7} \frac{7!}{k!(7-k)!}(1-.245)^k(.245)^{7-k} = 0.132$$

Four standby trains would provide

$$Q_D^v = 1 - \sum_{k=4}^{8} \frac{8!}{k!(8-k)!}(1-.245)^k(.245)^{8-k} = 0.0297$$

which gives

$$Q_E = 1 - (1-.009)(1-.0297) = 0.0384$$

or

$$A_E \cong 0.96$$

Thus, the design objective is met.

CONCLUSION

An overview of the KITT-1 computer algorithm for reliability analysis has been given. The algorithm has been modified to permit the handling of two elements common in process technology: (a) a time delay and; (b) redundant standby units. Use of the modified

TABLE 1

Program Name	Program Function	Comments
KONTROL	Main Program	Input of Primary Instructions. Loop control of each subtree (sybsystem)
KSORT	Identifies and sorts components by type	Identifies and sorts component types as either: 1. Non-repairable 2. Repairable 3. Inhibit Condition 4. Time delay
		* For Time Delays, information may be stored in sequential order or in an order prescribed by the programmer. Input of Time Delay information (e.g., values of Q and W) may be arbitrarily input.
KALC	Major Calculational Algorithm	If a time delay is found as a component or a cut set, program assumes Q and W are already stored in memory for use
	1. Calculates component data	Eq. (3) and (4) or (5) and (6) are used.
	2. Calculates cut set parameters	Eq. (7) and (8) are used.
	3. Calculates system parameters	Eq. (9) and (10) are used.
DELAY	Calculates system parameters with a time delay	Adjusts subsystem values using eq. (11) and (12).
REDUND	Calculates cut set reliability parameters for a set of redundant components.	Eq. (10, (18), and (19) are used depending upon cold or hot standby. Standby status set internally in program KALC.
NFACT	Calculates factorial	
BRAK	Adjust system parameters to account for simultaneous cut or path set failures	Not used when upper bound approximations are made. Subsequently, not used when time delays are present.

TABLE II

Unit	Name	(1/hr.)	τ (hr.)
1	Apron Feeder A	.003	25
2	Roll Crusher A	.0015	50
3	Belt Feeder A	.003	25
4	Collecting Conveyor	.001	25
5	Transport Conveyor	.0005	25
6	Tripper Conveyor	.0005	25
7	Coarse Ore Stockpile	0	-36 [1]
8	Apron Feeder B	.002	25
9	Secondary Crusher	.001	50
10	Belt Feeder B	.002	25
11	Single Deck Vibrating Screen	.003	15
12	Roll Crusher B	.001	50
13	Double Deck Vibrating Screen	.0003	15
14	Primary Crusher Train	0	-.000001
15	Secondary Crusher Train	0	-.000001
16	Shale Fines Storage	0	-7.35 [2]

---

[1] 500,000 tons/13,600 tons/hr. = 36 hrs.

[2] 100,000 tons storage at 13,600 tons/hr.

algorithm, has been demonstrated for a shale materials handling process having both elements.

ACKNOWLEDGMENTS

Support for this research was provided by Grant ENG-75-17613 from the National Science Foundation.

NOMENCLATURE

a	Component availability	---
A	Availability of unit or system	---
c	Capacity of unit	Units/time
MTTF	Mean time to failure	hr.
MTTR	Mean time to repair	hr.
n	Number of components	---
N_c	Number of cut sets	---
q	Q of a component	---
Q	Probability of failure at time t; Unavailability, unreliability	---
r	Number of units required to be operating	---
R	Probability of operation at time t; availability, reliability	---
t	Time	hr.
T	Time delay	hr.
w	W of a component	Failures/hr.
W	Expected number of failures/unit time; rate of failure	Failures/hr.
Z	$-r (\ln a)$	---
τ	Repair time	hr.
λ	Failure intensity (Failure rate of a component	$hr.^{-1}$
Λ	Failure intensity of a unit (cut set or system)	$hr.^{-1}$

Superscripts and Subscripts

v   Property of a cut set

—   Failed state

o   System property

i   Item (i) property

u,U   Upstream component, cut set, or system property

d,D   Downstream component, cut set, or system property

C   Cold standby

H   Hot standby

REFERENCES

1.   Barlow, R. E., and F. Proschan, Mathematical Theory of
      Reliability, John Wiley & Sons, New York (1965).

2.   Fussell, J. B., Henry, E. B., and N. H. Marshall. "MOCUS, A
      Computer Program to Obtain Minimal Sets from Fault Trees,"
      ANCR-1156 (1974).

3.   Fussell, J. B., "How to Hand Calculate System Reliability
      Characteristics," IEEE Trans. on Reliability, R-24, 3, August
      (1975).

4.   Henley, E. J., "Concept of Failure Distribution," Process and
      Equipment Reliability. AIChE Today Series (1977).

5.   _____, and H. Hoshin. "Effect of Storage Tanks on
      Plant Availability," Industrial and Engineering Chemistry
      Fundamentals, Vol. 16, 439, Nov. (1976).

6.   Inoue, K., Gandhi, S. L., and E. J. Henley, "Optimal Reliability
      Design of Process Systems," IEEE Transactions on Reliability,
      Vol. R-23, No. 1, 29, April (1974).

7.   Veseley,W.E., Narum, R. E., "PREP and KITT: Computer Codes
      for Automatic Synthesis of Fault Trees," IN-1349, Aug. (1970).

8.   Veseley,W.E., "A Time-Dependent Methodology for Fault Tree
      Evaluation," Nuclear Engineering and Design, Vol. 13, No. 2,
      337, August (1970).

9.   "Availability Manual," Imperial Chemical Industries Ltd., Corporate Laboratories, The Heath, Runcorn, England, Aug. 3 (1976).

10.   Henley, E. J., Kumamoto, H., "Reliability Engineering and Risk Assessment," Prentice Hall Book Co., Englewood Cliffs, NJ (1980).

ABOUT THE DEFINITION OF COHERENCY IN BINARY SYSTEM RELIABILITY ANALYSIS

A. Amendola, Commission of the European Communities, Joint Research Centre, Ispra Establishment, 21020 Ispra (Va), Italy
S. Contini, Sigen S.p.A., Via S. Caboto 5, Corsico, Milano, Italy

INTRODUCTION

This paper was stimulated by discussions which arose at the last NATO-ASI in Urbino and by Caldarola's new definition of coherency [1]. Moreover, the development of a procedure, for the analysis of a fault-tree constituted by AND-OR-NOT gates [2], showed the necessity of identifying the possible logic structures of actual physical systems.

In this paper, we show some simple examples of the so-called non-coherent systems, whose analysis leads to the conclusion that the terms "coherent" or "non-coherent" do not seem to be physically appropriate. Therefore, we propose to classify the systems simply according to the properties of their boolean functions, because these may have some effect on the methods required for their analysis.

The classical definition of coherency, for binary systems, was related to the monotonicity of the structure function [3]. A system was said to be coherent if its boolean function $\phi(x_1, x_2, ..., x_n)$ is monotonic (increasing), that is for each vector $X' = (x'_1, x'_2, ..., x'_n)$ which dominates another vector $X'' = (x''_1, x''_2, ..., x''_n)$, we get

$$\phi(x'_1, x'_2, ..., x'_n) \geqslant \phi(x''_1, x''_2, ..., x''_n)$$

and each component is relevant.

This definition was somewhat linked to the physical behaviour of the system, in the sense that usually a failure of a component cannot lead the system into a safer state. Systems described only by AND-OR operators belong to this group.

According to this definition, the exclusive OR is said to be non-coherent; in fact, its structure function is not monotonic. An example of an electrical system

79

with an exclusive OR was given by Fussell [4]. In general, the use of the NOT operator, results in a non-monotonic structure function. In these cases, the cut set definition is no more appropriate: the more appropriate term is the one of prime
implicant.

During the development of his methodology, Caldarola has noted that the definition of monotonic functions is doubtful for multistate systems [1]. Since his procedure requires the determination of the complete base of the prime implicants
and then the search for all irredundant bases (forms), he had the necessity to distinguish between the case in which the complete base is already irredundant from the
other ones. Therefore, he called the boolean functions which admit only one minimal
form to be coherent which is at the same time complete and irredundant.

We note that the exclusive OR is non-coherent according to the classical definition, and coherent according to Caldarola's.

In general, a boolean function may be classified as follows:

i)   monotonic functions;
ii)   non-monotonic functions:
       a)   functions which admit only one minimal form, which is at the same time
             complete and irredundant;
       b)   functions which admit only one minimal form, which is not complete;
       c)   functions which admit more than one minimal form.

The proposed classification results are useful for the choice of the proper way
to perform the logical analysis. Indeed, in general, the boolean function can be
analysed according to two different approaches: the first one, as already mentioned,
consists of the determination of the boolean disjunction of the complete set of
prime implicants. (We maintain here the clear notation of [1]); from this complete
base, all the irredundant expressions can be found, among which the simplest ones
can be identified. The second one permits the direct identification of one of the
irredundant forms, without determining the complete base. The second approach is
much faster than the first, and is not equivalent to it only in the case of iic), but it
contains all the information required for the numerical analysis.

Discussion of the analysis methods is not within the scope of this paper, which
is focused only on the possible logical structures.

SYSTEMS CHARACTERIZED BY A NON-COMPLETE MINIMAL FORM

We will not discuss systems characterized by monotonic functions, since every
usual fault-tree constituted by AND-OR gates results in this type of functions.
Moreover, we refer to reference [2,4] for the discussion of systems of type iia).
Systems, in which a component causes in certain situations a danger with its correct
action, may have a minimal form which is not complete. Consider, for instance, the
traffic light at the crossing of two monodirectional roads. Assume that it acts properly and is red for 1 and green for 2. What is the probability that a car "a", moving
towards 1 has an accident in such a situation? The accident occurs if "a" acts

properly and stops ($\overline{A}$) and a car "b" fails to stop (B), or, if "a" fails to stop (A) and a car "c" moving towards 2 is crossing (C). The boolean function results in:

$$AC + \overline{A}B.$$

This form is minimal but not complete, since it does not contain the prime implicant BC, as can be seen from its Karnaugh map:

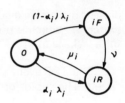

Fig. 1. Transition diagram.

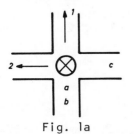

Fig. 1a

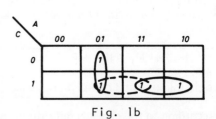

Fig. 1b

Such a system is non-coherent according to [1] and in this case the terminology would seem to be appropriate to its physical behaviour, because whatever the behaviour of "a" is, a dangerous situation exists.

Consider now Fig. 2. An electric line "a", charged inductively, has at its end a load "b" whose failure mode (B) is the short circuit. "z" is a protection against overvoltages which occur if the line fails open (A). A component located in 0 may be damaged if "b" is in short circuit with "a" safe ($\overline{A}B$) or if "a" fails open and "z" fails to protect (AZ). The logical function

$$AZ + \overline{A}B$$

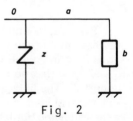

Fig. 2

is minimal but non complete, since it does not include the prime implicant BZ. In this case a dangerous situation (B) is transmitted through the safe state of "a". This is a very frequent case, but, normally, the probability of the safe state (such as A) is taken equal to 1, so that a "coherent" system is only an approximation for a real system.

By means of the following example (fig.3) we can show that, independently of numerical approximations, the terms coherency or non-coherency do not apply to the system physical behaviour.

Consider an electric load "c" in a room in which explosive mixture may be

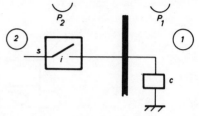

Fig. 3

present due to leakage (P_1). Let "c" be protected against short circuit by a fast switch "i" which is properly isolated "s" since a voltaic arc is an explosive trigger for a leakage mixture (P_2).

The TOP event we consider is the explosion in the case that "c" fails in short circuit. The explosion occurs if "i" fails to open and there is a leakage P_1 (IP_1), or if "I" does not fail to open (I), the isolator "s" fails (S) and there is a leakage P_2 (ISP_2). The function is

$$IP_1 + \bar{I}SP_2$$

and it would be non-coherent, since this minimal form is not complete. But, if $P_1 = P_2$, that is the room is the same (or a loss in 1 also affects 2 and vice versa), the function

$$IP_1 + \bar{I}SP_1 = IP_1 + P_1 S$$

is not only minimal and complete but even monotonic!

According to the classical definition, the case $P_1 = P_2$ is said to be coherent, whereas the case $P_1 \neq P_2$ is said to be non-coherent, even if the latter is safer than the former, that is, better designed.

SYSTEMS CHARACTERIZED BY MORE THAN ONE MINIMAL FORM

Systems, in which danger or abnormal loads arise from unbalanced situations, may have more than one minimal form. Consider Fig.4a, where in normal situations a load P_b is in equilibrium with two loads P_a and P_c so that no force exists at the support E. The links a, b and c may fail. An abnormal load in E occurs according to the following boolean expression (where X indicates the failed state and $\bar{X}$ the safe state of the component "x"), which is given in its complete disjunctive form.

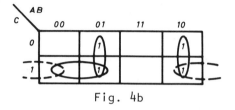

$P_b = P_a + P_c$

Fig. 4a

$$A\bar{B} + \bar{A}B + \bar{A}C + \bar{B}C.$$

From Fig.4b we can see that it has two minimal forms:

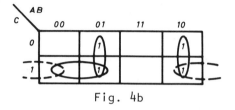

Fig. 4b

and, namely:

(1) $A\overline{B} + \overline{A}B + \overline{A}C$

(2) $A\overline{B} + \overline{A}B + \overline{B}C$

The occurrence probability does not change with the minimal form chosen for the calculation, as it can be easily verified.

We note that, if $P_a = P_b$ and $P_c = 0$, the minimal form is only one, namely

$A\overline{B} + \overline{A}B$

that is, the form of an exclusive OR (coherent according to (1)).

It must be noted that the state AB is a safe state but it is reached by passing through unsafe states. Therefore, this example may be of practical relevance only for systems in which abnormal loads lead to a failure after a given period of time. Such cases may be found in those mechanical structures where failure modes are creep deformations. Nevertheless, examples of systems having more than one minimal form, for which the safe state is reached without passing through unsafe states, can be found in a more detailed paper [2].

CONCLUSIONS

The above considerations have shown that, even if the approximation of neglecting the NOT operator results in a conservative evaluation of the probability of occurrence of a given TOP event, a complete and correct logical analysis of real systems requires a procedure able to handle the NOT gates.

The existence of systems described by boolean functions, which may have more than one minimal form, suggests the usefulness of a procedure able to analyse the so-called non-coherent systems. These procedures are necessary for multistate systems; the coherency or non-coherency of such systems is to be referred only to their boolean functions and cannot be predicted by "a priori" analysis or by an engineering judgement.

ACKNOWLEDGEMENTS

Thanks are due to Mr. Caldarola and Mr. Volta for their valuable contribution and suggestions.

REFERENCES

[1] Caldarola L., Fault-tree Analysis with Multistate Components, in this pro-
     ceeding.
[2] Amendola A., Contini S., Analysis of Logical Structures in System Reliability
     Assessment, J.R.C., Ispra Establishment, EUR-report (in preparation).
[3] Barlow R., Proshan F., Statistical Theory of Reliability and Life Testing,
     Holt, Rinehart and Winston, New York, 1975.
[4] Fussell J., Fault-tree Analysis - Concepts and Techniques, Proc. NATO Ad-
     vanced Study Institute on Generic Techniques of System Reliability
     Assessment, Liverpool, July 1973.

REGENERATION DIAGRAMS

G W PARRY

UNITED KINGDOM ATOMIC ENERGY AUTHORITY

SRD, CULCHETH, WARRINGTON

SUMMARY

The diagrammatic formalism developed to deal with component reliability problems is summarised. The effect of the time structure of failure and repair processes is discussed. An extention to a simple system calculation illustrates the incorrectness of one of the equations of kinetic tree theory.

1. INTRODUCTION

In this talk I will present a theoretical technique for solving component reliability problems which has been developed at SRD over the last year. The method, which derives from the use of Feynman diagrams in quantum field theory, has been described in detail in References 1, 2 and 3. Consequently, I will concentrate on the application to two problems and use this as a vehicle to elaborate on some points which are relevant to the understanding of the controversy, typified by the Vesely-Murchland dispute [4,5] over the validity of the equations used in the Kinetic Tree Theory of Vesely. [6]

The first problem is the calculation of the availability of a repairable component. This introduces the important concept of the time-structure of failure and repair processes. The second problem is the calculation of the unreliability of a simple system, namely a two component redundant system. This provides a counter-example to Vesely's proposed calculation of system reliability.

The above-mentioned technique has two major advantages:

(1)   It is diagrammatic and explicit and consequently avoids
       complicated probability arguments.

(2)   It treats both commonly used 'time structures' on a
       similar basis, and can also be used when the time struc-
       tures of the failure and repair process are different.
       eg Bad as Old for failure and Good as New for repair.

2.   NOTATION

      We will use the following notation for the quantities of interest
to this presentation.

(a) $q(t)$ — unavailability — the probability that the component
       is in a failed state at time t. $p(t) = 1-q(t)$ — availa-
       bility — the probability that the component is operational
       at time t.

(b) $\lambda(t)$ — conditional failure rate — the conditionality will
       be discussed in Section 4.

(c) $\omega_\lambda(t)$ — unconditional failure rate — $\omega_\lambda(t)dt$ is the proba-
       bility that the component fails in $(t, t + dt)$.

(d) $\mu(t)$ — conditional repair rate — the conditionality will
       be discussed in Section 4.

(e) $\omega_\mu(t)$ — unconditional repair rate — $\omega_\mu(t)dt$ is the proba-
       bility that the component is repaired in $(t, t + dt)$.

(f) $f_1(t)$ — cumulative distribution function of the time to
       first failure, ie $1-f_1(t)$ is the reliability.

      For the system characteristics capital letters will be used, the
lower case letters being reserved for component characteristics.

3.   REGENERATION DIAGRAMS — BASIC ELEMENTS

      There are four basic elements, each of which represents a proba-
bility:

(i)   Propagators

       $t_1 \overline{\qquad} t_2$ represents the probability of no failure in
                  (t_1, t_2).

       $t_1 \underline{\qquad} t_2$ represents the probability of no repair in
                  (t_1, t_2).

(ii) Flips (change of state)

t
↓   represents the probability of a failure in
           (t, t + dt).

t
↑   represents the probability of a repair in
           (t, t + dt).

When combined, these elements represent more complicated probabilistic statements so that for instance

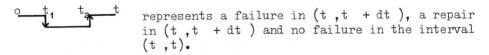

           represents a failure in $(t, t + dt)$, a repair
           in $(t, t + dt)$ and no failure in the interval
           (t, t).

When internal labelling is removed an integration over intermediate times is implied so that

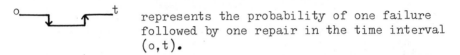

           represents the probability of one failure
           followed by one repair in the time interval
           (o, t).

To complete the definitions it is necessary to associate with
each diagram a mathematical expression to represent the relevant
probability but before doing this it is necessary to discuss the 'time
structure' of the failure and repair processes.

4.   TIME STRUCTURE

In Fig. 1 we draw three possibilities for the behaviour of the
function $\lambda(t)$ as the component under-goes failure and repair. The
first labelled 'As Good as New' (GN), following the notation of
Ascher,[7] is applicable to a component where repair is equivalent to
replacement by a new component. This is normally treated by Renewal
Theory.[8]   The second, labelled 'As Bad as Old' (BO), represents the
situation where, when the component is repaired, the failure rate is
as it would have been had the failure and repair not occurred. This
is the time dependence assumed by Veseley and would be applicable
possibly to the case where the "component" has many failure modes all
with approximately the same rate of occurrence and where failure and
repair of one mode does not significantly alter the overall failure
rate. The third possibility in Fig. 1 is labelled 'Not Quite as Bad
as Old' and is included to illustrate one of the infinite number of
alternatives to the first two. The important point to notice is
that the conditionality on the function $\lambda(t)$ is different for the GN
and BO cases. The time structure of the function $\mu(t)$ may be modelled
in similar ways.

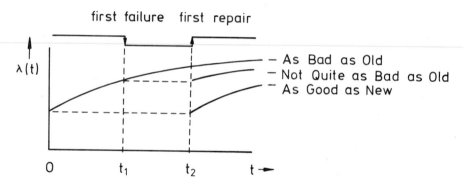

Fig. 1.   Time structure of λ (t)

For the GN the function $\lambda(t)dt$ represents the probability that the component fails in $(t, t + dt)$ given it did not fail in (o, t), whereas for the BO function $\lambda(t)dt$ represents the probability that the component fails in $(t, t + dt)$ given that it was working at time t. In the latter case it is irrelevant whether the component did not fail in (o, t), or whether it had one or more failures in (o, t). This difference in conditionality leads to a different mathematical equivalence for the elements of the regeneration diagrams as discussed in the next section.

5.   MATHEMATICAL EQUIVALENCE

Consider the process described by the diagram

The propagator $\overset{o\underline{\hspace{1cm}}t_1}{}$ is the same in both BO and GN schemes

ie, $\exp\left(-\int_{o}^{t_1}\lambda(t')dt'\right)$

and $\overset{t_1}{\downarrow}$ is given by $\lambda(t)dt$

But $t_1\underline{\hspace{1cm}}t_2$ is given by $\exp\left(-\int_{o}^{t_2-t_1}\mu(t')dt'\right)$ in GN and $\exp \left(- \int_{t_1}^{t_2} \mu(t')dt' \right)$ in BO

t_2

↑   is given by $\mu(t_2 - t_1)dt_2$ in GN

and $\mu(t_2)dt_2$ in BO

$t_2 \!-\!\!-\!^t$ is given by $\exp \left(- \int_0^{t-t_2} \lambda(t')dt' \right)$ in GN

and by $\exp \left(- \int_{t_2}^{t} \lambda(t')dt' \right)$ in BO

t

↓   is given by $\lambda(t-t_2)dt$ in GN

and by $\lambda(t)dt$ in BO

By defining the propagators and flips in the appropriate way therefore, the time structure of the failure and repair processes can be taken into account. In particular it will be noticed that for the GN scheme the change of time origin at each change of state is taken into account.

Note that for both GN and BO the reliability, or probability that no failure has occurred in (o,t), is given by

$$\exp \left(- \int_0^t \lambda(t')dt' \right) \tag{1}$$

6.   THE INTEGRAL EQUATION FOR THE AVAILABILITY

To demonstrate the use of the diagrams we will consider the derivation of the integral equation for the availability of a component subject to failure and repair. The availability, being the probability of the component working at time t is merely the sum of the probabilities represented by the following series of diagrams:

$$p(t) = \quad \overset{o}{\underline{\quad}}{}^{t} + \overset{o}{\overset{}{\underset{}{\sim}}}{}^{t} + \overset{o}{\overset{}{\underset{}{\sim}}}{}^{t} + \cdots \tag{2}$$

To sum this series of graphs it is sufficient to notice that the series may be factorized symbolically in the following way

$$p(t) = \overset{\circ\quad t}{\rule{1cm}{0.4pt}} + \left[\; \overset{\circ\quad t'}{\rule{1cm}{0.4pt}} + \overset{\circ}{\rule{0.3cm}{0.4pt}}\!\!\diagup\!\!\!\diagdown\!\!\overset{t'}{\diagup} + \overset{\circ}{\rule{0.3cm}{0.4pt}}\!\!\diagup\!\!\!\diagdown\!\!\diagup\!\!\!\diagdown\!\!\overset{t'}{\diagup} + \cdots \;\right].\left[\; \overset{t'}{\diagdown}\!\!\!\overset{t}{\diagup} \;\right]$$

(3)

where

$$-\;\overset{t'}{\diagdown}\;].\;[\;\overset{t'}{\diagdown}$$

implies an integration over the intermediate variable t'. Since the
first term in brackets in the second term on the RHS of Equation (3)
is the series of graphs representing $p(t')$ this represents an integral
equation for $p(t)$. In the BO time structure this is

$$p(t) = \exp\left(-\int_{\bullet}^{t} \lambda(t')dt'\right) +$$

$$\int_{0}^{t} p(t')\lambda(t')dt' \int_{t'}^{t} \exp\left(-\int_{t}^{t''}\mu(t_1)dt_1\right)\mu(t')dt''.$$

$$.\exp\left(-\int_{t''}^{t}\lambda(t_2)dt_2\right)$$

Equation (3) is only valid for the BO time structure. If GN is
being used the equation must be factorized immediately after a change
of state otherwise the argument of the element representing the change
of state is unknown. In this case therefore

$$p(t) = \overset{\circ\quad t}{\rule{1cm}{0.4pt}} + \left[\; \overset{\circ\quad t'}{\rule{0.6cm}{0.4pt}}\!\!\downarrow + \overset{\circ}{\rule{0.3cm}{0.4pt}}\!\!\diagup\!\!\!\diagdown\!\!\diagup\!\!\overset{t'}{\downarrow} + \overset{\circ}{\rule{0.3cm}{0.4pt}}\!\!\diagup\!\!\!\diagdown\!\!\diagup\!\!\!\diagdown\!\!\diagup\!\!\overset{t'}{\downarrow} + \cdots \;\right].\left[\;\rule{0.5cm}{0.4pt}\!\!\diagup\!\!\overset{t}{\rule{0.3cm}{0.4pt}}\;\right]$$

(4)

The first bracket in the second term on the RHS of Equation (4)
represents $\omega_\lambda(t')$ and Equation (4) therefore is an equation relating
to $p(t)$ to $\omega_\lambda(t)$. An integral equation for $\omega_\lambda(t)$ can be found in a
similar way by factorizing the series.

$$\omega_\lambda(t) = \overset{\circ\quad t}{\rule{0.6cm}{0.4pt}}\!\!\downarrow + \overset{\circ}{\rule{0.3cm}{0.4pt}}\!\!\diagup\!\!\!\diagdown\!\!\diagup\!\!\overset{t}{\downarrow} + \overset{\circ}{\rule{0.3cm}{0.4pt}}\!\!\diagup\!\!\!\diagdown\!\!\diagup\!\!\!\diagdown\!\!\diagup\!\!\overset{t}{\downarrow} + \cdots =$$

$$\overset{\circ\quad t}{\rule{0.6cm}{0.4pt}}\!\!\downarrow + \left[\; \overset{\circ\quad t'}{\rule{0.5cm}{0.4pt}}\!\!\downarrow + \overset{\circ}{\rule{0.3cm}{0.4pt}}\!\!\diagup\!\!\!\diagdown\!\!\diagup\!\!\overset{t'}{\downarrow} + \overset{\circ}{\rule{0.3cm}{0.4pt}}\!\!\diagup\!\!\!\diagdown\!\!\diagup\!\!\!\diagdown\!\!\diagup\!\!\overset{t'}{\downarrow} + \cdots \;\right].\left[\;\overset{t'}{\rule{0.5cm}{0.4pt}}\!\!\diagup\!\!\overset{t}{\downarrow}\;\right]$$

(5)

and this solution used to determine $p(t)$. The mathematical expressions for Equations (4) and (5) are

$$p(t) = \exp\left(-\int_{0}^{t}\lambda(t')dt'\right) +$$

$$\int_{0}^{t}\omega_\lambda(t')dt' \int_{t'}^{t}\exp\left(-\int_{0}^{t''-t'}\mu(t_1)dt_1\right)\mu(t''-t')dt''.$$

$$. \exp \left(- \int_{0}^{t-t''} \lambda(t_2)dt_2\right)$$

and

$$\omega_\lambda(t) = \exp\left(- \int_0^t \lambda(t')dt'\right) \lambda(t) +$$

$$\int_0^t \omega_\lambda(t')dt' \circ \int_{t'}^t \exp\left(- \int_0^{t''-t'} \mu(t_1)dt_1\right) \mu(t''-t')dt'.$$

$$. \exp\left(- \int_0^{t-t''} \lambda(t_2)dt_2\right) \lambda(t-t'')$$

7.   THE UNRELIABILITY OF A TWO COMPONENT REDUNDANT SYSTEM

In this section we will describe the extension of the diagrammatic method to calculate the unreliability of a two component redundant system. We shall restrict the discussion to constant repair rate μ and failure rate λ and identical components. This case may also be solved simply using Markov methods,[9] but the present calculation may be immediately adapted to an arbitrary time dependence for the repair rate in the GN scheme, and for both repair and failure rates in the BO scheme.

The failure of the system occurs when either component is in a failed state and the other subsequently fails. Graphically therefore,

$\Omega_\lambda^{(1)}$ — the probability of first system failure at time t =

$$+ \cdots + 1 \leftrightarrow 2 \qquad (6)$$

The x sign indicates that the probabilities represented by the upper and lower graph are multiplied together before integration over intermediate times and before the summation is performed, since the two series of graphs are highly correlated in the following sense. At all times before t, when component 1 fails component 2 must be working and while component 1 is failed component 2 must be working and vice versa. While component 1(2) is working component 2(1) may fail any number of times. These conditions are met if the propagator $\circ\!\!=\!\!\!=\!\!t'$ is merely $p(t')$ for a component, all other symbols having their usual meaning.

The series for $\Omega_\lambda^{(1)}$ may now be rewritten as

$$\Omega_\lambda^{(1)} = 2 \left[\quad + \quad + \cdots \right] \lambda$$

where

$$t_1 \rule{1cm}{0pt} t_2 = e^{-\lambda(t_2 - t_1)} \cdot p(t_2 - t_1), \quad t_1 \rule{1cm}{0pt} t_2 = e^{-u(t_2 - t_1)} e^{-\lambda(t_2 - t_1)}$$

$$t \downarrow = \lambda dt, \quad t \uparrow = \mu \, dt \tag{7}$$

Equation (7) may be solved by factorization of the series of diagrams as before.

$$= \quad + \left[\quad + \quad \cdots \right] \cdot \left[\quad \right] \tag{8}$$

Solving the integral equation by using Laplace Transforms and integrating $\Omega_\lambda^{(1)}$ yields $F_1(t)$

$$F_1(t) = \int_0^t \Omega_\lambda^{(1)}(t')dt' =$$

$$1 - \frac{R_2}{R_2 - R_1} e^{-R_1 t} + \frac{R_1}{R_2 - R_1} e^{-R_2 t} \tag{9}$$

with

$$R_1 + R_2 = 3\lambda + \mu$$

$$R_1 \cdot R_2 = 2\lambda^2$$

Vesely[6] claimed that $F_1(t)$ was given by

$$F_1(t) = 1 - \exp\left(-\int_0^t \Lambda(t')dt'\right) \tag{10}$$

where

$$\Lambda(t) = \frac{\Omega_\lambda(t)}{P(t)} \tag{11}$$

For the present case

$$\Lambda(t) = \frac{2\lambda(1-p(t))}{2-p(t)} \tag{12}$$

with

$$p(t) = \frac{\mu}{\lambda + \mu} + \frac{\lambda}{\lambda + \mu} \exp\left(-(\lambda+\mu)t\right) \tag{13}$$

Changing variables from t' to $p(t')$ it can be shown[10]

$$1 - \exp\left(-\int_0^t \Lambda(t')dt'\right) =$$

$$1 - \left[\angle\frac{2\lambda + \mu}{\lambda + \mu} - \frac{\lambda}{\lambda + \mu} \exp\left(-(\lambda+\mu)t\right) \angle \exp(-\lambda t)\right]^{\frac{2\lambda}{2\lambda + \mu}} \tag{14}$$

which is a very different form from Equation (9) and which therefore provides a counter example to Veseley's claim, and upholds Murchland's objection to Equation (10).

A numerical example of the difference between Equations (9) and (14) is given below.

$$\lambda = \mu = 1 \text{ unit} \quad t = 10 \text{ units, } F_1(t) = .9965$$
$$F_1(t) \text{ (Vesely)} \quad = .9983$$

$$\lambda = .1 \text{ unit} \quad \mu = 1 \text{ unit} \quad t = 10 \text{ units, } F_1(t) = .1337$$
$$F_1(t)(\text{Vesely}) \quad = .1412$$

8.   CONCLUSIONS

We have discussed briefly a diagrammatic method for solving reliability component problems. The method is an ideal vehicle for discussing the time structure of failure and repair processes. If time dependence of failure and repair rates is important it is imperative to specify the time structure assumed, as the structure of the equations is dependent on this assumption.

The time structure is the most important difference between the approach of Vesely and the renewal theory approach at the component level, and criticisms of Vesely's formalism based on renewal theory are not valid as the two formalisms represent different models. A more cogent point on which to criticize the Vesely approach might be to enquire whether Bad as Old models of components are indeed sensible. We have presented a calculation which explicitly displays the incorrectness of Vesely's formula for system unreliability. At the component level Vesely's calculation is correct since the function $\lambda(t)$ is a given function, independent of $\mu(t)$ and hence does not know about repair. $\Lambda(t)$ however is a function of the individual μ's and λ's and therefore does know about repair and cannot be used to calculate system reliability. The particular technical point is probably of no great significance in practise (since unreliability is not often used to describe the effectiveness of a system over a long time) but is an important point of principle.

REFERENCES

1. D H Worledge and G W Parry, An Operator Representation of Failure and Repair, Nucl Eng and Des 45 : 261 (1978).
2. G W Parry and D H Worledge, The Use of Regeneration Diagrams to Solve Component Reliability Problems, Nuc Eng and Des 45 : 271 (1978).
3. G W Parry and D H Worledge, The Downtime Distribution in Reliability Theory, Nucl Eng and Des 49 : 295 (1978).
4. J D Murchland, Comment on "A Time-Dependent Methodology for Fault Tree Evaluation," Nucl Eng and Des 22 : 167 (1972).
5. W E Vesely, Reply to J D Murchland's Comment, Nucl Eng and Des 22 : 170 (1972).
6   W E Vesely, A Time-Dependent Methodology for Fault Tree Evaluation, Nucl Eng and Des 13 : 337 (1970).
7. H E Ascher, Evaluation of Repairable System Reliability Using the "Bad as Old" Concept, IEEE Trans on Reliability, R17 no 2 : 108 (1968).
8. D R Cox, Renewal Theory - Methuen's Monographs on applied probability and statistics. Gen Editor - M S Bartlett, Methuen (1962).
9. J P Signoret, Use of Markov Processes for Reliability Problems - this course.
10. J D Murchland, Private Communication.

UNCERTAINTY PROPAGATION IN FAULT-TREE ANALYSIS

A. G. Colombo

Commission of the European Communities
Joint Research Centre - Ispra Establishment
Ispra, Italy

ABSTRACT

This paper deals with methods of investigating the propagation of the uncertainty from the lower level (primary event) to the higher level (top) of a complex system, such as a nuclear plant.

A numerical method to determine the probability distribution at each level of the fault-tree is illustrated.

1. INTRODUCTION

The failure probability of a complex system, such as a nuclear plant, is usually computed assuming fixed values for the failure parameters of the components. However, due to various causes of variability, a failure parameter is not a fixed value but a random variable.

Assuming for the plant an AND/OR fault-tree model, it follows that for investigating the propagation of the uncertainty from the primary event level to the top, one has to combine random variables. An OR gate with n inputs requires a sum of n random variables, an AND gate requires a product.

This paper discusses various methods of investigating the propagation of the uncertainty in a fault-tree. First, assuming that each failure parameter is defined by its mean and standard deviation, the coefficient of variation at the output of AND gates and the coefficient of variation at the output of OR gates are given. Expressions to derive a probability interval are also given.

Finally, assuming that each failure parameter is defined by its density, a numerical method to derive the probability distribution at each level of the fault-tree is illustrated.

2. UNCERTAINTY AT PRIMARY EVENT LEVEL

The major causes of variability of a failure parameter are the following: differences from component to component, different environmental conditions, different maintenance policies and different operational demands.

In each special situation the choice of the uncertainty distribution for a failure parameter should be based on rational considerations. In this paper we do not tackle this fundamental problem, which, in our opinion, requires basic research; we only discuss methods to propagate the uncertainty from the lower level to the top of a fault-tree.

To define the uncertainty at lower level we considered the following distributions: lognormal, loguniform and gamma. The lognormal is a partner to the normal distribution in the sense that, as the normal enters when the variation is characterized by increments, the lognormal enters when the variation is characterized by factors or percentages. It was adopted in WASH-1400[1]. This choice was mainly motivated by the fact that, in some cases where data were available, the lognormal gave adequate empirical fitting. The lognormal is certainly a distribution of interest in various cases. Nevertheless, it has at least two drawbacks: (i) it is defined in the interval $(0, \infty)$ whilst a failure parameter is surely greater than zero and takes a value on a limited range; (ii) it has a long tail which seems unrealistic in many situations. These drawbacks may be avoided by considering a loguniform distribution. This distribution is also defined on a logarithmic scale, moreover its interval of definition (A, B) may be chosen in a way that $(0 < A < B < \infty)$.

The third distribution we considered is the gamma. If a Bayesian approach is adopted to estimate the failure parameter at lower level, the gamma has the advantage of being a conjugate distribution in the case where a Poisson sampling distribution is assumed.

3. UNCERTAINTY PROPAGATION

3.1 Propagation of the Coefficient of Variation

Let X_1, X_2, ... X_n be the inputs to a gate, and $\mu_1, \mu_2, \ldots \mu_n$; $\sigma_1, \sigma_2, \ldots \sigma_n$; $c_1 = \sigma_1/\mu_1, c_2, \ldots c_n$, respectively the means, the standard deviations and the coefficients of variation of X_1, X_2, ... X_n. In addition, we assume μ_i, $\sigma_i \ll 1$, $(i=1, 2, \ldots n)$.

If the gate is an OR gate, it follows that the output has mean

$$\mu_s^{(n)} = \mu_1 + \mu_2 \ldots + \mu_n \tag{1}$$

and standard deviation

$$\sigma_s^{(n)} = (\sigma_1^2 + \sigma_2^2 \ldots \sigma_n^2)^{1/2} . \tag{2}$$

In the case of two inputs, the coefficient of variation of the output is

$$c_s^{(2)} = \frac{(\sigma_1^2 + \sigma_2^2)^{1/2}}{\mu_1 + \mu_2} \tag{3}$$

We also obtain

$$\frac{1}{\sqrt{2}} MIN(c_1, c_2) \leq c_s^{(2)} < MAX(c_1, c_2) . \tag{4}$$

This result shows that an OR gate reduces the uncertainty in the sense that the coefficient of variation of the output is lower than the largest coefficient of variation in input.

The coefficient of variation of the sum of n random variables which have the same coefficient of variation c is:

$$c_s^{(n)} = \frac{c}{n^{1/2}} \cdot \tag{5}$$

For an AND gate with two inputs, we obtain the output mean

$$\mu_p^{(2)} = \mu_1 \cdot \mu_2 \cdot \tag{6}$$

The output standard deviation and coefficient of variation are, respectively

$$\sigma_p^{(2)} = (\sigma_1^2 \sigma_2^2 + \mu_1^2 \sigma_2^2 + \mu_2^2 \sigma_1^2)^{1/2}, \tag{7}$$

$$c_p^{(2)} = (c_1^2 + c_2^2 + c_1^2 c_2^2)^{1/2} \cdot \tag{8}$$

We also obtain

$$MAX(c_1, c_2) < c_p^{(2)} \leqslant c_M (2 + c_M^2)^{1/2} \tag{9}$$

where

$$c_M = MAX(c_1, c_2).$$

Expression (9) shows that an AND gate increases the uncertainty. The coefficient of variation of the output is greater than the largest coefficient of variation in input.

The coefficient of variation of the product of n random variables which have the same coefficient of variation c is

$$c_p^{(n)} = \left[(c^2+1)^n - 1 \right]^{1/2} \cdot \tag{10}$$

3.2 Derivation of a Probability Interval

Let X be the random variable which describes the uncertainty at a given level of a fault-tree. Let μ and σ be, respectively, the mean and the standard deviation of X. Markov-type inequalities allow us to compute a probability interval for $X^{2,3}$.

In particular, X being a positive random variable, the Cantelli inequalities give us

$$Pr(X < d) \leq \frac{\sigma^2}{\sigma^2 + (\mu - d)^2} \qquad (0 < d \leq \mu) \qquad (11)$$

$$Pr(X < d) \geq 1 - \frac{\mu}{d} \qquad (\mu \leq d \leq \frac{\mu^2 + \sigma^2}{\mu}) \qquad (12)$$

$$Pr(X < d) \geq 1 - \frac{\sigma^2}{\sigma^2 + (\mu - d)^2} \qquad (\frac{\mu^2 + \sigma^2}{\mu} \leq d) \quad , \qquad (13)$$

where d is any positive number.

3.3 Propagation of the Uncertainty Distributions

Assuming that the distributions of the failure parameters are completely defined by their densities, one can combine such distributions and derive the distribution of the uncertainty of each level of the fault-tree. To do this, we have developed a new method to combine random variables which consists of a systematic combination of the random variables concerned, and which may be considered as an improvement of the Montecarlo technique.

The method we implemented in the computer code SCORE, is described in ref. 4. The main idea consists in approximating each random variable by a histogram with N equal probability intervals, of probability $1/N$. In order to get the sum or the product of two random variables, the intervals of the corresponding histograms are systematically combined (sum or product) generating N^2 intervals of probability $1/N^2$. Then, these N^2 intervals are reduced to N intervals of probability $1/N$.

4. PROPAGATION OF THE UNCERTAINTY DISTRIBUTION IN A FAULT-TREE - A NUMERICAL EXAMPLE

To investigate, by a numerical example, the propagation of the distributions of the uncertainties in a fault-tree, we refer to a 750 failure mode fault-tree. It does not refer to any real plant, however it allows us to discuss some problems which arise in real situations. The logic of our sample fault-tree is as follows: the plant fails if 3 systems fail, each system fails if one of 25 subsystems fails, each subsystem fails if two components fail, and each component has 5 failure modes (see Fig. 1).

We assume that all the component failure modes have the same time-independent failure rate (exponential law), and that the parameter of such a law is the random variable λ. Operation time is $T \ll 1/\lambda$, so that one can consider the same distribution for X (the probability distribution at component failure mode level) as for λ. As mentioned in chapter 2, the uncertainty distributions we have considered for λ are the following: lognormal, loguniform and gamma.

Assigning to the three distributions the same median M and the same 95-th percentile U, we have computed the failure distribution at each level of the fault-tree by the code SCORE. For details concerning the computation see ref. 4 and ref. 5. The results obtained show that:

- If the error factor e = U/M is small (< 3), then the choice of the uncertainty distribution for the failure parameter is not critical. At each level of the fault-tree we obtained approximately the same value for the median and for the 95-th percentile in the three cases.

- Increasing the error factor, the differences increase. E. g. for e = 10 and median M of the failure distribution at failure mode level = 10^{-3}, we obtained a 95-th percentile at plant level equal to $9.95 \cdot 10^{-8}$ in the case of loguniform prior for λ, and equal to $20.4 \cdot 10^{-8}$ in the case of lognormal prior for λ, (see Fig. 1).

Fig. 2 shows how the median of the failure distribution at plant level varies as a function of the error factor e at the failure mode level for the three distributions considered, and M = 10^{-3}. It confirms the above considerations and, in particular, when assuming a lognormal distribution at failure mode level, a median at plant level of about ten times greater than in the case of log-uniform is obtained.

LEVEL	MEDIAN			95-th PERCENTILE		
	LU	G	LN	LU	G	LN
Failure Mode	10^{-3}	10^{-3}	10^{-3}	10^{-2}	10^{-2}	10^{-2}
Component (OR of 5 Failure Modes)	$1.17\cdot10^{-2}$	$1.06\cdot10^{-2}$	$.94\cdot10^{-2}$	$2.57\cdot10^{-2}$	$2.95\cdot10^{-2}$	$3.7\cdot10^{-2}$
Subsystem (AND of 2 Components)	$1.20\cdot10^{-4}$	$1.05\cdot10^{-4}$	$.92\cdot10^{-4}$	$4.30\cdot10^{-4}$	$4.88\cdot10^{-4}$	$6.03\cdot10^{-4}$
System (OR of 25 Subsystems)	$3.93\cdot10^{-3}$	$3.91\cdot10^{-3}$	$4.18\cdot10^{-3}$	$5.21\cdot10^{-3}$	$5.67\cdot10^{-3}$	$7.53\cdot10^{-3}$
Plant (AND of 3 Systems)	$6.02\cdot10^{-8}$	$6.00\cdot10^{-8}$	$7.62\cdot10^{-8}$	$9.95\cdot10^{-8}$	$11.4\cdot10^{-8}$	$20.4\cdot10^{-8}$

Fig. 1 - Median and 95-th percentile at the various levels of a plant, considering three different distributions for the failure modes (LN = lognormal, LU = loguniform, G = Gamma)

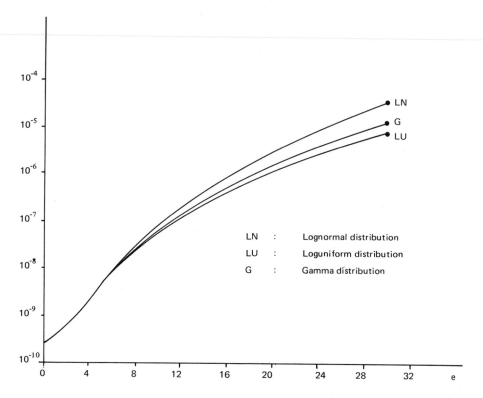

Fig. 2 - Median M of the failure distribution at plant level, as a
function of the error factor e at the failure mode level,
for the three distributions considered (median of the
failure distribution at failure mode level 10^{-3})

5. CONCLUSIONS

To conclude we make the following considerations:

- The analysis of the propagation of the uncertainties in a fault-
tree is an important problem which requires more investigation,
particularly in the nuclear field where the error factor of the
failure parameter distributions is very large.

- The code SCORE, which systematically combines random variables, is an efficient tool that may help in this task, at least
for numerical calculations.

- The choice of the uncertainty distribution for the failure parameters is still an open problem, which requires basic research.

6. REFERENCES

1. US Nuclear Regulatory Commission, "Reactor Safety Study. An Assessment of Accident Risks in US Commercial Nuclear Power Plants", WASH-1400, (NUREG-75/014), Washington D.C., October 1975
2. H.L. Royden, "Bounds on a Distribution Function when its First n Moments are Given", Ann. Math. Stat., vol. 24: 361-376 (1953)
3. Y.T. Lee and G.E. Apostolakis, "Probability Intervals for the Top Event Unavailability of Fault-Trees", UCLA-ENG 7663, University of California, Los Angeles, June 1976
4. A.G. Colombo and R.J. Jaarsma, "A Powerful Numerical Method to Combine Random Variables", to be published as EUR Report
5. A.G. Colombo, R.J. Jaarsma and L. Olivi, "On the Statistical Data Processing for a Safety Data System", Proceedings of the ANS Conference on Probabilistic Analysis of Nuclear Reactor Safety, Los Angeles, California, May 1978.

MULTISTATE SYSTEMS - LOGIC DIAGRAMS

Introduction by the Editors

The development and improvement of methodologies for the assessment of the risk from large technological systems have been the subjects of extensive investigations during the last decade. The release of the Reactor Safety Study [1] can be considered a milestone in the history of methodological developments. The report achieved a major goal in unifying, and actually applying to reactor systems, the various methods and techniques, which had been scattered in the journals and technical reports. Major methodological tools of the report were Fault Tree Analysis (FTA) and Event Tree Analysis (ETA). Commenting on these methodologies the Lewis Committee [2] stated: "Despite its shortcomings, WASH-1400 provides at this time the most complete single picture of accident probabilities associated with nuclear reactors. The fault-tree/event-tree approach coupled with an adequate data base is the best available tool with which to quantify these probabilities." Thus it is expected that these methodologies will play a major role in future risk analyses.

Fault tree analysis has been a popular subject of research even before the release of the Reactor Safety Study. One can distinguish two phases in FTA: the construction of a model of the system (the fault tree) using binary logic, and the probabilistic analysis of the tree. Due to its attractive mathematical problems the second phase has been the subject of many investigations, an early landmark paper being that of Vesely [3], which analyzed coherent fault trees with stochastically independent primary events. Many papers followed which improved and expanded Vesely's results.

As the methods for the analysis of fault trees became more and more sophisticated, it also became clear that their results could not be better than the fault tree itself. In other words, it was realized that a crucial question in FTA is how good a representation of the system is the fault tree used. This leads to two problems: the problem of completeness and that of adequate modelling.

Completeness is actually a misnomer because it implies that "all" the failure modes of a system must be built into the fault tree. This, of course, is impossible and the best that the analyst can hope for is to have included in the fault tree the "significant" failure modes, especially the ones that are the result of dependencies among components.

It became evident that a great deal of effort was duplicated, since many of the systems and components that various investigative teams analyzed were very similar, and that the findings of the groups as they developed fault trees were not widely available. This state of affairs led several investigators to attempt to automate the construction of fault trees. One of the earlier papers in this area is that of Fussell [4].

It is very important to emphasize that, although the computer automation of fault tree construction can greatly speed up this phase of FTA and readily allow the construction and investigation of very detailed fault trees, it should not be viewed as a replacement for the analyst's efforts. The insight and understanding provided by the analyst himself in carefully setting up the system and component models, as well as in choosing the appropriate TOP events, cannot be supplied by the computer. Furthermore, the fault tree so produced can only be as accurate and complete as the input provided by the analyst. If the automation of fault tree construction is viewed in this light, it can be seen as a useful tool in assisting the fault tree analyst and will become even more effective when combined with care and foresight in its use.

The paper by Salem and Apostolakis on "The CAT Methodology for Fault Tree Construction" discusses a methodology for the systematic construction of fault trees, which models the components via decision tables. The systematic modeling of the components led the investigators to acknowledge that there was a need to consider more than the traditional "good-bad" states since a component may be in one of several states, each of which may be important to the system. An essential feature of the methodology is that it is applicable to "static" or "synchronous" fault trees and that it traces the propagation of one signal (e.g. voltage or current, but not both). For most of the engineered safeguards of nuclear power plants such a methodology is adequate.

Reina and Squellati, in their paper on "L.A.M. Technique: Systematic Generation of Logical Structures in Systems Reliability Studies", consider the whole problem of modeling physical systems, whose configurations and the equations for the important variables (more than one) are known. Their method proceeds systematically from the functional and topological analysis of the system and its components to the construction of TOP conditions and the minimal sets that cause these top conditions to exist.

The paper by Garribba, Mussio and Naldi on "Multivalued Logic in the Representation of Engineering Systems" also discusses the whole problem of modelling and it utilizes operators as the fundamental models of components and subsystems. The trees do not contain the standard AND, OR and NOT gates, but more generalized ones.

The work that is contained in the preceding papers clearly indicates that, especially for process plants, simple binary component models are not adequate. Given fault trees with multistate components the existing probabilistic codes, which by at large can handle only coherent binary fault trees, are not useful. Caldarola, in his paper on "Fault Tree Analysis with Multistate Components", introduces what he calls a "Boolean algebra with restrictions on variables", which is a natural extension of the traditional Boolean Algebra. This allows the development of a complete theory for the probabilistic evaluation of fault trees, which also naturally utilizes previous work, e.g. in the identification of the shortest irredundant base of a Boolean function.

The question is now, where do we go from here? In the area of fault tree construction, it is clear that as the proposed methodologies are tested more in real life applications (and by analysts other than their developers) it will become clearer to a wider audience what the merits and drawbacks of each one are. As for the probabilistic analysis of fault trees with multistate components, it appears that Caldarola's work will play the role that Vesely's paper played ten years ago. Improvements and refinements will undoubtedly come, but at a slower pace, because the need for the analysis of such fault trees in the most general case is not so pressing as was the need to analyze coherent binary fault trees.

REFERENCES

[1]   U.S. Nuclear Regulatory Commission, "Reactor Safety Study", WASH-1400 (NUREG-75/014), NTIS, Springfield, Va. (Oct. 1975).
[2]   H.W. Lewis et al., Risk Assessment Review Group Report to the U.S. Nuclear Regulatory Commission, NUREG/CR-0400, NTIS, Springfield, Va. (Sept. 1978).
[3]   W.E. Vesely, "A time-dependent methodology for fault-tree evaluation", Nuclear Engineering and Design, 13: 337 (1970).
[4]   J.B. Fussell, "A formal methodology for fault-tree construction", Nuclear Science and Engineering, 52: 421 (1973).

THE CAT METHODOLOGY FOR FAULT TREE CONSTRUCTION

Steven L. Salem and George Apostolakis*

The Rand Corporation
Santa Monica, California 90406
*University of California
Los Angeles, California 90024

ABSTRACT

This paper presents a methodology for the systematic construction of fault trees based on decision tables. The presentation
is made through an example. The modeling capability of decision
tables is demonstrated and the construction of a fault tree from
the decision tables is shown in a step by step fashion.

INTRODUCTION

The automation of the construction phase of fault tree
analysis has attracted considerable attention in recent years.
Several methodologies have been proposed differing in the modeling
of components or variables and in their objectives (see, for
example, references 1-3 and other papers in this volume).

The present approach of Salem et al[4-5] consists of a scheme
which utilizes decision tables to model component behavior, a
method of describing the specific system configuration including
initial system states, and a means of defining a top event (or
events) of interest. Given these inputs, the decision table models
are used for the appropriate components within the system, and are
combined and edited to form a completed fault tree for the TOP
event desired. This fault tree may then be analyzed, either by
hand, or by any of several fault tree analysis codes, in order to
obtain the desired reliability (availability) information for the
TOP event. The methodology has been implemented in the CAT (Computer Automated Tree) code[6] and has been used to investigate

This research was supported by the Electric Power Research Institute

several systems, which include a residual heat removal system, a consequence limiting control system, and a containment spray recirculation system.

The current approach has several important features which make it especially useful in the analysis of nuclear systems, as well as of other, general types of systems. The decision table methodology is capable of modeling complex components of essentially any type, including mechanical, electrical and hydraulic. It can incorporate models for human interactions, environmental influences and provides a number of ways of treating common cause effects. Furthermore, the specific approach developed here allows the analysis of systems containing feedback loops, such as may be found in many types of control circuits in use in nuclear plants.

This paper presents the methodology through a simple example. The use and modeling capability of decision tables is discussed, as well as methods for constructing such tables. Finally, the construction of fault trees via decision tables is demonstrated.

DEVELOPMENT OF DECISION TABLES

Since the development of accurate decision table models is the basis for the construction of useful fault trees in this approach, we will concentrate on the development and use of such tables here. A typical two-out-of-three sensor system, shown in Figure 1, will serve as an example. In this system, a certain variable is monitored by three sensors, whose outputs will be defined as:

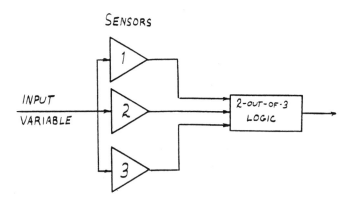

Figure 1   Two-out-of-three Sensor System

1.   input variable within normal range;
2.   input variable out of range.

Note that in this example, state 2 is used to represent the
sensor output when the input variable is either too high or too
low.   Three such sensors are input into a two-out-of-three logic
circuit which will produce the following output states:

1.   2 or more inputs within normal range;
2.   2 or more inputs out of range.

We proceed now to develop the decision tables necessary to
represent such components.   Table 1 is a simple decision table for
the sensor described above.   As this table indicates, both a variable which is too low (input = 0) and one which is too high (input = 2) will produce an out-of-range output (output = 2).   One
could equally well model a sensor which produced different outputs
for low and high inputs by changing the output state of row 1 to
a state of 0.

We will now expand this table to model internal failures of
the sensor.   In order to simplify what is to follow, we will consider only two-state variables (1 = normal, 2 = too high) which
might, for example, be useful for such applications as overpower,
overtemperature or overpressure sensors.   Let us consider two
generic types of failure: "fails-safe" and "fails-dangerous."
The first would represent the situation where an abnormal (out-of-
range) output would be produced, regardless of whether the input
variable was normal or out of range.   A "failed-dangerous" situation would occur if a normal output were produced by both a normal
and out-of-range input.   This situation is modeled by Table 2.

TABLE 1

Decision Table for Perfect Sensor With
Three Input States

Input	Output
0	2
1	1
2	2

TABLE 2

Decision Table for Sensor with Failure

Row No.	Input	Internal Mode	Output
1	1	0	1
2	1	1004	1
3	2	1004	1
4	2	0	2
5	1	1005	2
6	2	1005	2

The internal states are:

```
0    :  sensor good
1004 :  sensor failed-unsafe
1005 :  sensor failed-safe
```

Table 2 represents the following:

a)   a "good sensor will produce normal and out-of-range out-
     puts given normal and high inputs, respectively (rows 1,
     4);

b)   a "failed-unsafe" sensor will produce a normal signal
     regardless of the input (rows 2, 3);

c)   a "failed-safe" sensor will produce an "out-of-range"
     output regardless of the input (rows 5, 6).

These interpretations suggest useful simplifications of the
table. Let us define a state "-1" to represent a "don't care situation, such that:

A don't care situation occurs whenever a specific combination
of states of all but one input or internal column produces a unique
output state, independent of the state of the remaining input or
internal column.

In this example, an internal state of 1004 always produces an
output of 1, regardless of the input state. Thus rows 2 and 3 can
be combined into a single row with a "don't care" state for the
input. Similarly, rows 5 and 6 can be combined. The resulting
decision table is shown in Table 3.

Now let us see how maintenance and calibration errors can be
introduced into such a model. Although miscalibration errors could

TABLE 3

Reduced Decision Table for Sensor

Row	Input	Internal	Output
1	1	0	1
2	-1	1004	1
3	2	0	2
4	-1	1005	2

be considered as a subset of the failure states already defined, we may wish to distinguish between independent sensor failures and potential common cause calibration errors. The first step, then, is to define an additional internal column for calibration, with the states[6]:

0   :   correctly calibrated
5010:   setpoint too high (always produces "normal" output)
5011:   setpoint too low (always produces "out-of-range" output).

Before developing the decision table for such a sensor, we must consider the effects of the combination of calibration errors and internal failures on the output. Let us assume that a failed-safe sensor produces an out-of-range output regardless of the calibration; most significantly, this implies that a setpoint set "too high" will not produce a normal output if the sensor has failed safe. Similarly, we assume that a failed-dangerous sensor will always produce a normal output, regardless of the calibration. The complete decision table is shown in Table 4.

We can now reduce this table, in stages, considering the combinations of the three input and internal columns. First, it is seen that all rows with an input of 1 and internal state of 1004 produce an output state of 1, regardless of the calibration state (rows 7,8,9). Thus these three rows can be combined into the following row:

1 - 1 1004 1

Similar reductions apply to rows 10-12, 13-15, and 16-18. Furthermore, all rows with a calibration state of 5010 and internal state of 0 (rows 2, 5) produce an output state of 1, regardless of the input. Thus these two rows reduce to:

-1   5010   0   1

Finally, rows 3 and 6 can be similarly combined. These reductions combine to produce Table 5.

TABLE 4

Complete Decision Table for Sensor

Row	Input	Calibration	Internal	Output
1	1	0	0	1
2	1	5150	0	1
3	1	5011	0	2
4	2	0	0	2
5	2	5010	0	1
6	2	5011	0	2
7	1	0	1004	1
8	1	5010	1004	1
9	1	5011	1004	1
10	2	0	1004	1
11	2	5010	1004	1
12	2	5011	1004	1
13	1	0	1005	2
14	1	5010	1005	2
15	1	5011	1005	2
16	2	0	1005	2
17	2	5010	1005	2
18	2	5011	1005	2

TABLE 5

Partially Reduced Table for Sensor

Row	Input	Calibration	Internal	Output
1	1	0	0	1
2	-1	5010	0	1
3	2	0	0	2
4	-1	5011	0	2
5	1	-1	1004	1
6	2	-1	1004	1
7	1	-1	1005	2
8	2	-1	1005	2

TABLE 6

Fully Reduced Decision Table for Sensor

Row	Input	Calibration	Internal	Output
1	1	0	0	1
2	-1	5010	0	1
3	-1	-1	1004	1
4	2	0	0	2
5	-1	5011	0	2
6	-1	-1	1005	2

This table can be further reduced as follows. Since all rows
with calibration state = -1 and internal state = 1004 produce output state = 1 (rows 5,6), these two rows can be combined, using a
'don't care' input state. By a similar argument, rows 7 and 8 can
be combined. Thus we arrive at the following fully reduced table,
Table 6 (the rows have been rearranged to group rows with similar
output state).

We shall now see how this treatment of miscalibration can be
made to include the common cause miscalibration of several sensors
simultaneously. In actual use, the "internal" columns of decision
tables for different components represent independent failures.
Thus, for example, in the system of Figure 1 each sensor can be
good, failed-safe, or failed-unsafe independently of the other two.
On the other hand, the input to all three sensors must be identical,
since their inputs come from a common source. (If the inputs came
from independent sources, then they, too, would be independent).
This difference in treatment suggests two ways of handling calibration and maintenance errors.

First, these could be represented as random, independent events
by treating the "calibration" column as an internal failure column.
On the other hand, by considering the calibration column to be an
external input, coming from some external maintenance source, calibration errors can be treated either independently (by having an
independent maintenance source for each sensor), or dependently
(by having a common maintenance source for all sensors). The
decision table for such maintenance could be represented most
simply by Table 7.

A single maintenance personnel, modeled by Table 7 and "connected" to the calibration inputs of several sensors, would represent
a totally dependent (common cause) source of correct or incorrect
calibration. If both dependent and independent calibration errors
are desired, they can be handled in one of 4 ways:

1)   consider independent miscalibration as included in states
     1004 and 1005 of the internal failure column;

2)   add additional states representing miscalibration to this
     same internal column;

3)   add an internal miscalibration column in addition to the
     external miscalibration column;

TABLE 7

Decision Table for Sensor Calibration

Internal	Output
0	0
5010	5010
5011	5011

4)   develop an expanded calibration decision table, such as Table 8, which uses separate outputs for each sensor. For example, rows 1-3 represent dependent calibration, rows 4-9 represent independent calibration, and other rows can be added for various combinations, as suggested by row 10.

Clearly such a decision table can become very complicated, although it is very flexible. In most cases, the first two alternatives will be most useful, and the first of these will be used here.

CONSTRUCTION OF FAULT TREES FROM DECISION TABLES

Now it is possible to see how such a table can be used to see how such a table can be used to develop fault trees. Let us suppose we wish to develop the fault tree for the event "normal output from sensor." This event corresponds to rows 1, 2 and 3 of Table 6. Since any one of these rows will lead to this event, these rows are combined by OR logic, as in the figure below. To further develop row 1, we note that all three columns (input, calibration and internal) must have the appropriate state for the output state to be correct. Thus the three entries in row 1 are connected by an AND gate. The first entry (input) must be further developed since it comes from an external source, which will have its own decision table. This is also true for the calibration column, if it has been treated as an external input. Finally, the internal column (and the calibration column, if it is treated internally) represents a primary failure, and its development is

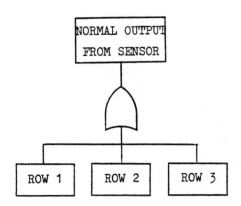

TABLE 8

Expanded Decision Table for Calibration

Row	Internal	Output 1	Output 2	Output 3
1	0	0	0	0
2	5010	5010	5010	5010
3	5011	5011	5011	5011
4	5100	5010	0	0
5	5101	0	5010	0
6	5102	0	0	5010
7	5103	5011	0	0
8	5104	0	5011	0
9	5105	0	0	5011
10	5106	5010	5010	0
⋮		etc.		

complete. Thus, row 1 becomes the following:

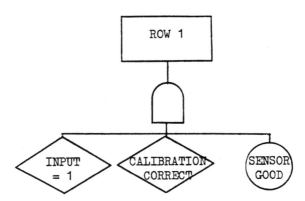

Similarly, row 2 becomes the AND of "calibration = 5010" and sensor good (the "don't care" input is ignored), and row 3 is then the single event "sensor failed-unsafe." The resulting tree for the event "normal output from sensor" is shown in Figure 2.

An additional fault tree can be constructed for the event "out-of-range" output from sensor. Using rows 4-6 of Table 6,

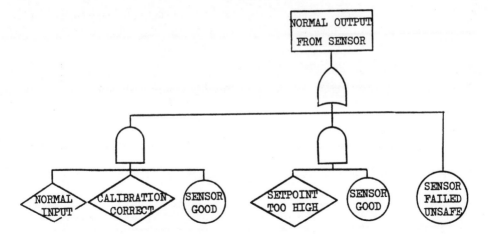

Figure 2. Fault Tree for Event "Normal Output From Sensor"

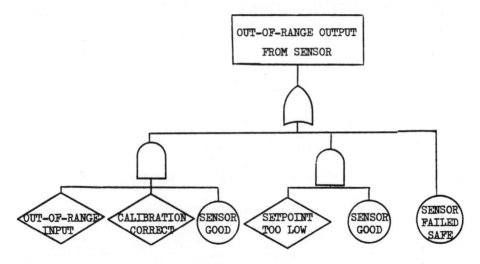

Figure 3. Fault Tree for Event "Out-of-Range Output from Sensor

the resulting fault tree is shown in Figure 3. In both Figures 2 and 3, we note the explicit appearance of "good" component states. Quite often, the inclusion of such states leads to a fault tree which is unnecessarily complex; furthermore, such states imply NOT type logic, which is not properly handled by some fault tree analysis codes. Thus, in those situations where the failure probabilities are small, we will often wish to eliminate good states, using the approximation: $P_{good} \approx 1$.

This is accomplished by replacing the "good (zero) states in decision tables by the "don't care" (-1) state. For example, Table 6
would then reduce to Table 9.

It must be emphasized that such a table is only valid for
small failure probabilities, and cannot be used if success trees
are to be generated. As an example of the effect of such a table,
the fault tree for the event "normal output from sensor", using
Table 9, is shown in Figure 4. By comparison with the complete
tree in Figure 2, two events and one gate have been eliminated.

USE OF BOUNDARY CONDITIONS

For any given event of interest, it is usually necessary to
specify initial or boundary conditions in existence within, or
external to the system. For example, the event "Normal Output
from Sensor," given the condition "out-of-range signal present"
would represent an undesirable event in most applications. Such
a boundary condition is handled as follows. For the event "normal
output," rows 1-3 of Table 9 (or 6) are used, as before. However,
now the out-of-range boundary condition (state 2 at the sensor
input) contradicts the input state (state 1) required for row 1
to be true. Thus, row 1 cannot occur and is eliminated. Rows
2 and 3 are still valid, since the input states are "don't care"
states. The resulting fault tree is shown in Figure 5. Note
that this is identical to Figure 4, with the deletion of the first
branch. This is equivalent to setting the event "normal input"
equal to "false" in Figure 4, which renders the output from the
AND gate false.

TABLE 9
DECISION TABLE FOR SENSOR
WITH GOOD STATES REMOVED

ROW	INPUT	CALIBRATION	INTERNAL	OUTPUT
1	1	0	-1	1
2	-1	5010 -	-1	1
3	-1	-1	1004	1
4	2	0	-1	2
5	-1	5011	-1	2
6	-1	-1	1005	2

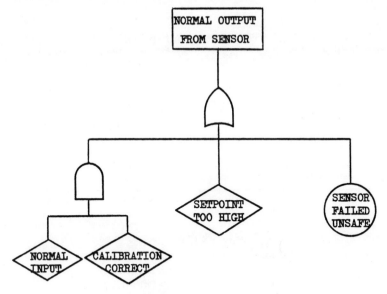

Figure 4.   Fault Tree for Event "Normal Output from Sensor,"
            with good states removed.

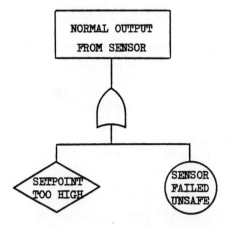

Figure 5.   Fault Tree for Event "Normal Output from Sensor"
            with out-of-range input present.

SAMPLE APPLICATION

We now return to the system of Figure 1 to show how a multiple-component system can be modeled. All three sensors will be represented by Decision Table 9. The 2-out-of-3 logic will be modeled to include the following:

1) failure modes will include both fail-safe and fail-unsafe modes,

2) one of the three sensor channels may be out for maintenance, in which case the logic becomes 1-out-of-2,

3) "good" states will be eliminated,

4) the maintenance state will be modeled as an internal mode with the following states:

> 200 – not under maintenance
> 201 – channel 1 under maintenance
> 202 – channel 2 under maintenance
> 203 – channel 3 under maintenance

Note that these states may be treated as inhibit conditions. Table 10 is the decision table for this component. In this table, the first 6 rows represent the 2-out-of-3 logic when not under maintenance, rows 7-9 represent 1-out-of-2 logic when channel 1 is under maintenance, etc.

Finally, the calibration for the three sensors will be modeled by Table 7. We will utilize a single maintenance "component" (i.e., a single source of maintenance) common to all sensors, to allow us to include common mode calibration errors. Figure 6 represents the complete system with the calibration "component" included.

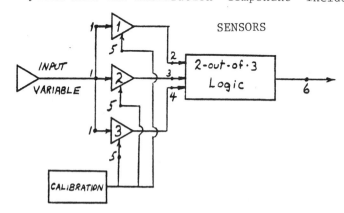

Figure 6.   Two-out-of-three Sensor System with Common Cause Calibration Component

TABLE 10
DECISION TABLE FOR
2-OUT-OF-3 LOGIC WITH MAINTENANCE

ROW	IN 1	IN 2	IN 3	MAINT IN	INT	OUT
1	1	1	-1	200	-1	1
2	1	-1	1	200	-1	1
3	-1	1	1	200	-1	1
4	2	2	-1	200	-1	2
5	2	-1	2	200	-1	2
6	-1	2	2	200	-1	2
7	-1	1	1	201	-1	1
8	-1	2	-1	201	-1	2
9	-1	-1	2	201	-1	2
10	1	-1	1	202	-1	1
11	2	-1	-1	202	-1	2
12	-1	-1	2	202	-1	2
13	1	1	-1	203	-1	1
14	2	-1	-1	203	-1	2
15	-1	2	-1	203	-1	2
16	-1	-1	-1	-1	1004	1
17	-1	-1	-1	-1	1005	2

NODE NUMBERING

     With the system developed and the decision tables for all
components now modeled, a node numbering scheme must be set up in
order to allow the inputting of the system configuration into the
CAT code if a computer generated fault tree is desired. One possibility is presented in Figure 6. Node 1 is the common input to all
three sensors. In this example, it will be defined as the output
from a general "signal source" modeled by Decision Table 11. In a
real system, this signal would, in fact, probably be the output
from some other subsystem. Nodes 2, 3 and 4 are the independent
outputs from the three sensors, as well as the inputs to the 2-out-
of-3 logic. Node 5 in the output from the calibration "component"
and the common calibration input to the three sensors. Finally,
node 6 is the output from the 2/3 logic. In a complete system,
this node might be connected either to an alarm system, or to some
type of automatic control system.

TABLE 11

General Signal Source

Internal	Output
0	0
1	1
2	2

TOP EVENT DEFINITION AND BOUNDARY CONDITIONS

In this example, we wish to examine two events for the complete system: "Normal Output from System with Out-of-Range Input", and "Out-of-Range Output from System with Normal Input." Both of these involve a simple TOP event and an additional boundary condition. For example, the first has the TOP event "Normal Output from System", which is equivalent to "output state = 1 at Node 6." The boundary condition, "Out-of-Range Input" is then "State = 2 at Node 1." The second event of interest, "Out-of-Range Output from System with Normal Input" has the TOP event "Output State = 2 at Node 6" and a boundary condition "State = 1 at Node 1."

DISCUSSION OF FAULT TREES

The fault tree produced by the CAT code for the event "Normal Output from System with Out-of-Range Input" is shown in Figure 7. The upper level structure of the tree is the OR of a number of possible sensor failure combinations under various maintenance possibilities. It was developed from the top down by starting with the TOP event (Output = 1, Node = 6). Since the 2-out-of-3 sensor output is connected to node 6, the upper level gate is developed from the Decision Table for the logic, Table 10. Since the TOP event requires an output state of 1, the top gate becomes an OR with rows 1-3, 7, 10, 13 and 16 as inputs. These seven inputs have been further developed to produce the seven branches of Figure 7. For example, Row 1 has a maintenance state of 200 (no maintenance), which has been indicated here as an inhibit (fixed probability) condition. State 1 at the first two inputs becomes: "state 1, node 2" and "state 1, node 3" which, from Figure 6, become "sensor 1, output = 1" and "sensor 2, output = 1". Each of these events has then been further developed down to the primary failure level, under the proper boundary condition: "out-of-range input". This produces lower level gates identical to that in Figure 5.

In a similar fashion, the fault tree in Figure 8 was produced for the event "Out-of-Range Output from System" with the boundary

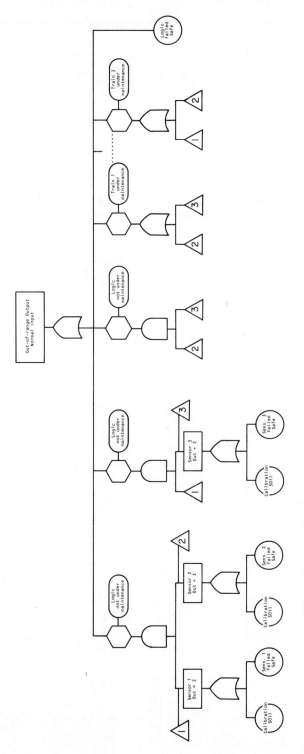

Fig. 7. Fault tree for event "Out-of-range output, normal input."

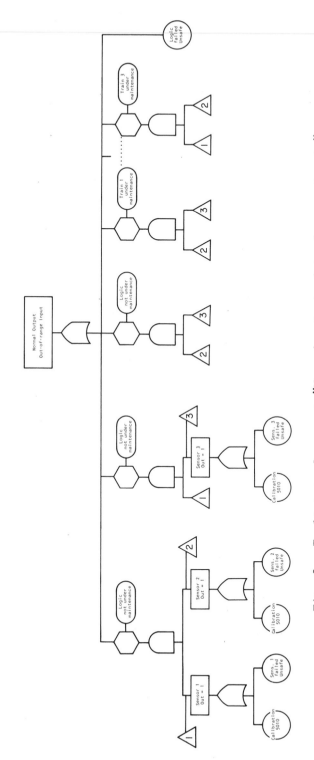

Fig. 8. Fault tree for event "Normal output, Out-of-range input."

condition "normal input to sensors." It is interesting to compare the two fault trees, since they point out very visibly an example of the trade-off between safety and availability which must often be made, and indicate the desirability of generating fault trees for different TOP events. Figure 7, important from a safety standpoint (e.g., "failure to scram" type events) has only one single failure branch (branch 7), as well as the common cause input "calibration 5010" (set-point too high). Figure 8, which is an important event for availability considerations (e.g., spurious shut-down), has additional single failure events ("sensor failed safe") when any one train is under maintenance. Furthermore, if a numerical evaluation were performed, the possibility of sensors being designed to fail "safe" rather than "unsafe" would further add to the probability of the TOP event of Figure 8.

These, of course, are well known design trade-offs associated with logic circuits of this type. However, these features point out the usefulness of a method which allows multiple events or the effects of varying boundary conditions to be readily modeled. For this example, only a single TOP event system state and a single boundary condition had to be changed; it would have been equally easy to examine events at other nodes in the system as well.

SUMMARY

This paper has presented the basic concepts of the CAT methodology of fault tree construction by following the decision table development and fault tree construction for a simple system. Although some of the advantages of such an approach are evident, the user must be cautioned that the accuracy and completeness of the results depend on the initial care used in developing the decision tables and system model. Thus, rather than a method for the "blind" construction of fault trees, this approach is intended as a systematic guide to the fault tree analyst and, in its computer-automated form, as a tool to assist in the rapid construction of such trees.

REFERENCES

1.   S. A. Lapp and G. J. Powers, "The Synthesis of Fault Trees", in: Nuclear Systems Reliability Engineering and Risk Assessment, J. B. Fussell and G. R. Burdick, eds., SIAM, Philadelphia (1977) pp 778-799.

2.   J. R. Taylor and E. Hollo, "Experience with Algorithms for Automatic Failure Analysis", same ref. as [1].

3.   J. B. Fussell, "A Formal Methodology for Fault Tree Construc-
      tion", Nucl. Sci. Eng., 52:421 (1973).

4.   S. L. Salem, G. E. Apostolakis, and D. Okrent, "A New
      Methodology for the Computer-Aided Construction of Fault
      Trees," Ann. Nucl. Energy, 4:417 (1977).

5.   S. L. Salem, J. S. Wu, and G. Apostolakis, "Decision Table
      Development and Application to the Construction of Fault
      Trees", Nucl. Technol., 42:51 (1979).

6.   S. L. Salem, J. S. Wu, and G. E. Apostolakis, "CAT: A
      Computer Code for the Automated Construction of Fault Trees,"
      EPRI Report NP-705, Electric Power Research Institute (1978).

L.A.M. TECHNIQUE: SYSTEMATIC GENERATION OF LOGICAL STRUCTURES

IN SYSTEMS RELIABILITY STUDIES

Giuseppe Reina   Giuseppe Squellati

Dept. of Biomathematics   ARS S.p.A.,
Inst. of Pharmacology,   Milan, Italy
University of Milan,
Via Vanvitelli 32, Milan, Italy

SUMMARY

A new approach for the reliability analysis of coherent and non-coherent systems is presented with regard to the problem of the systematic generation of failure logical structures. In particular, this methodology allows us to derive the logical behaviour of the system by means of the physical behaviour of its components.

To this end, suitable component failure-dependent analytical models are constructed to describe the component behaviour under normal and failure conditions. These models constitute, in their whole, a set of parametric equations describing the normal and failure behaviour of the whole system.

Starting from the considered component failure events, all the possible configurations of the system hypothetical failure structures are automatically generated in a controlled way. Now, by definition, to each given logical structure it corresponds a specific set of equations. Thus, the comparison of the corresponding numerical solution with analytically defined critical TOP conditions allows TOP and/or NON-TOP sets of events to be identified.

An application to the study of a simplified mixing circuit of an ethylene oxide production plant is presented.

INTRODUCTION

While a number of theoretical studies and computational techniques have been developed for the systems reliability assessments, only few works have been performed towards the investigation of methodologies for the systematic generation of systems logical structures (some basic references are given at the end of the report).

The usual methods for the definition of the system's logical behaviour are greatly affected by heuristic considerations.

In this paper we present a new approach to this problem where the logical structure of the systems is completely deduced by the analytical models which are at the basis of the physical behaviour of the system itself. In particular, the L.A.M. technique (Logical Analytical Methodology) allows us to derive the logical behaviour of the system by means of the physical behaviour of its components. The problem can better be specified by the following steps:

a) Definition, for each component, of analytical relations connecting all the physical variables which are characteristic of the component operating and failing modes. The failing modes are described by means of suitable parameters which basically represent the failure and degradation events.

b) Parametric solution of the resulting set of equations with respect to a prefixed TOP event and controlled automatic generation of the system TOP states. In this phase it is possible to localize the loops of the system which are given by the minimal sets of indipendent equations. This last search is however inessential for the TOP states generation but it may be of interest in engineering applications.

c) Direct probabilistic calculations of the generated "non-coherent" TOP structure.

The development of these points will be presented in the next sections. In particular we will be concerned with:

1) Functional and topological analysis of the system

2) Functional analysis of components
   a) Analysis under normal conditions

b) Analysis under failure conditions

3) Construction of the Components Operating and Failing Models
    and identification of the set of logical analytical equations
    representative of the system operating and failing modes

4) Identification of the TOP conditions for a required TOP EVENT

5) Controlled generation of the minimal "TOP Sets" and minimal
    "NON-TOP Sets" and direct calculation of the TOP probability.

1. FUNCTIONAL AND TOPOLOGICAL SYSTEM ANALYSIS

        The first step for the construction of the components
analytical models requires a global analysis both of the system
topological structure and of the components functional operating
modes. This analysis has to be aimed at the identification of the
physical variables which logically and analytically interconnect
the various components.

        Let us consider, as a very simple but didactic example, the
following flow rate control system:

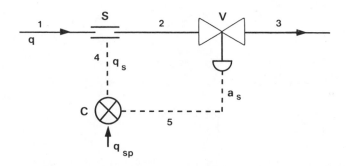

where   S = flow rate sensor

         C = flow rate controller

         V = control valve

        The input flow rate q is sensed by the flow sensor S
connected to the controller C by means of the signal line 4. Any
change of the flow rate q will produce a change of the signal
q_s from the sensor.

        The signal is received by the controller C and compared with
the set point flow rate q_{sp}. A signal area a_s from the controller

then causes the valve area to change to return to the initial flow conditions.

This first qualitative analysis allows us to go into details at a component level for the analytical description of each single component. The next step will be concerned with the study of the normal and failure behaviour of components.

2. FUNCTIONAL ANALYSIS OF COMPONENTS

2.1 Analysis of components under normal conditions

The previous qualitative analysis has now to be specified to give an analytical representation of the normal operating modes of each single component. In other words we must analyze the component normal behaviour and describe it in terms of analytical relations where, as "normal" conditions, we mean the component operating modes in absence of failures, degradations, etc.

For the considered sample case we have

SENSOR

    – Functional Scheme

    – Functional Relation

$$q_s = \alpha_s q$$

$$\begin{cases} q & \text{flow rate} \\ q_s & \text{flow rate signal} \\ \alpha_s & \text{constant of sensor} \end{cases}$$

CONTROLLER

    – Functional Scheme

    – Functional Relation

$$a_s = \begin{cases} 0 & \text{(under the lower bound of the proportional band)} \\ a_{sp} - \alpha_c(q_s - q_{sp}) & \text{(inside the proportional band)} \\ 1 & \text{(above the upper bound of the proportional band)} \end{cases}$$

where

  a_s fractional signal area imposed to the valve

  a_{sp} signal area corresponding to the set point flow
         rate signal q_{sp}

  α_c constant of the controller

CONTROL VALVE

  - Functional Scheme

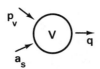

  - Functional Relation (for a linear characteristic valve)

$$q = \alpha_v a_s \sqrt{p_v} \quad \begin{cases} p_v & \text{differential valve pressure } p_{23} \\ \alpha_v & \text{constant of control valve} \end{cases}$$

Since we are mainly interested in the effects of "per-turbations" on the considered variables, it is advisable to change the components functional relations into a perturbed form.

This problem can be faced up to different levels of approximation depending on the specific analytical kind of the considered relations.

In general, given a multiple variables function $f(x_1, x_2, \ldots, x_n)$ we have

a) $\Delta f = f(x_1 + \Delta x_1, x_2 + \Delta x_2, \ldots, x_n + \Delta x_n) - f(x_1, x_2, \ldots, x_n)$
    (Exact)

b) $\Delta f \simeq (f(x_1 + \Delta x_1, x_2, \ldots, x_n) - f(x_1, x_2, \ldots, x_n)) +$
    $+(f(x_1, x_2 + \Delta x_2, \ldots, x_n) - f(x_1, x_2, \ldots, x_n)) +$
    $+\ldots+ (f(x_1, x_2, \ldots, x_n + \Delta x_n) - (f(x_1, x_2, \ldots, x_n)) =$
    $= \Sigma_i (\Delta f)_{x_i}$

c) $\Delta f \simeq \Sigma_i (\partial f / \partial x_i) \Delta x_i$

For quasi-linear relations, the form (c) is the most convenient because of its simplicity and linearity in the new incremental variables $\Delta x_1, \ldots, \Delta x_n$.

On the other hand, forms (a) and (b) are strictly required for strong non linear relations.

Let us note that, by a purely formal and logical point of view, the LAM methodology does not need necessarily the passage from non-perturbed to the perturbed form. However, this passage is, in general, particularly useful in view of our end problem (solution of a system of equations) because it allows us to reduce, in most cases, slightly non linear equations into a linear form.

Application of form (c) to our example gives

SENSOR

$$\Delta q_s = \alpha_s \, \Delta q \qquad\qquad (1)$$

CONTROLLER

$$\Delta a_s = \Delta a_{sp} + \alpha_c \, \Delta q_{sp} - \alpha_c \, \Delta q_s \qquad\qquad (2)(*)$$

CONTROL VALVE

$$\Delta q = \alpha_v \, \sqrt{p_v} \, \Delta a_s + [\alpha_v a_s/(2\sqrt{p_v})] \, \Delta p_v \qquad\qquad (3)$$

Relations (1), (2), (3) give the <u>normal</u> connections between the new incremental variables Δq, Δq_s, Δq_{sp}, Δa_s, Δa_{sp}, Δp_v.

The next step now concerns the analysis of the changes of the normal realations (1), (2), (3) when in presence of failures, degradations, etc.

(*) <u>Note</u> –   The exact perturbed form of the controller funtional relation would involve the discontinuities connected with the bounds of the proportional band. In fact, large variations of the variables a_{sp}, q_s, q_{sp} could lead to a_s values out of the proportional range. However, for sake of didactic simplicity, we will limit our analysis to the case of small variations inside of the proportional band.

2.2 - Analysis of components under failure conditions

Let us start from the normal operating modes of components and derive the failure effects in terms of "deviations" from the normal conditions as a consequence of failures, degradations, etc.

To this end, let us consider the following steps:

a) Qualitative Failure Modes and Effects Analysis

b) Quantitative Failure Effects Analysis of each single failure mode as deviations from the functional normal relations. Introduction of the "Event Variables"

c) Failure Effects Analysis of contemporary failure modes and introduction of the "Component States Operators"

STEP a) - This step is devoted to the study of the component failure modes and to a functional qualitative analysis of the effects of each single failure with respect to the normal conditions.
For the case considered let us assume:

SENSOR

Failure Modes	Failure Effects
- Sensor Stuck	Changes of q do not influence q_s
- Sensor Reversed action	Positive (Negative) changes of q cause negative (positive) changes of q_s

CONTROLLER

- Controller Reversed action	Positive (Negative) changes of q_s cause positive (negative) changes of a_s and positive (negative) changes of q_{sp}, a_{sp} cause negative (positive) changes of a_s
- Controller Stuck	Changes of q_s, q_{sp}, a_{sp} do not influence a_s
- Drift	Progressive changes of a_{sp}, q_{sp} with a corresponding change of a_s
- Controller fails low	Changes of a_{sp}, q_s, q_{sp} do not influence a_s and an additive negative change of a_s is produced

- Controller fails   Changes of a_{sp}, q_s, q_{sp} do not
  high   influence a_s and an additive
                      positive change of a_s is produced

CONTROL VALVE

- Valve stuck   Changes of a_s do not influence q

- Valve fails open   Changes of a_s do not influence q
                      and q rises to the value $\alpha_v \sqrt{p_v}$

- Valve fails closed Changes of a_s, p_v do not influence q,
                      and q goes to zero

STEP b) – This step is devoted to the quantification of the
            effects of __each single__ failure mode and to the
            introduction of the Event Variables.

            To each indipendent failure event we will associate a
            two state Event Variable and to each mutually exclusive
            failure event we will associate a multi-states vari-
            able.

            Let us note that, in general, we can change the
            structure of the normal equations (1), (2), (3), as a
            consequence of failures, both by changing the coeffi-
            cients of the indipendent incremental variables and/or
            by adding additional terms.

            For the considered case we have:

SENSOR

Failure Modes	Failure Effects	Event Variables
- Sensor Stuck	$\Delta q_s / \Delta q \leftarrow 0$	SS $\begin{array}{l} 0 \text{ non stuck} \\ 1 \text{ stuck} \end{array}$
- Sensor Reversed action	$\Delta q_s / \Delta q \leftarrow -\alpha_s$	SR $\begin{array}{l} 0 \text{ non reversed act.} \\ 1 \text{ reversed action} \end{array}$

Note: The formal notation $\Delta y / \Delta x \leftarrow k$ represents the amount k of
      variation of y as a consequence of a unit variation of x.

CONTROLLER

Failure Modes	Failure Effects	Event Variables

- Controller
  Reversed
  action

$$\Delta a_s / \Delta q_s \leftarrow \alpha_c$$
$$\Delta a_s / \Delta q_{sp} \leftarrow -\alpha_c$$
$$\Delta a_s / \Delta a_{sp} \leftarrow -1$$

CR 0 non reversed act.
    1 reversed action

- Drift

$$\Delta a_{sp} \neq 0, \Delta q_{sp} \neq 0$$

Already considered in the model

- Fails low

$$\Delta a_s / \Delta a_{sp} \leftarrow 0$$
$$\Delta a_s / \Delta q_{sp} \leftarrow 0$$
$$\Delta a_s / \Delta q_s \leftarrow 0$$
$$(\Delta a_s)_{\Delta=0} \leftarrow -a_{sp} +$$
$$+\alpha_c (q_s - q_{sp}) \equiv g_1$$

- Fails high

$$\Delta a_s / \Delta a_{sp} \leftarrow 0$$
$$\Delta a_s / \Delta q_{sp} \leftarrow 0$$
$$\Delta a_s / \Delta q_s \leftarrow 0$$
$$(\Delta a_s)_{\Delta=0} \leftarrow 1 + g_1 \equiv g_2$$

CF 0 OK
    1 fails low
    2 fails high
    3 stuck

- Control
  Stuck

$$\Delta a_s / \Delta a_{sp} \leftarrow 0$$
$$\Delta a_s / \Delta q_{sp} \leftarrow 0$$
$$\Delta a_s / \Delta q_s \leftarrow 0$$

Note: The formal notation $(\Delta y)_{\Delta=0} \leftarrow h$ represents the additive amount h of variation of y apart from changes of the independent variables.

CONTROL VALVE

Failure Modes	Failure Effects	Event Variables

- Valve fails
  open

$\Delta q / \Delta a_s \leftarrow 0$

$(\Delta q)_{\Delta=0} \leftarrow g_3$

$(g_3 = \alpha_v \sqrt{\overline{p_v}}(1-a_s))$

0 valve OK

- Valve fails
  closed

$\Delta q / \Delta a_s \leftarrow 0$

$\Delta q / \Delta p_v \leftarrow 0$

$(\Delta q)_{\Delta=0} \leftarrow g_4$

$(g_4 = - \alpha_v a_s \sqrt{\overline{p_v}})$

VF
1 fails open
2 fails closed
3 stuck

- Valve stuck

$\Delta q / \Delta a_s \leftarrow 0$

STEP C) — This step is devoted to the analysis of the effects of simultaneous failure modes and to the definition of the "Component State Operators".

The introduction of the Component State Operators allows us to describe the component operating and failing modes in a parametric form.

Each operator is constructed by means of decisional tables and it is given a form that implicitly contains both the whole possible states of the component and the corresponding effects on the functional relations.

For the considered case we have:

SENSOR

States of Component	Event variables SS	SR	Effects $\Delta q_s / \Delta q$
S_1	0	0	α_s (normal condition)
S_2	0	1	$- \alpha_s$
S_3	1	0	0
S_4	1	1	0

Component State Operator

$$OS(SS, SR; \Delta q_s / \Delta q; \quad \alpha_s, \ - \alpha_s, \ 0, \ 0)$$

Thus, the interpretation of the OS operator is as follows:

1) - It depends on the State Variables SS, SR

2) - It gives, for each state of the sensor described by the two state variables, the amount of variation of q_s corresponding to unit variation of q, i.e.

$$\Delta q_s = OS \ \Delta q$$

Thus, for example, in the case "Sensor Reversed Action" we have:

- SS = 0   SR = 1

- Relative effect: $\Delta q_s = - \alpha_s \Delta q$

CONTROLLER

States of Component	Event variables		Effects			
	CR	CF	$\Delta a_s / \Delta a_{sp}$	$\Delta a_s / \Delta q_{sp}$	$\Delta a_s / \Delta q_s$	$(\Delta a_s)_{\Delta=0}$
S_1	0	0	1	α_c	$-\alpha_c$	0
S_2	0	1	0	0	0	g_1
S_3	0	2	0	0	0	g_2
S_4	0	3	0	0	0	0
S_5	1	0	-1	$-\alpha_c$	α_c	0
S_6	1	1	0	0	0	g_1
S_7	1	2	0	0	0	g_2
S_8	1	3	0	0	0	0

Component State Operators

$$OC1(CR, CF; \ \Delta a_s / \Delta a_{sp}; \ 1,0,0,0,-1,0,0,0)$$

$$OC2(CR, CF; \ \Delta a_s / \Delta q_{sp}; \ \alpha_c,0,0,0,-\alpha_c,0,0,0)$$

$$OC3(CR, CF; \ \Delta a_s / \Delta q_s; \ -\alpha_c,0,0,0, \ \alpha_c,0,0,0)$$

$$VC4(CR, CF; \ (\Delta a_s)_{\Delta=0}; \ 0,g_1,g_2,0,0,g_1,g_2,0)$$

Note: The last operator is given a different name because of its
      additive action.

___

CONTROL VALVE

States of Component	Event variables VF	Effects		
		$\Delta q / \Delta a_s$	$\Delta q / \Delta p_v$	$(\Delta q)_{\Delta=0}$
S_1	0	g_5	g_6	0
S_2	1	0	g_6	g_3
S_3	2	0	0	g_4
S_4	3	0	g_6	0

$$[\; g_5 = \alpha_v \sqrt{p_v} \quad \text{and} \quad g_6 = \alpha_v a_s / (2\sqrt{p_v}) \;]$$

Component State Operators

$$OV1(VF; \; \Delta q / \Delta a_s \; ; \; g_5, 0, 0, 0)$$

$$OV2(VF; \; \Delta q / \Delta p_v \; ; \; g_6, g_6, 0, g_6)$$

$$VV3(VF; \; (\Delta q)_{\Delta=0}; \; 0, g_3, g_4, 0)$$

3 - CONSTRUCTION OF THE COMPONENT OPERATING AND FAILING MODELS

Now we are concerned with the construction of formal models
to synthetize in a parametric form all the previous considerations
about the components behaviour.

To this end, let us start from the normal relations (1),
(2), (3) and introduce the "Component State Operators".
It results:

SENSOR

$$\Delta q_s = OS(SS, SR) * \Delta q \tag{4}$$

CONTROLLER

$$\Delta a_s = OC1(CR, CF) * \Delta a_{sp} + OC2(CR, CF) * \Delta q_{sp} +$$
$$+ OC3(CR, CF) * \Delta q_s + VC4(CR, CF) \tag{5}$$

CONTROL VALVE

$$\Delta q = OV1(VF) * \Delta a_s + OV2(VF) * \Delta p_v + VV3(VF) \qquad (6)$$

Relations (4), (5), (6) describe in a <u>parametric form</u> (where the parameters are constituted by the Event Variables) the components normal and failure behaviour and represent the starting point for the generation of the system failure states.

In this representation the parameters are constituted both by the Component State Operators and by those perturbative variables which have to be prior assigned a value in order to make the system of equations determined.

In this respect, the incremental variables Δa_{sp}, Δq_{sp}, Δp_v will be considered as parameters which will be given the following values

$$\Delta a_{sp} = \begin{array}{ll} 0 & \text{normal conditions} \\ -\Delta_1 & \text{set point area negative drift} \\ \Delta_1 & \text{set point area positive drift} \end{array}$$

$$\Delta q_{sp} = \begin{array}{ll} 0 & \text{normal conditions} \\ -\Delta_2 & \text{set point flow rate negative drift} \\ \Delta_2 & \text{set point flow rate positive drift} \end{array}$$

$$\Delta p_v = \begin{array}{ll} 0 & \text{normal conditions} \\ -\Delta_3 & \text{negative valve pressure change} \\ \Delta_3 & \text{positive valve pressure change} \end{array}$$

Owing to their particular nature, these parameters will be handled in the same way of events. To this end, let us associate the following Event Variables:

$$DASP \quad \begin{array}{ll} 0 & \Delta a_{sp} = 0 \\ 1 & \Delta a_{sp} = -\Delta_1 \\ 2 & \Delta a_{sp} = +\Delta_1 \end{array}$$

$$DQSP \quad \begin{array}{ll} 0 & \Delta q_{sp} = 0 \\ 1 & \Delta q_{sp} = -\Delta_2 \\ 2 & \Delta q_{sp} = +\Delta_2 \end{array}$$

$$
\text{DPV} \quad
\begin{array}{ll}
0 & \Delta p_v = 0 \\
1 & \Delta p_v = -\Delta_3 \\
2 & \Delta p_v = +\Delta_3
\end{array}
$$

and introduce the following State Operators

$$\text{ODASP}(\text{DASP}; \Delta a_{sp}; 0, -\Delta_1, +\Delta_1)$$

$$\text{ODQSP}(\text{DQSP}; \Delta q_{sp}; 0, -\Delta_2, +\Delta_2)$$

$$\text{ODPV} \ (\text{DPV}; \ \Delta p_v \ ; \ 0, -\Delta_3, +\Delta_3)$$

The system of equations thus becomes

$$\Delta q_s = \text{OS} * \Delta q \tag{4'}$$

$$\Delta a_s = \text{OC1} * \text{ODASP} + \text{OC2} * \text{ODQSP} + \text{OC3} * \Delta q_s + \text{VC4} \tag{5'}$$

$$\Delta q = \text{OV1} * \Delta a_s + \text{OV2} * \text{ODPV} + \text{VV3} \tag{6'}$$

The parametric solution of the set of equations (4'), (5'), (6') with respect to a prefixed TOP condition (for example $\Delta q \leq \Delta q_0$) will then give the system behaviour as a function of the operating and failing states of its components.

Thus, for example, in the case: "Valve stuck", "Sensor Reversed Action" and "Critical increase of pressure", the Event Variables take the following set of values:

SS	SR	CR	CF	VF	DPV	DASP	DQSP
0	1	0	0	3	2	0	0

and, in correspondence, the system of equations becomes:

1) $\Delta q_s = \text{OS}(\text{SS}=0,\text{SR}=1) * \Delta q = -\alpha_s * \Delta q$

2) $\Delta a_s = \text{OC1}(\text{CR}=0,\text{CF}=0) * \text{ODASP}(\text{DASP}=0) + \text{OC2}(\text{CR}=0,\text{CF}=0) *$

$\qquad * \text{ODQSP} \ (\text{DQSP}=0) + \text{OC3}(\text{CR}=0,\text{CF}=0) * \Delta q_s +$

$\qquad + \text{VC4}(\text{CR}=0,\text{CF}=0) = -\alpha_c \Delta q_s$

3) $\Delta q = \text{OV1}(\text{VF}=3) * \Delta a_s + \text{OV2}(\text{VF}=3) * \text{ODPV}(\text{DPV}=2) +$

$\qquad + \text{VV3}(\text{VF}=3) = g_6 * \Delta_3$

Thus, by solving this particularized set of equations with respect to the variables interested in the TOP conditions, we are able to test if the simultaneous events "Valve Stuck", "Sensor Reversed Action" and "Critical increase of pressure" constitute a TOP set of events for the system. Obviously, this procedure is completely automatized in a controlled way in LAM algorithm for each combination of events.

4. IDENTIFICATION OF THE TOP CONDITIONS

As previously stated, the parametric solution of the set of equations representative of the whole system requires the identification of TOP conditions in terms of analytical con- straints between the relating variables. This allows us to easily obtain different TOP configurations simply by a change of the analytical constraints.

In the considered sample case, the system has the task to control the flow rate q. Then the TOP condition can be represented by

$$\Delta q \leq - \varepsilon \qquad \text{or} \qquad \Delta q \geq \varepsilon \qquad (7)$$

where ε is the limit flow rate tolerance.

Then the problem is reduced to the parametric solution of the set of equations (4'), (5'), (6') and to the numerical comparison of the TOP condition (7) with the resulting Δq value given by

$$\Delta q = (\xi + \eta * OV1)/(1 - OS * OV1 * OC3) \qquad (8)$$

where

$$\xi = OV2 * ODPV + VV3$$

$$\eta = OC1 * ODASP + OC2 * ODQSP + VC4$$

Any set of events (described by the Event Variables) that cause the TOP condition to hold thus defines a TOP set and the union of all TOP sets gives the logical failure representation of the system.

5. CONTROLLED GENERATION OF THE TOP SETS AND DIRECT TOP
    PROBABILITY CALCULATION

        As it can be easily pointed out, the combinatorial
non-controlled parametric solution of the set of equations which
synthetically represent the logical system behaviour, leads in
general to such a large amount of work that practical results can
hardly be produced. Thus, the computational aspects of the LAM
methodology are of primary importance.

        The LAM algorithm performs a controlled ordered generation
of TOP sets up to an arbitrary prefixed order. In other words the
algorithm starts from the generation of TOP sets constituted by
single failure events (order 1 sets), and proceeds in a controlled
way up to the desired order. It is worth-while to point out that
each TOP set consists of both failure and safe states. Indeed a
TOP set consists of those combinations of events (not necessarily
only failure events) that cause the TOP condition to hold. In this
respect the order of each TOP set is relative only to the failure
events while the TOP set itself implicitly involves safe events.
Thus, for instance, a TOP set of order 2 consists of the following
complete set of Event Variables

SS	SR	CR	CF	VF	DPV	DASP	DQSP
1	0	0	0	0	2	0	0

        (sensor stuck)   (critical pressure increase)

where this particular combination of failure events represents a
given external critical perturbation.

        Then, in the LAM algorithm, each complete set of events
constitutes the input for the system set of equations, and the set
itself is defined as a TOP set only if the solution of the
equations fulfills the TOP conditions.

        This particular procedure allows the probability calcul-
ations to be performed in a direct way by simply adding the TOP
sets probabilities.

        In fact, because of the exhaustive form of each TOP set, it
results that the compound event described by a generic TOP set is
mutually exclusive with any other considered TOP set. Moreover,
because of the indipendence, by construction, of each primary event
described by the Event Variables, the TOP sets probabilities can

be simply calculated as a product of the probabilities associated to each primary event.

This is of primary importance because it allows us to calculate the probability of the final TOP event in a direct and exact way without involving any hard procedure characteristic of general "non-coherent" logical functions. In fact, usual methods can easily handle only "coherent" systems, i.e. when disregarding the logical .NOT. operator. Now, the specific procedure followed by the LAM methodology, allows us to handle both coherent and non coherent systems and, in particular, allows us to extract all the events which are connected with the logical .NOT. operator (NON-TOP sets).
Specifically, because of their engineering interest, the LAM algorithm points out only the minimal TOP sets and the minimal NON-TOP sets where a NON-TOP set of order n is a complete set of primary events consisting of n single failure events which, in their whole, do not constitute a final TOP but where k of these $(1 \leq k \leq n-1)$ are a TOP for the system. Finally, a TOP (NON-TOP) set is said to be minimal if it does not contain a TOP (NON-TOP) set of lower order.

Yet, we have not examined the question concerning the parametric solution of the system of equations.

Apart from any numerical technique, it is worth while to mention the sequentialization method which may result, in many applications, to great advantage and efficiency.

In a few words, when some equation contains only a subset of the whole set of variables, then, under certain conditions, it is possible to get the solution by solving sequentially m subsets of independent equations thus reducing the initial generic $(n \times n)$ system into m $(n' \times n')$ sub-systems $(n' \leq n)$.

This may be of decisive importance particularly in non-linear problems. Moreover, by this method, it is possible to determine the presence of loops in the physical system which are characterized by the minimal sets of independent equations.

6. SAMPLE CONTROL LOOP: LAM RESULTS

The failure logical structure of the flow rate control loop as resulting by the LAM methodology is shown in tables 2, 3, 4 and a summary table (Tab.1) relative to the considered Event Variables has been added in order to make the reading easier.

Since the logical structure is a direct consequence of numerical comparisons between assigned TOP conditions and the solution of sets of equations, the numerical values of the constants of the models have to be given. In this respect, typical values coming from the operating field have been used.

TAB. 1. - Summary Table of the Event Variables

SS	0	Sensor in safe state
	1	Sensor Stuck
SR	0	Sensor not reversed action
	1	Sensor reversed action
CR	0	Controller not reversed action
	1	Controller reversed action
CF	0	Controller in safe state
	1	Controller fails low
	2	Controller fails high
	3	Controller stuck
VF	0	Control valve in safe state
	1	Control valve fails open
	2	Control valve fails closed
	3	Control valve stuck
DASP	0	$\Delta a_{sp} = 0$
	1	$\Delta a_{sp} < 0$
	2	$\Delta a_{sp} > 0$
DQSP	0	$\Delta q_{sp} = 0$
	1	$\Delta q_{sp} < 0$
	2	$\Delta q_{sp} > 0$
DPV	0	$\Delta p_{v} = 0$
	1	$\Delta p_{v} < 0$
	2	$\Delta p_{v} > 0$

TAB. 2 - LAM: Failure logical structure of the flow rate

Control loop – Order 1 minimal sets

TOP set	CF	1	
TOP set	CF	2	
TOP set	VF	1	
TOP set	VF	2	
TOP set	DASP	1	
TOP set	DASP	2	
TOP set	DQSP	1	
TOP set	DQSP	2	

Total sets = 15

TOP sets = 8

Minimal TOP sets = 8

Minimal NON–TOP sets = 0

TAB. 3 - LAM: Failure logical structure of the flow rate

Control loop – Order 2 minimal sets

	TOP set	SS	1	DPV	1
	TOP set	SS	1	DPV	2
	TOP set	SR	1	DPV	1
	TOP set	SR	1	DPV	2
	TOP set	CR	1	DPV	1
	TOP set	CR	1	DPV	2
NON	TOP set	CF	1	VF	3
NON	TOP set	CF	2	VF	3
NON	TOP set	CF	3	DASP	1
NON	TOP set	CF	3	DASP	2
NON	TOP set	CF	3	DQSP	1
NON	TOP set	CF	3	DQSP	2
	TOP set	CF	3	DPV	1

TAB. 3 (cont'd)

TOP set	CF	3	DPV	2
NON TOP set	VF	3	DASP	1
NON TOP set	VF	3	DASP	2
NON TOP set	VF	3	DQSP	1
NON TOP set	VF	3	DQSP	2
TOP set	VF	3	DPV	1
TOP set	VF	3	DPV	2
NON TOP set	DASP	1	DQSP	2
NON TOP set	DASP	2	DQSP	1

Total sets   =   96

TOP sets   =   74

Minimal TOP sets   =   10

Minimal NON-TOP sets   =   12

TAB. 4 - LAM: Failure logical structure of the flow rate

Control loop - Order 3 minimal sets

| NON TOP set | SR | 1 | CR | 1 | DPV | 1 |
| NON TOP set | SR | 1 | CR | 1 | DPV | 2 |

Total sets   =   342

TOP sets   =   278

Minimal TOP sets   =   0

Minimal NON-TOP sets   =   2

7. SHORT CONSIDERATIONS ON THE SAMPLE CASE AND GENERAL COMMENTS

1) The total number of states for the flow rate control system results to be N = 3456 as it can be easily deduced by considering the states of the involved Event Variables.

2) Order 1 TOP sets are constituted only by those events that directly influence the flow rate q. Failure events such as "Sensor stuck", Valve stuck", etc. do not appear in order 1 because, obviously, they need a simultaneous change of the system physical conditions (valve pressure variations).

3) TOP and NON-TOP sets of Order 2 and 3 are, in this simple case, very intuitive and probably they might have been easily obtained also by means of heuristic techniques.
   However, it is worth while to point out that in more complex systems any heuristic consideration about NON-TOP events becomes rapidly impracticable.
   This difficulty is generally evaded by simplifying the analysis of non-coherent systems by means of coherent techniques thus obtaining conservative probability results. However, in this way, the design and maintainability costs may be, when in presence of high failure probabilities, severely overestimated and, moreover, all the interesting engineering information deriving from NON-TOP sets considerations are lost.

4) The running time up to Order 6 has been of about 4 sec. CPU (UNIVAC 1108).

5) Till now, in addition to several sample tests, the LAM technique has been applied to five real cases relative to significant subsystems of nuclear, chemical and mechanical plants. A sixth more recent application has concerned the study of a dynamic mechanical case (level control loop).

6) Since the most relevant part of the time spent in the LAM analysis is relative to the construction of the "components operating and failing models", a library of generalized models for usual industrial components is being implemented.

7) At present, subprograms for the controlled generation of TOP and NON-TOP sets are generally available and a standard computer input formalization is under study.

L.A.M.   APPLICATION:

FAILURE ANALYSIS OF A SIMPLIFIED

ETHYLENE OXIDE PRODUCTION PLANT:

MIXING CIRCUIT

DESCRIPTION OF THE SYSTEM

The case considered in this sample application is relative to an ethylene oxide production plant.

We have schematized, in a very simplified but didactic way, an oxygen-ethylene mixing circuit.

Oxygen flow rate passes across the stop valve SV, it is controlled by the flow rate control loop constituted by the sensor S, the controller C and the control valve CV; then it goes into the mixer where it is mixed with ethylene.

An O_2 concentration threshold analyser controls the mixture composition: when it becomes explosive, a stop action is transmitted to the shut-down logic.

The ethylene oxidization takes place in a reactor, whose outlet temperature is controlled by three independent thermo-couples, connected in a 2/3 logic with the shut-down logic.

When the outlet reactor temperature exceeds the set point temperature, an alarm signal is transmitted to the shut-down logic.

A positive signal either from the O_2 detector or from the thermocouples is converted by the shut-down logic in a shut action of the stop valve.

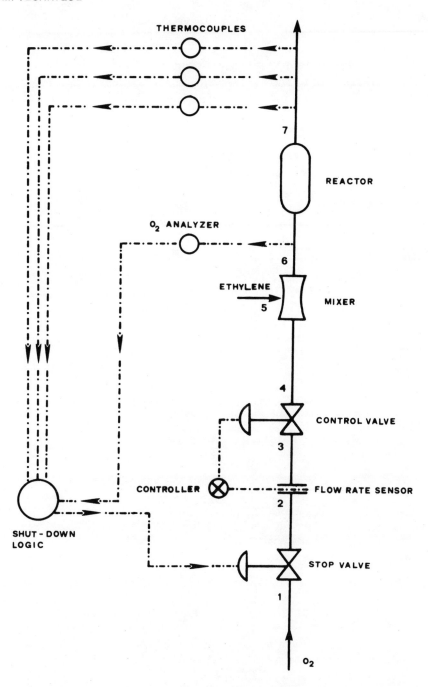

Fig. 1 – Scheme of the Ethylene Oxide Mixing Circuit.

STOP VALVE

In the system's normal operating state, the stop valve is in "open" position. If the shut-down logic orders the oxigen flow rate to stop, then tension V reaches the threshold value V_o closing the valve.

Functional relations in normal conditions

$$P_2 = (P_1 - \frac{Q_{o_2}^2}{K^2}) \cdot [1 - H(V,V_o)] + P_7 \cdot H(V,V_o)$$

where:

K	= valve constant
V	= tension relative to the stop signal
V_o	= tension threshold relative to the stop signal
P_1	= inlet valve pressure
P_2	= outlet valve pressure
Q_{o_2}	= oxygen flow rate
P_7	= outlet circuit pressure

$$H(x,x_o) = \text{step function: } H(x,x_o) \begin{cases} 0 & x < x_o \\ 1 & x \geq x_o \end{cases}$$

and in terms of incremental variables, it follows

$$\Delta P_2 = g_1 \cdot \Delta P_1 + g_2 \cdot \Delta Q_{o_2} + g_3 \cdot \Delta P_7 + g_4$$

where:

$$g_1 = 1 - H(V + \Delta V, V_o)$$
$$g_2 = - 2g_1 Q_{o_2} /K^2$$
$$g_3 = 1 - g_1$$
$$g_4 = (p_7 - p_1 + Q_{o_2}^2 /K^2) \cdot [H(V + \Delta V, V_o) - H(V, V_o)]$$

Single failure modes and effect analysis

Failure modes	Failure effects	Event variables
Actuator stuck	$(\Delta p_2)_v \leftarrow 0$	SA 0 non stuck 1 stuck

Valve fails open	$(\Delta p_2)_v \leftarrow 0$
	 $\Delta p_2 / \Delta p_1 \leftarrow 1$
	 $\Delta p_2 / \Delta Q_{o_2} \leftarrow -2Q_{o_2} /K^2$
	 $\Delta p_2 / \Delta p_7 \leftarrow 0$
		SSV 0 valve OK
		       1 valve fails
		          open

Simultaneous failure modes and effect analysis

States of component	Event variables		Effects			
	SA	SSV	$\Delta p_2 / \Delta p_1$	$\Delta p_2 / \Delta Q_{o_2}$	$\Delta p_2 / \Delta p_7$	$(\Delta p_2)_v$
S_1	0	0	g_1	g_2	g_3	g_4
S_2	0	1	1	$-2Q_{o_2} /K^2$	0	0
S_3	1	0	1	"	0	0
S_4	1	1	1	"	0	0

Stop valve state operators

OVB1   (SA, SSV; $\Delta p_2 / \Delta p_1$; g_1, 1, 1, 1)

OVB2   (SA, SSV; $\Delta p_2 / \Delta Q_{o_2}$; g_2, $-2Q_{o_2}/K^2$, $-2Q_{o_2}/K^2$, $-2Q_{o_2}/K^2$)

OVB3   (SA, SSV; $\Delta p_2 / \Delta p_7$; g_3, 0, 0, 0)

VVB4   (SA, SSV; $(\Delta p_2)_v$; g_4, 0, 0, 0)

Stop valve operating and failing model

$$\Delta p_2 = \text{OVB1} \cdot \Delta p_1 + \text{OVB2} \cdot \Delta Q_{o_2} + \text{OVB3} \cdot \Delta p_7 + \text{VVB4}$$

SENSOR

D.P. cell and linearization devices are synthetized in the oxigen flow rate sensor. Therefore sensor signal QS transmitted to the controller is proportional to the oxigen flow-rate.

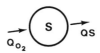

Functional relations in normal conditions

$$QS = \alpha_s \cdot Q_{o_2}$$

where:

α_s = sensor constant

QS = sensor signal

Q_{o_2} = oxigen flow rate

and, in terms of incremental variables, it follows:

$$\Delta QS = \alpha_s \cdot \Delta Q_{o_2}$$

Single failure modes and effect analysis

Failure modes	Failure effects	Event variables
Sensor Stuck	$\Delta QS/\Delta Q_{o_2} \leftarrow 0$	SS 0 sensor OK 1 sensor stuck

Simultaneous failure modes and effect analysis

States of component	Event variables	Effects
	SS	$\Delta QS/\Delta Q_{o_2}$
S_1	0	α_s
S_2	1	0

Sensor state operator

$$OS\ (SS;\ \Delta QS/\Delta Q_{o_2}\ ;\ \alpha_s,\ 0)$$

Sensor operating and failing model

$$\Delta QS = OS \cdot \Delta Q_{o_2}$$

CONTROLLER

In this simplified case we have assumed that the controller action is of proportional type. Namely, as a flow-rate change is sensed, the controller produces a corresponding corrective proportional change of valve position in order to keep the set-point flow-rate unchanged.

Functional relations in normal conditions

$$A = A_{sp} - \alpha_r \cdot (QS - QSP)$$

where:

A   = fractional area signal

A_{sp} = fractional set point area signal

α_r = controller constant

QS   = flow rate signal

QSP = flow rate set point signal

and, in terms of incremental variables, it follows

$$\Delta A = -\alpha_r \cdot \Delta QS + \alpha_r \cdot \Delta QSP$$

Single failure modes and effect analysis

Failure modes	Failure effects	Event variables
controller stuck	$\Delta A/\Delta QS \leftarrow 0$ $\Delta A/\Delta QSP \leftarrow 0$	
controller reversed action	$\Delta A/\Delta QS \leftarrow \alpha_r$ $\Delta A/\Delta QSP \leftarrow -\alpha_r$	
controller out of set point	$\Delta QSP \neq 0$	-

SC   0   contr. OK
SC   1   contr. stuck
2   contr. rev. act.

Simultaneous failure modes and effect analysis

States of component	Event variables	Effects	
	SC	$\Delta A/\Delta QS$	$\Delta A/\Delta QSP$
S_1	0	$-\alpha_r$	α_r
S_2	1	0	0
S_3	2	α_r	$-\alpha_r$

Controller state operators

$\quad$ OR1 (SC; $\Delta A/\Delta QS$; $-\alpha_r$, 0, α_r)

$\quad$ OR2 (SC; $\Delta A/\Delta QSP$; α_r, 0, $-\alpha_r$)

Controller operating and failing model

$\quad \Delta A = OR1 \cdot \Delta QS + OR2 \cdot \Delta QSP$

CONTROL VALVE

$\quad$ This valve controls the oxygen flow-rate in the mixing circuit. It receives the signal from the controller which produces a corresponding change in the flow area in order to keep the oxygen flow rate unchanged.

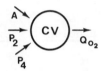

Functional relations in normal conditions

$$Q_{O_2} = K_1 \cdot A \cdot (p_2 - p_4)^{1/2}$$

where:

$\quad K_1 \quad$ = constant of the valve

$\quad A \quad$ = fractional signal area

$\quad p_2 \quad$ = inlet pressure

$\quad p_4 \quad$ = outlet pressure

$\quad Q_{O_2} \quad$ = oxygen flow rate

and, in terms of incremental variables, it follows

$$\Delta Q_{O_2} = g_5 \cdot \Delta A + g_6 \cdot \Delta p_2 + g_7 \cdot \Delta p_4$$

where:

$$g_5 = K_1 (p_2 - p_4)^{1/2}$$
$$g_6 = (K_1 A/(p_2 - p_4)^{1/2})/2$$
$$g_7 = - g_6$$

Single failure modes and effect analysis

Failure modes	Failure effects	Event variables	
valve stuck	$\Delta Q_{o_2}/\Delta A \leftarrow 0$	SCV	0 valve OK
			1 valve stuck

Simultaneous failure modes and effect analysis

States of component	Event variables	Effects
	SCV	$\Delta Q_{o_2}/\Delta A$
S_1	0	g_5
S_2	1	0

Control valve state operator

OVR (SCV; $\Delta Q_{o_2}/\Delta A$; g_5, 0)

Control valve operating and failing model

$$\Delta Q_{o_2} = OVR \cdot \Delta A + g_6 \cdot \Delta p_2 + g_7 \cdot \Delta p_4$$

MIXER

This component carries out the mixing of the oxygen and ethylene.

It has been schematized as a three ways collector whose inputs are the oxygen and ethylene flow-rates and the output is the oxygen-ethylene mixture.

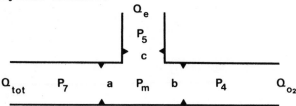

Load losses are localized in both inlet sections and in the outlet mixture section. Oxygen concentration in the mixture must be less than a prefixed critical value since, otherwise, an explosive mixture will be produced.

In this example we assume that this critical value can be reached only in consequence of oxygen and ethylene changes of pressures and flow-rates, not taking into consideration possible mechanical failures.

Moreover, changes of oxygen and ethylene flow rates change the control valve outlet pressure P_4.

Therefore this component will be characterized by two functional relations: one related to the oxygen concentration and the other to the control valve outlet pressure.

Functional relations in normal conditions

1) $P_4 = Q_{tot}^2/K_c^2 + Q_{o_2}^2/K_a^2 + P_7$

where:

$$Q_{tot} = Q_{O_2} + Q_e$$

$$K_a = \text{inlet oxygen load loss}$$

$$K_c = \text{outlet mixture load loss}$$

$$Q_{O_2} = \text{oxygen flow-rate}$$

$$Q_e = \text{ethylene flow-rate}$$

2) $$\varrho = Q_{O_2}/Q_{tot}$$

where:

ϱ = concentration of O_2 in the output mixture

and, in terms of incremental variables, it follows

1) $\Delta p_4 = g_8 \cdot \Delta Q_{O_2} + g_9 \cdot \Delta Q_e + \Delta p_7$

where:

$$g_8 = 2Q_e/K_c^2 + 2Q_{O_2}(K_a^2 + K_c^2)/K_a^2 K_c^2$$

$$g_9 = 2(Q_e + Q_{O_2})/K_c^2$$

2) $\Delta \varrho = g_{10} \cdot \Delta Q_{O_2} + g_{11} \cdot \Delta Q_e$

where:

$$g_{10} = Q_e/(Q_e + Q_{O_2})^2$$

$$g_{11} = -Q_{O_2}/(Q_e + Q_{O_2})^2$$

Mixer operating model

$$\Delta p_4 = g_8 \cdot \Delta Q_{O_2} + g_9 \cdot \Delta Q_e + \Delta p_7$$

$$\Delta \varrho = g_{10} \cdot \Delta Q_{O_2} + g_{11} \cdot \Delta Q_e$$

ANALYZER

This component compares the oxygen concentration in the mixer output with the critical explosive value. When this threshold value is reached an electronic signal $V_a = V_0$ is transmitted to the shut-down-logic.

Functional relations in normal conditions

$$V_a = V_0 \cdot H(\varrho, \varrho_0)$$

where:

V_a = output signal from the analyzer

V_0 = threshold signal characteristic of the stop valve

ϱ_0 = threshold concentration

and, in terms of incremental variables, it follows

$$\Delta V_a = V_0 \cdot [H(\varrho + \Delta\varrho, \varrho_0) - H(\varrho, \varrho_0)]$$

Single failure modes and effect analysis

Failure modes	Failure effects	Event variables	
detector stuck	$(\Delta V_a)_\varrho \leftarrow 0$	SDA	0 detector OK 1 detector stuck
comparator stuck	$(\Delta V_a)_\varrho \leftarrow 0$	SCA	0 comparator OK 1 comparator stuck

Simultaneous failure modes and effect-analysis

States of component	Event variables		Effects
	SDA	SCA	$(\Delta v_a)_\varrho$
S_1	0	0	g_{12}
S_2	0	1	0
S_3	1	0	0
S_4	1	1	0

where:

$$g_{12} = v_0 \cdot [H(\varrho + \Delta\varrho, \varrho_0) - H(\varrho, \varrho_0)]$$

Analyzer state operator

$$VA(SDA, SCA; (\Delta v_a)_\varrho; g_{12}, 0, 0, 0)$$

Analyzer operating and failing model

$$\Delta v_a = VA$$

REACTOR

Chemical process relations are not considered in this simple model.

We have only considered the event which directly affects the safety of the system, i.e., the effect of an internal fire in the reactor.

Functional relations in normal conditions

Not considered.

Single Failure modes and effect analysis

Failure modes	Failure effects	Event variables
internal fire in reactor	$\Delta T \leftarrow T_c - T$	IFRT $\quad$ 0 $\quad$ reactor OK $\quad\quad\quad$ 1 $\quad$ internal fire

where:

T_c = critical temperature

Simultaneous failure modes and effect analysis

States of component	Event variables	Effects
	IFRT	ΔT
S_1	0	0
S_2	1	$T_c - T$

Reactor state operator

$$VRT(IFRT; \Delta T; 0, T_c - T)$$

Reactor operating and failing model

$$\Delta T = VRT$$

THERMOCOUPLES

Three thermocouples in 2/3 logic are connected with the outlet pipe of the reactor.

If the reactor temperature exceeds the safety threshold T_c, a signal $V_o/2$ is forwarded to the shut down logic from each thermocouple.

Functional relations in normal conditions

$$VT_i = V_o \cdot H(T, T_c)/2 \qquad (i = 1, 2, 3)$$

where:

VT_i = i-th thermocouple tension signal

T = reactor temperature

T_c = critical threshold temperature

V_o = threshold signal characteristic of the stop valve

and, in terms of incremental variables, it follows

$$\Delta VT_i = g_{13}$$

where:

$$g_{13} = V_o \cdot \left[H(T + \Delta T, T_c) - H(T, T_c) \right]/2$$

Single failure modes and effect analysis

Failure modes	Failure effects	Event variables		
i-th thermocouple stuck	$(\Delta VT_i)_T \leftarrow 0$	ST_i	0	non stuck
			1	stuck
i-th thermocouple out of set point	$(\Delta VT_i)_T \leftarrow g_{14}$	STS_i	0	set point OK
			1	out of set pint

where:

$$g_{14} = V_o \cdot \left[H(T + \varDelta T, T_{c_i}) - H(T, T_{c_i}) \right] / 2$$

(T_{c_i} = false set point temperature for the i-th thermo-couple)

Simultaneous failure modes and effect analysis

States of components	Event variables		Effects
	ST_i	STS_i	$(\varDelta VT_i)_T$
S_1	0	0	g_{13}
S_2	0	1	g_{14}
S_3	1	0	0
S_4	1	1	0

Reactor state operator

$$VTM_i(ST_i, STS_i; (\varDelta VT_i)_T; g_{13}, g_{14}, 0, 0)$$

Thermocouple operating and failing model

$$\varDelta VT_i = VTM_i$$

SHUT-DOWN LOGIC

This component is the "core" of the shut-down system.

It receives the signals both from the analyzer and the three thermocouples.

If signals from either the analyzer or at least from two thermocouples are received, a shut-down action is generated and a stop impulse V is transmitted to the stop valve.

The shut down logic operation has been simulated by performing the sum of the input signals. Thus, while the signal (V_o) from the analyzer is sufficient in itself to operate the stop valve, signals from only one thermocouple $(V_o/2)$ at a time do not produce any effect.

Functional relations in normal conditions

$$V = VT1 + VT2 + VT3 + V_a$$

where:

V = output signal to the stop valve

V_a = analyzer signal

VT1,VT2,VT3 = thermocouples signals.

and, in terms of incremental variables, it follows

$$\Delta V = \Delta VT1 + \Delta VT2 + \Delta VT3 + \Delta V_a$$

Single failure modes and effect analysis

Failure modes	Failure effects	Event variables
Analyzer logic stuck	$\Delta V/\Delta V_a \leftarrow 0$ SDLA	0 analyzer logic OK 1 analyzer logic stuck
i-th thermocouple logic stuck	$\Delta V/\Delta VT_i \leftarrow 0$ SDLT	0 therm. logic OK 1 therm. logic stuck

Simultaneous failure modes and effect analysis

States of component	Event variables		Effects	
	SDLA	SDLT	$\Delta v/\Delta v_i$	$\Delta v/\Delta v_a$
S_1	0	0	1	1
S_2	0	1	0	1
S_3	1	0	1	0
S_4	1	1	0	0

Shut-down logic state operators

OLB1 (SDLA, SDLT; $\Delta v/\Delta v_i$; 1, 0, 1, 0)

OLB2 (SDLA, SDLT; $\Delta v/\Delta v_a$; 1, 1, 0, 0)

Shut-down logic operating and failing model

ΔV = OLB1 . $\Delta VT1$ + OLB1 . $\Delta VT2$ + OLB1 . $\Delta VT3$ + OLB2 . ΔV_a

TOP CONDITIONS

In this example we have considered two TOP conditions:

1) Oxygen concentration in the outlet mixer mixture must not exceed the critical value ϱ_o. Thus TOP condition is reached when:

$$\Delta \varrho \geq \varrho_o - \varrho$$

2) If a fire in the reactor is generated, the shut-down system must stop the oxygen flow rate. Thus TOP conditions is reached when

$$\Delta T \geq T_c - T$$
$$\Delta Q_{O_2} \geq 0$$

where:

$\quad\quad$ T $\;$ is the reactor outlet temperature

$\quad\quad$ T_c is the critical threshold temperature

SUMMARY TABLE OF THE EVENT VARIABLES

SA	0	stop valve actuator in safe state
	1	stop valve actuator stuck
SSV	0	stop valve in safe state
	1	stop valve fails open
SS	0	flow rate sensor safe
	1	flow rate sensor stuck
SC	0	controller in safe state
	1	controller stuck
	2	controller reversed
SCV	0	control valve in safe state
	1	control valve stuck
SDA	0	analyzer detector in safe state
	1	analyzer detector stuck
SCA	0	analyzer comparator in safe state
	1	analyzer comparator stuck
IFRT	0	reactor in safe state
	1	internal fire in the reactor
ST_i	0	i-th thermocouple in safe state
	1	i-th thermocouple stuck
STS_i	0	i-th thermocouple not out of set point
	1	i-th thermocouple out of set point
SDLA	0	analyzer S.D. logic in safe state
	1	analyzer S.D. logic stuck

SUMMARY TABLE OF THE EVENT VARIABLES (cont'd)

SDLT   0   thermocouples S.D. logic in safe state
        1   thermocouples S.D. logic stuck

DP1   0 $\Delta p_1 = 0$
      1   $\Delta p_1 < 0$
      2   $\Delta p_1 > 0$

DP7   0 $\Delta p_7 = 0$
      1   $\Delta P_7 < 0$
      2   $\Delta P_7 > 0$

DQE   0 $\Delta Q_e = 0$
      1   $\Delta Q_e < 0$
      2   $\Delta Q_e > 0$

DQSP   0 $\Delta Q_{sp} = 0$
       1   $\Delta Q_{sp} < 0$
       2   $\Delta Q_{sp} > 0$

RELIABILITY DATA

Events		Failure Rate λ(F/y)	Repair Rate μ(R/y)	State Probability P_∞
SA	0			$9.999658 \cdot 10^{-1}$
	1	.15	4380	$3.42 \cdot 10^{-5}$
SSV	0			$9.999316 \cdot 10^{-1}$
	1	.15	2190	$6.84 \cdot 10^{-5}$
SS	0			$9.991514 \cdot 10^{-1}$
	1	1.86	2190	$8.486 \cdot 10^{-4}$
SC	0			$9.998813 \cdot 10^{-1}$
	1	.26	2190	$5.935 \cdot 10^{-5}$
	2			$5.935 \cdot 10^{-5}$

RELIABILITY DATA (cont'd)

SCV	0		$9.9974 \cdot 10^{-1}$
	1	.57	2190	$2.6 \cdot 10^{-4}$
SDA	0		$9.968138 \cdot 10^{-1}$
	1	7.	2190	$3.1862 \cdot 10^{-3}$
SCA	0		$9.998813 \cdot 10^{-1}$
	1	.26	2190	$1.187 \cdot 10^{-4}$
IFRT	0		$9.95025 \cdot 10^{-1}$
	1	.05	10	$4.975 \cdot 10^{-3}$
ST_i	0		$9.998174 \cdot 10^{-1}$
	1	.4	2190	$1.826 \cdot 10^{-4}$
STS_i	0		$9.99429 \cdot 10^{-1}$
	1	5.	8760	$5.71 \cdot 10^{-4}$
SDLA	0		$9.999989 \cdot 10^{-1}$
	1	.01	8760	$1.1 \cdot 10^{-6}$
SDLT	0		$9.999989 \cdot 10^{-1}$
	1	.01	8760	$1.1 \cdot 10^{-6}$
DP1	0		$9.9943 \cdot 10^{-1}$
	1	10.	17520	$2.85 \cdot 10^{-4}$
	2			$2.85 \cdot 10^{-4}$
DP7	0		
	1	"	"	"
	2			
DQE	0		
	1	"	"	"
	2			
DQSP	0		
	1	"	"	"
	2			

LAM output: Symplified Ethylene Oxide Production Plant

Mixing Circuit – TOP Condition: $\Delta \varrho \geq \Delta \varrho_c$

Order 1 minimal sets

Total sets	=	25
TOP sets	=	0
Minimal TOP sets	=	0
Minimal NON–TOP sets	=	0
TOP probability	=	0.

Order 2 minimal sets

TOP set	SA	1	DQE	1
TOP set	SA	1	DQSP	2
TOP set	SSV	1	DQE	1
TOP set	SSV	1	DQSP	2
TOP set	SDA	1	DQE	1
TOP set	SDA	1	DQSP	2
TOP set	SCA	1	DQE	1
TOP set	SCA	1	DQSP	2
TOP set	SDLA	1	DQE	1
TOP set	SDLA	1	DQSP	2

Total sets	=	295
TOP sets	=	10
Minimal TOP sets	=	10
Minimal NON–TOP sets	=	0
TOP probability	=	.19221–05

<u>LAM output (cont'd)</u>

<u>Order 3 minimal sets</u>

		SA/SSV/SS		2nd		3rd	
	TOP set	SA	1	SS	1	DP1	2
	TOP set	SA	1	SS	1	DP7	1
	TOP set	SA	1	SC	1	DP1	2
	TOP set	SA	1	SC	2	DP1	2
	TOP set	SA	1	SC	1	DP7	1
	TOP set	SA	1	SC	2	DP7	1
NON	TOP set	SA	1	SC	1	DQSP	2
	TOP set	SA	1	SC	2	DQSP	1
NON	TOP set	SA	1	SC	2	DQSP	2
	TOP set	SA	1	SCV	1	DP1	2
	TOP set	SA	1	SCV	1	DP7	1
NON	TOP set	SA	1	SCV	1	DQSP	2
	TOP set	SA	1	DP1	2	DP7	1
NON	TOP set	SA	1	DP1	1	DQE	1
NON	TOP set	SA	1	DP1	1	DQSP	2
NON	TOP set	SA	1	DP7	2	DQE	1
NON	TOP set	SA	1	DP7	2	DQSP	2
NON	TOP set	SA	1	DQE	1	DQSP	1
NON	TOP set	SA	1	DQE	2	DQSP	2
	TOP set	SSV	1	SS	1	DP1	2
	TOP set	SSV	1	SS	1	DP7	1
	TOP set	SSV	1	SC	1	DP1	2
	TOP set	SSV	1	SC	2	DP1	2
	TOP set	SSV	1	SC	1	DP7	1
	TOP set	SSV	1	SC	2	DP7	1
NON	TOP set	SSV	1	SC	1	DQSP	2
	TOP set	SSV	1	SC	2	DQSP	1
NON	TOP set	SSV	1	SC	2	DQSP	2
	TOP set	SSV	1	SCV	1	DP1	2
	TOP set	SSV	1	SCV	1	DP7	1
NON	TOP set	SSV	1	SCV	1	DQSP	2
	TOP set	SSV	1	DP1	2	DP7	1
NON	TOP set	SSV	1	DP1	1	DQE	1
NON	TOP set	SSV	1	DP1	1	DQSP	2
NON	TOP set	SSV	1	DP7	2	DQE	1
NON	TOP set	SSV	1	DP7	2	DQSP	2
NON	TOP set	SSV	1	DQE	1	DQSP	1
NON	TOP set	SSV	1	DQE	2	DQSP	2
	TOP set	SS	1	SDA	1	DP1	2

LAM output

Order 3 minimal sets (cont'd)

	TOP set	SS	1	SDA	1	DP7	1
	TOP set	SS	1	SCA	1	DP1	2
	TOP set	SS	1	SCA	1	DP7	1
	TOP set	SS	1	SDLA	1	DP1	2
	TOP set	SS	1	SDLA	1	DP7	1
	TOP set	SC	1	SDA	1	DP1	2
	TOP set	SC	2	SDA	1	DP1	2
	TOP set	SC	1	SDA	1	DP7	1
	TOP set	SC	2	SDA	1	DP7	1
NON	TOP set	SC	1	SDA	1	DQSP	2
	TOP set	SC	2	SDA	1	DQSP	1
NON	TOP set	SC	2	SDA	1	DQSP	2
	TOP set	SC	1	SCA	1	DP1	2
	TOP set	SC	2	SCA	1	DP1	2
	TOP set	SC	1	SCA	1	DP7	1
	TOP set	SC	2	SCA	1	DP7	1
NON	TOP set	SC	1	SCA	1	DQSP	2
	TOP set	SC	2	SCA	1	DQSP	1
NON	TOP set	SC	2	SCA	1	DQSP	2
	TOP set	SC	1	SDLA	1	DP1	2
	TOP set	SC	2	SDLA	1	DP1	2
	TOP set	SC	1	SDLA	1	DP7	1
	TOP set	SC	2	SDLA	1	DP7	1
NON	TOP set	SC	1	SDLA	1	DQSP	2
	TOP set	SC	2	SDLA	1	DQSP	1
NON	TOP set	SC	2	SDLA	1	DQSP	2
	TOP set	SCV	1	SDA	1	DP1	2
	TOP set	SCV	1	SDA	1	DP7	1
NON	TOP set	SCV	1	SDA	1	DQSP	2
	TOP set	SCV	1	SCA	1	DP1	2
	TOP set	SCV	1	SCA	1	DP7	1
NON	TOP set	SCV	1	SCA	1	DQSP	2
	TOP set	SCV	1	SDLA	1	DP1	2
	TOP set	SCV	1	SDLA	1	DP7	1
NON	TOP set	SCV	1	SDLA	1	DQSP	2
NON	TOP set	SDA	1	IFRT	1	DQE	1
NON	TOP set	SDA	1	IFRT	1	DQSP	2
	TOP set	SDA	1	DP1	2	DP7	1
NON	TOP set	SDA	1	DP1	1	DQE	1
NON	TOP set	SDA	1	DP1	1	DQSP	2
NON	TOP set	SDA	1	DP7	2	DQE	1
NON	TOP set	SDA	1	DP7	2	DQSP	2

LAM output

Order 3 minimal sets (cont'd)

NON TOP set	SDA	1	DQE	1	DQSP	1
NON TOP set	SDA	1	DQE	2	DQSP	2
NON TOP set	SCA	1	IFRT	1	DQE	1
NON TOP set	SCA	1	IFRT	1	DQSP	2
TOP set	SCA	1	DP1	2	DP7	1
NON TOP set	SCA	1	DP1	1	DQE	1
NON TOP set	SCA	1	DP1	1	DQSP	2
NON TOP set	SCA	1	DP7	2	DQE	1
NON TOP set	SCA	1	DP7	2	DQSP	2
NON TOP set	SCA	1	DQE	1	DQSP	1
NON TOP set	SCA	1	DQE	2	DQSP	2
NON TOP set	IFRT	1	SDLA	1	DQE	1
NON TOP set	IFRT	1	SDLA	1	DQSP	2
TOP set	SDLA	1	DP1	2	DP7	1
NON TOP set	SDLA	1	DP1	1	DQE	1
NON TOP set	SDLA	1	DP1	1	DQSP	2
NON TOP set	SDLA	1	DP7	2	DQE	1
NON TOP set	SDLA	1	DP7	2	DQSP	2
NON TOP set	SDLA	1	DQE	1	DQSP	1
NON TOP set	SDLA	1	DQE	2	DQSP	2

Total sets	=	2185
TOP sets	=	194
Minimal TOP sets	=	50
Minimal NON-TOP sets	=	51
TOP probability	=	.19332-05

LAM output: Simplified Ethylene Oxide Production Plant

Mixing Circuit – TOP Conditions: $\Delta T \geq T_c - T$ and $\Delta Q_{o_2} \geq 0$

Order 1 minimal sets

Total sets	=	25
TOP sets	=	0
Minimal TOP sets	=	0
Minimal NON-TOP sets	=	0
TOP probability	=	0.

Order 2 minimal sets

TOP set	SA	1	IFRT	1
TOP set	SSV	1	IFRT	1
TOP set	IFRT	1	SDLT	1

Total sets	=	295
TOP sets	=	3
Minimal TOP sets	=	3
Minimal NON-TOP sets	=	0
TOP probability	=	.50777-06

Order 3 minimal sets

NON TOP set	SA	1	IFRT	1	DP1	1
NON TOP set	SA	1	IFRT	1	DP7	2
NON TOP set	SA	1	IFRT	1	DQSP	1
NON TOP set	SSV	1	IFRT	1	DP1	1
NON TOP set	SSV	1	IFRT	1	DP7	2

LAM output

Order 3 minimal sets (cont'd)

NON TOP set	SSV 1	IFRT 1	DQSP 1	
TOP set	IFRT 1	ST1 1	ST2 1	
TOP set	IFRT 1	ST1 1	ST3 1	
TOP set	IFRT 1	ST1 1	STS2 1	
TOP set	IFRT 1	ST1 1	STS3 1	
TOP set	IFRT 1	ST2 1	ST3 1	
TOP set	IFRT 1	ST2 1	STS1 1	
TOP set	IFRT 1	ST2 1	STS3 1	
TOP set	IFRT 1	ST3 1	STS1 1	
TOP set	IFRT 1	ST3 1	STS2 1	
TOP set	IFRT 1	STS1 1	STS2 1	
TOP set	IFRT 1	STS1 1	STS3 1	
TOP set	IFRT 1	STS2 1	STS3 1	
NON TOP set	IFRT 1	SDLT 1	DP1 1	
NON TOP set	IFRT 1	SDLT 1	DP7 2	
NON TOP set	IFRT 1	SDLT 1	DQE 1	
NON TOP set	IFRT 1	SDLT 1	DQSP 1	
NON TOP set	IFRT 1	SDLT 1	DQSP 2	

Total sets	=	2185
TOP sets	=	67
Minimal TOP sets	=	12
Minimal NON-TOP sets	=	11
TOP probability	=	.52037−06

REFERENCES

1. R. G. BENNETS, On the analysis of fault trees, IEEE Trans. on Rel., R-24/3 (1975).
2. Z. W. BIRNBAUM, Theory of Reliability for Coherent Structures, Report 41, Dept. of Mathematics, University of Washington, Seattle, (1965).
3. D. B. BROWN, A computerized algorithm for determining the reliability of redundant configurations, IEEE Trans. on Rel., R-20, 121:124 (1971).
4. A. CARNINO, Safety Analysis Using Fault-Trees, NATO Advanced Study Inst. on Generic Techniques of System Reliability Assessment, Nordhoff Publishing Company (1974).
5. A. G. COLOMBO, Cadi - A Computer Code for System Availability and Reliability Evaluation, Report EUR 49400 (1973).
6. A. G. COLOMBO, G. VOLTA, Sensitivity Analysis in Systems Reliability Evaluation, J.R.C. Annual Report, Ispra (1973).
7. A. G. COLOMBO, G. VOLTA, Multistep Reliability Analysis and Optimization of Complex Systems, Proc. of the OECD-NEA Specialist Meeting on Reliability, Liverpool (1974).
8. J. B. FUSSELL, Fault tree analysis: concepts and techniques, NATO Advanced Study Inst. on Generic Techniques of System Reliability Assessment, Nordhoff Publishing Company (1974).
9. J. B. FUSSELL, Synthetic tree model: A formal methodology for fault tree construction, Aerojet Nuclear Report ANCR 01098 (1973).
10. J. B. FUSSELL, A Formal Methodology for Fault Tree Construction, Nuc. Sc. and Eng., 52 (1973).
11. J. B. FUSSELL, W. E. VESELY, A New Methodology for Obtaining Cut Sets for Fault Trees, Trans. Am. Nucl. Soc., 15 (1972).
12. J. B. FUSSELL, G. J. POWERS, R.G. BENNETTS, Fault Trees: A State of the Art Discussion, IEEE Trans. on Rel. R-23/1 (1974).
13. S. L. GANDHI, K. INOUE, E.J. HENLEY, Computer Aided System Reliability Analysis and Optimization, Proc. of the IFIP Working Conference on Principles of Computer Aided Design, Eindoven (1972).
14. S. GARRIBBA, G. REINA, G. VOLTA, Repair Processes: Fundamental and Computation, EUR 5232e Ispra (1974).
15. S. GARRIBBA, G. REINA, G. VOLTA, Availability of Repairable Units when Failure and Restoration Rates Age in Real Time, IEEE Trans. on Rel., R-25 (1976).

16. S. GARRIBBA, P. MUSSIO, F. NALDI, G. REINA, Determinazione Diretta degli Insiemi Minimi di taglio di Alberi Logici, CESNEF IN-006 (1974).

17. S. GARRIBBA, P. MUSSIO, F. NALDI, G. REINA, G. VOLTA, Efficient Construction of Minimal Cut Sets from Fault Trees, IEEE Trans. on Rel. R-26/2 (1977).

18. S. GARRIBBA, P. MUSSIO, F. NALDI, G. REINA, G. VOLTA, Dicomics: An Algorithm for Direct Computation of Minimal Cut Sets of Fault Trees, EUR 5481e, Ispra (1976).

19. S. GARRIBBA, G. REINA, Fault Tree Sensitivity Analysis for Reliability Calculation in Nuclear Power Plants, IAEA RC 1651/RB (1976).

20. B. J. GARRICK, Principles of Unified Systems Safety Analysis, Nucl. Eng. and Des., 13,245:321 (1974).

21. W. Y. GATELEY, D.W. STODDARD, R. L. WILLIAMS, GO: A Computer Program for Reliability Analysis of Complex Systems, Kaman Sciences Corporation, Colorado Springs, KN-67-704(R) (1968).

22. D. F. HAASL, Advanced Concept in Fault Tree Analysis, System Safety Symposium (available from the University of Washington Library), Seattle (1965).

23. F. J. HENLEY, R.A. WILLIAMS, Graph Theory in Modern Engineering, Academic Press, New York (1973).

24. R. B. HURLEY, Probability maps, IEEE Trans. on Rel., R-12, 39:44 (1963).

25. B. V. KOEN, Méthodes Nouvelles pour l'Evalutation de la Fiabilité: Reconnaissance des Formes, CEA-R-4368 (1972).

26. H. E. KONGSO, REDIS: a Computer Program for System Reliability Analysis by Direct Simulation, International Symposium on Reliability of Nuclear Power Plants, Innsbruck, IAEA-SM-195/17 (1975).

27. H. E. LAMBERT, Systems Safety Analysis and Fault Tree Analysis, UCID-16238 (available from the Lawrence Livermore Laboratories, Livermore, Calif.) (1973).

28. P. M. LIN, G. E. ALDERSON, Symbolic Network Functions by a Single Path Finding Algorithm, Proc. 7th Allerton Conf. on Circuits and Systems, 196:205, Univ. of Illinois, Urbana (1969).

29. P. M. LIN, B. J. LEON, T. C. HUANG, A New Algorithm for Symbolic System Reliability Analysis, IEEE Trans. on Rel., R-25/1 (1976).

30. C. W. MCKNIGHT, Automatica Reliability Mathematical Model,

North American Aviation, Downey California, NA 66-838 (1966).

31. K. B. MISRA, An Algorithm for the Reliability Evaluation of Redundant Networks, IEEE Trans. on Rel., R-19, 146: 151 (1970).

32. D. S. NIELSEN, O. PLATZ, B. RUNGE, A Cause-Consequence Chart of a Redundant Protection System, IEEE Trans. on Rel. R-24,8:13 (1975).

33. D. S. NIELSEN, The Cause-Consequence Diagram Method as a Basis for Quantitative Reliability Analysis, ENEA/CREST Meeting on Applicability of Quantitative Reliability Analysis of Complex Systems and Nuclear Plants in its Relation to Safety, Munich (1971).

34. D. S. NIELSEN, Use of Cause-Consequence Charts in Practical Systems Analysis, Conference on Rel. and Fault Tree Analysis, Berkeley, California (1974).

35. P. K. PANDE, Computerized Fault Tree Analysis: TREEL and MICSUP, Operation Research Center, Univ. of California, Berkeley, ORC 75-3 (1975).

36. E. PHIBBS, S. H. KUWAMOTO, An Efficient Map Method for Processing Multistate Logic Trees, IEEE Trans. on Rel., R-21,93:98 (1972).

37. E. PHIBBS, S. H. KUWAMOTO, Fault Tree Analysis, IEEE Trans. on Rel., R-23,226 (1974).

38. G. J. POWERS, S. A. LAPP, Quantitative Safety Assessment of Chemical Processes, U.S.-Japan Joint Seminar on Application of Process System Engineering to Chemical Technology Assessment, Kyoto, Japan, (1975).

39. G. J. POWERS, F.C. TOMPKINS Jr., Fault Tree Synthesis for Chemical Processes, AICHE Journal, 20/2,376 (1974).

40. G. J. POWERS, F. C. TOMPKINS Jr., A Synthesis Strategy for Fault Trees in Chemical Processing Systems: Loss Prevention, Chem. Eng. Progress Techn. Manual, 8, AICHE, New York (1974).

41. G. J. POWERS, F. C. TOMPKINS Jr., Computer Aided Synthesis of Fault Trees for Complex Processing System, Proc. NATO Advanced Study Inst. on Systems Reliability, Liverpool (1973).

42. G. REINA, Sul problema della descrizione e della rappresentazione di un sistema: Approccio logico analitico per la costruzione di alberi degli eventi e fault trees, Proc. of the ANIPLA Meeting on Reliability, Milan (1977).

43. G. REINA, G. SQUELLATI, LAM: A New Logical Analitical Methodology for Synthetic System Representation, Institute on Safety and Risk Assessment in Chemical Plants, Sogesta, Urbino, Italy (1978).

44. G. REINA, Codice DSC per l'analisi probabilistica di Sistemi Complessi, ARS RT 75/19 (1974).

45. E. T. RUMBLE, F. L. LEVERENZ, R.C. ERDMANN, Generalized Fault Tree Analysis for Reactor Safety, EPRI 217-2-2, Palo Alto (1975).

46. S. L. SALEM, G. E. APOSTOLAKIS, D. OKRENT, A Computer-Oriented Approach to Fault-Tree Construction, EPRI NP-288, Palo Alto (1976).

47. S. L. SALEM, G. E. APOSTOLAKIS, D. OKRENT, A New Methodology for the Computer-Aided Construction of Fault Trees, Annals of Nuclear Energy, 4,417:433 (1977).

48. S. N. SEMANDERES, ELRAFT: A Computer Program for the Efficient Logic Reduction Analysis of Fault Trees, IEEE Trans. on Nucl. Sc., NS-18/1,481:487 (1971).

49. R. J. SHROEDER, Fault Trees for Reliability Analysis, R 70-15078 ASQC 821:844, Proc. of the Annual Symposium on Rel., Los Angeles (1970).

50. J. R. TAYLOR, Sequential Effects in Failure Mode Analysis, Conference on Rel. and Fault Tree Analysis, Berkeley (1974).

51. J. R. TAYLOR, A Semiautomatic Method for Qualitative Failure Mode Analysis, CSNI Specialist Meeting on the Development and Application of Rel. Tech. to Nuclear Plants, Riso M1707 (1974).

52. J. R. TAYLOR, E. HOLLO, Algorithms and Programs for Consequence Diagram and Fault Trees Construction, Riso M1907 (1977).

53. W. J. VAN SLYKE, D. E. GRIFFING, ALLCUTS: A Fast Comprehensive Fault Tree Analysis Code, Atlantic Richfield Hanford Company, Richland, Washington, ARH-ST-112 (1975).

54. W. E. VESELY, A Time-Dependent Methodology for Fault Tree Evaluation, Nuc. Eng. and Des., 13 (1970).

55. W. E. VESELY, R. E. NARUM, PREP and KITT: Computer Codes for the Automatic Evaluation of a Fault Tree, Idaho Nuclear Report N-1349 (1970).

56. O. WING, P. DEMETRIOU, Analysis of Probabilistic Network, IEEE Trans. Comm. Tech., COM-12, 38:40 (1964).

57. E. R.WOODCOCK, The Calculation of Reliability of Systems: The Program NOTED, UKAEA Authority Health and Safety Branch, Risley, Warrington, England, AHSB (S) R 153 (1971).

ACKNOWLEDGEMENTS

The authors are very grateful to Dr. G. Volta for his helpful advice and, particularly, to Mr. R. Rossetti for his kind forbearance in typing the manuscript.

MULTIVALUED LOGIC IN THE REPRESENTATION OF ENGINEERING SYSTEMS

S. Garribba, CESNEF, Instituto Ing. Nucleare, Politecnico di Milano,
Via G. Ponzio 34/3, Milano, Italy 20133
P. Mussio and F. Naldi, CNR, Via E. Bassini 15, Milano, Italy 20133

ABSTRACT

The paper deals with the construction process of a reliability-oriented system representation made in terms of a multivalued logical tree (MVLT) which computes logical statements. The propositional variables of these logical statements assume values related with the behaviours of the system, and of its subsystems and components. When fed by a set of values for input variables, the MVLT gives the instantaneous value of the proposition it represents. A formal procedure of system decomposition and recomposition can be designed for the automatic construction of the MVLT. Foundations of this procedure are provided and solutions discussed for two cases. Merits of MVLT seem to lay on a better control of information to retain in the representation of the system, high degree of compactness, evidence given to the correspondence between logical structures and physical behaviours.

1. INTRODUCTION

The construction of a reliability-oriented representation of an engineered system presumes the recognition and observation of the system and its characteristics. A model is selected expressing those properties, attributes and connections that are deemed of interest. Then the model will entail a representaion of the system, that is some set of mathematical equations or relations. It is clear that even in the case equations or relations depict the model perfectly, if the model is not a complete description of the physical system, the representation "might not tell us very much about the system, no matter how carefully we develop it" [1]. Furthermore, in view of the complexity of practical systems, we cannot avoid that representations of the system and of its components contain some intrinsic approximation.

The construction process of an approximate representation of the system may thus follow three interconnected steps or phases. First, having assumed models for the entire system and its parts, is system decomposition where subsystems or components are identified, each one limited by some (set of) physical boundaries.

Second is the phase where representations are developed and suitable approximations found for all subsystems and components. Finally, these separate representations must be reassembled to provide the approximate representation of the entire system. Since it is reliability-oriented, this representation should be able to provide statements of the type "system is operating safety", "system is out of order and safe", "system is failed and unsafe", and so on.

It occurs that in the search for components and their representations, the models selected need review and changements. In this respect, it may be said that system decomposition and component modeling are iterative and ask for continuous checks of coherence. Similarly, when the different representations of components are pieced together, conditions of congruence ought to be set in such a way that representations are readjusted and their values relocated.

Representations we are looking for will be given in terms of logical trees. In principle, a logical tree is a combinatorial machine (with no memory or storage), which is designed for the computation of logical statements. The propositional variables of these statements take values on a set of variables regarding the representations of the subsystems of components. In the formulation of a model for the system it has to be assumed that all information is simultaneous. In this sense it will be said that logical tree provides synchronic representations of the system.

2. SYSTEM DECOMPOSITION AND SEARCH FOR REPRESENTATIONS

Attention will be concentrated on the class of technological systems. Indeed, systems and subsystems that will be dealt with are designed by engineers and constructed to perform some mission where objectives can be clearly stated. Aim is the definition of some outcome space or representation which can be used for reliability assessment and computation. In particular we shall be interested in certain structures of outcome space. By outcome space we mean the set of all possible event points or behaviours which could be taken by the system and its subsystems under given conditions. Behaviours are defined formally in terms of couples of states and transition functions, satisfying certain rules to be stated. It is understood that, provided the outcome space has been obtained, we admit the possibility of a probability space defined by a sigma field of events and a probability measure.

Let us admit that after system observation models can be conceived which allow to start a procedure of decomposition of the system into subsystems or parts or components. This procedure will be based upon three conditions: (i) system and subsystems must be physically limited by a closed surface; (ii) inputs and outputs towards the environment and other subsystems must be finite and completely determinable, thus enabling the analyst to consider the subsystem as disconnected from other subsystems or components; (iii) subsystems ought to be described in terms of a deterministic dynamic representation, as shown in what follows.

In view of their complexity, it may happen that subsystems should be broken up further into new subsystems. If this is the case, they will be called non-terminal in contrast with terminal or atomic subsystems. A question arises: how to determine the resolution level where the procedure of decomposition should come to a halt. In practice, this level will depend both upon representation requirements set by the analyst and by the type of experimental data which are available.

A deterministic dynamic representation of a system and subsystems (technological systems are a particular case) can be specified by means of five sets (T, U, Ω, Y, S)

and two functions ϕ and η [1]. $\cdot$T is the time set (i.e. time instants are indexed by numbers $t \in T$); U is the input set (i.e. instantaneous values of all input functions $u(t)$ lie in U); Ω is the set of admissible input functions from T to U (if input functions $u(t) \in \Omega$ it will be $u(t) \in U$); Y is the output set (i.e. the set of all output functions $y(t)$; S is the set of internal or state variables or memory configurations $s(t)$. The function $\phi : T \times T \times S \times \Omega \rightarrow S$ is called the state transition map.

Let us consider two times t_0 and t_1 ($t_0 \leqslant t_1$), an initial state $s(t_0)$ and an input function $u(t) \in \Omega$ restricted to the subset $[t_0 t_1)$. If we start the system in the state $s(t_0)$ at t_0 and apply $u_{[t_0, t_1)}$, the state transition function allows to determine the state $s(t_1)$ which is reached by the system at t_1, $s(t_1) = \phi(t_0, t_1, s(t_0), u_{[t_0, t_1)})$. On the other hand, the output mapping $\eta : T \times S \times U$ specifies the output of the system at t_1, $y(t_1) = \eta(t_1, s(t_1), u(t_1))$.

Let us refer to any time interval in T, we may say that the behaviour of the system is normal if and only if for all $u(t) \in \Omega$ the state variable $s(t)$ and the output remain within bounds which are fixed by the designer. Now reliability analysis and computation require the consideration of cases where one or all these bounds are exceeded. The corresponding behaviour of the system is referred to as abnormal, up-set, perturbed, unsafe, etc. Precisely, if a new function, say $u'(t)$, is applied to the system which was previously described by means of $(T, U, \Omega, Y, S, \phi, \eta)$, a new representation has to be defined in terms of $(T, U', \Omega', Y, S', \phi', \eta')$, where $u'(t) \in \Omega'$.

Similarly, if due to any reason a subsystem undergoes some changements and so does its representation, the representation of the whole system will change. This even if Ω remains the accepted set of input functions. In this case, the designer is led to the definition of a new set $(T, U, \Omega, Y, S'', \phi'', \eta'')$. Every new set S'', ϕ'', η'' might have common subsets with each one of S, ϕ, η.

Now all these circumstances can find a formal account if the behaviour of the system is defined in terms of the couple (S, ϕ). It is clear indeed that the couple (S, ϕ) determines uniquely the trajectories $s(t)$ followed by the system under the action of any forcing input function $u(t) \in \Omega$.

3. CONSTRUCTION OF THE MULTIVALUED LOGICAL TREE

Once representations for subsystems or components have been ascertained, the analyst is able to describe the system by means of some flowgraph, where specific symbols are associated with each component and connecting arrows designate infor-mation flows and functional relations. Evidence will be given to the goals that are assigned to the system and to the interconnections that the system may have with other systems or with its environment. The hope is that given the knowledge of the behaviour of all the components and inputs to the system, we are able to evaluate the behaviour of the entire system [2,3]. Indeed the sets of states and of transition functions of the system will be subsets of the cartesian product of sets of states and transition functions for the components (and external inputs). The inte-rest, however, is in finding a way to reassemble the components (or to reconnect the system), for our purpose is to transform the disconnected collection of representations of components into a representation for the system. This representation for the sys-tem should tell the analyst about conditions (behaviours) that are needed in order to verify whether some statements about the system are true.

In principle, the mapping of component representations into the system can be performed along two directions. System may be traced backwards (i.e. from consequence to causing events or moving from the behaviour of the system towards the behaviours of the components and external inputs) or forwards (i.e. from cause to consequence [4]).

We will consider in what follows a representation for the system where behaviour of the system and its components are made to correspond with values from a discrete set B^r with cardinality r. System is then traced backwards until a multivalued logical tree (MVLT) is obtained. Criteria of partition are established to divide the continuum into a number of regions. These criteria will take into account the nature of the problem, the availability of data, the need for more or less refined descriptions. The partition will originate a discrete or approximate representation for the components and the system. We may remark that any variable could be used to denote different behaviours $b_h \in B^r$ (h = 1, .., r). For instance, if r = 3, $b_1 = -1$ may stay for the unsafe behaviour (or for a disruptive occurrence), $b_2 = 0$ may denote the safe operation (or normal operation), $b_3 = +1$ may indicate other critical operation modes.

Since we admit that states and state transition functions are exhaustive and mutually exclusive, the result is that system and components are defined by a single behaviour at any time instant in T. In this respect, the representation of the system which ensues may be called synchronic since it corresponds with a picture of the system and its components taken at a single time instant. Given correspondence between behaviours and values from B^r, the approximate representation of the system consists essentially of mapping the (behaviours of the components) into the system. This means a statement of re-evaluation (or re-location) of behaviours, and of inputs in B^n, together with an incidence relation which indicates the terminal variables (i.e. inputs and outputs) which are shared by two or more components. This incidence relation is provided in terms of logical operators. Any dyadic logical operator is represented by an oriented truth table or logical gate. Obviously, it is always possible to translate these logical operators in terms of general decision tables and viceversa. The use of this technique has been shown in [5]. Distinct operators will be denoted by different Greek letters. Rules can be stated for the reduction of m-adic operators (i.e. having a number of entries higher than two) to a logical tree linking dyadic operators only.

4. SAMPLE CASE

Let us refer to the electric circuit of Fig. 1. Different models can be made to correspond with the situations which may occur in this system. It is admitted that the circuit is driven by a sinusoidal voltage generator G. Now, if frequency is increased, for description purposes, instead of lumped variables models, one should use distributed variables. Conversely, if electrical current is augmented beyond a certain value, one should allow for dependence of parameters upon the temperature. To determine the specific models which apply, it is convenient to refer to the phase space. In the phase space co-ordinates are the state variables and time does not appear explicitly. Time indeed is considered as a parameter along any trajectory or sequence of states followed by the system and its components. We choose effective current, i_e, and frequency f as state variables. Correspondingly, the phase space will be $I_e \times F$, where $i_e \in I_e$ and $f \in F$ (Fig. 2). This space is divided into five mutually exclusive regions R_j (j = 1, ..., 5), each one characterized by a specific model. It must be

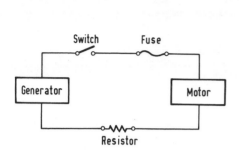

Fig. 1 : Sample system. An electric circuit

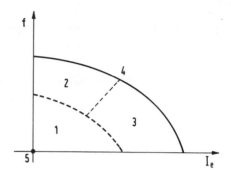

Fig. 2 : Phase space for the sample system

remarked that these five regions cannot be defined by means of neat or unique boundaries. Rather, the responsibility for tracing partitions on the $I_e \times F$ plane lays upon
the designer or the analyst. In our notation R_1 is the region of low frequencies and
low currents. R_2 is the region of high frequencies and low currents. R_3 is the region
where because of high currents resistance and impedance values may change in time.
Finally, R_5 corresponds with the situation where circuit is open, whereas R_4 denotes a region which is viewed as unsafer or non-operable under all respects.

Given any region R_j, there will be a state transition function
$\phi_j^{(s)}(t_0, t, s(t_0), u_{[t_0, t)}) = s(t)$. $s(t) \in S_j$ [1] is a vector whose components are instantaneous current $i(t)$ and frequency $f(t)$. $u_{[t_0, t)}$ is the voltage applied from t_0
to t. In region R_1 from the equivalent RL network of Fig. 3 we get the first-order
differential equation $Ri(t) + L \, di(t)/dt = u(t)$, where $i(t_0) = i_0$, $R = r_s + r_F + r_R$
and $L = \ell_M$. It can be readily verified that the solution is

$$i(t) = i_0 \exp[-(t-t_0)R/L] + \frac{1}{L} \int_{t_0}^{t} u(x) \exp[-(t-x)R/L] \, dx$$

Once $i(t)$ is given, $I_e(t)$ will be also known. On the other hand, frequency $f(t)$
would be obtained from the expansion of $u(t)$ in a Fourier series. This analysis
shows that in R_1 the circuit can be decomposed into five elements or components:
fuse, resistance, switch, generator and motor. Along the same line of reasoning one
should consider in R_3 a model where resistance and inductance depend upon the
current, and in R_2 a distributed elements model. Obviously, the lumped constant
model adopted in R_1 turns out to be a particularization.

Let us think of R_1 as of the region of normal operation for the circuit. If the
circuit contains some control as far as trajectories in the phase space approach region
like R_2, R_3, etc., which are unwanted, this control will intervene to bring back the
system to R_1. In this respect, we will limit our attention to the case where frequency
control is unimportant. Then interest will be on the I_e axis only. If the trajectories
approach R_3 the fuse is expected to blow and the trajectory of the circuit would
jump to R_5. In this region state transition function is represented by the identity
function ϕ_5, for any shift is excluded. As a result, it will be $I_e = 0$ and $f = 0$.
However, if the system when approaching R_3 does not cause the fuse to blow, or
the fuse blows only after a certain amount of time has elapsed, the trajectory will
enter R_3. In R_3, since the comparatively high value assumed by the current, resistance and inductance would heat up and damage.

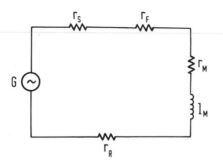

Fig. 3 : Equivalent network for the sample system

In consideration of the needs of the user, the behaviours of interest in the circuit can be associated with values drawn from B^4 as follows. First, is normal operation of the circuit and its components (value of 0). Next, three types of failed behaviour are of importance. Namely, behaviour is failed safe if trajectories remain in R_2 or circuit lies open in R_5 (value of +1); behaviour anticipates a future failure when trajectories are in R_3 so that components undergo some degradation effects due to high currents (value of +2); finally, behaviour is considered failed unsafe if circuit is blocked in some position different from R_5 (value of −1). As a result, one has the representation shown by Table 1.

Table 1 : Behaviours of the network for the sample case

States \ Functions	ϕ_1	ϕ_2	ϕ_3	ϕ_5
$s \in S_1$	0	0	0	−1
$s \in S_2$	−	+1	−	−1
$s \in S_3$	−	−	+2	−1
$s \in S_4$	−	−	−	−1
$s \in S_5$	0	0	0	+1

ϕ_1 : Transitions represented by lumped elements model
ϕ_2 : Transitions represented by distributed elements model
ϕ_3 : Transitions represented by models where parameters depend upon current
ϕ_5 : Transitions not allowed (identify function)

Entries are states S_j $(j = 1, ..., 5)$ and state transition functions ϕ_j. It can be noted that there are a few combinations (i.e. behaviours) which are not allowed by the nature of the problem.

The representation of the circuit will be given by a MVLT where the behaviours of the single components are combined according to suitable logical operators defined on the base of the structure of the system. To construct the tree of behaviours, components must be represented. The fuse has the scope of protecting the circuit from overloads. We will exclude the consideration of the case of high frequencies. Thus, in its normal operation the fuse is expected to blow when voltage exceeds V_{MAX}. If defective, the fuse would blow for voltages lower than V' (where $V' < V_{MAX}$) or for voltages higher than V'' (where $V'' > V_{MAX}$). Correspondingly, three state transition functions can be defined as in Table 2a.

Table 2a : Behaviours of fuse

Functions / States	ϕ_1	ϕ_2	ϕ_3
$s \in S_1$	0	1	-1
$s \in S_2$	$-$	1	-1
$s \in S_3$	$-$	$-$	-1
$s \in S_4$	$-$	$-$	$-$
$s \in S_5$	0	1	-1

$$\phi_1 \quad : \quad \begin{cases} i_F = \dfrac{V_F}{r_F}, \ V_F \leqslant V_{MAX} \\[2mm] i_F = 0, \ V_F > V_{MAX} \end{cases}$$

$$\phi_2 \quad : \quad \begin{cases} i_F = \dfrac{V_F}{r_F}, \ V_F \leqslant V' < V_{MAX} \\[2mm] i_F = 0, \ V_F > V' \end{cases} \qquad \text{Anticipated interruption}$$

$$\phi_3 \quad : \quad \begin{cases} i_F = \dfrac{V_F}{r_F}, \ V_{MAX} < V_F \leqslant V'' \\[2mm] i_F = 0, \ V'' < V_F \end{cases} \qquad \text{Delayed interruption}$$

Behaviours result from combinations with the state variables. After relocation of values it seems convenient to recognize normal (0), defective safe (+1) and defective unsafe (−1) behaviours. Similarly, it seems fair to assume for the resistor that resistance is constant (ϕ_1) or depends upon the current (ϕ_3). Combinations with state variables will give behaviours whose values after relocation from B^4 are as in Table 2b.

Table 2b : Behaviours of switch

States / Functions	ϕ_1	ϕ_3
$s \in S_1$	0	0
$s \in S_2$	0	0
$s \in S_3$	0	+1
$s \in S_4$	−	−
$s \in S_5$	0	0

$$\phi_1 \; : \; \frac{V}{r_R}$$

$$\phi_3 \; : \; \frac{V}{r_R(i)}$$

On the other hand, switch is characterized by a state variable which assumes two extreme or bounding states and for normal operation these two states must be reversible. Then ϕ_1 is a mapping from the permissive or closed (state) position to the non-permissive or open (state) position and viceversa. This mapping can go back and forth upon demand. ϕ_2 maps from the open state into the closed state, where this latter state is absorbing or non-reversible. Conversely, ϕ_3 maps from the closed state into the open state, where this state has no return. The behaviours are quoted in Table 2c.

Table 2c : Behaviours of resistor

States / Functions	ϕ_1	ϕ_2	ϕ_3
open	0	1	−1
closed	0	1	−1

$S = \{\text{open, closed}\}$

$\phi_1 \; : \quad T \times T \times \Omega \times S \rightarrow S$

$\phi_2 \; : \quad T \times T \times \Omega \times S \rightarrow \text{closed}$

$\phi_3 \; : \quad T \times T \times \Omega \times S \rightarrow \text{open}$

Now, since the interconnections of the components in the circuit, after relocation of values, we have the logical operators of Table 3. These operators are then combined into the MVLT, expressing the behaviour of the system (Fig. 4). From MVLT it would be possible to obtain binary logical trees one for each of the four

Table 3 : Multivalued logic operators for interconnections of
components in the sample case

FUSE

α	1	0	1
1	−1	−1	1
0	−1	0	1
1	−1	−1	1

SWITCH (row label)

RESISTOR

β	1	0
1	1	1
0	0	0
−1	1	1

γ (row label)

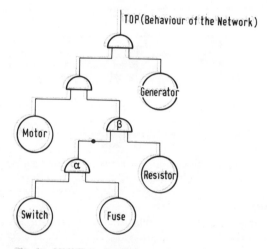

Fig. 4 : MVLT for behaviours of the sample system

behaviours entailed by the root.

5. HTGR CORE AUXILIARY COOLING SYSTEM - PLANT PROTECTING SYSTEM (PPS)

Reference is made to a high temperature gas-cooled reactor (HTGR) containing a single plant protective system (PPS). In the event of design basis depressurization coupled with loss of main loop cooling, the PPS is designed to shut down the entire main cooling system and to activate the auxiliary cooling system. In a simplified version, the PPS is assumed to consist of five different, independent detection modules [6]. It is assumed that there is only one detection module of each of the five types (Fig. 5). These modules are designed for events as follows: (i) low helium pressure; (ii) low helium flow rate; (iii) low steam temperature; (iv) high helium moisture content; (v) high containment pressure.

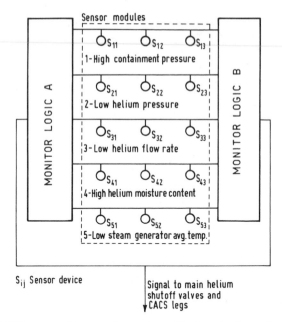

Fig. 5 : HTGR core auxiliary cooling system. Plant protective system (PPS) [6]

If one of these five events is detected and monitored, an appropriate signal will activate the core auxiliary cooling system (CACS). In its turn, each one of the five sensor/monitor modules contains three independent sensor devices, any two of which are assumed to be needed to sense the event before signal is sent to the corresponding monitor module. The original signal is picked by the sensor devices and forwarded to the independent monitor logics A and B for the evaluation according to a two out of three criterion. If 2 out of 3 criterion is met, then the monitor device individually signals each main helium shut off valve and each CACS leg. The schematic of the monitor logic is in Fig. 6.

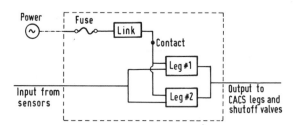

Fig. 6 : Schematic of a monitor logic

The assumption is that the CACS fails to initiate if the sensor system fails to detect the need for the CACS to initiate or if the sensor signal fails to be monitored. The sensor system will fail to detect the need for the CACS (unsafe failure) if any of the five sensor modules fails to detect the need. In this context, it is worthwhile to consider for the PPS three behaviours. PPS may operate safe (value 0), or fail unsafe, i.e. fail to activate the CACS when required (value -1), or fail safe, i.e. initiate the

CACS when not required (value +1).

Let us now briefly consider transfer functions ϕ's for each component. Particularly, let ϕ_0 denote the case where the component may change from one state to another on demand and viceversa. Let ϕ_1 stay for the case where the component may only pass from its active or operating state to its non operating state, and ϕ_2 stay for the case where the component is blocked in one of its states and no transition can occur. In addition, ϕ_3 will refer to the case where the component changes its state randomly, due to the effect of some curious or perturbing behaviour in the absence of any external demand or stimulus.

Behaviours for the component being studied, are then established as in Table 4. It is admitted that the indicator is characterized by a variety of states where someones correspond to the indicator in operation and others correspond to the indicator out of operation. Given these tables of behaviours, it is possible to construct the logical operators of Table 5. In particular, it may be remarked that the use of the value 2 in the operators allows to consider situations where, notwithstanding the presence of the failures, the system still maintains a regular or safe behaviour. For instance, in the case of two simultaneous failures, they compensate each other and produce a system which is intrinsically non coherent. It can be also noted that the introduction of values 2 and −2 in operators offers an easy way to describe a logic of the type two out of three. Finally, there is a number of combinations in operator and where the occurrence of combinations of two behaviours causes a contradiction. These situations are marked as "don't care" (DC), where "don't care" signifies behaviour whose realization is physically impossible.

Provided that the flow chart of the system is known and logical operators have been obtained, one is able to trace the corresponding logical tree of behaviours (Figs. 7, 8). This MVLT compacts all the information which would have been contained in two binary fault trees (one for each type of failure). Obviously the complete expression of these binary fault trees would have required an extensive use of the NOT (as well as AND and OR) operators.

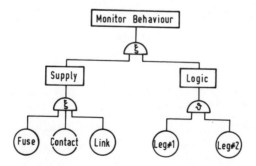

Fig. 7: MVLT for behaviours of monitor logic

Table 4 : Behaviours of components of the monitor (i.e. transmitter, indicator and link) and of sensor

TRANSMITTER

States	Functions ϕ_0	ϕ_2
in operation	0	1
out-of-operation	0	−1

INDICATOR

States	Functions ϕ_0	ϕ_2
X_1	0	1
X_2	0	1
.	.	.
.	.	.
X_N	0	1

LINK

States	Functions ϕ
connected	0
disconnected	1
other states	−1

SENSOR

States	Functions ϕ_0	ϕ_1	ϕ_3
in operation	0	−1	1
out-of-operation	0	−1	1

Table 5 : Multivalued logical operators expressing interconnections among components and subsystems of PPS

MONITOR

η	0	1	1
0	0	1	-1
1	1	1	0
1	-1	0	-1
2	0	0	0

(row label: SENSOR)

μ

λ	0	1	-1	2
0	0	1	-1	2
1	1	1	2	2
-1	-1	2	-1	2
2	2	2	2	2

(row label: μ)

$\nu(S_{ij}, S_{ik})$

μ	0	1	-1	2	-2
0	0	0	0	1	.. 1
1	0	1	DC	1	DC
-1	0	DC	-1	DC	.. 1

(row label: SENSOR S_{ih})

SENSOR S_{ik}

ν	0	1	-1
0	0	1	-1
1	1	2	DC
-1	-1	DC	-2

(row label: SENSOR S_{ij})

C_j **LOGIC**

ξ	0	1	-1
0	0	1	-1
1	1	1	-1
-1	-1	-1	-1

(row label: SUPPLY C_i)

MONITOR

ϑ	0	1	-1
0	0	1	0
1	1	1	0
-1	0	0	-1

(row label: MONITOR)

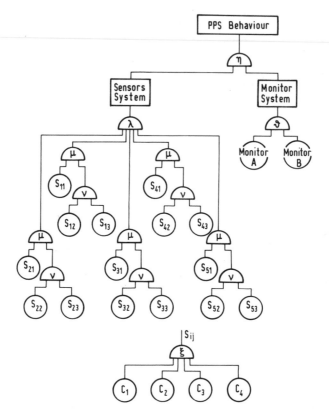

Fig. 8 : MVLT for behaviours of PPS

6. CONCLUSION

The procedure presented seems to help to clarify some limits encountered in the representation of systems and to provide indications for further development. The thesis has emerged that fault trees as used for reliability computations can be interpreted as consisting of a particular combination of statements whose variables are behaviours of the system and its components or inputs. As we move along the time axis, we do not specify when these behaviours should occur but we ask that they are synchronic for they must occur at the same instant. In this sense fault tree hardly provides a dynamic representation or simulation of the system.

As a final step we are left with the analysis of multivalued logical trees. Two types of problems are of interest. First is the problem of finding the path sets or combinations of primary events (behaviours and terminal variables) by which a specified behaviour of the entire system may occur. Second is the problem of estimating the probability associated with this behaviour of the entire system. With regard to this latter problem, it may happen that some of the combinations of primary events have more weight than others and it is beneficial to be able to determine those combinations that are of greatest importance.

In principle, the analysis of MVLTs can be performed through a direct computation of the tree, where multivalued logical operators are handled by the use of especially designed algorithms. Alternatively, it may be easier to transform the MVLT in into an equivalent forest of binary logical trees (BLTs). After this transformation has been performed, the analyst can adopt algorithms that have proved to be useful for that class of trees [2,7]. The possibility of reducing a MVLT to a forest of BLTs hints at a substantial equivalence of multivalued and two-valued representations.

REFERENCES

[1] L. Padulo and M.A. Arbib, "System theory. A unified state-space approach to continuous and discrete systems", W.B. Saunders, Philadelphia, Pa.(1974).

[2] S. Garribba, P. Mussio, F. Naldi and G. Volta, "System reliability and multiple-valued logic", CESNEF - IN 012, Politecnico di Milano, Milano, Italy (Feb. 1978).

[3] S. Contini, S. Fumagalli, P. Mussio, F. Naldi, S. Garribba and G. Volta, "Multiple-valued logic in modelling of nuclear safety systems and automated search for fault states", Paper XIII-2 in vol. 3 of "Proc. of the Topical Meeting on Probabilistic Analysis of Nuclear Reactor Safety", ANS, La Grange Park, III. (May 1978).

[4] J.R. Taylor, "A semi-automatic method for qualitative failure mode analysis", Risoe M-1707, Research Establishment Risoe, Roskilde, Denmark (Aug. 1974).

[5] S.L. Salem, G.E. Apostolakis and D. Okrent, "A computer-oriented approach to fault-tree construction", EPRI-NP-288, Electric Power Research Institute, Palo Alto, Calif. (1976).

[6] K.A. Solomon, D. Okrent and W.E. Kastenberg, "A prediction of the reliability of the cooling system for a high pressure gas-cooled reactor", UCLA-ENG-7495, Univ. of California, Los Angeles, Calif. (Jan. 1975).

[7] L. Caldarola, "Fault-tree analysis with multistate components", Paper VIII-1, in Vol. 3 of "Proc. of the Topical Meeting on Probabilistic Analysis of Nuclear Reactor Safety", ANS, La Grange Park, III.(May 1978).

FAULT TREE ANALYSIS WITH MULTISTATE COMPONENTS

L. Caldarola[1]

Institut für Reaktorentwicklung Kernforschungszentrum Karlsruhe

Postfach 3640, D-7500 Karlsruhe, Federal Republic
of Germany

ABSTRACT

A general analytical theory has been developed which allows
one to calculate the occurrence probability of the top event of a
fault tree with multistate (more than two states) components.

It is shown that, in order to correctly describe a system with
multistate components, a special type of boolean algebra is required.
This is called "boolean algebra with restrictions on variables" and
its basic rules are the same as those of the traditional boolean
algebra with some additional restrictions on the variables. These
restrictions are extensively discussed in the paper.

Important features of the method are the identification of the
complete base and of the smallest irredundant base of a boolean
function which does not necessarily need to be coherent. It is shown
that the identification of the complete base of a boolean function
requires the application of some algorithms which are not used in
today's computer programmes for fault tree analysis.

---

[1]Principal Scientific Officer of the Commission of the European
Community; delegated to the Kernforschungszentrum Karlsruhe.

The problem of statistical dependence among primary components is discussed. The paper includes a small demonstrative example to illustrate the method. The example includes also statistical dependent components.

INTRODUCTION

The evaluation of the occurrence probability of the top event of a fault tree can be carried out by means of simulation methods (Monte Carlo-type methods) or by means of analytical methods. Numerical simulation allows reliability information to be obtained for systems of almost any degree of complexity. However, this method provides only estimates and no parametric relation can be obtained. In addition, since the failure probability of a system is usually very low, precise results can be achieved only at the expense of very long computational times.

Analytical methods give more insight and understanding because explicit relationships are obtainable. Results are also more precise because these methods usually give the exact solution of the problem. In 1970 Vesely[1] gave the foundations of the analytical method for fault tree analysis. However, Vesely's method can be applied only to coherent systems with binary (two states) components. Another important limitation of the method is that the boolean function which describes the top variable of the fault tree must not contain negated variables. Since there are components (like a switch) which have more than two states, and since the technique of multistate super-components can be used to remove statistical dependencies from the fault tree[3], a theory has been developed at the nuclear research center of Karlsruhe[2,3] to handle systems with multistate components. One interesting feature of the method is that the boolean function which describes the top variable of the fault tree does not necessarily need to be coherent. In addition boolean functions containing negated variables can be treated.

In this paper a formalization of the theory by means of the so called "boolean algebra with restriction on variables" has been developed. In addition the basic and important boolean operations of this special type of boolean algebra are described. The paper also includes a small demonstrative example to illustrate the method.

1.   BOOLEAN ALGEBRA WITH RESTRICTIONS ON VARIABLES. DEFINITION OF FAULT TREE

Let us consider a variable which can take discrete values (states) only. The set of all possible values, which the variable can take, constitute the state space associated to that variable. Each value of the variable is called member or element of the state space. The variable can take only one value of its state space at a time. The value taken by the variable at a given time is called event.

Variables can be classified in two large categories: primary variables and non-primary variables.

A variable is called primary variable if and only if the occurrence probabilities of all members of its state space are as such already available. A primary variable can be the variable associated to a primary component of a complex system, such as a pump, a relay etc. Probability data associated to the occurrence of the states (failed, not failed etc.) of these components are in fact in general available from data banks. The values which a primary variable can take are called primary events. A non-primary variable can be, for instance, the variable associated to a complex system such as the emergency core cooling system of a nuclear power plant. Probability data related to the events "system failed", "system intact", are in fact as such in general not available.

We consider a system at a fixed moment in time. The state of the system at a given time obviously depends upon the state at that time of each individual component belonging to the system. We now select a special set of states of the system (i.e. the set of all failed states) and call it "top" (with small letters). We associate to it a boolean variable which we call TOP (with capital letters). The variable TOP will take the value 1 (true) if the system occupies one of the states belonging to the selected set and the value 0 (false) otherwise.

Any non-primary variable can be chosen as TOP variable. The chosen set of states "top" is called partition of the state space of the system. If we want now to calculate the occurrence probability of the event

$$\text{top} \quad \equiv \quad \left\{ \text{TOP} = 1 \right\}$$

we must first dissect the TOP variable into combinations of primary variables, that is to express the TOP variable as a proper function of the primary variables. The occurrence probability of the event $\left\{ \text{TOP} = 1 \right\}$ can then be calculated as a function of the occurrence probabilities of the primary events.

Due to the complexity of the systems, the operation of dissection of the TOP variable into combinations of primary variables is in general carried out in steps. The TOP variable is first dissected into combinations of simpler non-primary variables (intermediate variables). These intermediate variables are in turn dissected into combinations of even simpler intermediate variables and so on. The process of dissection comes to an end when all combinations are combinations of primary variables only.

The process of dissection can be carried out in a graphic form by constructing a fault tree of the chosen TOP variable.

A fault tree is a logic model which shows in diagrammatic form the connections between the TOP variable and the primary variables.

A more precise definition of a fault tree can be given by making use of the graph theory.

"A fault tree is a finite directed graph without loops. Each vertex may be in one of several states. For each vertex a function is given which specifies its states in terms of the states of its predecessors. Those vertices without predecessors are considered the independent variables of the fault tree." [4]

We are following the graphical terminology of Berge[5] here. In the technical literature a vertex with predecessors is currently called gate. The output variable of a gate is called (improperly) output event of the gate. An input variable to a gate is called predecessor of (again improperly) input event to the gate. In the technical literature the improper terms TOP event, primary event are also currently used. One should instead use the more correct terms TOP variable and primary variable. In fact the word event is used (in the set theory and in the propositional calculus) to indicate a value or a set of values of a variable. We shall use the correct mathematical terminology here.

Note that in the above definition of fault tree the term "independent variable" is used and not "primary variable". The word independent in this context means "logically independent", that is each input variable to the tree can take any value of its sample space independently from the values taken by the other input variables. The truth table of the fault tree contains all possible combinations among the values of the input variables. Each row of the truth table represents a state of the system. If all primary components of the system are characterized by only two states (inact and failed), we assign to each primary component a boolean variable which takes the value 1 if the component is failed and the value 0 if the component is intact. These are the primary variables which are pairwise mutually logically independent. The primary variables in this case are also independent variables.

If the fault tree has m binary primary components, that is m input variables, the truth table of the fault tree has 2^m rows.

The function which links the output to the inputs of a gate are boolean functions. The basic gates are the AND (conjunction), OR (disjunction) and the NOT (negative) gates.

Let us first consider an AND gate with two inputs, namely A and B (Fig. 1-1)

AND Gate   Truth Table

Inputs		Output
A	B	S
0	0	0
0	1	0
1	0	0
1	1	1

Fig. 1-1.   AND Gate $(S = A \wedge B)$

The truth table of Fig. 1-1 gives the value of the output S for each pair of values of the two predecessors A and B. This truth table can be expressed in words as follows

"Output takes the value 1 if and only if all predecessors take the value 1, and the value 0 if at least one of its predecessors takes the value 0."

We now order the values 1 and 0 in that we say, for instance the 1 is larger than 0

$$1 > 0$$

We can synthetize the AND operation as follows

$$S = \min (A; B)$$

which means that S takes the smallest between the values of A and B.

Fig. 1-2 shows the OR gate with associated truth table.

OR Gate   Truth Table

Inputs		Output
A	B	S
0	0	0
0	1	1
1	0	1
1	1	1

Fig. 1-2.   OR Gate $(S = A \vee B)$

Also in this case the truth table of Fig. 1-2 can be expressed in words as follows

" Output takes the value 1 if at least one of the predecessors takes the value 1 and the value 0 if and only if all predecessors take the value 0."

If we put 1 > 0, we can write in the case of the OR gate

$$S = \max (A; B)$$

which means that S takes the largest between the values of A and B.

Fig. 1-3 shows the NOT gate with associated truth table.

NOT Gate

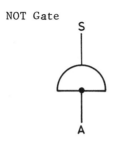

Truth Table

Inputs	Output
A	S
0	1
1	0

Fig. 1-3.   NOT Gate $(S = \bar{A})$

In words

"Output takes the value 1 if predecessor takes the value 0 and viceversa."

In a fault tree the truth tables of each gate are properly combined to get the truth table of the TOP. We show this by means of an example.

We consider the simple fault tree of Fig. 1-4 (Example No.1). Each one of the two OR gates will be characterized by a truth table of the type of Fig. 1-2. The outputs of the two OR gates will be the inputs to the AND gate, which has a truth table of the type shown in Fig. 1-1. By properly combining the three truth tables one finally gets the overall truth table of the fault tree. This truth table has 16 rows (Fig. 1-5).

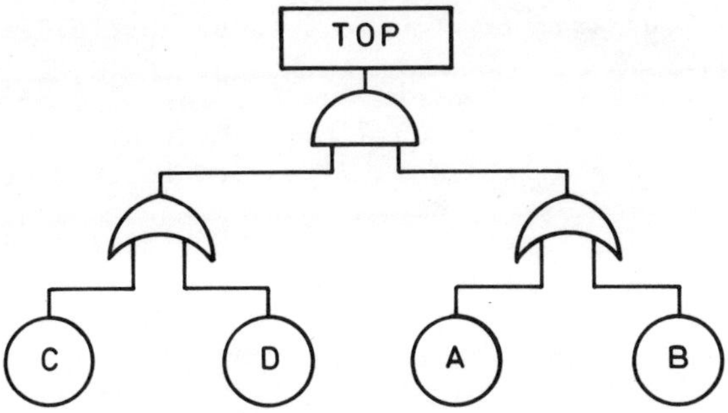

Fig. 1-4. Fault Tree - TOP = (C V D) ∧ (A V B)

	Row Number	Inputs				Output
		A	B	C	D	TOP
+	1	0	0	0	0	0
	2	0	0	0	1	0
+	3	0	0	1	0	0
	4	0	0	1	1	0
+	5	0	1	0	0	0
	6	0	1	0	1	1
+	7	0	1	1	0	1
	8	0	1	1	1	1
	9	1	0	0	0	0
—	10	1	0	0	1	1
	11	1	0	1	0	1
—	12	1	0	1	1	1
	13	1	1	0	0	0
—	14	1	1	0	1	1
	15	1	1	1	0	1
—	16	1	1	1	1	1

Fig. 1-5.
Complete truth table of the fault tree of Fig. 1-4 (Example No.1)

In the previous example we have assumed that all primary components are binary. There are however primary components which are characterized by more than two states. For instance an electrical switch is characterized by at least three states, namely (1) intact, (2) failed in closed position and (3) failed in open position.

One could in this case assign to each primary component a multivalued variable characterized by a number of values equal to the number of states of the primary component. Each value of the variable corresponds to a specific state of the primary component. These multivalued variables are the primary variables. They are pairwise mutually logically independent. Primary variables and independent variables are also in this case identical. The function which links the output to the input of a gate is a logic function which is in general not boolean. This way of thinking is consistent with the definition of fault tree given above. There is however, a considerable drawback, namely that a more complicated multivalued logic must be developed. The basic gates are not any more simply the AND, OR and NOT gates as in the case of the boolean algebra. New basic gates must be found. Some authors[6] are following this way of thinking. We want to follow another path instead. We want to have primary variables which are binary.

Let us consider the state space of a primary component. A state belonging to the state space of a primary component is called primary state. The event of the primary component occupying a given state of its state space at a given time is called primary event.

A primary component will be indicated by the small letter c followed by an integer positive number (c1; c2; c3 etc.). In general we shall have cj with j=1;2...; m, where "m" is the total number of primary components contained in the system.

A state of a primary component will be indicated by the same notation of the primary component to which it belongs followed by a positive integer number as an index. (cj_1; cj_2; cj_3 etc.) In general we shall have cj_q with q=1;2;...nj, where nj is the total number of states belonging to primary component cj. We can now associate to each state cj_q a boolean variable Cj_q which takes the value 1 (true) if primary component cj occupies state cj_q and the value 0 (false) if cj does not occupy cj_q.

The event

$$\left\{ Cj_q = 1 \right\} \equiv cj_q$$

indicates that primary component cj occupies state cj_q.

Conversely, the event

$$\left\{ Cj_q = 0 \right\} \equiv \bigcup_{k=1}^{nj} cj_k \qquad\qquad k \neq q$$

indicates that primary component cj does not occupy state cj_q and therefore occupies one of its other possible states.

Note the one to one correspondance between state cj_q (small c) and boolean variable Cj_q (capital C) associated to it. We obviously have

$$cj_q = \left\{ Cj_q = 1 \right\} \quad \text{and} \quad \overline{cj}_q \equiv \left\{ Cj_q = 0 \right\}$$

We shall say that the primary state cj_q belongs to component cj ($cj_q \in cj$). The word "primary component" (with small c) is here intended as the set of all possible states which the component can occupy.

We shall also say that the variable Cj_q belongs to Component Cj ($Cj_q \in Cj$). The word "primary Component" (with capital C) means here the complete set of variables associated to its states.

The binary variables Cj_q are the primary variables. They are however not any more pairwise mutually independent.

Since a primary component must occupy one of its states and can occupy only one state at a time, the variables Cj_q must obviously satisfy the following two types of restrictions.

Restriction Type 1   The disjunction of all binary variables associated to the same primary Component is always equal to 1

$$\bigvee_{q=1}^{nj} Cj_q = 1 \tag{1-1}$$

The notation "1" in Eq. 1-1 means "true". Eq.1 must be read as follows. The proposition "at least one of the variables Cj_q (q=1; ;...nj) takes the value 1" is true.

Restrictions Type 2   The conjunction of two different binary variables associated to the same primary Component is always equal to 0.

$$Cj_q \wedge Cj_k = 0 \qquad q \neq k \tag{1-2}$$

The notation "0" in Eq. 1-2 means "false". Eq. 2 must be read as follows. The proposition "both variables Cj_q and Cj_k ($q \neq k$) take the value 1" is false.

Note that there is only one restriction type 1 and $\dfrac{nj(nj-1)}{2}$ restrictions type 2.

Note also that Eqs. 1-1 and 1-2 can be translated straightforward in the equivalent equations among states. We have obviously

Restriction Type 1

$$\bigcup_{q=1}^{nj} cj_q = 1 \tag{1-1a}$$

and

Restrictions Type 2

$$cj_q \cap cj_k = 0 \qquad q \neq k \tag{1-2a}$$

Eqs. 1-1a and 1-2a have been obtained respectively from
Eqs. 1-1 and 1-2 by carrying out the following simple operations.

Capital C   is replaced by   small c
Disjunction operator $\vee$ "   "   "   Union operator $\cup$
Conjunction operator $\wedge$ "   "   "   Intersection operator $\cap$

Note that the notation "1" and "0" in Eqs. 1-1a and 1-2a have
a different meaning. They indicate respectively the "universal set"
and the "empty set". Eq. 1-1a means therefore that the union of all
states of a primary component constitutes an universal set, that is
its complete state space. Eq. 1-1b means that the intersection of
two different states of a primary component constitutes an empty
set.

Since we have introduced primary variables which are not any
more pairwise mutually independent, we have to slightly modify the
definition of a fault tree.

"A fault tree is a finite directed graph without loops.
Each vertex may be in one of several states. For each
vertex a function is given which specifies its states
in terms of the states of its predecessors. Those
vertices without predecessors are the primary variables
of the fault tree. The primary variables may satisfy some
conditions (called restrictions) which are associated to
the fault tree."

Since a fault tree does not contain loops, it follows that
the restrictions contain primary variables only. We shall limit

ourselves to consider fault trees characterized by a boolean TOP
variable and boolean primary variables which satisfy restrictions
of the types given respectively by the Eqs. 1-1 and 1-2.

We consider now the truth table of the TOP variable.

Restriction type 1 means that the primary events

$$\left\{ Cj_q = 0 \right\} \quad ; \quad \left\{ Cj_2 = 0 \right\} \quad ; \quad \left\{ Cj_{nj} = 0 \right\}$$

cannot co-exist all together at the same time. This is equivalent
saying that all the rows of the truth table in which the variables
Cj_1; Cj_2; Cj_3... take simultaneously the value 0 are <u>prohibited</u>
and <u>must</u> be deleted.

The restrictions type 2 mean that the primary events

$$\left\{ Cj_q = 1 \right\} \quad \text{and} \quad \left\{ Cj_k = 1 \right\} \quad , \quad q \neq k$$

cannot co-exist at the same time. This is equivalent saying that
all the rows of the truth table in which both the two input variables Cj_q and Cj_k take the value 1 are <u>prohibited</u> and <u>must</u> be
deleted. The following two examples will make this point clearer.

Let us consider the fault tree of Fig. 1-4 and let us assume
that the primary variables A and D belong both to the same primary
Component which is characterized by two states (Example No. 2).
Eqs. 1-1 and 1-2 become respectively

$$A \lor D = 1 \qquad\qquad\qquad (1-3)$$
$$A \land D = 0 \qquad\qquad\qquad (1-4)$$

Eq. 1-3 tells us that the events $\left\{ A = 0 \right\}$ and $\left\{ D = 0 \right\}$
cannot co-exist. If we now look at the complete truth table of
the fault tree (Fig. 1-5) we notice that the rows 1; 3; 5 and 7
are <u>prohibited</u> because in these rows A and D have both the value 0.
These rows <u>must</u> therefore be deleted.

Eq. 1-4 tells us that the events $\left\{ A = 1 \right\}$ and $\left\{ D = 1 \right\}$
cannot co-exist. This is equivalent saying that the rows No. 10;
12; 14 and 16 (Fig. 1-5) are also <u>prohibited</u> and <u>must</u> be deleted.
The truth table of the fault tree of Fig. 1-4 with the additional
conditions 1-3 and 1-4 will be reduced to that of Fig. 1-6 which
contains eight rows only.

The input (primary) variables of the truth table of Fig. 1-6
are not all pairwise mutually independent. In fact the eight rows
containing the combinations of values (0;0) or (1;1) for the
variables A and D do not appear in the truth table of Fig. 1-6.

Row Number	Inputs				Output
	A	B	C	D	TOP
1	0	0	0	1	0
2	0	0	1	1	0
3	0	1	0	1	1
4	0	1	1	1	1
5	1	0	0	0	0
6	1	0	1	0	1
7	1	1	0	0	0
8	1	1	1	0	1

Fig. 1-6.   Truth Table of Example No.2

It is sometimes possible however to reduce the number of the primary variables and to get the independent variables only. In the case of example No. 2 this is possible.

We notice that Eqs. 1-3 and 1-4 can be reduced to the following equation.

$$D = \overline{A} \qquad\qquad (1-5)$$

Eq. 1-5 means that, once a value has been assigned to the variable A, the variable D takes a defined value according to the truth table of Fig. 1-3 (NOT Gate). For this reason the column corresponding to the variable D in the truth table of Fig. 1-6 is redundant and can be deleted. The value of the TOP is in fact completely determined if the values of the primary variables A; B; C have been previously chosen. The truth table of Fig. 1-6 can be further reduced by deleting the column of the primary variable D (Fig. 1-7).

Row Number	Inputs			Output
	A	B	C	TOP
1	0	0	0	0
2	0	0	1	0
3	0	1	0	1
4	0	1	1	1
5	1	0	0	0
6	1	0	1	1
7	1	1	0	0
8	1	1	1	1

Fig. 1-7.   Truth Table of Example No. 2 (Final)

Conversely one could keep the variable D as independent variable and delete in Fig. 1-6 the column corresponding to the variable
A which would now be redundant.

Let us consider again the fault tree of Fig. 1-4 and let us
assume that the primary variables A and D belong both to the same
primary Component (as in example No. 2) but that this component is
characterized now by three states and that the primary variable
associated to the third state (call it E) is not present in the
fault tree (example No. 3). In this case Eqs. 1-1 and 1-2 become
respectively

$$A \lor D \lor E = 1 \tag{1-6}$$

and

$$A \land D = 0 \ (1\text{-}7a) \qquad A \land E = 0 \ (1\text{-}7b) \qquad D \land E = 0 \qquad (1\text{-}7c)$$

The rows 10; 12; 14; 16 of the truth table of Fig. 1-5 are
prohibited because the events $\{A=1\}$ and $\{D=1\}$ cannot co-exist
at the same time (Eq. 1-7a). By deleting these rows one obtains
the truth table of Fig. 1-8 which contains 12 rows only.

Row Number	Inputs				Output
	A	B	C	D	TOP
1	0	0	0	0	0
2	0	0	0	1	0
3	0	0	1	0	0
4	0	0	1	1	0
5	0	1	0	0	0
6	0	1	0	1	1
7	0	1	1	0	1
8	0	1	1	1	1
9	1	0	0	0	0
10	1	0	1	0	1
11	1	1	0	0	0
12	1	1	1	0	1

Fig. 1-8.   Truth Table of Example No. 3.

Note that in this case we don't make any use of the restrictions given by Eqs. 1-6; 1-7a and 1-7c because the primary variable E is not explicitly contained in the fault tree.

The input variables of the truth table of Fig. 1-8 are not all
pairwise mutually independent. In fact the four rows which contain
the combination of values (1; 1) for the variables A and D do not

appear in the truth table of Fig. 1-8. In this case however it is not possible to reduce the number of primary variables as in the case of Example No. 2. In fact no column in the truth table of Fig. 1-8 is redundant.

In conclusion the following rule can be stated (Rule No. 1)

"The truth table of the TOP variable of a fault tree can be obtained from the complete truth table (in which all primary variables present in the fault tree are assumed to be pairwise mutually independent) by deleting the prohibited rows and the redundant columns. The restrictions allow one to identify these prohibited rows and redundant columns. Each survived row corresponds to a specific state of the system. The survived primary variables may or may not be pairwise mutually independent."

We notice that we have defined primary variables which are binary as in the classical boolean algebra, but not necessarily pairwise mutually independent. We shall therefore introduce the term "boolean algebra with restrictions on variables" to indicate an algebra in which the basic (primary) variables are boolean but not necessarily pairwise mutually independent. The classical boolean algebra can be considered as a particular case of this boolean algebra with restrictions on variables in that the basic variables are all pairwise mutually independent.

We now consider the states of the partition top. Each state of the partition top can be expressed by the smallest cartesian product of primary states. This expression of the state is called smallest form of the state. Consider, for instance, the row 7 of the truth table of Fig. 1-8 (Example No. 3).

$$\text{System event No. 7} = \left\{ B{=}1 \right\} \times \left\{ C{=}1 \right\} \times \left[\left\{ A{=}0 \right\} \cap \left\{ D{=}0 \right\} \right] \quad (1\text{-}8)$$

Note that Equation 1-8 is obtained (1) by grouping all events which belong to the same component and linking them with the intersection operator $\cap$ and (2) by linking all groups with the cartesian product operator x. In fact the events $\left\{ A{=}0 \right\}$ and $\left\{ D{=}0 \right\}$ belong to the same component and must therefore be grouped together.

We now want to eliminate the groups.

From Eq. 1-6 we get

$$E = \overline{A \lor D} = \overline{A} \land \overline{D} \quad (1\text{-}9)$$

From Eq. 1-9 we get

$$\left\{ E{=}1 \right\} \equiv \left\{ \overline{A} \land \overline{D}{=}1 \right\} \equiv \left\{ \overline{A}{=}1 \right\} \cap \left\{ \overline{D}{=}1 \right\} \quad (1\text{-}10)$$

We have the following identities

$$\left\{ \overline{A}=1 \right\} \quad \equiv \quad \left\{ A=0 \right\} \tag{1-11}$$

and

$$\left\{ \overline{D}=1 \right\} \quad \equiv \quad \left\{ D=0 \right\} \tag{1-12}$$

Taking into account Eqs. 1-11 and 1-12, Eq. 1-10 becomes

$$\left\{ A=0 \right\} \cap \left\{ D=0 \right\} \quad \equiv \quad \left\{ E=1 \right\} \tag{1-13}$$

Taking into account Eq. 1-13, Eq. 1-8 becomes

$$\text{System event No. 7} = \left\{ B=1 \right\} \times \left\{ C=1 \right\} \times \left\{ E=1 \right\} \tag{1-14}$$

Note that Eq. 1-14 does not contain any more the intersection operator $\cap$ and all events contain the symbol 1.

We now introduce the notation for the states of primary components (small letters). We have

$$\left\{ B=1 \right\} \quad \equiv \quad b \tag{1-15}$$

$$\left\{ C=1 \right\} \quad \equiv \quad c \tag{1-16}$$

$$\left\{ E=1 \right\} \quad \equiv \quad e \tag{1-17}$$

Taking into account Eqs. 1-15, 1-16, 1-17, Eq. 1-14 becomes

$$\text{System event No. 7} = bxcxe \tag{1-18}$$

The expression on the right side of Eq. 1-18 is the smallest form of system state No. 7.

We can now state the following definition

" The smallest form of a state of a system is defined by the cartesian product of the states occupied by each single primary component belonging to the system."

We now go back to Eq. 1-14 which we can now write in a more compact form.

$$\begin{aligned} \text{System event No. 7} &= \left\{ B=1 \right\} \times \left\{ C=1 \right\} \times \left\{ E=1 \right\} \\ &= \left\{ B \wedge C \wedge E = 1 \right\} \end{aligned} \tag{1-19}$$

From Eqs. 1-18 and 1-19, we get

$$bxcxe = \left\{ B \wedge C \wedge E = 1 \right\} \tag{1-20}$$

Before discussing Eq.1-20, we want to introduce some new terms.
A variable which results from the conjunction of primary variables
is called monomial. A monomial containing two or more primary variables
belonging to the same primary Component is obviously equal to zero
(restrictions type 2). A non-zero monomial containing a number of
primary variables equal to the number of primary components present
in the system is called "complete monomial". For instance, the variable $B \wedge C \wedge E$ of Example 3 is a complete monomial". For a given
system the number of complete monomials is equal to the number of
its states.

Eq. 1-20 tells us that, given the complete monomial $B \wedge C \wedge E$,
one obtains the minimal form of the corresponding state bxcxe by
carrying out the following operations

$$
\begin{array}{ccccc}
B & \text{is replaced by} & b \\
C & " & " & " & c \\
E & " & " & " & e \\
\end{array}
$$

conjunction
operator $\wedge$ " " " cartesian product operator x

We can now state the following rule (Rule No. 2).

"The smallest form of a state of a system is obtained
from its corresponding complete monomial by replacing
each primary variable by its associated primary state
and each conjunction operator ($\wedge$) by the cartesian
product operator (x).

Conversely we have

"A complete monomial of a system is obtained from the
minimal form of its corresponding system state by
replacing each primary state by its associated primary
variable and each cartesian product operator (x) by the
conjunction operator ($\wedge$)."

Going back to the truth table of Fig. 1-18 (Example No. 3),
we select the rows for which TOP = 1. These are the rows No. 6,
7, 8, 10 and 12. Each selected row respresents a state of the
system for which the equation TOP = 1 is satisfied. We now find
the smallest form of each row. In order to do that we must introduce the states $\bar{b}$ and $\bar{c}$ which satisfy the restrictions respectively
with b and c.

$$b \cup \bar{b} = 1 \ (1\text{-}21a) \ ; \quad b \cap \bar{b} = 0 \tag{1-21b}$$
and
$$c \cup \bar{c} = 1 \ (1\text{-}22a) \quad c \cap \bar{c} = 0 \tag{1-22b}$$

The smallest forms of the rows 6, 7, 8, 10 and 12 are given in the
following table (Fig. 1.9).

System state	Smallest form
6	b x $\bar{c}$ x d
7	b x c x e
8	b x c x d
10	a x $\bar{b}$ x c
12	a x b x c

Fig. 1.9   Smallest form of system states (from the truth table of Fig. 1.8).

By making use of the above table we can now write

$$\text{top} = (\text{bx}\bar{\text{c}}\text{xd}) \cup (\text{bxcxe}) \cup (\text{bxcxd}) \cup (\text{ax}\bar{\text{b}}\text{xc}) \cup (\text{axbxc}) \quad (1\text{-}23)$$

Eq. 1-23 can be written as follows

$$\left\{ \text{TOP} = 1 \right\} = \left\{ B \wedge \bar{C} \wedge D{=}1 \right\} \cup \left\{ B \wedge C \wedge E{=}1 \right\} \cup \left\{ B \wedge C \wedge D{=}1 \right\} \cup$$
$$\cup \left\{ A \wedge \bar{B} \wedge C{=}1 \right\} \cup \left\{ A \wedge B \wedge C{=}1 \right\} \quad (1\text{-}24)$$

Eq. 1-24 can be written in a more compact form

$$\left\{ \text{TOP}{=}1 \right\} = \left\{ (B \wedge \bar{C} \wedge D) \vee (B \wedge C \wedge E) \vee (B \wedge C \wedge D) \vee (A \wedge \bar{B} \wedge C) \vee (A \wedge B \wedge C) = 1 \right\}$$
$$(1\text{-}25)$$

From Eq. 1-25 we also get

$$\text{TOP} = (B \wedge \bar{C} \wedge D) \vee (B \wedge C \wedge E) \vee (B \wedge C \wedge D) \vee (A \wedge \bar{B} \wedge C) \vee (A \wedge B \wedge C) \quad (1\text{-}26)$$

Eqs. 1-23 and 1-26 tell us that given the variable TOP as a disjunction of complete monomials (Eq. 1-26) one obtains the expression of the partition top (Eq. 1-23) by carrying out the following operations

TOP is replaced by top
A   "   "   "   a
B   "   "   "   b
$\bar{B}$ "   "   " $\bar{b}$
C   "   "   "   c
$\bar{C}$ "   "   " $\bar{c}$
D   "   "   "   d
E   "   "   "   e

conjunction operator $\wedge$ "   "   " cartesian product operator x
disjunction operator $\vee$ "   "   " union operator $\cup$

The disjunction of complete monomials of a boolean function is called "disjunctive canonical form" of the function.

Now we can state the following rule (Rule No. 3)

"If the variable TOP is given in its disjunctive canonical form, the corresponding partition top is obtained by replacing each complete mononomial by the corresponding smallest form of system state and each disjunction operator (V) by the union operator (U)."

Conversely we have

"If the partition top is given in the form of union of smallest forms of states the corresponding disjunctive canonical form of the variable TOP is obtained by replacing each smallest form of state by the corresponding complete monomial and each union operator (U) by the disjunction operator (V)."

We notice that the disjunction operator V is always replaced by the union operator U. The conjunction operator $\wedge$ instead is replaced by the intersection operator U in the case of the restrictions type 2 (Eqs. 1-2 and 1-2a) and by the cartesian product operator x in the case of the complete monomials. This fact however does not cause any problem. In fact any complete monomial is a non-zero monomial which corresponds to a specific state of the system. A state is for definition a non-empty set. Since the restrictions are only used to identify the zero monomials of a boolean function that is the prohibited rows of the corresponding truth table and both are <u>always</u> deleted, it is impossible to get smallest forms of system states containing the intersection operator, and/or complete monomials which contain two or more primary variables belonging to the same component.

In conclusion the boolean algebra with restrictions on variables allows us to operate on boolean variables in a way similar to the classical boolean algebra, but with the additional complication of the restrictions. Once that the boolean expression of the TOP variable has been found, the rules No. 2 and 3 allow one to easily identify the smallest form of the states of the partition top.

The advantage of using boolean variables instead of states is obviously that of having a more flexible instrument to operate. We show this point by developing Eq. 1-26. We notice that

$$(B \wedge \bar{C} \wedge D) \; V \; (B \wedge C \wedge D) = (B \wedge D) \qquad (1\text{-}27)$$

and

$$(A \wedge \bar{B} \wedge C) \; V \; (A \wedge B \wedge C) = (A \wedge C) \qquad (1\text{-}28)$$

Taking into account Eqs. 1-27 and 1-28, Eq. 1-26 becomes

$$\text{TOP} = (B \wedge D) \vee (A \wedge C) \vee (B \wedge C \wedge E) \tag{1-29}$$

We also notice that

$$E = \overline{A} \wedge \overline{D} \tag{1-30}$$

and therefore

$$(B \wedge D) \vee (B \wedge C \wedge E) = B \wedge \left[D \vee (C \wedge \overline{A} \wedge \overline{D}) \right] = (B \wedge D) \vee (B \wedge C \wedge \overline{A}) \tag{1-31}$$

Taking into account Eq. 1-31, Eq. 1-29 becomes

$$\text{TOP} = (B \wedge D) \vee (A \wedge C) \vee (B \wedge C \wedge \overline{A}) \tag{1-32}$$

We have

$$(A \wedge C) \vee (B \wedge C \wedge \overline{A}) = C \wedge \left[A \vee (B \wedge \overline{A}) \right] = (C \wedge A) \vee (C \wedge B) \tag{1-33}$$

Taking into account Eq. 1-33, Eq. 1-32 becomes finally

$$\text{TOP} = (B \wedge D) \vee (A \wedge C) \vee (C \wedge B) \tag{1-34}$$

The partition top is simply given by

$$\text{top} = \left\{ (B \wedge D) \vee (A \wedge C) \vee (C \wedge B) = 1 \right\} \tag{1-35}$$

Note that the expression of the partition top given by Eq. 1-35 (i.e. by using the boolean variables) is much simpler and much more compact than the equivalent expression given by Eq. 1-23 (i.e. by using the set theory).

2. FAULT TREE SYMBOLOGY

The graphical symbology of a fault tree which is being used here is derived from that proposed by Fussell[7] with some modifications and some additional symbols.

The symbols have been organized in two tables, namely

A.   Table of Variables (Fig. 2-1)
B.   Table of Basic Gates (Fig. 2-2)

The two tables are selfexplanatory so that only few additional comments are needed for a correct use of the symbols contained in them.

1.   The House (Table of Variables) is used to modify the structure of the fault tree. If the House is given the value O, the whole branch of the fault tree under the AND gate (to which the House is input) is cancelled out. If the House is given

No.	Symbol	Denomination	Meaning
1	*(rectangle)*	Rectangle	Variable Description
2	 *(circle)*	Circle	A primary variable belonging to an independent component.
3	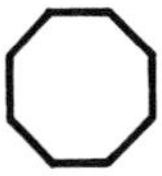 *(octagon)*	Octagon	A primary variable belonging to a dependent component
4	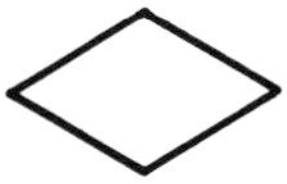 *(diamond)*	Diamond	A non-primary variable which would require dissection in more basic variables, but that for some reasons has not been further dissected.
5	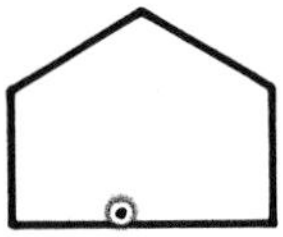 *(house)*	House	A variable whose sample space contains only one member, that is a variable which is constant and always takes either the value 1 or 0. Note: this symbol is used only as input to an AND gate.
6	 *(triangle)*	Transfer IN	A connecting or transfer symbol indicating a variable entering the fault tree.
7	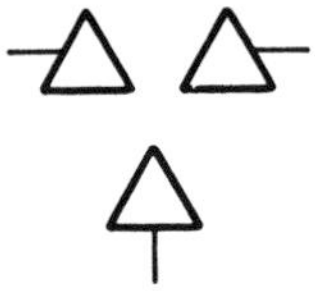 *(triangles)*	Transfer OUT	A connecting or transfer symbol indicating a variable going out from the fault tree.

Fig. 2-1.   Table of variables

No.	Symbol	Denomination	Boolean Notation	Output/Inputs Relationship	Rules for the Generation of the Truth Table
1		NOT	$B=\bar{A}$	$B=1-A$	Output takes the value 1 if predecessor takes the value 0 and vice versa.
2		AND	$B=\bigwedge_{i=1}^{n} \bar{A}_i$	$B=\min(A_1;A_2\cdots;A_n)$	Output takes the value 1 if and only if all predecessors take the value 1, and the value 0 if at least one of the predecessors takes the value 0.
3		OR	$B=\bigvee_{i=1}^{n} \bar{A}_i$	$B=\max(A_1;A_2\cdots;A_n)$	Output takes the value 1 if at least one of the predecessors takes the value 1, and the value 0 if and only if all predecessors take the value 0.

Note: A marked point at the input of the input of a gate means that the input variable is negated before entering the gate.

Fig. 2-2.   Table of Basic Gates.

the value 1 no modification of the structure of the fault tree
occurs.

2. Transfer IN and Transfer OUT (Table of Variables) are used in
    the case in which a variable is at the same time an output
    (Transfer OUT) from a gate and input (Transfer IN) to some
    other gates which are located (in the drawing of the fault tree)
    far away one from the other.

3. If an input to a gate (Tables of Basic Gates) is marked with
    a point, it means that the input variable is complemented
    (negated) before entering the gate.

    For instance we have

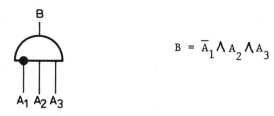

$$B = \bar{A}_1 \wedge A_2 \wedge A_3$$

3. CONSTRUCTION OF A FAULT TREE. AN EXAMPLE

    Fig. 3-1 shows a very simplified electric power supply system
(EPSS) consisting of the bus bars C which are supplied either by the
external network B or by the electric generator A. Network and electric generator are connected in parallel to the bus bars respectively through the electrically operated circuit breakers F and L. The
dotted lines (with arrows) indicate that the position (open or
closed) of each circuit breaker depends upon the state (failed or
intact) of the component to which the circuit breaker is associated.

    The circuit breakers in Fig. 3-1 are shown in the position
open (coil deenergized). In normal operating conditions both
circuit breakers F and L are closed (coil energized) and the generator A supplies electric power to the bus bars C as well as to the
external network B. If the generator A fails the circuit breaker L
opens and the external network feeds the bus bars C. If the network
B fails the circuit breaker F opens and the generator A feeds the
bus bars C only. The function of each circuit breaker is that of
disconnecting its associated component (conditioning component)
when this fails. If the circuit breaker fails to open, no electric
voltage will be available at the bus bars C. In addition B may
cause by failing the failure of A and vice versa (a failure of A
may cause B to fail). Components A and B are said to be correlated.

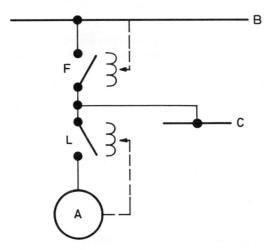

Fig. 3-1.   Schematic diagram of a simplified electric
power supply system (EPSS)

The primary components with associated states are shown in the
table of Fig. 3-2. Here for each primary component the conditioning
components are listed in the homonymous column. The correlated
components, which are each other statistically dependent (in our
example A and B), are also shown.

Note that in our example the conditioning components of F and
L are also primary components. However, in general the conditioning
components may be not primary (i.e. the variables belonging to
them are not primary). In.this case additional information must be
given to identify these conditioning components.

We can now proceed to define the TOP variable. The EPSS is
failed if no electric voltage is available at the bus bars C. We
have therefore

    TOP = No voltage at bus bars C

We observe that the absence of voltage at the bus bars C is caused
either by the failure of the bus bars C or by the fact that no
voltage arrives at C. In this way we have dissected the TOP variable
into the disjunction of two other variables namely "bus bars C
failed" and "no voltage at the input of bus bars C". This dissection
is graphically shown in Fig. 3-3, where the OR gate GO1 has the TOP
as output and the other two above defined variables as input.

Primary Component		Conditioning Components	Correlated Components	State	
Denomination	Symbol			Denomination	Symbol of associated primary variable
Generator	A		B	Failed	A_1
				Intact	A_2
Network	B		A	Failed	B_1
				Intact	B_2
Bus bars	C			Failed	C_1
				Intact	C_2
Circuit Breaker F	F	B		Failed open	F_1
				Failed closed	F_2
				Intact	F_3
Circuit Breaker L	L	A		Failed open	L_1
				Failed closed	L_2
				Intact	L_3

Fig. 3-2.   Table of the primary components of the EPSS.

We point out that the probability data associated to the variable "bus bars C failed" are available from reliability data banks. This variable is therefore a primary variable. We call it C_1 and we draw a circle in Fig. 3-3 because C is statistically independent (see table of Fig. 3-2). We now dissect the variable "No voltage at the input of bus bars C".

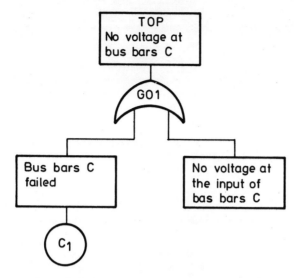

Fig. 3-3. Partial fault tree of the EPPS (1st step)

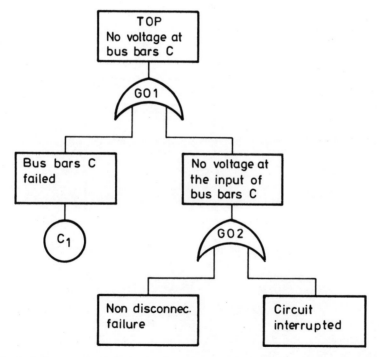

Fig. 3-4. Partial fault tree of the EPPS (2nd step)

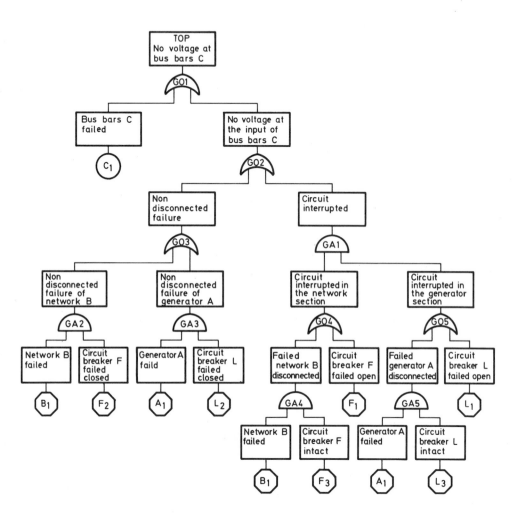

Fig. 3-5.   Fault tree of the EPSS.

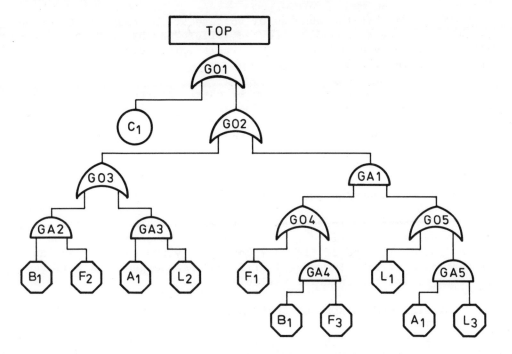

Fig. 3-6.   Fault tree of the EPPS (without variable descriptions)

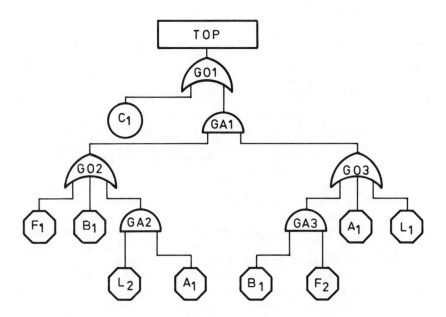

Fig. 3-7.   Fault tree of the EPPS (Alternative)

We notice that the absence of voltage at the bus bars C can be caused either by a "non-disconnected failure" or by an "interruption of the continuity of the electric circuit". This dissection is whown graphically in Fig. 3-4.

The process of dissection can be carried further on until all variables are primary variables. The complete fault tree is shown in Fig. 3-5. Note that the variables A_1; B_1; L_1; L_2; L_3; F_1; F_2 and F_3 are all represented by octagons because they belong to dependent components.

The fault tree of Fig. 3-5 has been redrawn in simplified form in Fig. 3-6 without rectangles (i.e. variable descriptions).

Since there are in general, different possible ways of dissecting the variables, different fault trees of the same TOP can be drawn. The fault tree of Fig. 3-7 has exactly the same TOP variable of that of Fig. 3-6. In general different people generate different fault trees for the same TOP variable.

4.   MODIFIED FAULT TREE. OCCURRENCE PROBABILITY OF THE PRIMARY
      EVENTS

Given a boolean variable A, we define as expectation of A ($E\{A\}$) the occurrence probability of the event $\{A=1\}$, that is

$$E\{A\} = P\{A=1\} \qquad\qquad (4-1)$$

where $P\{...\}$ means occurrence probability of the event under brackets.

The probability data related to the primary variables of the system described in the previous section are given in the table of Fig. 4-1. Here we assume that all failure rates of the primary components are constant. The transition rates are identified as follows. The primary variable of the row refers to the state before the transition (state of departure). The number of the column identifies the state after the transition (state of arrival).

The components A and B have transitions which are correlated. If B fails (transition $B_2 \rightarrow B_1$) there is a constant probability K_A that A fails too (transition $A_2 \rightarrow A_1$). In this case the transition $B_2 \rightarrow B_1$ is the conditioning transition and the transition $A_2 \rightarrow A_1$ is the conditioned transition. This is shown in the table of Fig. 4-1. The table shows also that if A fails (conditioning transition $A_2 \rightarrow A_1$) there is a constant probability K_B that B fails too (conditioned transition $B_2 \rightarrow B_1$).

Fig. 4-1.   Table of the input probability data of the primary variables (System of Fig. 3-1).

Primary Component	Conditioning Variable	Primary Variable	Transition rates (hours^{-1})			Correlated transitions		
			1	2	3	Conditioning Transition	Conditioned Transition	Conditional Probability
A		A_1	λ_A	μ_A				
		A_2				$B_2 \rightarrow B_1$	$A_2 \rightarrow A_1$	K_A
B		B_1	λ_B	μ_B				
		B_2				$A_2 \rightarrow A_1$	$B_2 \rightarrow B_1$	K_B
C		C_1	λ_c	μ_c				
		C_2						
F	B_1	F_1			ρ_1			
		F_2			ω_1			
		F_3	ν_1	σ_1				
	B_2	F_1			ρ_2			
		F_2			ω_2			
		F_3	ν_2	σ_2				
L	A_1	L_1			η_1			
		L_2			α_1			
		L_3	ε_1	ς_1				
	A_2	L_1			η_2			
		L_2			α_2			
		L_3	ε_2	ς_2				

We introduce the following symbol

$$\lambda_A = \text{transition rate of } A_2 \rightarrow A_1$$

$$\mu_A = \quad " \quad " \quad " \quad A_1 \rightarrow A_2$$

$$\lambda_B = \quad " \quad " \quad " \quad B_2 \rightarrow B_1$$

$$\mu_B = \quad " \quad " \quad " \quad B_1 \rightarrow B_2$$

We can now draw the state diagram of the super-component G characterized by the four states which one obtains by intersecting the state of A and B in all possible ways. The state diagram of super-component G is shown in Fig. 4-2.

With reference to the state diagram of Fig. 4-2, we can now express the primary variables of components A and B as functions of the primary variables of G. We have

$$A_1 = G_1 V G_3 \tag{4-2}$$

$$A_2 = G_2 V G_4 \tag{4-3}$$

$$B_1 = G_1 V G_2 \tag{4-4}$$

$$B_2 = G_3 V G_4 \tag{4-5}$$

We now replace in fault tree of Fig. 3-6 the primary variables A_1 and B_1 with the new primary variables G_1; G_2; G_3 and G_4 by making use of Eqs. 4-2 and 4-4. The new fault tree is shown in Fig. 4-3.

In the fault tree of Fig. 4-3 the primary variables A_1 and B_1 have been replaced respectively by the OR Gates GO7 (inputs G_1 and G_3) and GO6 (inputs G_1 and G_2). Note that the primary variables G_1; G_2 and G_3 are represented by circles because they belong to an independent super-component. In fact their expectations can be calculated by solving the state diagram of Fig. 4-2. The new primary veriables have been introduced also in the fault tree of Fig. 3-7 (See Fig. 4-4).

The expectations of the primary variables G_1; G_2; G_3 and G_4 can easily be calculated by means of the very well known methods of state analysis.

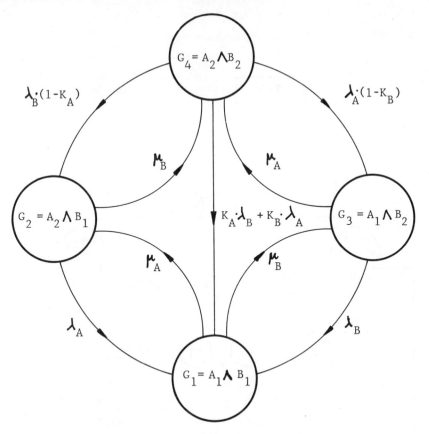

Fig. 4-2.   State   diagram of super-component G

We go back to the table of Fig. 4-1 and we consider the circuit breaker F. The circuit breaker F is a bipolar switch with conditioning variables B_1 and B_2. The theory of the bipolar switch has been fully developed by the author in[11]. Here only some important points of the model are recalled. Since a bipolar switch has three states, there will be three primary variables, namely (in the case of F)

F_1 associated to state f_1 (failed open)

F_2 "   "   " f_2 (failed closed)

F_3 "   "   " f_3 (intact)

We shall assume that the two failed states of the switch don't communicate directly with each other. This means that the switch must be repaired before failing again. This is exactly what happens in practice. Failure and repair rates (i.e. transitions rates) of

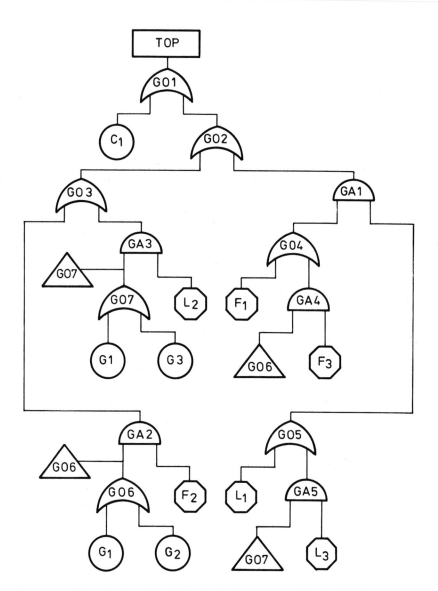

Fig. 4-3. Modified fault tree of the EPSS.

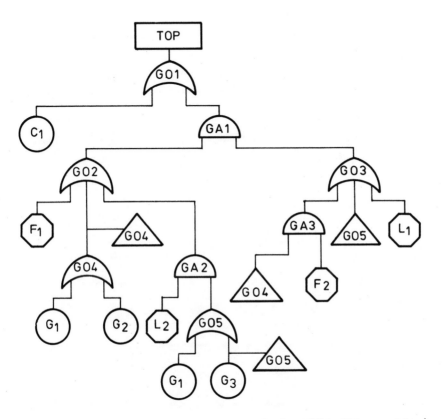

Fig. 4-4. Modified fault tree of the EPPS (Alternative).

the switch will be in general dependent upon its position i.e. upon the state of the network B (intact or failed). They are conditional transition rates.

In the case of a bipolar switch a procedure has been used[11] which is quite different from that used in the case of supercomponent G.

In this case in fact it is possible to identify a conditioning component B and a dependent component F. For this reason we define first the conditional expectation of a dependent variable (say F_k) given a conditioning variable (say B_q) as the occurrence probability of the event $\{F_k = 1\}$ given the event $\{B_q = 1\}$

$$E\left\{F_k \mid B_q\right\} = P\left\{F_k = 1 \mid B_q = 1\right\} \tag{4-6}$$

One can easily calculate the conditional expectations of the primary variables F_1; F_2; and F_3 by means of the analysis developed in[11].

In[11] it has been demonstrated that the following relationships hold under some conditions which are always satisfied in the practical cases (for instance, repair rates must be order of magnitudes larger than failure rates). The relationships are

$$E\left\{F_k \mid B_q \wedge Y\right\} \cong E\left\{F_k \mid B_q\right\} \tag{4-7}$$

(k=1; 2;3)   (q=1; 2)   where Y is an arbitrary

boolean function which does not contain any literal of F.

$$E\left\{F_k \mid G_1\right\} \cong E\left\{F_k \mid G_2\right\} \cong E\left\{F_k \mid B_1\right\} \tag{4-8}$$

$$E\left\{F_k \mid G_3\right\} \cong E\left\{F_k \mid G_4\right\} \cong E\left\{F_k \mid B_2\right\} \tag{4-9}$$

(k=1; 2; 3)

In the case of circuit breaker L, one can also write expressions similar to (4-13) to (4-15). We have

$$E\left\{L_k \mid A_q \wedge Y\right\} \cong E\left\{L_k \mid A_q\right\} \quad \text{(k=1; 2;3) (q=1; 2)} \tag{4-10}$$
where Y is an arbitrary
boolean function which does not contain any literal of L.

$$E\left\{L_k \mid G_1\right\} \cong E\left\{L_k \mid G_3\right\} \cong E\left\{L_k \mid A_1\right\} \tag{4-11}$$

$$E\left\{L_k \mid G_2\right\} \cong E\left\{L_k \mid G_4\right\} \cong E\left\{L_k \mid A_2\right\} \tag{4-12}$$

5.   BOOLEAN OPERATIONS

5.1 Generalities

The reader must become acquainted with some terms which are currently used throughout this paper.

In the following primary variables will be also called literals. A boolean function can be expressed in the form of a disjunction of conjunctions of literals (disjunctive form). A conjunction of literals belonging to a disjunctive form of a boolean function will be called shortly "monomial". A monomial X of the disjunctive form of a boolean function (TOP) is said to be an implicant of the TOP. It must satisfy the following boolean identy.

$$\text{TOP} \wedge X = X \tag{5-1}$$

Let X_j and X_k be two monomials. We say that X_k subsumes X_j if every literal of X_j is contained in X_k. This is the same as saying that X_k is an implicant of X_j, that is

$$X_j \wedge X_k = X_k \tag{5-1}$$

A disjunctive form of a boolean function will be called "normal disjunctive form" if its monomials satisfy the following four properties.

1.   Each monomial (X) must be a non-zero monomial ($X \neq 0$, i.e. no pair of mutually exclusive literals must be contained in it)

2.   Each monomial must not contain any literal (primary variable) more than once (no repeated literals).

3.   Monomials must not subsume pairwise each other.
      $(X_j \neq X_j \wedge X_k \neq X_k)$

4.   Monomials must not contain negated literals .

Each negated literal must have been previously replaced by the corresponding disjunction of all remaining literals belonging to the same primary component, that is

$$\overline{A_i} = \bigvee_{k=1}^{n} A_k \quad k \neq i \quad (i=1;\ 2;\ \ldots;n) \tag{5-2}$$

A boolean function can have in general many normal disjunctive forms. For a given fault tree, there is a particular normal disjunctive form of its TOP variable which is associated to that fault tree. We shall call it "associated normal disjunctive form".

We say that a monomial X_j is a "prime implicant" (minimal cut set) of the boolean function TOP if (1) X_j implies the TOP $(X_j \wedge TOP = X_j)$ and (2) any other monomial Y subsumed by X_j (i.e. obtained from X_j be deleting one of its literals) does not imply the TOP $(Y \wedge TOP \neq Y)$.

We shall call any disjunction of prime implicants, which is equivalent to the function TOP , a "base of the function TOP". The disjunction of all prime implicants has this property. We shall call it the "complete base". We shall describe as an "irredundant base" a base which ceases to be a base if one of the prime implicants occuring in it is removed (deleted). Boolean functions may have many irredundant bases. We shall call "smallest irredundant base" the irredundant base having the smallest number of prime implicants. There may be more than one base with the smallest number of prime implicants.

If a boolean function has only one base, which is at the same time complete and irredundant, the boolean function is said to be coherent. The identification of an irredundant base (or one of the smallest irredundant bases) of the boolean function TOP of a fault tree is carried out in three steps:

Step No. 1   Identification of the associated normal disjunctive form.

Step No. 2   Identification of the complete base starting from the associated normal disjunctive form.

Step No. 3   Extraction of an irredundant base (or one of the smallest irredundant bases) from the complete base.

After having identified an irredundant base of the TOP variable, some other transformations are carried out to get the boolean function in a form suitable for probability calculations. We have

Step No. 4   Expression of the TOP as a disjunction of pairwise mutually exclusive boolean functions (keystone functions).

Step No. 5   Identification of the conditioning variables to be associated to each keystone function.

The purpose of step No. 4 is that of getting an expression of the TOP which facilitates the operation of expectation. This will become clear in section 6 of this paper.

5.2   Step No. 1 - Identification of the Associated Normal Disjunctive Form

The Variables of the fault tree are first ordered in a list (table of variables). The literals are first listed. The acceptance criterion of a variable (gate) in the list is the following: the variable is accepted only and only if the input variables to the gate have already been accepted. If the gate satisfies the acceptance criterion is written in the list. The ordering process comes to an end when all variables have been written in the list.

By simple inspection of the fault tree of Fig. 3-6 we get the table of variables of Fig. 5-1.

The algorithm to identify the monomials of the associated normal disjunctive form is the so called "downward algorithm" which is based on the principle already described in[7] by Fussell and in[8]. Some additional features have been incorporated in the original downward algorithm so that the NOT gate and multistate components can be handled. The algorithm begins with the TOP and systematically goes down through the tree from the highest to the lowest variable, that if from the bottom to the top of the ordered list of variables. The fault tree is developed in a table (table of monomials). The elements of the table are variables. Each row of the table is a monomial. The numbers of the elements contained in a row is called length of the row. Each time an OR gate is encountered new rows will be produced (so many as the number of input variables to the gate). Each time an AND gate will be encountered the length of the rows (in which the gate appears) will be increased. Each time a NOT gate is encountered the input variable to the gate receives a negation mark. If a negated non primary variable will be dissected, the gate type will be replaced by its dual type (AND will be changed into OR and viceversa) and the negation mark is transmitted to all input variables of the gate. If a primary variable is negated, it is replaced by an OR gate which has as input variables all the remaining primary variables belonging to the same primary component.

The process of dissection comes to an end when all the elements of the table of monomials are primary variables (literals).

In addition the three following simplification rules are applied:

1.   Delete zero monomials, that is rows which contain at least one pair of mutually exclusive literals.
$Cj_q \wedge Cj_k = 0$ for $q \neq k$ (exclusion law).

2.   Delete the repeated literals of a monomial (row).
$Cj_q \wedge Cj_q = Cj_q$ (idempower law).

Ordering Numbers	Variable	Boolean Relationship	Predecessors	Successors
1	C_1	-	-	GO1
2	G_1	-	-	GO6;GO7
3	G_2	-	-	GO6
4	G_3	-	-	GO7
5	L_1	-	-	GO5
6	L_2	-	-	GA3
7	L_3	-	-	GA5
8	F_1	-	-	GO4
9	F_2	-	-	GA2
10	F_3	-	-	GA4
11	GO6	OR	$G_1;G_2$	GA2;GA4
12	GO7	OR	$G1;G3$	GA3;GA5
13	GA5	AND	$GO7;L_3$	GO5
14	GA4	AND	$GO6;F_3$	GO4
15	GA3	AND	$L_2;GO7$	GO3
16	GA2	AND	$GO6;F_2$	GO3
17	GO4	OR	$F_1;GA4$	GA1
18	GO5	OR	$L_1;GA5$	GA1
19	GA1	AND	GO4;GO5	GO2
20	GO3	OR	GA2;GA3	GO2
21	GO2	OR	G 03;GA1	GO1
22	GO1(TOP)	OR	$C_1;GO2$	-

Fig. 5-1.   Table of variables of the fault tree of Fig. 4-3.

3. Delete any subsuming monomial, that is any row which contains
   all elements or another row.
   $X_a \lor X_b = X_a$ if $X_a \land X_b = X_b$ (absorption law).

At the end of the process each row of the table of monomials is a monomial and the disjunction of all monomials is the normal disjunctive form of the TOP associated to the fault tree under considerations.

We now apply the above described procedure to the table of variables of Fig. 5-1. The example is self explanatory. We have

Ordering Number	Boolean Identity	Table of Monomials
	TOP = GO1	GO1
22	GO1 = C_1 VGO2	C_1 / GO2
21	GO2 = GO3 VGA1	C_1 / GO3 / GA1
20	GO3 = GA2 VGA3	C_1 / GA2 / GA3 / GA1
19	GA1 = GO4 $\wedge$ GO5	C_1 / GA2 / GA3 / GO4 GO5
18	GO5 = L_1 VGA5	C_1 / GA2 / GA3 / GO4 L_1 / GO4 GA5

and so on.

At the end of the process the table of monomials will look as follows (Fig. 5-2).

We can therefore write the following boolean identity for the TOP (we indicate from now on the conjunction by means of the simpler multiplication symbol ".").

$$\text{TOP} = C_1 \vee F_2 \cdot G_1 \vee F_2 \cdot G_2 \vee L_2 \cdot G_1 \vee L_2 \cdot G_3 \vee G_1 \cdot F_3 \cdot L_1 \vee G_2 \cdot F_3 \cdot L_1 \vee$$

$$\vee F_1 \cdot G_1 \cdot L_3 \vee F_1 \cdot G_3 \cdot L_3 \vee F_1 \cdot L_1 \vee G_1 \cdot F_3 \cdot L_3 \qquad (5-3)$$

If we now apply the same above procedure to the fault tree of Fig. 4-4, we get

$$\text{TOP} = C_1 \vee L_1 \cdot F_1 \vee F_1 \cdot G_3 \vee G_3 \cdot L_2 \vee L_1 \cdot G_2 \vee G_1 \vee F_2 \cdot G_2 \qquad (5-4)$$

C_1		
F_2	G_1	
F_2	G_2	
L_2	G_1	
L_2	G_3	
G_1	F_3	L_1
G_2	F_3	L_1
F_1	G_1	L_3
F_1	G_3	L_3
F_1	L_1	
G_1	F_3	L_3

Fig. 5-2.   Table of monomials of the fault tree of Fig. 3-6.

The two expressions 5-3 and 5-4 look very different. However they are the same boolean function. This will be shown in the next section. Here we can say that it is not possible to prove whether or not two boolean functions are equal by making use only of algorithms which calculate normal disjunctive forms of boolean functions.

5.3   Step No. 2 - Identification of the complete base

Various algorithms for the identification of the complete base of a boolean function (step No. 2) are available from the litera- ture[9]. An algorithm due to Nelson[10] is particularly convenient. This algorithm consists simply in complementing (negating) a normal disjunctive form of a boolean function TOP (which from now on we also call ϕ) and then in complementing its complement $\overline{\phi}$. After each of the two complement operations, the three simplification rules (section 5.2) are applied to the result.

Nelson's algorithm can be described as follows

1. Complement ϕ, expand $\bar{\phi}$ into disjunctive form, apply simplification rules and call the result $\bar{F}$.

2. Complement $\bar{F}$, expand F into disjunctive form, apply simplification rules and call the result K.

The disjunction of the monomials of K is the complete base of the boolean function ϕ.

We now apply the Nelson algorithm to our case, that is to Eq. 5-3. By complementing Eq. 5-3, we can write

$$\overline{TOP} = \bar{C} \cdot (\bar{F}_2 \vee \bar{G}_1) \cdot (\bar{F}_2 \vee \bar{G}_2) \cdot (\bar{L}_2 \vee \bar{G}_1) \cdot (\bar{L}_2 \vee \bar{G}_3) \cdot$$
$$\cdot (\bar{G}_1 \vee \bar{F}_3 \vee \bar{L}_1) \cdot (\bar{G}_2 \vee \bar{F}_3 \vee \bar{L}_1) \cdot (\bar{F}_1 \vee \bar{G}_1 \vee \bar{L}_3) \cdot$$
$$\cdot (\bar{F}_1 \vee \bar{G}_3 \vee \bar{L}_3) \cdot (\bar{G}_1 \vee \bar{L}_1) \cdot (\bar{G}_1 \vee \bar{F}_3 \vee \bar{L}_3) \qquad (5\text{-}5)$$

Now we have

$$\bar{C}_1 = C_2 \qquad (5\text{-}6)$$

$$\bar{G}_k = \bigvee_{q=1}^{4} Gq \qquad k \neq q \qquad (k=1; \; 2; \; 3; \; 4) \qquad (5\text{-}7)$$

$$\bar{F}_k = \bigvee_{q=1}^{3} F_q \qquad k \neq q \qquad (k=1; \; 2; \; 3) \qquad (5\text{-}8)$$

and

$$\bar{L}_k = \bigvee_{q=1}^{3} Lq \qquad k \neq q \qquad (k=1; \; 2; \; 3) \qquad (5\text{-}9)$$

By taking into account Eqs. 5-6 to 5-9, Eq. 5-5 becomes

$$\overline{TOP} = C_2 \cdot (F_1 \vee F_3 \vee G_2 \vee G_3 \vee G_4) \cdot (F_1 \vee F_3 \vee G_1 \vee G_3 \vee G_4) \cdot$$
$$\cdot (L_1 \vee L_3 \vee G_2 \vee G_3 \vee G_4) \cdot (L_1 \vee L_3 \vee G_1 \vee G_2 \vee G_4) \cdot$$
$$\cdot (G_2 \vee G_3 \vee G_4 \vee F_1 \vee F_2 \vee L_2 \vee L_3) \cdot (G_1 \vee G_3 \vee G_4 \vee F_1 \vee F_2 \vee L_2 \vee L_3) \cdot$$
$$\cdot (F_2 \vee F_3 \vee G_2 \vee G_3 \vee G_4 \vee L_1 \vee L_2) \cdot (F_2 \vee F_3 \vee G_1 \vee G_2 \vee G_4 \vee L_1 \vee L_2) \cdot$$
$$\cdot (F_2 \vee F_3 \vee L_2 \vee L_3) \cdot (G_2 \vee G_3 \vee G_4 \vee F_1 \vee F_2 \vee L_1 \vee L_2) \qquad (5\text{-}10)$$

We execute the operations of Eq. 5-10 and we apply the three simplification rules. We get

$$\overline{TOP} = C_2 \cdot G_2 \cdot F_1 \cdot L_2 \vee C_2 \cdot G_2 \cdot F_1 \cdot L_3 \vee C_2 \cdot G_2 \cdot F_3 \cdot L_2 \vee C_2 \cdot G_2 \cdot F_3 \cdot L_3 \vee$$
$$\vee C_2 \cdot G_3 \cdot F_2 \cdot L_1 \vee C_2 \cdot G_3 \cdot F_2 \cdot L_3 \vee C_2 \cdot G_3 \cdot F_3 \cdot L_1 \vee C_2 \cdot G_3 \cdot F_2 \cdot L_3 \vee$$
$$\vee C_2 \cdot G_4 \cdot F_2 \vee C_2 \cdot G_4 \cdot F_3 \vee C_2 \cdot G_4 \cdot L_2 \vee C_2 \cdot G_4 \cdot L_3 \qquad (5\text{-}11)$$

We now complement $\overline{TOP}$ and we execute all operations including the application of the three simplification rules. We get finally

$$TOP = C_1 \vee L_1 \cdot F_1 \vee F_1 \cdot G_3 \vee G_3 \cdot L_2 \vee L_1 \cdot G_2 \vee G_1 \vee F_2 \cdot G_2 \qquad (5\text{-}12)$$

Eq. 5-12 is the complete base of the TOP.

We notice that Eq. 5-12 and 5-4 (that is the fault trees of Figs. 4-3 and 4-4) have the same TOP. The knowledge of the complete base of a boolean function is important also because offers the possibility to find out if two or more fault trees have the same TOP.

We can state the following criterion

"If two boolean functions have the same complete base they are identical".

Nelson's algorithm was improved by Hulme and Worrell[11] to reduce the computing time. A modified Nelson's algorithm has been developed at Karlsruhe[3]. The execution times of the three algorithms are compared in the table of Fig. 5-3. The examples have been taken from[11].

5.4   Step No. 3 - Extraction of an Irredundant Base (or One of the Smallest Irredundant Bases) from the Complete Base.

Various algorithms for the extraction of the smallest irredundant base of a boolean function from its complete base are available from the literature[9].

We consider a method, which may be called the method of the expansion coefficients. The basic principles of this method have been described in[3].

A fast algorithm based on this principle has been developed at Karlsruhe[3] which allows one to identify the smallest irredundant base of a boolean function. The table of Fig. 5-4 gives the required execution times for the examples 3 to 7 of the table 5-3.

Example	Number of prime implicants in complete base	CPU time (sec)		
		Nelson algorithm (CDC6600)	Sandia algorithm (CDC 6600)	Karlsruhe algorithm (IBM370/168)
1	4	0.158	0.156	0.11
2	3	0.367	0.182	not performed
3	15	221.418	0.391	0.26
4	15	1413.580	0.388	0.26
5	32	5300[1]	3.868	0.42
6	61	4600[1]	303.657	1.03
7	87	6000[1]	417.371	1.12

[1] These entries indicate times at which execution was terminated without completing the algorithm.

Fig. 5-3.   Computational times of different types of Nelson Algorithms.

Example	Number of prime implicants in complete base	Number of prime implicants in smallest irredundant base	CPU time needed to identify smallest irredundant base (secs)
3	15	7	0.24
4	15	8	0.23
5	32	12	0.49
6	61	17	6.07
7	87	19	19.51

Fig. 5-4.   Computational times of the algorithm for the extraction of the smallest irredundant base.

An even faster algorithm for the extraction of an irredundant base (which is not necessarily the smallest) has been developed at Karlsruhe. This algorithm will be described elsewhere.

Since the boolean function of our example is coherent, the complete base is already irredundant and the algorithm for the extraction of an irredundant base does not need to be applied.

5.5   Step No. 4 - Expression of the TOP as a Disjunction of
      Pairwise Mutually Exclusive Boolean Functions

   We have the TOP as disjunction of the prime implicants "X_j"
(irredundant base).

$$TOP = \bigvee_{j=1}^{N} X_j \qquad (5\text{-}13)$$

where

   N = total number of prime implicants belonging to the
        irredundant base.

   We now want to transform Eq. 5-13 in an expression of the
type

$$TOP = \bigvee_{i=1}^{Q} Y_i \qquad (5\text{-}14)$$

where Y_i are boolean functions (called keystone functions) which
are pairwise mutually exclusive, that is satisfy the conditions

$$Y_i \cdot Y_k \equiv 0 \quad i \neq k \quad (i; k = 1; 2...;Q) \qquad (5\text{-}15)$$

In addition each Y_i results to be of the form

$$Y_i = M_i \cdot \bigvee_{s=1}^{n_i} P_{is} \quad (i = 1; 2...;Q) \qquad (5\text{-}16)$$

where the M_i and the P_{is} are non-zero boolean monomials satisfying the following conditions

$$M_i \cdot M_k = 0 \quad i \neq k \quad (i; k = 1; 2...;Q) \qquad (5\text{-}17)$$

$$\bigvee_{i=1}^{Q} M_i = 1 \qquad (5\text{-}18)$$

-    the monomials P_{is} are pairwise logically independent, that is
if a literal A_q Appears in a monomial P_{is}, no other literal belonging to the same component will appear in any other monomial P_{ir}
($r \neq s$ r;s = 1;2...;n_i).

-    each monomial P_{is} is logically independent with M_i.

The last two conditions can be expressed in the following way

If $\qquad$ $A_q \cdot P_{is} = P_{is}$

then $\qquad$ $0 \neq A_q \cdot M_i \neq M_i$ and

$\qquad\qquad$ $0 \neq A_q \cdot P_{ir} \neq P_{ir} \qquad r \neq s$

AND

If $\qquad$ $A_q \cdot M_i = M_i$

then $\qquad$ $0 \neq A_q \cdot P_{is} \neq P_{is}$

In other words a component A can appear only once in a keystone function Y_i: either in the monomial M_i or in one of the monomials P_{is}.

A fast algorithm has been developed at Karlsruhe to identify the keystone functions Y_i (keystone algorithm). By applying the keystone algorithm to our example (Eq. 5-12) we get

$$TOP = \bigvee_{i=1}^{4} Y_i \qquad\qquad (5\text{-}19)$$

where

$$Y_1 = G_1 \qquad\qquad (5\text{-}20)$$

$$Y_2 = G_2 \cdot (C_q \vee L_1 \vee F_2) \qquad\qquad (5\text{-}21)$$

$$Y_3 = G_3 \cdot (C_1 \vee F_1 \vee L_2) \qquad\qquad (5\text{-}22)$$

$$Y_4 = G_4 \cdot (C_1 \vee L_1 \cdot F_1) \qquad\qquad (5\text{-}23)$$

5.6   Step No. 5 - Identification of the Conditioning Variables to be associated to each Keystone Function.

Each keystone function receives marks for the identification of the conditioning variables associated to the statistically dependent variables which appear in it.

A fast algorithm (called "marking algorithm") has been developed at Karlsruhe for the identification of these conditioning variables. By applying this algorithm to our example we get the following table (Fig. 5-5)

Keystone Function	Statistically Dependent Primary Variable	Conditioning Variable
Y_1	-	-
Y_2	L_1	$A_2 = G_2 \vee G_4$
	F_2	$B_1 = G_1 \vee G_2$
Y_3	F_1	$B_2 = G_3 \vee G_4$
	L_2	$A_1 = G_1 \vee G_3$
Y_4	L_1	$A_2 = G_2 \vee G_4$
	F_1	$B_2 = G_3 \vee G_4$

Fig. 5-5.   Table of the conditioning variables to be
associated to each keystone function

6.   CALCULATION OF THE OCCURRENCE PROBABILITY OF THE TOP EVENT

We now want to calculate the expectation of the TOP variable,
that is the occurrence probability of the event $\{TOP = 1\}$.

$$E\left\{TOP\right\} = P\left\{TOP = 1\right\} \tag{6-1}$$

Taking into account Eqs. 5-13 and 5-15 we can write

$$E\left\{TOP\right\} = \sum_{i=1}^{Q} E\left\{Y_i\right\} \tag{6-2}$$

In our example (Eqs. 5-20 to 5-23 and table of Fig. 5-5) we can
write

$$E\left\{Y_1\right\} = E\left\{G_1\right\} \tag{6-3}$$

$$E\left\{Y_2\right\} = E\left\{G_2 \cdot (C_1\ L_1\ F_2)\right\} =$$
$$= E\left\{G_2 \cdot C_1\right\} + E\left\{G_2 \cdot L_1\right\} + E\left\{G_2 \cdot F_2\right\} -$$
$$- E\left\{G_2 \cdot C_1 \cdot L_1\right\} + E\left\{G_2 \cdot C_1 \cdot F_2\right\} + E\left\{G_2 \cdot L_1 \cdot F_2\right\} +$$
$$+ E\left\{G_2 \cdot C_1 \cdot L_1 \cdot F_2\right\} \tag{6-4}$$

Taking into account Eqs. 4-7; 4-8; 4-10; and 4-12 and the table of Fig. 5-5, we can write

$$E\left\{G_2 \cdot C_1\right\} = E\left\{G_2\right\} \cdot E\left\{C_1\right\} \tag{6-5}$$

$$E\left\{G_2 \cdot L_1\right\} = E\left\{G_2\right\} \cdot E\left\{L_1 | G_2\right\} = E\left\{G_2\right\} \cdot E\left\{L_1 | A_2\right\} \tag{6-6}$$

$$E\left\{G_2 \cdot F_2\right\} = E\left\{G_2\right\} \cdot E\left\{F_2 | G_2\right\} = E\left\{G_2\right\} \cdot E\left\{F_2 | B_1\right\} \tag{6-7}$$

$$E\left\{G_2 \cdot C_1 \cdot L_1\right\} = E\left\{C_1\right\} \cdot E\left\{G_2 \cdot L_1\right\} = E\left\{C_1\right\} \cdot E\left\{G_2\right\} \cdot E\left\{L_1 | G_2\right\} =$$
$$= E\left\{C_1\right\} \cdot E\left\{G_2\right\} \cdot E\left\{L_1 | A_2\right\} \tag{6-8}$$

$$E\left\{G_2 \cdot C_1 \cdot F_1\right\} = E\left\{C_1\right\} \cdot E\left\{G_2\right\} E\left\{F_1 | B_1\right\} \tag{6-9}$$

$$E\left\{G_2 \cdot L_1 \cdot F_2\right\} = E\left\{G_2 \cdot L_1\right\} \cdot E\left\{F_2 | G_2 L_1\right\} =$$
$$= E\left\{G_2\right\} \cdot E\left\{L_1 | G_2\right\} \cdot E\left\{F_2 | G_2\right\} =$$
$$= E\left\{G_2\right\} \cdot E\left\{L_1 | A_2\right\} \cdot E\left\{F_2 | B_1\right\} \tag{6-10}$$

$$E\left\{G_2 \cdot C_1 \cdot L_1 \cdot F_2\right\} = E\left\{G_2\right\} \cdot E\left\{C_1\right\} \cdot E\left\{L_1 | A_2\right\} \cdot E\left\{F_2 | B_1\right\} \tag{6-11}$$

Taking into account Eqs. 6-5 to 6-11, Eq. 6-4 becomes finally

$$E\left\{Y_2\right\} = E\left\{G_2\right\} \cdot \left[E\left\{C_1\right\} + (1 - E\left\{C_1\right\}) \cdot E\left\{L_1 | A_2\right\} + \right.$$
$$\left. + (1 - E\left\{C_1\right\})(1 - E\left\{L_1 | A_2\right\}) E\left\{F_2 | B_1\right\}\right] \tag{6-12}$$

In a similar way one gets

$$E\left\{Y_3\right\} = E\left\{G_3\right\} \cdot \left[E\left\{C_1\right\} + (1 - E\left\{C_1\right\}) \cdot E\left\{F_1 | B_2\right\} + \right.$$
$$\left. + (1 - E\left\{C_1\right\})(1 - E\left\{F_1 | B_2\right\}) E\left\{L_2 | A_1\right\}\right] \tag{6-13}$$

and

$$E\left\{Y_4\right\} = E\left\{G_4\right\} \cdot \left[E\left\{C_1\right\} + (1 - E\left\{C_1\right\}) E\left\{L_1 | A_2\right\} \cdot E\left\{F_1 | B_2\right\}\right] \tag{6-14}$$

By replacing Eqs. 6-3; 6-12; 6-13 and 6-14 into Eq. 6-2 (with Q=4) one finally gets the occurrence probability of the TOP event.

7.   CONCLUSIONS

Following conclusions can be drawn:

1.   The theory described in this paper is a powerful tool for the analysis of fault trees containing multistate (more than two states) primary components as well as statistically dependent primary components. This means that a very wide spectrum of problems which are met in practice can now be solved analytically by applying this theory.

2.   A special type of boolean algebra has been developed to allow one to handle multistate primary components. This is the boolean algebra with restrictions on variables. Its basic rules have been described in this paper.

3.   The problem of statistical dependence has been solved either (1) by removing it, that is by replacing in the fault tree the statistically dependent primary variables by means of ad hoc new defined primary variables or (2) by defining some conditioning variables and evaluating separately the associated necessary conditional probabilities.

      General criteria to establish which one of the two methods should be chosen have not been given in the paper. They are illustrated in Reference[11].

4.   General criteria for the identification of the most convenient conditioning variables are given also in Reference[11]. The choice depends upon the type of statistical dependence and upon the way in which this statistical dependence enters in the fault tree.

5.   The concept of expectation of a boolean variable and of conditional expectation of a boolean variable have been introduced in this paper in a rather intuitive way just pointing out the close relationship between conditional expectation and conditional probability. In Reference[11] a formalization of the concept is developed.

6.   A computer programme based on the above theory has been developed at Karlsruhe and is now being tested. Two sample problems

have been solved by using this programme.

A system was given to three different people. Three different fault trees were generated for the same TOP variable.
The three associated disjunctive forms (output from the downward algorithm) were calculated and they looked each other
remarkably different (large differences in the total number
of monomials as well as in their composition). However, it
was possible to verify that the three functions were identical
by calculating the complete base (output of the Nelson algorithm),
which resulted to be exactly the same for all three fault trees.

The second problem was chosen because it contained three different types of dependecies which are commonly met in practice,
namely (1) common mode failure, (2) components characterized
by failure rates which depend upon the occurrence of some non-
primary events and (3) the case of a component whose repair
affects the operation of another component. The computer
programme solved the problem successfully.

7.   A new definition of coherency has been given in this paper.
     We recall it again

     "A boolean function is said to be coherent if it is
     characterized by only one base which is at the same
     time complete and irredundant."

The question arises whether or not all technical systems are
coherent. Some authors[13] have demonstrated that there are
examples of systems which are non-coherent.   Non-coherent
boolean functions may also be generated, when one analyses the
problem of a transition from one partition of a system to
another.   These boolean functions are rather special because
they describe the space at the boundary between the two partitions.   The computer programme developed at Karlsruhe can
handle coherent as well as non-coherent boolean functions.

8.   ACKNOWLEDGEMENTS

     The author wishes to thank Dr. Wenzelburger (IRE, Karlsruhe)
for the fruitful discussions on the theory developed in this paper.

9.   REFERENCES

1.   W.E. Vesely, 1970, "A time dependent methodology for fault tree
     evaluation", Nucl. Eng. Des. 13, 337-360.

2. L. Caldarola, A. Wickenhäuser, 1977,"Recent Advancaments in
    fault tree methodology at Karlsruhe", International Conf. on
    Nucl. Systems Reliability Engineering and Risk Assessment,
    Gatlingburg, SIAM, 518-542.

3. L. Caldarola, 1978, "Fault tree analysis of multistate systems
    with multistate components", ANS Topical Meeting on Probabilistic
    Analysis of Nuclear Reactor Safety, Los Angeles, California,
    Paper VIII.1.

4. J.D. Murchland, G. Weber, 1972, "A moment method for the
    calculation of a confidence interval for the failure probability
    of a system", IEEE Proceedings Annual Symposium on Reliability.

5. C. Berge, 1962, "The theory of graphs", Methuen and John Wiley.

6. P. Mussio, S. Garriba, S. Fumagalli,1979, "Multiple valued
    logic in system representation", NATO ASI.

7. J.B. Fussell, 1973,"Fault tree analysis: Concept and techniques",
    NATO Conference on Reliability, Liverpool, England.

8. L. Caldarola, A. Wickenhäuser, 1977, "The Karlsruhe computer
    program for the evaluation of the availability and reliability
    of complex repairable systems", Nucl. Eng. Des. 43, 463-470.

9. J. Kuntzmann, 1967,"Fundamental Boolean Angebra," Blackie and
    Sons Ltd.

10. R.J. Nelson, 1954,"Simplest normal truth functions," the
    Journal of Symbolic Logic, vol. 20, Nr. 2, 105-108.

11. B.L. Hulme, R.B. Worrell, 1975,"A prime implicant algorithm
    with factoring," IEEE Transaction on computers, vol. C-24,
    Nr. 11, 1129-1131.

12. L. Caldarola, 1979, "Generalized fault tree analysis combined
    with state analysis", (being published).

13. A. Amendola, S. Contini, 1979, "about the definition of co-
    herency in binary system reliability analysis." This issue.

SECTION 3

MULTISTATE SYSTEMS - OTHER METHODS

Introduction by the Editors

This section contains papers showing a number of the latest developments and applications of generic methods, not based on logic diagrams, for solving reliability problems.

Some of these methods like the ones based on Markov processes and in general on stochastic processes, have been extensively used in the reliability field since the origin of this dicipline. What has been changed in the recent years is the possibility to apply these methods to large and complex systems.

Some other methods like the Response Surface Methodology (RSM), have been originally developed and used in other fields. The interest in reliability studies has grown only in the last two or three years.

We have to stress the fact that the methods shown in this section are complementary to the "logical diagrams" methods. In many cases, for solving real problems, the two types of methods have to be used together. In other cases the use of methods based on logic diagrams or on other techniques (Markov and non-Markov continuous time stochastic processes) depends on the degree of complexity of the system and on the degree of accuracy of the results seached for.

The first paper by Foglio Para and Garribba on "Reliability Analysis of a Repairable Single Unit under General Age Dependance" considers the case of units or components whose properties change due to some global effect. Situations are treated where hazard rates are influenced by total elapsed calendar time, total accumulated on-time (or down-time), and a number of transitions. The problem can be solved by a set of partial differential or integral equations and the Chapman-Kolmogrov set results as a specialization.

The three following papers deal with Markov processes. The paper by Blin et al. on "Use of Markov Processes for Reliability Problems", gives a tutorial introduction to homogeneous Markov processes and shows an application to an engineered system. The paper by Somma, "Some Considerations on the Markov Approach to Reliability", shows a way to tackle the analysis of systems leading to very large Markov transition matrix. The paper by Wenzelburger, "How to Use the Minimal Cut Sets of Fault-Tree in Markov Modelling", suggests a possible coupling of the fault-tree technique with the Markov process approach in view of the automatization of the construction of the transition matrix.

Next is the paper by Olivi on "Response Surface Methodology in Risk Analysis". RSM is a general approach to the problems in which a yield variable y varies in the same pattern according to the levels of one or more stimulus variable x. In practice, this approach becomes essential when complex modes of failure depending on many continuous variables have to be analyzed. The paper gives a comprehensive state of the art of this technique as applicable to risk analysis.

The paper by Inagaki, "Optimization Problems in System Supervision" shows how Markov processes can be applied to an optimization problem of great interest in plant operation.

The last paper by Krogull also deals with a problem of great practical interest: the evaluation of systems maintainability using raw maintainability data.

In conclusion, looking at the future of these generic methods, the papers suggest an increasing application of the Markov processes and a higher integration of the various methods. Certainly RSM will become in the near future an increasingly important chapter of reliability theory.

RELIABILITY ANALYSIS OF A REPAIRABLE SINGLE UNIT UNDER GENERAL AGE-DEPENDENCE

A. Foglio Para and S. Garribba

CESNEF, Istituto di Ingegneria Nucleare, Politecnico di Milano, Via G. Ponzio, 34/3, Milano, Italy 20133

ABSTRACT

The case is considered of a single two-state unit which undergoes a symmetric alternating process of failure and restoration. It is admitted that under general circumstances aging may be described in terms of total elapsed calendar-time, total accumulated on-time (or down-time) and, possibly, upon the number of transitions. Thus it is of utmost importance to be able to calculate and find explicit analytic expressions for the p.d.f. of total on-time (or total down-time) at a given time instant. The solution of the problem relies upon a set of integral equations. This set can be easily reduced to a set of partial differential equations. The solutions appear to be rather simple and manageable for a number of cases of practical interest. Finally, relations are established with the Chapman-Kolmogorov equations describing the non-homogeneous Markov repair process.

1. INTRODUCTION

We first introduce some assumptions, notation and terminology that will be used through the entire paper. Then let us refer to a single unit as a component or a part of the system whose operation and performance are analyzed independently from other parts or components. It is admitted that the unit may be found in various (internal) states. State identifies a particular situation, or operating mode, or configuration, or behaviour of the unit. In practical cases, states are expressed by sets of attributes and propositions.

We will assume that, once they have been ascertained, states are exhaustive for they offer a full description of the behaviour of the unit and mutually exclusive for the unit may be in a single state at a time. In what follows the possible states x_j of the unit belong to a discrete set $X = \{x_1, ..., x_j, ..., x_J\}$ called the phase space of the unit, j being in the sigma field of events.

Assume that the unit changes in time and its evolution is of stochastic nature.

The stochastic process $\{x_j(t);\ t \in T\}$ is a family of random variables where time t takes values in the index set T of the process. All processes we consider in the following are continuous-time processes with $T = \{t \mid t \geq t_0\}$.

Transitions among states and permanences can be represented by means of oriented graphs. A few examples are sketched in Fig.1.

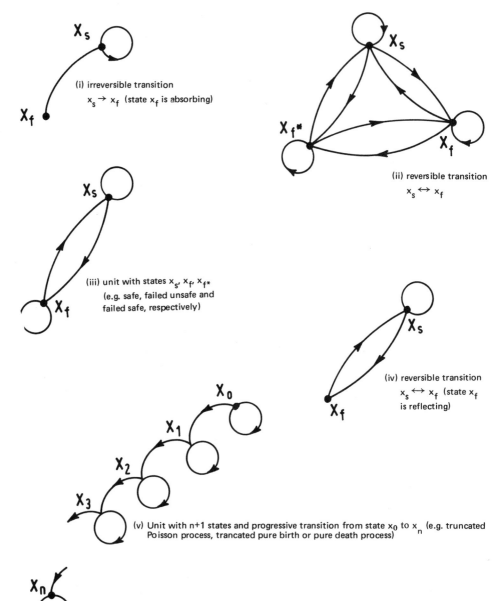

(i) irreversible transition
$x_s \to x_f$ (state x_f is absorbing)

(ii) reversible transition
$x_s \leftrightarrow x_f$

(iii) unit with states x_s, x_f, x_{f*}
(e.g. safe, failed unsafe and failed safe, respectively)

(iv) reversible transition
$x_s \leftrightarrow x_f$ (state x_f is reflecting)

(v) Unit with n+1 states and progressive transition from state x_0 to x_n (e.g. truncated Poisson process, trancated pure birth or pure death process)

Fig. 1 :   Oriented graphs showing recurrent transitions among states

Branches indicate the paths that unit may follow. Nodes indicate the states. In the (X, T) plane it is possible to draw the sample functions or realization. Given a two-state unit, Fig.2 shows two particular sample functions. Specifically, in the following, we will consider random point processes, where each occurrence time has associated with it the random variable x taking alternatingly the two values x_s and x_f in the two subsets of states X_s and X_f. The cartesian product holds $X = X_s \cdot X_f$. For purposes of representation the variable of state x(t) is set at $x_s = 1$ if the unity is operating and at $x_f = 0$ if the unit is under restoration or regeneration.

Let us denote by $\tau'_1, \tau''_1, \tau'_2, \tau''_2, \tau'_3, \ldots$ the times or life lengths spent successively in the states x_s and x_f.

$\{\tau'_n\}$ and $\{\tau''_n\}$, with $n = 1, 2, 3, \ldots$, are sequences of non-negative random variables $(\tau'_0 = \tau''_0 = 0)$.

The instants:

$$t'_n = t_0 + \tau'_1 + \tau''_1 \ldots + \tau'_n, t'_0 = t_0, \qquad (1.1)$$

correspond with the failures of the unit and the instants,

$$t''_n = t_0 + \tau'_1 + \tau''_1 + \ldots \tau'_n + \tau''_n, t''_0 = t_0, \qquad (1.2)$$

represent the restorations (or regenerations).

Furthermore, under many practical circumstances, it is found of interest to count the number of points (i.e. the number of transitions) in the subsets X_s and X_f on which the point process is defined.

Thus let denote by $\{N'(t); t \geqslant t_0\}$ and $\{N''(t); t \geqslant t_0\}$ two counting processes where N' and N'' are statistical variables representing the number of transitions performed from the safe into the failed state and from the failed into the safe state, respectively.

During the intervals $t''_{n-1} \leqslant t \leqslant t'_n$ we think of a failure act or process defined by a failure (hazard) rate (or age-specific failure rate) λ_n in such a way that the product $\lambda_n dt$ is the probability that the unit fails from t to $t + dt$, given that the unit is safe at time t. Because random point processes are supposed conditionally orderly, the probability of there being no point (no failure) from t to $t + dt$ is approximated to order dt by $1 - \lambda_n dt$. On the other hand, during the intervals $t'_n \leqslant t \leqslant t''_n$ we consider a restoration act or process characterized by a restoration (hazard) rate μ_n.

The product $\mu_n dt$ is the probability of a restoration occurring from t to $t + dt$ provided that the unit is failed at the instant t.

In our treatment we will refer to cases where any external preventive action of maintenance is absent. Thus it is sufficient for the description to introduce two random intensity processes $\lambda; t \geqslant t_0$ and $\mu; t \geqslant t_0$ for the states x_s and x_f, respectively. Obviously, the sample paths of the intensity processes will depend on the realizations of the alternating (base) random point process. The intensities characterize the infinitesimal behaviour or the time microstructure of the point process conditional on its previous global behaviour or macrostructure.

2. A FEW SIMPLE MODELS

We term our random point process a self-exciting point process if the corresponding intensity processes are defined as [1]:

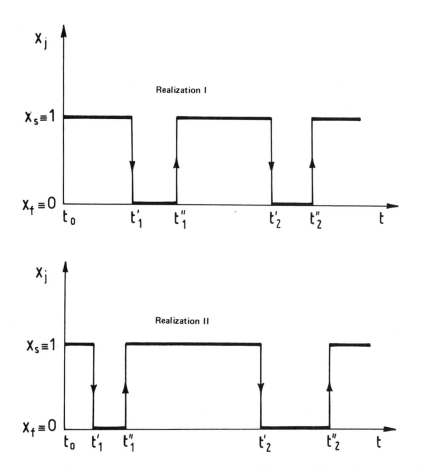

Fig. 2 : Two particular sample functions for the process (ii) of Fig. 1 (reversible transition)

$$\lambda = \lambda(N'_n, t; t''_{n-1}, t'_{n-1}, ..., t'_1), t''_{n-1} \leqslant t \leqslant t'_n, \tag{2.1}$$

$$\mu = \mu(N''_n, t; t'_n, t''_{n-1}, ..., t'_1), t'_n \leqslant t \leqslant t''_n,$$

where $n = 1, 2, ..., N'_n = N''_n = n-1, t''_0 = t_0$, and $x(t_0) = x_s$.

Now the reliability-oriented characterization of this process would require that answers are provided for a number of questions. Some are:

(i)   Evaluation of the pointwise marginal availability $P_s(t)$ (or unavailability $P_f(t)$), that is the probability $P\{x(t) = x_s\}$ that the unit is in the state x_s at a given instant of time $t \geqslant t_0$. Since events x_s and x_f are non-compatible, it is $P_s(t) + P_f(t) = 1$.
There may be sometimes the need of evaluating the pointwise conditional availability $P_{s|f}(t|\bar{t})$ expressing the probability $P\{x(t) = x_s | x(\bar{t}) = x_f\}$ that the component is in the state x_s at t, given that the unit lies in the state x_f at $\bar{t} \geqslant t_0$. In many cases $P_{s|f}(t|\bar{t})$ differs from the probability $P_{s|f*}(t|\bar{t}) = P\{x(t) = x_s | x(t) = x_{f*}\}$ that the unit is in the state x_s at t given that the unit enters the state x_f at $\bar{t} \geqslant t_0$.

(ii) Search for the probability density function (p.d.f.) of the total on-time φ (or down-time ψ) accumulated by the unit during the time interval $[t_0, t)$. Obviously, it will be $0 \leqslant \varphi \leqslant t-t_0$ (and $\varphi + \psi = t-t_0$). If we denote this p.d.f. by $Q(t, \varphi)$, a relation would hold of the type

$$\int_0^{t-t_0} \varphi Q(t, \varphi) \, d\varphi = \int_{t_0}^t P_s(u) \, du.$$

(iii) Computation of the (marginal) number of visits $N_{s\to f}(t_0, t)$ from x_s to x_f in $[t_0, t)$. N is a random number. Expected number of steps will then be expressed as $M_{s\to f}(t_0, t)$. Conditional numbers can also be considered.

(iv) Computation of interval reliability or probability that at a specified time instant the unit is safely operating and will continue to operate for an interval of duration, say T. Having defined a new random variable, namely the forward recurrence time to failure $\xi(t)$, we will write

$$P\{\xi(t) > T\} = P\{N_{s\to f}(t, t+T) = 0\}$$

(v)   Search, in the case of preventive maintenance, of the optimum maintenance policy or strategy; that is definition of a specific class of maintenance policies that minimizes total cost, maximizes availability, or in general contains the best value of a prescribed objective function.

However, when proposed in these general terms, the solution to all these problems tends to be overly complicated for many applications. Therefore one is led to search for simpler models that may provide adequate treatment. Indeed in many practical situations only a few of the most recent transition times tend to influence the future evolution of the unit. It is also of interest to remark that would failure and restoration rates be thoroughly constant, any model entailed by the set (2.1) degenerates to a two-state homogenous Markov process.

    A fundamental role is played by those policies of restoration where after the failure the unit is replaced by a new one which starts its life taking on part of its original properties. Then a (non-homogeneous, symmetric) 1-memory self-exciting process has

$$\lambda = \lambda\,(N'_n,\,t;\ t{-}t''_{n-1}) \tag{2.2}$$

$$\mu = \mu\,(N''_n,\,t;\ t{-}t'_n)$$

This process reduces to a (homogeneous modified) renewal process or semi-Markov process if

$$\lambda = \lambda(t{-}t''_{n-1}) \equiv \lambda_{n-1}(\Delta t) \tag{2.3}$$

$$\mu = \mu(t{-}t'_n) \equiv \mu_r(\Delta t)$$

More specifically, it reduces to an ordinary renewal process if in addition for all $n = 1, 2, \ldots$ $\lambda_{n-1}(\Delta t) = \lambda_0(\Delta t)$ and $\mu_n(\Delta t) = \mu_1(\Delta t)$, that is the interarrivals of each type are identically distributed. In cases of increasing failure rate (IFR) and decreasing resoration rate (DRR) it may be said that after the transition the unit is good as new.

Conversely, one is led to the consideration of a (non-homogeneous, symmetric) 0-memory self-exciting point process, where

$$\lambda = \lambda\,(N'_n,\,t) \tag{2.4}$$

$$\mu = \mu\,(N''_n,\,t)$$

The unit is without aftereffect or of a Markov type. The probability of its being situated at time t in a state $x_i(t)$ under the condition that the life of the unit up to time $\bar{t}$ $(\bar{t} < t)$ is completely known, depends only on the state of the unit at time t. Particularly, we have a repair process in calendar time (or real time), or a non-homogeneous Markov process if

$$\lambda = \lambda\,(t) \tag{2.5}$$

$$\mu = \mu\,(t)$$

and a bounded birth-and-death process, or a binary process if

$$\lambda = \lambda\,(N') \tag{2.6}$$

$$\mu = \mu\,(N'')$$

Again, in this case of IFR and DRR after the transitions the unit continues its life in a condition which may be referred to as bad as old.

A multitude of different models could be imagined so as to match arrangements occurring in the operation and maintenance practice of engineered systems. Cases may be also sought where the failure process and the restoration process have non-symmetric microstructures. In many practical instances, however, simple renewal, repair and binary processes represent a sort of a starting point. These processes indeed can be actually treated in their analytical aspects, so as to throw some light on more intrigued situations.

3. HAZARD RATES IN THE PRESENCE OF PHENOMENA OF WEAR OR AGING

When plotting and examining data of failure and restoration reliability analysts may be led to recognize that units or components change due to effects of wear and aging. Hazard rate (or intensities) may be influenced by the total elapsed calendar time (or real time), and/or they may change according to the total accumulated on-time or down-time (or effective times) and/or they may be affected by the number of transitions during the life of the unit. The existence of different classes of hazard dependences for different types of equipment and failure modes is verified by the experience and recognized in the literature [2-4]. Let us refer to the case of a component (like a pump, a shaft, a piece of pipe, etc.) where failure occurs because of some mechanisms induced by corrosion. In reliability analysis one may ask to be able to treat separately cases where failure is mainly due to (static) corrosion, which is effective during the entire calendar life of the components, and cases where failure depends upon stress or fretting action. More specifically, in this latter situation, one should be able to take into account the time during which the component is effectively under stress or moving. On a different side, the situation may occur of a component (like a valve, a light bulb, a switch, etc.) where failure tends to be connected with the number of times the component is turned on or off (see Fig.3).

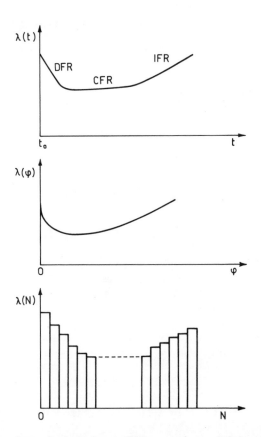

Fig. 3 :   General dependences for hazard rates. Failure rate λ vs. total elapsed calender time, total accumulated on-time, total accumulated number of transitions. In all diagrams it has been assumed to be able to recognize regions of decreasing, constant and increasing failure rate (DFR, CFR and IFR, respectively). Arbitrary units.

Having in mind these situations and many others which can be easily imagined, it seems of the utmost interest to be able to describe a symmetric process of failure and restoration where the intensity process has a sort of a global memory of the past and takes the form

$$\lambda = \lambda \, (N, \, t, \, \varphi) \tag{3.1}$$

$$\mu = \mu \, (N, \, t, \, \varphi)$$

where $N = N' + N''$.

Then let us start with a model where λ and μ do not depend in any way on the realization of φ. We have the 0-memory self-exciting point process (2.4)

$$\lambda = \lambda \, (N, \, t) \tag{3.2}$$

$$\mu = \mu \, (N, \, t)$$

which is a Markov process. Define by $P_s(N, t)$ the probability of finding the unit after N transitions in its safe state at time t and similarly define by $P_f(N, t)$ the probability that the unit is in its failed state after it suffered a number of transitions equal to N. The Chapman-Kolmogorov set of equations would hold in the form

$$\frac{dP_s(N, t)}{dt} = -\lambda \, (N, t) \, P_s(N, t) + \mu \, (N-1, t) \, P_f(N-1, t) \tag{3.3}$$

$$\frac{dP_f(N-1, t)}{dt} = +\lambda \, (N-2, t) \, P_s(N-2, t) - \mu \, (N-1, t) \, P_f(N-1, t)$$

where $N = 2, 4, 6, \ldots$ and for $N = 0$

$$\frac{dP_s(0, t)}{dt} = -\lambda \, (0, t) \, P_s(0, t) \tag{3.4}$$

with $P_s(0, 0) = 1$. The solution would be found as for the non-homogeneous birth-and-death process studied by Kendall [5]. Next is the model where intensities do not depend upon the number of transitions

$$\lambda = \lambda \, (t, \, \varphi) \tag{3.5}$$

$$\mu = \mu \, (t, \, \varphi)$$

This model underlies a non-Markov process which will be referred to as a repair process in accumulated on-time (or effective time) and in calendar time (or real time). In our knowledge this type of model has not found consideration in the literature. Our aim will be then of finding solutions for the problem of computation of p.d.f. of total on-time and pointwise marginal availability. Ultimately we hope to be able to combine the treatments of models (3.3) and (3.5) in order to provide answers to more general case implied by (3.1).

4. LIMITING VALUES AND CONDITIONS OF NORMALIZATION

Let us suppose that the unit starts at time instant $t_0 = 0$ in its safe state x_s and experiences failure and restoration processes whose intensities are given $\lambda = \lambda \, (t, \varphi)$ and $\mu = \mu \, (t, \varphi) = \mu'(t, \psi)$. At a particular (calendar-time) instant t the unit will be found in its safe or failed state with pointwise probabilities $P_s(t)$ and $P_f(t) = 1 - P_s(t)$ respectively. Now for the case where $\lambda = \lambda(t)$ and $\mu = \mu(t)$, $P_s(t)$ and $P_f(t)$ can be easily calculated by the use of the well-known Chapman-Kolmogorov set of equations [2].

However, the case of dependence upon accumulated total on time φ or, what is equivalent, upon accumulated total down time ψ requires a special analytical treatment. To this purpose let us introduce the φ-conditional reliability function of the unit $R(\bar{t}, t|\varphi)$, that is the interval reliability function of the unit over $[\bar{t}, t)$, given that the unit is safe at time instant $\bar{t}$ and the total on-time accumulated in $[0, \bar{t})$ is φ. We have

$$R(\bar{t}, t|\varphi) = \exp\left[-\int_{\bar{t}}^{t} \lambda(u, u - \bar{t} + \varphi)\, du\right] \tag{4.1}$$

Similarly, let us introduce the φ-conditional maintainability function of the unit $S(\bar{t}, t|\varphi)$, that is the probability of no restoration in $[t, t)$, given the accumulated on-time φ in $[0, \bar{t})$,

$$S(\bar{t}, t|\varphi) = \exp\left[-\int_{\bar{t}}^{t} \mu(u, \varphi)\, du\right] \tag{4.2}$$

Then refer to the stochastic cumulative process $\{\varphi(t); t \geqslant t_0\}$ and denote by $Q(t, \varphi)$ its first-order p.d.f. (see Fig. 4).

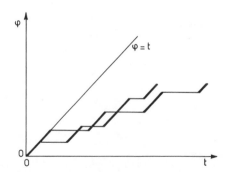

Fig. 4 : Typical realizations for the stochastic process of cumulated on-time $\{\varphi(t); t \geqslant 0\}$
Heavy line marks tracts where the unit is in its safe state.

The probability $P(t, \varphi)\, d\varphi$ that the unit has accumulated a total on-time ranging from φ to $\varphi + d\varphi$, given that the unit has experienced at least one transition (i.e. one failure) in the time interval $[0, t)$, will be found from the relation $P(t, \varphi) = Q(t, \varphi) - R(0, t|0)\, \delta\, (t - \varphi)$, where δ is the delta function. It is also useful to consider the decomposition $P(t, \varphi) = P^S(t, \varphi) + P^F(t, \varphi)$. The two additional first-order p.d.f.'s $P^S(t, \varphi)$ and $P^F(t, \varphi)$ are introduced to express the probability that φ is in $[\varphi, \varphi + d\varphi)$ given that the unit has experienced at least one failure in $[0, t)$ and it lays at time t in the safe or in the failed state, respectively. It may be recalled that all these p.d.f.'s are defined only for $0 \leqslant \varphi \leqslant t$. The limiting values of $P^S(t, \varphi)$, $P^F(t, \varphi)$ and $P(t, \varphi)$ for $\varphi = 0$ and $\varphi = t$ can be easily computed. If $\varphi = 0$, it results

$$PS(t, 0) = 0 \tag{4.1a}$$

$$PF(t, 0) = \lambda(0, 0) \cdot S(0, t \mid 0) \tag{4.1b}$$

$$P(t, 0) = \lambda(0, 0) \cdot S(0, t \mid 0) \tag{4.1c}$$

The relation (4.1b) refers to the case in which the unit fails at the time $t = 0$ immediately, without being repaired until time t is reached.
Conversely, for $\varphi = t$ one has

$$PS(t, t) = R(0, t \mid 0) \cdot \int_0^t \lambda(u, u) \cdot \mu(u, u) \cdot du \tag{4.2a}$$

$$PF(t, t) = R(0, t \mid 0) \cdot \lambda(t, t) \tag{4.2b}$$

$$P(t, t) = R(0, t \mid 0) \cdot [\lambda(t, t) + \int_0^t \lambda(u, u) \cdot \mu(u, u) \cdot du] \tag{4.2c}$$

Relations (4.2a) and (4.2c) take into account the probability that would unit fails at a particular time u, it is repaired immediately.
On the other hand, the normalization conditions hold in the form:

$$\int_0^t PS(t, \varphi) \cdot d\varphi = P_s(t) - R(0, t \mid 0) \tag{4.3a}$$

$$\int_0^t PF(t, \varphi) \cdot d\varphi = P_f(t) \tag{4.3b}$$

$$\int_0^t P(t, \varphi) \cdot d\varphi = 1 - R(0, t \mid 0) \tag{4.3c}$$

5. INTEGRAL AND DIFFERENTIAL EQUATIONS FOR $PS(t, \varphi)$ AND $PF(t, \varphi)$

It is easy to verify that the differential probabilities $PS(t, \varphi)$ and $PF(t, \varphi)$ are connected by the set of integral equations,

$$PS(t, \varphi) = \int_{t-\varphi}^t PF(y, \varphi - t + y) \cdot \mu(y, \varphi - t + y) \cdot R(y, t \mid \varphi - t + y) dy \tag{5.1}$$

$$PF(t, \varphi) = \int_{\varphi}^t PS(y, \varphi) \cdot \lambda(y, \varphi) \cdot S(y, t \mid \varphi) dy + R(0, \varphi \mid 0) \cdot$$
$$\lambda(\varphi, \varphi) \cdot S(\varphi, t \mid \varphi) \tag{5.2}$$

In this set the current integration variable y stays for the instant at which the last transition occurred.
Given the definitions (4.1) and (4.2), the reliability and maintainability functions which occur in the set (5.1 - 5.2) have the expressions:

$$R(y, t \mid \varphi - t + y) = \exp[-\int_y^t \lambda(u, \varphi - t + u) du]$$

$$S(y, t \mid \varphi) = \exp[-\int_y^t \mu(y, \varphi) du]$$

$$R(0, \varphi \mid 0) = \exp\left[-\int_0^\varphi \lambda(u, u)\,du\right]$$

$$S(\varphi, t \mid \varphi) = \exp\left[-\int_\varphi^t \mu(u, \varphi)\,du\right]$$

Now it is supposed that the failure and restoration hazard rates are continuous functions together with their first order derivatives. Therefore p.d.f.'s $PS(t, \varphi)$ and $PF(t, \varphi)$ will be continuous and differentiable. We can calculate the partial derivatives $\partial PS/\partial t$, $\partial PF/\partial t$, $\partial PS/\partial \varphi$, $\partial PF/\partial \varphi$.
We have:

$$\frac{\partial PS(t, \varphi)}{\partial t} = PF(t, \varphi) \cdot \mu(t, \varphi) \cdot R(t, t \mid \varphi) - PF(t - \varphi, 0) \cdot$$

$$\cdot \mu(t - \varphi, 0),\; R(t - \varphi, t \mid 0) +$$

$$+ \int_{t-\varphi}^t \frac{\partial}{\partial t}\, [PF(y, \varphi - t + y) \cdot \mu(y, \varphi - t + y) \cdot$$

$$\cdot R(y, t \mid \varphi - t + y)]\,dy \tag{5.3a}$$

$$\frac{\partial PS(t, \varphi)}{\partial \varphi} = PF(t - \varphi, 0) \cdot \mu(t - \varphi, 0) \cdot R(t - \varphi, t \mid 0) +$$

$$+ \int_{t-\varphi}^t \frac{\partial}{\partial \varphi}\,[PF(y, \varphi - t + y) \cdot \mu(y, \varphi - t + y) \cdot$$

$$\cdot R(y, t \mid \varphi - t + y)]\,dy \tag{5.3b}$$

Noting that in the integrands of equations (5.3) t and φ enter with opposite signs (with the exception of the upper limit of the reliability integral), their sum gives simply $-\lambda(t, \varphi) \cdot PS(t, \varphi)$. We are then led to the partial differential equation

$$\frac{\partial PS(t, \varphi)}{\partial t} + \frac{\partial PS(t, \varphi)}{\partial \varphi} = -\lambda(t, \varphi) \cdot PS(t, \varphi) + \mu(t, \varphi) \cdot PF(t, \varphi) \tag{5.4}$$

In a similar way we have

$$\frac{\partial PF(t, \varphi)}{\partial t} = \lambda(t, \varphi) \cdot PS(t, \varphi) \cdot S(t, t \mid \varphi) +$$

$$\int_\varphi^t \frac{\partial}{\partial t}\, [PS(y, \varphi) \cdot \lambda(y, \varphi) \cdot S(y, t \mid \varphi)]\,dy +$$

$$+ R(0, \varphi \mid 0) \cdot \lambda(\varphi, \varphi) \cdot \frac{\partial}{\partial t} S(y, t \mid \varphi) \tag{5.5}$$

and through the use of (5.2) it ensues

$$\frac{\partial PF(t, \varphi)}{\partial t} = \lambda(t, \varphi) \cdot PS(t, \varphi) - \mu(t, \varphi) \cdot PF(t, \varphi) \tag{5.6}$$

This equation after summation with (5.4) gives

$$\frac{\partial P(t, \varphi)}{\partial t} + \frac{\partial PS(t, \varphi)}{\partial \varphi} = 0 \tag{5.7}$$

Finally, it can be also shown that $\partial PF / \partial \varphi$ satisfies the integro-differential form,

$$\frac{\partial PF(t, \varphi)}{\partial \varphi} = - \lambda(\varphi, \varphi) \cdot PS(\varphi, \varphi) \cdot S(\varphi, t \mid \varphi) +$$

$$+ \int_{\varphi}^{t} \frac{\partial}{\partial \varphi} [\lambda(y, \varphi) \cdot PS(y, \varphi) \cdot S(y, t \mid \varphi)] \, dy +$$

$$+ \frac{\partial}{\partial \varphi} [R(0, \varphi \mid 0) \cdot \lambda(\varphi, \varphi) \cdot S(\varphi, t \mid \varphi)] \tag{5.8}$$

It is instructive to integrate the fundamental set of partial differential equations (5.4) and (5.6) with respect to the total accumulated on-time φ,

$$\frac{dP_s(t)}{dt} + PF(t, t) = - \int_{0}^{t} \lambda(t, \varphi) \, PS(t, \varphi) \cdot d\varphi +$$

$$+ \int_{0}^{t} \mu(t, \varphi) \, PF(t, \varphi) \cdot d\varphi \tag{5.9}$$

$$\frac{dP_f(t)}{dt} - PF(t, t) = + \int_{0}^{t} \lambda(t, \varphi) \, PS(t, \varphi) \cdot d\varphi$$

$$- \int_{0}^{t} \mu(t, \varphi) \, PF(t, \varphi) \, d\varphi \tag{5.10}$$

To this end use has been made of the time derivatives of the normalization conditions (4.3a) and (4.3b) which read as follows:

$$PS(t, t) + \int_{0}^{t} \frac{\partial PS(t, \varphi)}{\partial t} \, d\varphi = \frac{dP_s(t)}{dt} - \frac{dR(0, t \mid 0)}{dt}$$

$$PF(t, t) + \int_{0}^{t} \frac{\partial PF(t, \varphi)}{\partial t} \, d\varphi = \frac{dP_f(t)}{dt}$$

In the particular case where hazard rates depend only upon the calendar time t, it is easy to verify that equations (5.9) and (5.10) reduce to the set of forward Chapman-Kolmogorov equations.

6. ANALYTICAL EXPRESSIONS FOR ON-TIME DENSITY FUNCTIONS IN SOME CASES OF INTEREST

There are cases where it is possible to compute the p.d.f.'s $PS(t, \varphi)$ and $PF(t, \varphi)$ in a closed form through a direct procedure, without searching for the solutions of the integral equations (5.1) and (5.2) or of the differential equations (5.4) and (5.6). Let us first consider the simple case where both λ and μ are constant. This case has found consideration in the work performed on the subject by other authors like Takacs [6], Gnedenko et al. [7], Parry and Worledge [8]. It can be shown that

$$PS(t, \varphi) = \sum_1^\infty \frac{\lambda^n}{n!} \cdot \varphi^n \cdot \exp\left[-\lambda\varphi\right] \frac{\mu^n \cdot (t-\varphi)^{n-1}}{(n-1)!} \exp\left[-\mu(t-\varphi)\right] \qquad (6.1)$$

$$PF(t, \varphi) = \sum_1^\infty \frac{\lambda^n \varphi^{n-1}}{(n-1)!} \exp\left[-\lambda\varphi\right] \cdot \frac{\mu^{n-1}(t-\varphi)^{n-1}}{(n-1)!} \exp\left[-\mu(t-\varphi)\right] \qquad (6.2)$$

In fact, if the unit is safe at the time t, the number of transitions that occurred is even, because every failure is followed by a restoration. Referring to the case of 2n transitions ($n = 1, 2, 3...$), $PS(t, \varphi)$ is given by the probability of n failures in the interval $(0, \varphi)$ multiplied by the p.d.f. that the sum of n restoration intervals lasts $t - \varphi$. In its turn $PF(t, \varphi)$ is obtained from the probability of $n - 1$ restorations in the interval $(0, t - \varphi)$ multiplied by the p.d.f. that the sum of n working intervals is φ.

The same type of calculation finds a straightforward application to the case where $\lambda = \lambda(\varphi)$ and $\mu = \mu(t - \varphi)$.

Indeed, if the failure hazard rate λ remains constant during the restorations periods, the different on-time intervals can be considered contiguous, and the probability of n failures in $[0, \varphi)$ is given by

$$\frac{\left[\int_0^\varphi \lambda(u)\,du\right]^n}{n!} \exp\left[-\int_0^\varphi \lambda(u)\,du\right]$$

Whereas the differential probability that n working intervals last exactly φ is given by

$$\frac{\left[\int_0^\varphi \lambda(u)\,du\right]^{n-1}}{(n-1)!} \lambda(\varphi) \cdot \exp\left[-\int_0^\varphi \lambda(u)\,du\right]$$

Thoroughly similar considerations apply to restoration intervals, so that

$$PS(t, \varphi) = \sum_1^\infty \frac{\left[\int_0^\varphi \lambda(u)\,du\right]^n}{n!} \exp\left[-\int_0^\varphi \lambda(u)\,du\right] \cdot \frac{\left[\int_0^{t-\varphi} \mu(u)\,du\right]^{n-1}}{(n-1)!} \cdot$$

$$\cdot \mu(t-\varphi) \exp\left[-\int_0^{t-\varphi} \mu(u)\,du\right] \qquad (6.3)$$

$$PF(t, \varphi) = \sum_{1}^{\infty} \frac{[\int_{0}^{\varphi} \lambda(u)\, du]^{n-1}}{(n-1)!} \cdot \lambda(\varphi) \cdot \exp\left[-\int_{0}^{\varphi} \lambda(u)\, du\right] \cdot$$

$$\cdot \frac{[\int_{0}^{t-\varphi} \mu(u)\, du]^{n-1}}{(n-1)!} \exp\left[-\int_{0}^{t-\varphi} \mu(u)\, du\right] \tag{6.4}$$

Clearly, these formulae can be simplified and applied also to the case where $\lambda = \lambda(\varphi)$ and μ is constant or to the case where λ is constant and $\mu = \mu(t - \varphi)$.

7. DIFFERENTIAL EQUATIONS FOR THE MOMENTS OF THE ON-TIME DENSITY FUNCTIONS

Let $M_n(t)$ denote the n-th order moment of the on-time p.d.f.. It is

$$M_n(t) = \int_{0}^{t} \varphi^n \cdot P(t, \varphi) \cdot d\varphi + t^n \cdot R(0, t \mid 0) \tag{7.1}$$

where $n = 1, 2, 3, ...,$ t is fixed and the last term expresses the probability that the system remains in the safe state without any failure during $[0, t)$. In its turn, $M_n(t)$ is the sum of the two n-th order moments

$$M_n^S(t) = \int_{0}^{t} \varphi^n \cdot P^S(t, \varphi) \cdot d\varphi + t^n \cdot R(0, t \mid 0) \tag{7.2a}$$

$$M_n^F(t) = \int_{0}^{t} \varphi^n \cdot P^F(t, \varphi) \cdot d\varphi \tag{7.2b}$$

We may first compute the derivatives with respect to time t for the two components of the n-th order moment. In the case of $M_n^S(t)$ it results

$$\frac{dM_n^S(t)}{dt} = t^n \cdot P^S(t, t) + \int_{0}^{t} \varphi^n \cdot \frac{\partial P^S(t, \varphi)}{\partial t} \cdot d\varphi + n \cdot t^{n-1} \cdot R(0, t \mid 0) -$$

$$- \lambda(t, t) \cdot t^n \cdot R(0, t \mid 0)$$

Now equation (5.4) allows the expansion and computation of the term

$$\int_{0}^{t} \varphi^n \frac{\partial P^S(t, \varphi)}{\partial t}\, d\varphi,$$

so that through the use of (4.2b) it ensues:

$$\frac{dM_n^S(t)}{dt} = n \cdot M_{n-1}^S(t) - \int_{0}^{t} \lambda(t, \varphi) \cdot \varphi^n \cdot P^S(t, \varphi) \cdot d\varphi +$$

$$+ \int_{0}^{t} \mu(t, \varphi) \cdot \varphi^n \cdot P^F(t, \varphi) \cdot d\varphi - t^n \cdot P^F(t, t) \tag{7.3}$$

Similar calculations are carried out for $M_n^F(t)$. We obtain, because of (4.2b) and (5.6)

$$\frac{dM_n^F(t)}{dt} = t^n \cdot P^F(t, t) + \int_0^t \lambda(t, \varphi) \cdot \varphi^n \cdot P^S(t, \varphi) \cdot d\varphi -$$

$$- \int_0^t \mu(t, \varphi) \cdot \varphi^n \cdot P^F(t, \varphi) \cdot d\varphi \qquad (7.4)$$

Therefore by summing up (7.3) and (7.4), we have the recurrence relation

$$\frac{dM_n(t)}{dt} = n \cdot M_{n-1}^S(t) \qquad (7.5)$$

with the initial conditions $M_n^S(0) = M_n^F(0) = M_n(0) = 0 \ (n = 1, 2, ...)$. Finally, it is immediate to obtain

$$M_0^S(t) = P_s(t) - R(0, t \mid 0) + R(0, t \mid 0) = P_s(t),$$

$$M_0^F(t) = P_f(t),$$

$$M_0(t) = 1 \qquad (7.6)$$

From the previous relations it is also immediate to find

$$\frac{dM_1(t)}{dt} = 1 \cdot P_s(t), \ \text{ or } \ M_1(t) = \int_0^t P_s(u) \cdot du \qquad (7.7)$$

This relation, which has been already anticipated in chapter 2, means that the expectation value of the total on-time in $[0, t)$ is obtained by integrating the pointwise availability $P_s(t)$ from 0 to t.

Equations (7.5) show that in order to obtain the moment $M_n(t)$ one has to know the moment $M_{n-1}^S(t)$. Thus, going backwards, one is led to the need of computing $P^S(t, \varphi)$.

The previous considerations are valid in the most general case, where hazard rates λ and μ depend both on calendar time and accumulated on-time.

However, let us consider briefly the important case where hazard rates depend only upon calendar time t. We have:

$$\frac{dM_n^S(t)}{dt} = n \cdot M_{n-1}^S(t) - \lambda(t) \cdot M_n^S(t) + \mu(t) \cdot M_n^F(t),$$

$$\frac{dM_n^F(t)}{dt} = + \lambda(t) \cdot M_n^S(t) - \mu(t) \cdot M_n^F(t) \qquad (7.8)$$

In this case, owing to the fact that $M_0^S(t) = P_s(t)$ may be deduced directly from the Chapman-Kolmogorov equations, it appears that recurrence relations (7.8) would allow the direct computation of partial moments $M_n^S(t)$ and $M_n^F(t)$ without any explicit knowledge of the p.d.f.'s $P^S(t, \varphi)$ and $P^F(t, \varphi)$.

8. MOMENTS OF MISSION TIME DENSITY FUNCTIONS

Thus far the attention has been focused on the cumulative stochastic process $\{\varphi(t); t \geqslant 0\}$ and its first-order p.d.f.'s. In some circumstances it may be of interest to consider the inverse process $\{t(\varphi); t \geqslant \varphi \geqslant 0\}$ which also results of a cumulative type. In this respect, $P^S(t, \varphi)\,dt$ can be interpreted as the probability that calendar time t is in $[t, t+dt)$, the unit is in its safe state and cumulated on-time reaches the value φ. This, provided that at least one failure has been experienced for $t' \in [0, \varphi]$. In short, $P(t, \varphi)$ might be referred to as mission p.d.f., where mission is given by φ.

If for all $\varphi' \in [0, \varphi]$ and $t > 0$ it is

$$\lambda(t, \varphi') < \infty \quad \text{and} \quad \mu(t, \varphi') > 0 \tag{8.1}$$

the normalization condition holds

$$\int_{\varphi}^{\infty} P^S(t, \varphi)\,dt = 1 - R(0, \varphi \mid 0) \tag{8.2}$$

The form (8.2) recalls closely (4.3c). It is interesting to remark that (8.1) establishes a sufficient prerequisite for the existence of the mission p.d.f. As far as (8.1) is valid, there is always the possibility of defining in correspondence with the two extremes

$$\lambda_* = \max\ \{\lambda(t, \varphi')\} \qquad \text{and} \qquad \mu_* = \min\ \{\mu(t, \varphi')\}$$

$$\varphi' \in [0, \varphi],\ t > 0 \qquad\qquad\qquad \varphi' \in [0, \varphi],\ t > 0$$

a p.d.f. $P^S_*(t, \varphi)$ which would result non-zero for $0 \leqslant \varphi \leqslant t < \infty$. It is also clear that the prerequisite implied by λ_* and μ_* is not less stringent than the one implied by (8.1).

Next is the problem of finding an expression for $\int_{\varphi}^{\infty} P^F(t, \varphi)\,dt$. From equation (5.6) we obtain

$$\int_{\varphi}^{\infty} P^F(t, \varphi)\,dt = \int_{\varphi}^{\infty} \frac{\lambda(t, \varphi)}{\mu(t, \varphi)}\ P^S(t, \varphi)\,dt - \int_{\varphi}^{\infty} \frac{1}{\mu(t, \varphi)}\ \frac{\partial P^F(t, \varphi)}{\partial t}\,dt$$

and after integration by parts

$$\int_{\varphi}^{\infty} P^F(t, \varphi)\,dt = \int_{\varphi}^{\infty} \frac{\lambda(t, \varphi)}{\mu(t, \varphi)}\ P^S(t, \varphi)\,dt + \frac{\lambda(\varphi, \varphi)}{\mu(\varphi, \varphi)}\ R(0, \varphi \mid 0) +$$

$$+ \int_{\varphi}^{\infty} P^F(t, \varphi)\ \frac{\partial}{\partial t}\ \frac{1}{\mu(t, \varphi)}\ dt \tag{8.3}$$

Obviously, we must always admit that restrictions (8.1) are valid. In the case hazard rates depend upon cumulated on-time only, it is

$$\int_{\varphi}^{\infty} P^F(t, \varphi)\,dt = \frac{\lambda(\varphi)}{\mu(\varphi)} \tag{8.4}$$

Let us now consider the moments of the p.d.f. $P^S(t, \varphi)$ and $P^F(t, \varphi)$ along the t co-ordinate (i.e. with φ fixed). We introduce the new symbols

$$M_n^S(\varphi) = \int_\varphi^\infty t^n P^S(t, \varphi)\, dt + \varphi^n R(0, \varphi \mid 0) \tag{8.5a}$$

$$M_n^F(\varphi) = \int_\varphi^\infty t^n P^F(t, \varphi)\, dt \tag{8.5b}$$

and the sum

$$M_n(\varphi) = M_n^S(\varphi) + M_n^F(\varphi) \tag{8.6}$$

where $n = 0, 1, 2, \ldots$ The calculation of $M_n^S(\varphi)$ can be performed in two steps. After differentiation of (8.5a) one has

$$\frac{dM_n^S(\varphi)}{d\varphi} = -\varphi^n P^S(\varphi, \varphi) + \int_\varphi^\infty t^n \frac{\partial P^S(t, \varphi)}{\partial\varphi}\, dt + \frac{d}{d\varphi}[\varphi^n R(0, \varphi \mid 0)]$$

Then by the use of (5.7) one finds the recursive relations

$$\frac{d\, M_n^S(\varphi)}{d\varphi} = n\, M_{n-1}(\varphi) \tag{8.7a}$$

with initial conditions

$$M_n^S(0) = 0 \qquad (n = 1, 2, 3, \ldots) \tag{8.7b}$$

The similarity between equations (8.7a) and (7.5) is apparent. Now one is led to seek an expression for $M_n^F(\varphi)$. It is possible to move from equation (8.3) to obtain:

$$M_n^F(\varphi) = \int_\varphi^\infty \frac{\lambda(t, \varphi)}{\mu(t, \varphi)} t^n P^S(t, \varphi)\, dt + \frac{\lambda(\varphi, \varphi)}{\mu(\varphi, \varphi)} \varphi^n R(0, \varphi \mid 0) +$$

$$+ \int_\varphi^\infty P^F(t, \varphi) \frac{\partial}{\partial t} \frac{t^n}{\mu(t, \varphi)}\, dt \tag{8.8a}$$

with initial conditions

$$M_n^F(0) = \int_0^\infty t^n \lambda(0, 0)\, S(0, t \mid 0)\, dt \tag{8.8b}$$

for $n = 1, 2, 3, \ldots$ Then, in the case hazard rates do not depend upon calendar time, equation (8.8a) would become

$$M_n^F(\varphi) = \frac{\lambda(\varphi)}{\mu(\varphi)} M_n^S(\varphi) + \frac{n}{\mu(\varphi)} M_{n-1}^F(\varphi) \tag{8.9}$$

with $n = 1, 2, 3, \ldots$ Particularly, if hazard rates are constant, it is found $M_0^S(\varphi) = 1$, $M_0^F(\varphi) = \lambda/\mu$, $M_1^S(\varphi) = \varphi(\lambda + \mu)/\mu$, $M_1^F(\varphi) = \lambda[\varphi(\lambda + \mu) + 1]/\mu^2$ and so on.

9. CONCLUSIONS

The treatment of chapters 4 through 8 provides the basis for the consideration and possible solutions of the problem underlying the intensity process (3.1). By following the same line of reasoning which led to equations (5.1 - 5.2), we may write the new set which follows:

$$P^S(N, t, \varphi) = \int_{t-\varphi}^{t} P^F(N-1, y, \varphi - t + y) \cdot \mu(N-1, y, \varphi - t + y) \cdot$$

$$\cdot R(N, y, t \mid \varphi - t + y)\, dy \tag{9.1}$$

$$P^F(N-1, t, \varphi) = \int_{\varphi}^{t} P^S(N-2, y, \varphi) \cdot \lambda(N-2, y, \varphi) \cdot$$

$$\cdot S(N-1, y, t \mid \varphi)\, dy \tag{9.2}$$

where $N = 2, 4, 6, \ldots$ and for $N = 0$

$$P^S(0, t, \varphi) = R(0, 0, t \mid 0)\, \delta(t-\varphi) = R(0, t \mid 0)\, \delta(t-\varphi) \tag{9.3}$$

Symbols have a rather obvious meaning. Particularly, it may be of interest to note the relations $\sum_{N}^{0,2,4\ldots} P^S(N, t, \varphi) = P^S(t, \varphi)$ and $\sum_{N}^{1,3,5\ldots} P^F(N, t, \varphi) = P^F(t, \varphi)$. The set of equations (9.1 - 9.2) would be solved according to a procedure similar to the one which has been followed in chapters 5, 7 and 8 for the case where aging was independent upon the number of transitions.

REFERENCES

1. D.L. Snyder, "Random point processes", J. Wiley and Sons, New York, N.Y. (1975).
2. S. Garribba, G. Reina and G. Volta, "Availability of repairable units when failure and restoration rates age in real time", IEEE Trans. on Reliability, R-25: 88 (1976).
3. A. Bendell and S. Humble, "Operating history and failure and degradation tendencies", IEEE Trans. on Reliability, R-27: 75 (1976).
4. G.W. Parry and D.H. Worledge, "The use of regeneration diagrams to solve component reliability problems, Nucl. Engng. and Design, 45:271 (1978).
5. D.G. Kendall, "On the generalized birth-and-death process", Ann. Math. Statist., 19:1 (1948).
6. L. Takács, "On certain sojourn time problems in the theory of stochastic processes", Acta Math. Acad. Sci. Hung., 8: 169 (1957).
7. B.V. Gnedenko, Yu. K. Belyayev and A.D. Solovyev, "Mathematical methods of reliability theory", Academic Press, New York, N.Y. (1969) (transl. of "Matematicheskiye Metody v Teorii Nadezhnosti", Nauka Press, Moscow (1965)).
8. G.W. Parry and D.H. Worledge, "The downtime distribution in reliability theory", Nucl. Engng. and Design, 49 : 295 (1978).

USE OF MARKOV PROCESSES FOR RELIABILITY PROBLEMS

A. Blin, A. Carnino, J.P. Georgin, J.P. Signoret

C.E.A. - C.E.N. - F A R
DSN/SETS/BEPS
BP n°6   92260 Fontenay-aux-Roses (France)

ABSTRACT

It is not possible to use methods such as fault tree analysis, to assess the reliability or the availability of time-evolutive systems. Stochastic processes have to be used and among them the Markov processes are the most interesting ones.

The basic theory of Markov processes is described in this paper in connection with reliability problems. Then the MARK-GE code developed by the French CEA is presented with an example of reliability assessment of a complex system : AC power supply of a 900 MW PWR.

INTRODUCTION

Methods such as "Fault-tree analysis" do not fit to assess reliability and availability of time-evolutive systems. So, dynamic methods have been developed to deal with this problem and the most interesting ones use stochastic process theory[1,2,3].

Among stochastic processes, the Markov processes are very useful because they can easily deal with a large range of problems appearing in reliability assessments[4].

Markov processes have been developed since the beginning of the 20th century but until 1925 they were only of theoretical interest. Since this time Markov processes have been extensively used to deal with problems ranging from statistical mechanics and queueing processes to ... modern music (Xenakis) !

Of course, Markov processes are currently used to assess reliability and availability of time-evolutive systems. They lead to models very easy to use and fitting very well with reality.

We intend in this paper, using an example, to show how the Markov theory can be introduced and how it can be used in reliability assessments.

A computer code MARK-GE[6] has been developed at the French Commissariat à l'Energie Atomique on the basis of Markov processes and an example of complex system reliability computations[7] is given using the MARK-GE code.

MARKOV PROCESSES THEORY[1,2,3,4]

Practical Example

Markov theory is rather a mathematical one. So, to help understanding we are going to take a very simple example to link theory to physical reality.

Let us consider a system made of 2 running pumps. Only 1 pump is necessary to perform the function and when a pump has failed, repairs start at once. When the repairs are finished the pump is started.

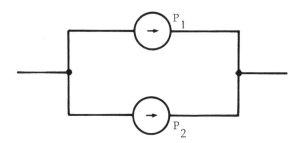

State Space

Each pump has 2 states :

- running state
- failure state

Therefore the whole system has 2x2 = 4 states which can be shown as follows :

For example, state n°2 corresponds to the case where pump n°1 is running and pump n°2 has failed.

The set of the 4 states so-defined is called "State space" of the system :

$$E = \{ 1, 2, 3, 4 \}$$

Probability Space

Now, if we watch the evolution of the system, we shall see the system jumping from one state to another as the time increases. So, we shall obtain a step function $\omega(t)$ like the following figure:

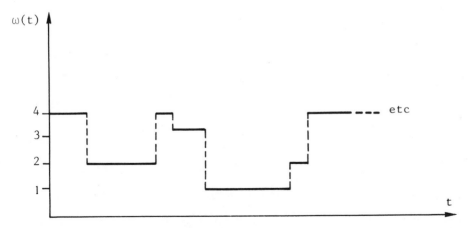

The set of all these step-functions $\omega(t)$ is the set of all the possible evolutions of the system. Each $\omega(t)$ is a possible outcome and is an elementary event for the system time-evolution.

This set of elementary event is called "sample space".

$$\Omega = \{\omega(t)\}_{t \in \mathbb{R}^+}$$

A σ-algebra $\mathbf{a}$ can be associated with Ω which contains all the possible combinations (U,Λ etc...) of elementary events $\omega(t)$.

A probability can be defined on (Ω, a) :

$$P : a \to [\ 0,1\ ] \subset \mathbb{R}^+$$

Then, (Ω, a, P) is a "Probability space".

This probability space is the mathematical frame into which our reliability studies will be performed.

Stochastic Processes

For each $\omega \epsilon \Omega$ and $t \epsilon \mathbb{R}^+$, let $X_t(\omega)$ be an element of the state space E.

1°/ <u>For a fixed value t of the time.</u>

$$\Omega \xrightarrow{\quad X_t \quad} E$$

$$\omega \longmapsto X_t(\omega)$$

$X_t(\omega)$ is a "random variable" taking values in E. Then for the example $X_t(\omega)$ = 1, 2, 3 or 4.

The collection of all these random variables when the time spreads from 0 to infinity is called : "Stochastic process".

$$X = \{X_t \ ; \ t \epsilon \mathbb{R}^+\}$$

The stochastic process X has a continuous time parameter and a state space E.

2°/ <u>For a fixed outcome ω</u>

$$\mathbb{R}^+ \xrightarrow{\quad X_t \quad} E$$

$$t \longmapsto X_t(\omega)$$

This function is called "sample path" ; it is the evolution of the system along the time for a given outcome ω.

Connection with Reliability Assessment

If we want to calculate the availability of the system given as example, we have to calculate the probability that the system is in the states n°2, 3 or 4 at the time t.

So : $A(t) = P(\omega/X_t(\omega) = 2, 3, 4)$

With a more simple notation we have :

$$A(t) = P(X_t = 2, 3, 4)$$

In the same way, unavailability is given by :

$$I(t) = P(X_t = 1)$$

If now, we want to calculate the reliability of the system, we have only to take into account the outcomes which have never been in the state n°1 which is the system failure before the time t :

Then ; $R(t) = P(X_t = 2, 3, 4/X_u \neq 1, \; u \leq t)$.

All these considerations show that stochastic processes are very interesting to use for reliability and availability calculations.

Markov Processes

Let us suppose we have watched the system evolution until time t and we now want to predict the future evolution since this time t. If this future evolution depends only on the state at time t and not at all on the past history before t, the stochastic process is a "Markov process" :

$X = \{X_t \; ; \; t \in \mathbb{R}^+\}$ $\Updownarrow$ is a Markov process

$$P(X_{t+s} = j/X_u, \; u \leq t) = P(X_{t+s} = j/X_t)$$

In addition, if this probability depends only on s but not on t, the Markov process is "time-homogeneous".

$X = \{X_t \; ; \; t \in \mathbb{R}^+\}$ is a time-homogeneous Markov process (or more simply "homogeneous Markov process)

$$P(X_{t+s} = j/X_t = i) = P(X_s = j/X_o = i) = P_s(i,j).$$

The probability to jump from i to j in a time s depends on i and s but not on the way state n°i has been reached before.

$P_s(i,j)$ is called "transition function" of the Markov process.

For our example, homogeneous Markov process can be used if the pump failure and repair rates are constant. This need will be shown later. From now we are going to work only with homogeneous Markov processes.

Sojourn Intervals

At time time t, the system is in a given state ; it stays there for a random time W_t before jumping to another state.

W_t is defined by :

$$W_t(\omega) = \inf \{ S > 0 / X_{t+s}(\omega) \neq X_t(\omega) \}$$

The cumulative distribution function of W_t is :

$$F(V) = P(W_t \leq V / X_t = i)$$

(we suppose here that the system is in state n°i at the time t).

We can define : $\overline{F}(V) = 1 - F(V) = P(W_t > V / X_t = i)$

The event $\{W_t > u+V\}$ is equal to the event $\{W_t > u, W_{t+u} > V\}$

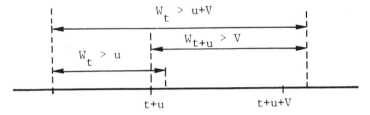

Let us put down : $A = \{W_t > u\}$; $B = \{W_{t+u} > V\}$; $C = \{X_t = i\}$

Therefore : $\overline{F}(u + V) = P(A\ B / C) = \dfrac{P(A\ B\ C)}{P(C)}$

$$= \frac{P(AC)}{P(C)} \cdot \frac{P(ABC)}{P(AC)} = P(A/C) \cdot P(B/AC)$$

$P(A/C) = P(W_t > u / X_t = i) = \overline{F}(u)$

$P(B/AC) = P(W_{t+u} > V / W_t > u, X_t = i)$

but $\{W_t > u, X_t = i\} = \{X_{t+u} = i\}$

then : $P(B/AC) = P(W_{t+u} > V / X_{t+u} = i) = \overline{F}(V)$

and : $\overline{F}(u+V) = \overline{F}(u) . \overline{F}(V)$

This implies that $\overline{F}(u)$ is an exponential law with a constant parameter $\lambda(i)$ which depends only on the state i.

$$\overline{F}(u) = e^{-\lambda(i)u} \quad \Longleftrightarrow \quad F(u) = 1 - e^{-\lambda(i)u}$$

In an homogeneous Markov process, the sojourn intervals are random variables with exponential laws. This shows why constant failure and repair rates are needed for using a Markov process to assess our example.

States Nature

Absorbing states : $\lambda(i) = 0$; if i is an absorbing state it is impossible to jump from it to another state. When i is reached the system stays there indefinitely.

Stable states : $0 < \lambda(i) < \infty$; if i is a stable state the system will jump to another state after a finite time.

Instantaneous states : $\lambda(i) = \infty$; if i is an instantaneous state it is impossible to stay herein. Instantaneous states occur only when the state space is not finite, so there are no instantaneous states in reliability calculation.

In availability calculation, all the states are stable ; in reliability calculation, absorbing states are needed.

Markov Chain

The system jumps from state to state as the time increases. We can define :

T_n : time of the n th jump

$Y_n = X(T_n)$: state of the system at the n th jump.

The collection of the random variables $\{Y_n ; n \in \mathbb{N}\}$ is a stochastic process with a discrete time parameter. It is called the "Markov chain" associated with the previous Markov process.

The sojourn intervals are given by :

$$T_{n+1} - T_n = W_{T_n}$$

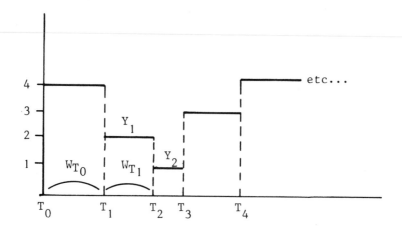

It is now interesting to calculate the probability to jump from state i to state j with a sojourn interval higher than a given value u. That is to say :

$$P(Y_{n+1} = j, \quad W_{T_n} > u \; / \; Y_n = i)$$

In the same way as previously using $P(AB/C)$, it is possible to write this probability :

$$P(Y_{n+1} = j/Y_n = i) . \; P(W_{T_n} > u \; / \; Y_{n+1} = j, \; Y_n = i)$$

Because the process is time homogeneous, we have :

$$P(Y_{n+1} = j/Y_n = i) = P(Y_1 = j/Y_0 = i) = Q(i,j)$$

Because the future cannot interfere with the present, we have :

$$P(W_{T_n} > u/Y_{n+1} = j, \; Y_n = i) = P(W_{T_n} > u/Y_n = i) = e^{-\lambda(i)u}$$

Then :

$$P(Y_{n+1} = j, \; W_{T_n} > u/Y_n = i) = Q(i,j) \; e^{-\lambda(i)u}$$

This implies :

$$P(Y_{n+1} = j, \; W_{T_n} \leqslant u/Y_n = i) = Q(i,j) \left[1 - e^{-\lambda(i)u} \right]$$

It is easy to interprete this last result. Being in state n°i, an exponential random time is awaited before jumping. When the jump occurs, there is the probability $Q(i,j)$ that the next state is j.

Q(i,j) is called the "transition matrix" of the Markov chain Y.

Generator and Basic Equations

Generally, we know the initial state of the system or the pro-bability to be in a given state at time $t = 0$ and it is interesting to evaluate at $t > 0$ the probability of being in a given state. So, we want to calculate :

$$P(X_t = j/X_o = i) = P_i(X_t = j) = P_t(i,j)$$

Let T_1 be the time of the first jump. Two cases have to be considered :

$$T_1 > t$$

$$T_1 \leqslant t$$

In the first case, no jump occurs before t and the system stays in the initial state i.

In the second case, one jump at least occurs before the time t.

We can write :

$$P_t(i,j) = P_i(X_t = j, T_1 > t) + P_i(X_t = j, T_1 \leqslant t)$$

- If $T_1 > t$, then $X_t = X_o = i$

$$P_i(X_t = j, T_1 > t) = I(i,j) \ e^{-\lambda(i)t}$$

$$\text{where} \quad I(i,j) = \begin{cases} o & \text{if} \quad i \neq j \\ 1 & \text{if} \quad i = j \end{cases}$$

- If $T_1 \leqslant t$:

If Y_1 is the state of the system after the first jump, this knowledge is enough to calculate the probability to be in state j at the time t ; that is a duration $t-T_1$ further.

$$P_i \ (X_t = j/Y_1, \ T_1) = P_{t-T_1} (Y_1, \ j)$$

If s is the time of the first jump, the probability to jump from i to another state between s and s+ds is :

$$d \ (1 - e^{-\lambda(i)s}) \ = \ \lambda(i) \ e^{-\lambda(i)s} \ ds$$

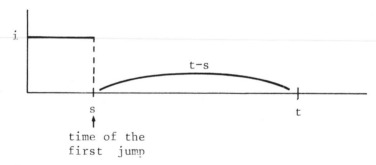

time of the
first jump

When the jump occurs, there is the probability $Q(i,k)$ that the next state is k. Then, the probability to be in state n°j at the time t is :

$$P_{t-s} (k,j) = P_k(X_{t-s} = j).$$

Gathering all these results yields :

$$P_i(X_t = j, T_1 \leq t) = \int_0^t \lambda(i)e^{-\lambda(i)s} \sum_k Q(i,k)P_k(X_{t-s}= j) \, ds$$

and the whole formula :

$$P_t(i,j)=I(i,j)e^{-\lambda(i)t} + \int_0^t \lambda(i)e^{-\lambda(i)s} \sum_k Q(i,k)P_k(X_{t-s}= j) \, ds$$

Making the change of variable $u = t - s$ and derivating, we obtain :

$$\frac{d}{dt} P_t(i,j) = \sum_k \left[-\lambda(i) I(i,k) + \lambda(i) Q(i,k) \right] P_t(k,j).$$

We can write :

$$\frac{d}{dt} P_t(i,j) = \sum_k A(i,k) P_t(k,j)$$

where :

$$A(i,k) = \begin{cases} -\lambda(i) & i = k \\ \lambda(i)Q(i,k) & i \neq k \end{cases}$$

The matrix $A(i,k)$ is called "generator" of the Markov process.

To use the above equation in computer codes, it is interesting to alter it.

$$P(X_t = i) = \sum_k P(X_t = i/X_0 = k) \cdot P(X_0 = k)$$

Let $\pi_t(i) = P(X_t = i)$ be the probability to be in state n°i at time t.

Therefore :

$$\pi_t(i) = \sum_k P_t(k,i) \; \pi_o(k)$$

$$\frac{d}{dt} \pi_t(i) = \sum_k \pi_o(k) \frac{d}{dt} P_t(k,i)$$

$$= \sum_k \pi_o(k) \sum_j P_t(k,j) A(j,i)$$

$$= \sum_j A(j,i) \sum_k \pi_o(k) P_t(k,j)$$

$$= \sum_j A(j,i) \pi_t(j)$$

This result can be put into the following matrix form :

$$\frac{d}{dt} \pi_t = \pi_t A$$

Or, using the transpose matrix of A :

$$\frac{d}{dt} \pi_t = {}^tA \; \pi_t$$

This last equation will be used in computer codes.

Necessity of Elementary Exponential Laws

Let us suppose that the system is in state n°i. In our example, independent phenomena make the system jump out to another state at random times.

Let T_{ij} be the random time after which the system could jump from i to j. It is obvious that the real time of jumping T_i will be the lowest T_{ij}.

Then : $T_i = \inf_j (T_{ij})$

But, we have shown :

$$P(T_i > t) = e^{-\lambda(i)t}$$

This implies that the random variables T_{ij} have exponential laws. That can be shown with 2 independent phenomena which could make the system jump from state n°1 to state n°2 and 3.

$$T_1 = \inf(T_{12}, T_{13})$$

Let f and g be the probability density functions of T_{12} and T_{13}

$$\begin{cases} P(T_{12} > t) = \overline{F}(t) = \int_t^\infty f(u)\,du \\[2ex] P(T_{13} > t) = \overline{G}(t) = \int_t^\infty g(u)\,du \\[2ex] P(T_1 > t) = \overline{R}(t) = e^{-\lambda(i)t} \end{cases}$$

$$P(T_1 > t) = P(T_{12} > t,\, T_{13} > T_{12}) + P(T_{13} > t,\, T_{12} > T_{13})$$

$$= \int_t^\infty f(u)\,\overline{G}(u)\,du \qquad + \int_t^\infty g(u)\,\overline{F}(u)\,du$$

$$= \int d(\overline{F}.\overline{G})$$

$$= \overline{F}(t).\overline{G}(t)$$

Then : $\overline{R}(t) = \overline{F}(t)\,\overline{G}(t)$

But, $\overline{R}(t)$ is an exponential law, therefore :

$$\overline{R}(t+s) = \overline{R}(t).\overline{R}(s) = \overline{F}(t).\overline{G}(t).\overline{F}(s).\overline{G}(s)$$

$$= \overline{F}(t+s)\,\overline{G}(t+s)$$

$\overline{F}$ and $\overline{G}$ being independent, this equation implies :

$$\overline{F}(t+s) = \overline{F}(t)\,\overline{F}(s)$$

$$\overline{G}(t+s) = \overline{G}(t)\,\overline{G}(s)$$

$\overline{F}$ and $\overline{G}$ have to be exponential laws if $\overline{R}$ is an exponential law. This result can be generalized and we have :

$$\lambda(i) = \sum_j \lambda_{ij}$$

Each λ_{ij} is the constant parameter of an exponential law corresponding to a given phenomenon.

For our example, the system jumps are due to failure and repair of the pumps. So, the failure and repair rates have to be constant if we want to use the Markov process theory to assess system reliability.

To summarize, Markov model can be used to assess system reliability only if elementary phenomena which can occur have exponential laws.

Generator Determination

Considering again the previous example :

Let λ_1 and λ_2 be the constant failure rates of each pump

Let μ_1 and μ_2 be the constant repair rates of each pump

Let D_1 and D_2 be the running durations of each pump

Let R_1 and R_2 be the repair durations of each pump

We have seen :

$$A(i,j) = \begin{cases} -\lambda(i) & i = j \\ \lambda(i)\, Q(i,j) & i \neq j \end{cases}$$

$\underline{A(1,1)\ determination}$: $\lambda(1)$ determines the transition from the state 1 to either state 2 or 3 by repairing the failed pumps.

The system jumps out of the state n°1 at $T = \inf(R_1, R_2)$

$$P(T \leq t) = 1 - e^{-\lambda(1)t} = 1 - e^{-(\mu_1 + \mu_2)t}$$

Then :

$$\lambda(1) = \mu_1 + \mu_2$$
$$A(1,1) = -(\mu_1 + \mu_2)$$

In the same way, we obtain :

$$\lambda(2) = \mu_2 + \lambda_1$$
$$A(2,2) = -(\mu_2 + \lambda_1)$$
$$\lambda(3) = \mu_1 + \lambda_2$$
$$A(3,3) = -(\mu_1 + \lambda_2)$$
$$\lambda(4) = \lambda_1 + \lambda_2$$
$$A(4,4) = -(\lambda_1 + \lambda_2)$$

$\underline{A(1,2)\ determination}$:
$$A(1,2) = \lambda(1)\, Q(1,2)$$

Q(1,2) is the probability to jump from 1 to 2 when the jump occurs. This occurs only if the jump from 1 to 3 has not taken place before, so :

$$Q(1,2) = P(R_1 < R_2)$$

$$Q(1,2) = \int_0^\infty \mu_1 \, e^{-\mu_1 u} \, e^{-\mu_2 u} \, du = \frac{\mu_1}{\mu_1 + \mu_2} = \frac{\mu_1}{\lambda(1)}$$

Then : $A(1,2) = \mu_1$

In the same way, we find :

$$A(1,3) = \mu_2$$

$$A(2,1) = \lambda_1$$

$$\vdots$$

etc

$$\vdots$$

Finally, we obtain :

$$A(i,j) = \begin{bmatrix} -(\mu_1 + \mu_2) & \mu_1 & \mu_2 & 0 \\ \lambda_1 & -(\mu_2 + \lambda_1) & 0 & \mu_2 \\ \lambda_2 & 0 & -(\lambda_2 + \mu_1) & \mu_1 \\ 0 & \lambda_2 & \lambda_1 & -(\lambda_1 + \lambda_2) \end{bmatrix}$$

The sum of the elements of each row is zero. This is a feature of a Markov matrix.

This matrix deals with the form :

$$\frac{d}{dt} \pi_t = \pi_t \, A$$

that is :

$$(\ldots \frac{d}{dt} \pi_t \ldots) = (\ldots \pi_t \ldots) \begin{pmatrix} A \end{pmatrix}$$

If we want to use the alternative formula :

$$\frac{d}{dt} \pi_t = {}^t A \, \pi_t = M \, \pi_t$$

that is :

$$\left[\begin{array}{c} \vdots \\ \dfrac{d}{dt}\,\pi_t \\ \vdots \end{array} \right] = (^t A) \left[\begin{array}{c} \vdots \\ \pi_t \\ \vdots \end{array} \right]$$

We have to transpose the matrix A :

$$M = {}^t A = \begin{bmatrix} -(\mu_1 + \mu_2) & \lambda_1 & \lambda_2 & 0 \\ \mu_1 & -(\mu_2 + \lambda_1) & 0 & \lambda_2 \\ \mu_2 & 0 & -(\lambda_2 + \mu_1) & \lambda_{1.} \\ 0 & \mu_2 & \mu_1 & -(\lambda_1 + \lambda_2) \end{bmatrix}$$

Markov Diagrams

What is important in order to describe the Markov process is in fact the elementary parameters of the exponential laws. This leads to a graphic description called "Markov diagram".

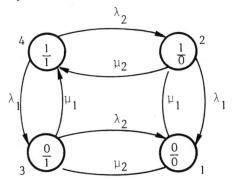

The whole information is contained in such a diagram :

- all the possible states of the system
- all the possibilities of jumping (transition) from a state to another one.

This diagram allows one to find directly the matrix A. As it is normally used on its transposed form, to avoid any ambiguity we are going to use the following notation :

$a_{i \leftarrow j}$: transition from j to i. This element is in i th row
        j th column.

Using the diagram, it is easy to determine each $a_{i \leftarrow j}$.

$\underline{a_{i \leftarrow i}}$, $a_{i \leftarrow i}$ is equal to the sum with the minus sign
                    of all the arrows leaving state n°i.

                    For example $a_{4 \leftarrow 4} = - (\lambda_1 + \lambda_2)$

$\underline{a_{i \leftarrow j}, \quad i \neq j}$

                    $a_{i \leftarrow j}$ is equal to the value of the arrow going
                         from j to i.

                    For example $a_{2 \leftarrow 1} = \mu_1$.

Then, it is very easy do draw the Markov diagram and to determine
the matrix A without any knowledge of the Markov theory.

Availability and Reliability Assessment

To assess system availability, all the possible evolutions of
the system have to be taken into account, so, the above Markov diagram can be used without any modifications.

To assess system reliability, only the possible evolutions of
the system which never reach the state of failure have to be taken
into account. Then, we have to remove all the evolutions which after
reaching the failure state, have jumped again to a running state.
To achieve this, it is necessary to prevent the system from jumping
from the failure state when reached. Proceeding this way, we shall
find the probability to be in a running state without having passed
through the failure state, that is the system reliability.

So, we have to put the failure state into an absorbing state.
This is very easy by removing the arrows, in order to prevent the
system to jump out of this state.

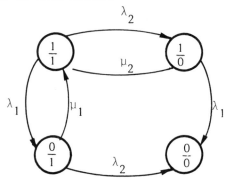

This implies the next matrix :

$$
(a_{i \leftarrow j}) = \begin{bmatrix} 0 & \lambda_1 & \lambda_2 & 0 \\ 0 & -(\mu_2+\lambda_1) & 0 & \lambda_2 \\ 0 & 0 & -(\mu_1+\lambda_2) & \lambda_1 \\ 0 & \mu_2 & \mu_1 & -(\lambda_1+\lambda_2) \end{bmatrix}
$$

The column of zeros is characteristic of the absorbing state.

COMPUTER CODE MARK-GE[6]

Homogeneous Markov processes results can be used to realize computer codes. The computer code called MARK-GE has been developed on these bases by the French C.E.A. in order to assess reliability and availability of dynamic systems.

The dynamic system behaviour is described, as we have shown it, by the following equation :

$$
\frac{d}{dt} \pi_t = M \pi_t
$$

$\frac{d}{dt} \pi_t$ and π_t are column vectors and M is the matrix A in its transposed form.

This equation is classically resolved by :

$$
\pi_t = e^{Mt} \pi_o
$$

π_o is the initial conditions vector which contains the probabilities to be in any state i at time t = 0.

π_t is the vector of the system states at time t.

If the matrix M is diagonalizable, we have :

$$
M = B.\ D.\ B^{-1}
$$

with :

D = diagonal matrix found by determinating eigenvalues of M.

B = matrix of corresponding eigenvectors.

Then $\pi_t = B.\ e^{Dt}.\ B^{-1} \pi_o$

This last equation is used in MARK-GE code to compute the probability to be in each state at time t.

The inputs of the code are :

M   : Matrix corresponding to the Markov diagram of the studied system.

π_o : Initial conditions.

T_1, T_2... T_n : Values of the time for which a computation is wanted.

The outputs of the code are the probabilities to be in each state at the times T_i. So, by combining these probabilities, it is very easy to calculate reliability (or unreliability) and availability (or unavailability) depending on the problem.

The maximum number of states is currently 30 but it could easily be increased to 100. The maximum number of time values is also currently fixed to 30.

LOSS OF AC POWER SUPPLY OF A NUCLEAR REACTOR[7]

A typical problem for which Markov theory can be used is AC power supply reliability assessment of nuclear reactors. We have used it, with the MARK-GE code, in the case of AC power supply of a 900 MW PWR.

AC Power Supply

The electrical supply of a 900 MW PWR is shown in figure n°1. There are 2 offsite power sources, the main one and the auxiliary one, and 2 onsite power generators (diesels).

During normal operation of the plant, offsite power sources are used and onsite diesels are in stand-by position. If the loss of the offsite sources occurs, then the 2 diesels are automatically started.

The 4 power sources are redundant and each can take the whole load of the plant thus, the AC power supply of the plant is available if at least one of the 4 sources is available.

After a preliminary analysis, the detailed AC power scheme has been reduced to the following equivalent scheme which is very simple:

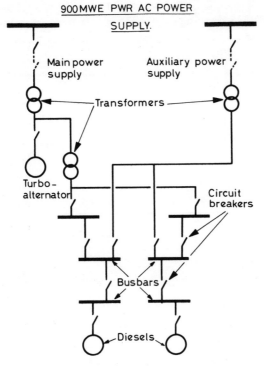

Figure 1.   900 MWE Pwr AC Power Supply.

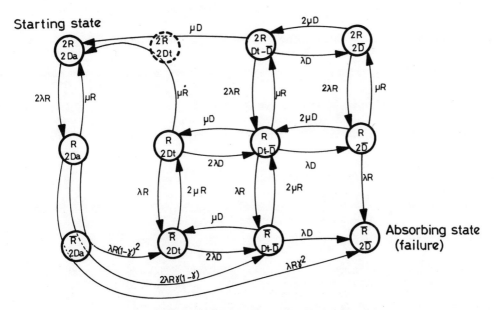

Figure 2.   Reliability Markov Diagram.

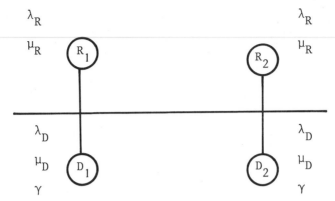

R$_1$: Main offsite power source.

R$_2$: Auxiliary offsite power source.

D$_1$, D$_2$: Onsite diesel generators.

In R$_1$ we have included transformers, switches and bus bars, so λ_R is an equivalent failure rate and μ_D an equivalent repair rate. As R$_2$ is very close to R$_1$ we use the same parameters λ_R and μ_R for R$_2$.

When a diesel is running, its failure rate is λ_D ; when it has failed, its repair rate is μ_D ; when a stand-by diesel is started, there is a probability that it fails, this probability not to start on demand is γ.

The calculation of these parameters has given :

$$\begin{cases} \lambda_R = 1.2 \times 10^{-4} \ h^{-1} \\ \mu_R = 6 \quad \times 10^{-2} \ h^{-1} \end{cases} \quad \text{offsite power sources}$$

$$\begin{cases} \lambda_D = 7 \quad \times 10^{-4} \ h^{-1} \\ \mu_D = 6 \quad \times 10^{-3} \ h^{-1} \\ \gamma = 3 \quad \times 10^{-2} \end{cases} \quad \text{onsite power sources}$$

Reliability Study

It is now possible to draw the Markov diagram corresponding to the AC power supply reliability. It is shown in figure n°2.

We have the notations :

   2R :   2 offsite power sources available.

   R   :   only 1 offsite power source available.

   $\overline{R}$:   0 offsite power source available.

   D_a :   Stand-by diesel.

   D_t :   Running diesel.

   $\overline{D}$:   Failed diesel.

The starting state is $2R-2D_a$ because the 2 AC power sources are available and then the two diesel generators are in stand-by position.

The failure state is $\overline{R} - 2\overline{D}$ because the 4 electrical power sources have failed. Since we want to assess the system reliability, we have put this state into an absorbing state.

There are 2 states which cannot actually exist, $\overline{R} - 2D_a$ and $2R - 2D_t$; we have called them "transparent states".

When the second offsite power source fails, the system jumps to the state $\overline{R} - 2D_a$ but it cannot stay there because the diesels are immediately started. There is at once a jump either to the state $\overline{R} - 2D_t$ with the probability $(1 - \gamma)^2$, or to the state $\overline{R} - D_t - \overline{D}$ with the probability $2\gamma(1-\gamma)$ or to the absorbing state with the probability γ^2 depending on the number of diesels which have not failed to start.

When the system jumps to the state $2R - D_t$, it cannot stay there because the diesels are stopped immediately.

Therefore, the Markov diagram has 10 different states to be taken into account.

Because of the absorbing state, this Markov diagram leads to assess the system reliability.

IV.2 - Common cause failures study

In the previous reliability study, we have not taken into account the common cause failures which could occur on the offsite power sources.

When common cause failure occurs, both the main and the auxiliary power sources fail. We have to introduce the following new parameters :

λ_{RMC} : Common cause failure rate

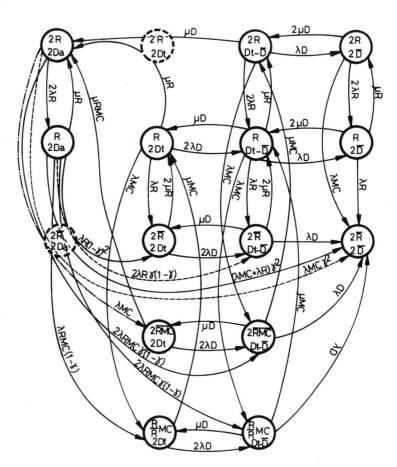

Figure 3.   Common Cause Failure Markov Diagram.

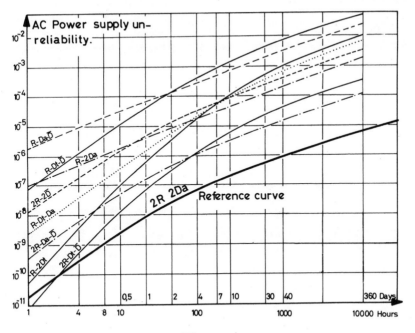

Figure 4

TIME (hours)		1	4	12	168 Week	1000	8 760 Year
λRMC	10^{-8} h^{-1}	$2.0\,10^{-11}$	$20\,10^{-10}$	$1.5\,10^{-9}$	$8.0\,10^{-8}$	$5.3\,10^{-7}$	$4.7\,10^{-6}$
	10^{-7} h^{-1}	$1.0\,10^{-10}$	$5.3\,10^{-10}$	$2.5\,10^{-9}$	$9.4\,10^{-8}$	$6.1\,10^{-7}$	$5.5\,10^{-6}$
	10^{-6} h^{-1}	$9.2\,10^{-10}$	$8.7\,10^{-9}$	$1.2\,10^{-8}$	$2.3\,10^{-7}$	$1.4\,10^{-6}$	$1.2\,10^{-5}$
Without common cause failure.		$1.1\,10^{-11}$	$1.7\,10^{-10}$	$1.4\,10^{-9}$	$7.9\,10^{-8}$	$5.2\,10^{-7}$	$4.7\,10^{-6}$

Figure 5.   Common Cause Failure Sensitivity Study.

μ_{RMC} :   Common cause repair rate.

The previous Markov diagram has to be modified to take into account the offsite common cause failure and new states are needed to describe the system behaviour. This is shown in figure n°3.

We have the following notations :

2 $\overline{R}_{MC}$:   the 2 offsite power sources have failed because of the common cause failure.

$\frac{R}{R}$ MC :   One offsite power source has failed before the common cause failure occurs failing the second offsite power source.

The diagram taking into account common mode failures seems quite complex, but in fact is not very difficult to achieve.

Computing this Markov diagram gives the system reliability when common cause failure can occur on offsite power sources.

In the same way, any kind of common cause failures could be taken into account by building the corresponding Markov diagram.

Results

Many results can be found from such a study. Figure n°4 shows some of them.

The reference curve gives the system reliability in terms of the time. The other curves have been drawn in the case of one or several power sources being definitely lost. For example the curve 2R - D_t - $\overline{D}$ means that one diesel is lost without any possibility of repair. With this kind of curve the influence of the loss of each power source is clearly brought to light.

When a parameter is not very accurately known, it is very easy to perform sensibility studies. In particular, that is the case of common cause failures for which we have looked for the minimum value under which they can be neglected (figure n°5).

As the computation time is very short it is possible to perform many calculations in order to realize very detailed analysis of the system reliability.

APPROXIMATIONS[5]

The AC power supply study has needed some approximations to be achieved. In fact that is the same for all complex systems. If the number of states is too high, the matrix M becomes too large and computation problems appear. To cope with these computation problems, it is necessary to reduce the number of states to be taken into account by using approximations.

A way to reduce the number of states is the calculation of equivalent failure and repair rates for some subsystems.

We can, for example, replace a series subsystem of n components by an equivalent single component with the following parameters :

$$\lambda = \sum_i \lambda_i$$

$$\mu = \lambda / (\sum_i \frac{\lambda_i}{\mu_i})$$

In the same way, we have for a parallel subsystem of n components :

$$\lambda = (\pi_i \frac{\lambda_i}{\mu_i}) (\sum_i \mu_i)$$

$$\mu = \sum_i \mu_i$$

Therefore, it is possible to reduce drastically the number of states used in the Markov diagram. These approximations are very accurate and lead to a good assessment of the system reliability.

CONCLUSION

Most of the practical reliability assessment problems can be approached by the Markov processes. Markov processes are very easy to use when the number of states is not too big, otherwise approximations are needed.

However, when the failure rates and mainly the repair rates cannot be considered as constant, Markov processes are not very suitable and other stochastic processes should be used[5] such as, for example, semi-Markov processes. These ones can be defined, after[1], as : "a system which moves from one state to another with random sojourn times in between ; the successive states visited form a Markov chain, and a sojourn time has a distribution which depends on the state being visited as well as the next state to be entered". Remark that "such a process becomes a Markov process if the distributions of the sojourn times are all exponential independant of the next state". Until these new models have been developed further, no doubt Markov processes will still help reliability engineers.

LIST OF MAIN SYMBOLS

E	: State space	$\mathbb{R}^+$	: Set of positive numbers
$\omega(t)$	: Step function	$i,j\ldots$	: States
Ω	: Sample space	W_t	: Sojourn interval
P	: Probability function	F	: c.d.f. of W_t
$X_t(\omega)$	Random variable	$\lambda(i)$	: Transition rate
X	: Stochastic process	$A(i,k)$	: Markov process generator
$A(t)$	: System availability	λ_i	: Failure rate
$I(t)$	: System unavailability	μ_i	: Repair rate
$R(t)$	: System reliability	M	: t_A

REFERENCES

1. E. Cinlar, Introduction to stochastic processes Prentice hall, Inc. (1975).
2. M. Girault, Processus aléatoires. Dunod (1965).
3. B. Gnédenko, Y. Béliaev, A. Soloviev, Méthodes Mathématiques en théorie de la fiabilité. Editions de Moscou (1972).
4. M. Corazza, Techniques mathématiques de la fiabilité prévisionnelle. Cepadues Edition (1975).
5. M. Gondran, A. Pages, Evaluation de la fiabilité des systèmes, Eyrolles, (to be published).
6. A. Blin, Notice de présentation et d'utilisation du programme MARK-GE. Note Technique SETSSR n°236 (1978), (available from Département de Sûreté Nucléaire, C.E.N. Fontenay-aux-Roses B.P. 6, 92260 France).
7. J.F. Greppo, M. Boursier, A. Carnino, A. Blin, Détermination par une approche probabiliste, d'une règle d'exploitation des alimentations de 6,6 kV des réacteurs à eau sous pression (tranches 900 MWe). Paper I.A.E.A., SM-195/11, Vienna (1975).

SOME CONSIDERATIONS ON THE MARKOV APPROACH TO RELIABILITY

Roberto SOMMA

Selenia S.p.A.

Via Tiburtina km. 12.400, Roma, Italy

ABSTRACT: The dimension of the transition rate matrix is a big problem in solving reliability problems using the Markov approach; this limitation can be partially overcome by using the sparsity and structure properties of this matrix, the problem is presented in the first part of this paper. The second part is a brief outline of a computer program to solve automatically the stationary Markov description of systems. The third part contains a discussion about what is the system behaviour described by a non stationary Markov process.

1. INTRODUCTION

Markov processes, introduced at the beginning of this century by the Russian mathematician A.A.Markov, are a well known approach to face and solve system reliability problems.
The basic theory of Markov processes is contained in a number of classical texts dealing with stochastic processes, e.g. [1],[2],[3]; a presentation in terms of system theory has been performed by the author and his colleagues, it is contained in [4].

A basic question arises when one tries to solve a problem by using a Markov approach; namely: is the problem under consideration suitably described by a Markov model? To answer this question is the purpose of the third
part of this paper.

Once that the suitability of the Markov model has been decided, one obtains
a mathematical model to   solve. This model is represented by a set
of first order linear differential equations (one for each system state), so
one has to face the problem of system complexity, i.e. the problem of the
dimension of the equation set. The use of a computer appears as the only
way for the solution.

The problem of dimension and some suggestions to face it are discussed in
the first part of this contribution, while the second part is devoted to the
description of a computer program.

2.   THE PROBLEM OF THE DIMENSION

If a problem is described in terms of a stationary Markov process, its solution is found by solving the following stationary differential equation
(basic equation):

$$\dot{\underline{p}}(t) = \Lambda \, \underline{p}(t) \quad , \qquad (2.1)$$

where Λ is the well known <u>transition rate matrix</u>, i.e. its general entry
λ_{ij} is the transition (failure or repair) rate of the component whose change
causes the system transition   from state $\underline{s}_j$ to state $\underline{s}_i$.
A big problem is represented by the system complexity, which reflects on
the equation set dimension, N. It is well known, in fact, that the number
of states for a system of n two-states components is given by:

$$N = 2^n \quad , \qquad (2.2)$$

and that the transition rate matrix is a NxN matrix.

For example if n=10, the possible system states are N=1024 and the transition rate matrix entries are NxN=1048576.

To handle such a quantity of data one can look at two characteristics of
Λ , namely its sparsity and its structure.

Let us examine these two properties:

a) Sparsity.

   This property refers to the number of non-zero entries of Λ .

With a single transition the system can pass from a state to another state
that differs for the condition of only one component. Thus, for an n-com-
ponent system the possible one-step transitions are n; there is, of course,
the possibility of remaining in the starting state, then the transition
rates are (n+1) for each state, for a total of:

$$2^n(n+1) \qquad\qquad (2.3)$$

non-zero entries in the Λ matrix.

The case of eq.(2.3) refers to the situation in which any possible transition is allowed, i.e. the case in which availability evaluation with multiple repair on-line is concerned. The above is the case in which Λ matrix
is the less empty.

The most empty case is that in which reliability without maintenance is
concerned. It is easy to show that this case corresponds to a lower tri-
angular Λ matrix, having:

$$2^{n-1}(n+2) - 1 \qquad\qquad (2.4)$$

non-zero entries.

For a 10-components system eq.s (2.3) and (2.4) give respectively
11264 and 6143 non-zero entries instead of 1048576.

These figures show what is the possible saving in computer storage.

b) Structure [5].

This property refers to the knowledge of the position of the non-zero entries.

The structural property of the transition rate matrix can be evidentiated
by adopting the following system states identification method:
let us associate to any system state the decimal number which is the complement to 2^n of the decimal number corresponding to the binary number
giving the state representation; i.e. if for a 3-components system a
state is:

$$1\ 0\ 1\ =\ 5 \quad,$$

the state number is:

$$2^3 - 5 = 3 \quad,$$

then:

$$\underline{s}_3 = 1\ 0\ 1 \ .$$

The application of this rule to a 3-components system gives the following
system states table:

Tab.1: States for a System of
3 components

State	Decimal	C	B	A
s_1	7	1	1	1
s_2	6	1	1	0
s_3	5	1	0	1
s_4	4	1	0	0
s_5	3	0	1	1
s_6	2	0	1	0
s_7	1	0	0	1
s_8	0	0	0	0

The corresponding transition rate matrix for the multiple repair availability evaluation is:

$$
\begin{bmatrix}
-\Sigma_1 & \mu_A & \mu_B & & \mu_C & & & \\
\lambda_A & -\Sigma_2 & & \mu_B & & \mu_C & & \\
\lambda_B & & -\Sigma_3 & \mu_A & & & \mu_C & \\
& \lambda_B & \lambda_A & -\Sigma_4 & & & & \mu_C \\
\lambda_C & & & & -\Sigma_5 & \mu_A & \mu_B & \\
& \lambda_C & & & \lambda_A & -\Sigma_6 & & \mu_B \\
& & \lambda_C & & \lambda_B & & -\Sigma_7 & \mu_A \\
& & & \lambda_C & & \lambda_B & \lambda_A & -\Sigma_8
\end{bmatrix}
$$

where the main diagonal entry $-\Sigma_i$ is the opposite of the sum of the same column entries.

The above structure is general as can be noted observing that each state s_{-2k} differs from the s_{-2k-1} (k=1, 2, ...) only in the last component and this creates the main diagonal 2x2 blocks. Successive pairs of states differ for the condition of the component before the last and this fact creates the (2x2) blocks of diagonal form, and so on for the higher po—wers of 2.

Of course if reliability is concerned or if a different maintenance policy is adopted, some μ entries will disappear (they become zero).

3.   THE AUTOMATIC SOLUTION OF THE BASIC EQUATION

The results of sect.2 have been used in Selenia during the analysis phase of the project C.A.R.A. (Computer Aided Reliability Analysis) whose aim is to obtain a computer package for the automatic reliability analysis.

The program is able to handle systems of 1000 states in order to evaluate their Reliability and Availability, for both single or multiple maintenance, as function of time.

In order to face the input problem due to the large number of data, a pro—gram phase is devoted to the construction of the transition rate matrix star—ting from a topological description of the reliability block diagram; this re—duces the human work to a minimum.

A brief description of this phase is given here below, for detailed informa—tions the reader is referred to the last paper of [4] .

The steps of the program are presented in fig.1:

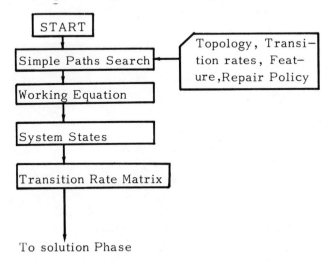

To solution Phase

Fig.1: Flow graph of the program C.A.R.A.

Blocks description:

a) Input.

The input block contains the topological description of the system, the
transition rates of the components, the feature to compute (i.e.: R(t)
or A(t)) and the assumed maintenance policy (i.e.: single or multiple
or no repair).

b) Simple path search.

A simple path is a sequence of system's components connecting the input
to the output of the reliability block diagram, in which a node (junction
point of the components) appears only once. There are a number of ways
to find all possible system paths, in [4] there is the description of a
method based on the connection matrix associated to the system topolo
gical description.

c) Working equations.

A system is able to work if there is at least a simple path with all
unfailed components. Then one can obtain a working equation defined as
follows:

A working equation is a logic function formed by the OR of the system
simple paths. Each simple path is formed by one component or by the
AND of two or more components. The system is able to perform its opera—
tion if, by substituting component symbols with 1 or 0 depending whether
the component works or is failed, the logic expression takes value 1, if
the value is 0 the system is failed.

d) States and their description.

The knowledge of the working equation allows a complete description of
all possible system states. In fact, by simply counting different symbols
in the equation one has the number of components in the system (this in—
formation may be supplied by the input or derived from the initial topolo—
gical description). If a component has two operative conditions, namely
working (1) or failed (0), the possible system states are 2^n, where n is
the number of components. Using the working equation it is possible to
associate to each state its operative condition. Therefore a table is ob—
tained describing all possible states.

e) Construction of the transition rate matrix.

As noted in the previous section, the general off—diagonal entry of the
transition rate matrix is the failure or the repair rate of the component,
the transition of which causes the system transition from the state identi—
fied by the column index to that identified by the row index. Therefore,
once the system states table has been obtained, the transition rate mat—
rix can be constructed. This is done by placing at the intersection of
the j-th column and the i-th row the failure or repair rate of the compo—
nent which is in different operative conditions in the states s_j and s_i ;

the main-diagonal entries are given by the opposite of the sum of the off-diagonal entries in the same column.
Obviously not any transition is possible, in fact the feature to be computed and the maintenance policy limit the number of transitions; in particular if reliability is concerned no repair transition is possible starting from failed states; if single maintenance is foreseen only one reapir rate can appear in the same column.

4.   PHYSICAL MEANING OF THE MARKOV ASSUMPTION [6]

The Markov assumption means that the system has not memory of what happened before the state it presently occupies; it, possibly, knows how much time has been spent since the system inizialization (time varying process). To show what this does mean in practice, let us refer to the following simple example.
Consider a 2-components system; let t_1, t_2 and t_3 be the instants in which the following events occur:

at t_1:	component A fails
at t_2:	component B fails
at t_3:	repair of A is completed ;

let us assume that components A and B have the time varying transition rates shown in fig.2.

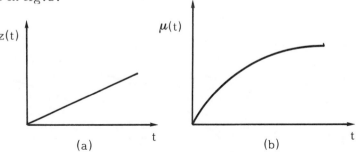

(a)   (b)

Fig.2: Transition rates of A and B. (a) failure. (b) repair

A very simple reasoning shows that the system evolution and its Markov model are as in fig.3, where failure and repair are shown separately. Fig.3 shows that if a non-stationary process is of concern, the Markov model is not a suitable representation of the system evolution; namely, it is pessimistic for failure processes and optimistic for repair ones; it corresponds to the situation known as "as bad as old". Of course if transition rates are costant, there is a perfect coincidence between system evolution and its markovian description, as can be easily seen from fig.3.

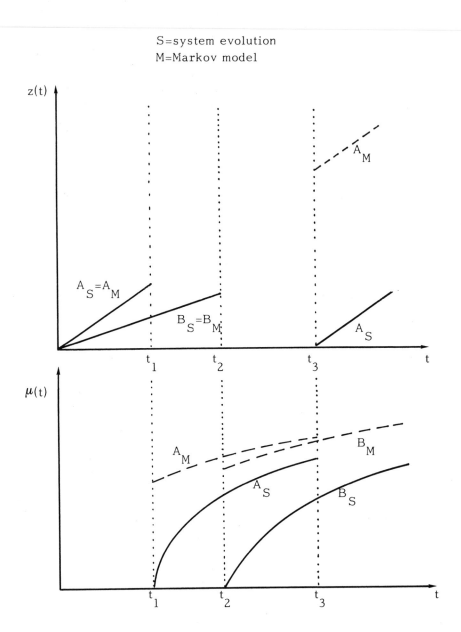

Fig.3: System behaviour and its Markov description

A description "as good as new", if applied to a single component, is the well known Renewal Theory approach [7] . The application of this concept to particular systems (parallel redundancies) can be found in [8] .

5.   CONCLUSION

The results of the present paper may be summarized as follows:
- non stationary Markov processes are not a suitable description for sys—
  tem with non costant transition rates;
- even in the case of stationary Markov processes there are problems ari—
  sing from the dimension of the transition rate matrix, they can be partial—
  ly overcome by considering the sparsity and the structure of the matrix;
- reliability problems can be automatically solved by using suitable compu—
  ter programs.

LIST OF SYMBOLS:

$\underline{p}(t)$ = System states probability vector
Λ = Transition rate matrix
$\underline{s}_i$ = i-th system state
λ_{ij} = Transition rate from $\underline{s}_j$ to $\underline{s}_i$
N = Number of system states
n = Number of components in the system
λ_X = Constant failure rate of component X
μ_X = Constant repair rate of component X
Σ_i = Sum of the off-diagonal entries of the i-th column of Λ matrix
$z_X(t)$ = Time varying failure rate of component X
$\mu_X(t)$ = Time varying repair rate of component X

                              REFERENCES
1. J.L.DOBB: Stochastic Processes – Wiley,1953
2. W.FELLER: An Introduction to Probability Theory and its Applications –
          ₁Wiley,1950
3. L.TAKACS: Stochastic Processes – Methuen, 1960
4. Rivista Tecnica Selenia, Vol.4, n.3 (1977) – Special issue on "System
          Reliability: The Markov Approach"
5. V.AMOIA, M.SANTOMAURO: Computer Oriented Reliability Analysis of
          Large Electrical Systems –Summer Symp. on Circuit Theory,
          Prague, 1977
6. V.AMOIA, E.CARRADA, R.SOMMA: Il punto di vista Markoviano e quel—
          lo Integrale per l'affidabilità dei sistemi – X° Convegno Naziona—
          le A.I.C.Q., Torino, Oct.1978

7. D.R.COX: Renewal Theory – Wiley, 1962

8. R.A.HALL, H.DUBNER, L.B.ADLER: Reliability of Non-exponential
     Redundant Systems – Proceedings of the 1966 Ann. Symp.
     on Reliability, San Francisco, Jan. 1966

HOW TO USE THE MINIMAL CUTS OF FAULT TREE ANALYSIS IN MARKOV MODELLING

HEINZ WENZELBURGER

Institut für Reaktorentwicklung, Kernforschungszentrum Karlsruhe,
Postfach 3640, D 7500 Karlsruhe, Federal Republic of Germany

ABSTRACT AND INTRODUCTION

This contribution has been stimulated by the NATO Conference at Sogesta and worked out there. It is an attempt to clarify the concepts of a fault tree and of minimal cuts in Markov-modelling of binary systems. These concepts which are currently used in reliability theory are still meaningful if we describe a binary system by a time evolutive process instead of a statical fault tree. So it seems to us worth-wile to demonstrate by a fairly simple example what can be done with these concepts in Markov modelling. Formal proofs and further examples will be given by the author elsewhere. [1]

The result will be that we can use the minimal cuts of a fault tree model to identify in a formal way the failed states relevant in the corresponding Markov model. This may be helpful for the evaluation of a Markov model related to a larger binary system by means of a computer code involving the following two problems:

(i) Automatization of the construction of the transition matrix A of a Markov process.

(ii) Calculation of the eigenvalues of the transition matrix A.

A lot of work has been done in numerical mathematics to solve problem (ii). By contrast not much work has been done to solve problem (i).[2] The main purpose of this paper is a tutorial one.

AN EXAMPLE

The example we have chosen is a two-out-of-three system, a little more complicated than the first one Signoret discussed in his lecture.[3] Our notation is similar to that of Barlow and Proschan[4] and that of Signoret.[3] There is but one difference: We use the structure function for failure and not that for success.

At first we describe a fault tree model of our system which then we generalize to a Markov model. The procedure of generalizing is not unique,[1] it depends upon the assumptions made with regard to repair, redundancy, maintenance etc.

1. Deterministic Description

The flow diagram of our example is displayed in fig. 1. It is a system consisting of three pumps. The system fails if two or more pumps have failed. We can represent this system either graphically by a fault tree or algebraically by a structure function $\varphi(x)$ for failure (fig. 2). There is however, rigorous equivalence between these two representations if and only if we compare events, i.e. the top event {system failed} with the event $\{ \varphi(x) = 1 \}$.

2. Probabilistic Description by Fault Tree Analysis

To obtain any probabilistic model for our example we have to replace the deterministic Boolean variables (small letters)

$$x_i = \begin{cases} 0 \\ 1 \end{cases} \text{pump } i \begin{cases} \text{intact} \\ \text{failed} \end{cases} \quad i = 1,2,3 \quad (1)$$

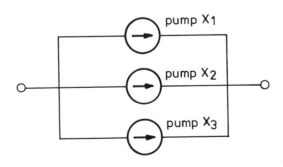

Fig. 1. Flow diagram

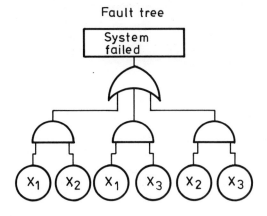

Fault tree

Structure function
for failure

$$\varphi (x) = (x_1 \wedge x_2)$$
$$\vee (x_1 \wedge x_3) \vee (x_2 \wedge x_3)$$

Minimal cuts:

$$x_1 \wedge x_2, \quad x_1 \wedge x_3, \quad x_2 \wedge x_3$$

Equivalence

Graphic representation   Algebraic representation

Fig. 2.   Deterministic description of a 2-out-of-3 System

and

$$\varphi (x) = \begin{cases} 0 \\ 1 \end{cases} \text{system} \begin{cases} \text{intact} \\ \text{failed} \end{cases}, \qquad (1')$$

$$x: = (x_1, x_2, x_3)$$

by random Boolean variables (capital letters). This is straightforward in the case of a statical or steady-state model, i.e. in
fault tree analysis. Defining here the reliability R of the system
(see Barlow[4] p.20) by

Reliability: = probability that the system is working correctly

we have in our example, assuming no repair and statistically independent components (pumps)

$$R = P \left[\; \Phi(X) = 0 \; \right] = 1 - P \left[\; \Phi(X) = 1 \; \right]$$

$$= 1 - \left[P_1 P_2 + P_1 P_3 + P_2 P_3 - 2\, P_1 P_2 P_3 \right] \; , \tag{2}$$

whereas $X: = (X_1, X_2, X_3)$ and

$$P \left[\; X_i = 1 \; \right] = P_i \; ; \quad P \left[\; X_i = 0 \; \right] = 1 - P_i, \quad i = 1,2,3.$$

The probability $\overline{R} := 1 - R$ is called unreliability and the corresponding event, i.e. $\left\{ \Phi(X) = 1 \right\}$, is called top event. Since
there is no repair in our example, we do not need to distinguish
between the reliability and the availability.

3. Probabilistic Description by a Markov Process

3.1 Some remarks on Markov modelling

If we assume our system to be time evolutive, we can do
modelling by various stochastic processes. One of the simpler
stochastic processes we can use are the continuous time Markov
processes with a finite number of states.[5,6] They can be represented by a so-called Markov or transition rate diagram. We can
establish this diagram for a system, if we know the number of its
states and the transition rates of its states transitions.

All states in Markov processes of this type are stable, being
either non-absorbing or absorbing. (See e.g. Karlin[6] for a
rigorous definition of "stable"). This may be described as follows:
if the system is in a non-absorbing state, it will jump to another
state after a finite time. However, if the system is in absorbing
state, it will never leave it. The waiting time of the system in a
non-absorbing state has an exponential distribution.

The Markov diagrams (i.e. processes!), the one for the
availability and the other for the reliability of the system, subsequently called A-diagrams and R-diagrams respectively, are
different. More precisely, A-diagrams (processes)consist of non-
absorbing states (system is either operating or non-operating)only,
R-diagrams (processes), by contrast consist of non-absorbing states
(system is operating) and absorbing states (system failed). Markov
models and traditional fault tree models of systems with binary
components have in general a different number of states.[1]

3.2 A Markow model for our example

To obtain a Markov model for our example we make the following additional assumptions:

(1)   Three repair men, one for each pump.

(2)   Transitions only between states, where exactly one
       pump changes its state (Poisson assumption).

Starting from the fault tree model, our example has $2^3 = 8$ states, because each of the three pumps can be either in a running or a failed state. Assumption (1) has been made to retain these 2^3 states also in the Markov model. Of course, each failed pump will repaired immediately after failure and then started again without delay.

Now we can define the Markov processes for our example in a formal way. We introduce the set of random variables (stochastic process)

$$X = \{ \ X_t, \ \ 0 \leq t < \infty \ \} \tag{3}$$

$$X := (X_1, X_2, X_3) \quad ,$$

where

$$X_i = \{ \ X_{it}, \ \ 0 \leq t < \infty \ \} \qquad i = 1,2,3 \tag{x}$$

is the real random variable of the component i (pump i) with

$$X_{it} = \begin{cases} 0 \\ 1 \end{cases} \text{pump i at time t} \begin{cases} \text{intact} \\ \text{failed} \end{cases} \cdot$$

In the case of the A-process the state space E^3 of X consists in 8 elementary events, namely

$$E^3 = \{ \ (0,0,0), \ (0,0,1), \ \dots \ , \ (1,1,0), \ (1,1,1) \ \} \tag{5}$$

The realization $X_t = (1,1,0)$ for example means that the system is at time t in a state, pumps 1 and 2 having failed and pump 3 being intact.

To establish the Markov diagrams (fig. 3) of the A- and R-processes we identify the operating and failed states by the following procedure:

operating states: sum of vector components of X less than
                   or equal to one,

failed states: sum of vector components of X greater than
                   or equal to two.

This is no general procedure to identify this type of states of a system, but it may be modified to apply to k-out-of-n systems.

Using this procedure we have in our example for the availability at time t defined by

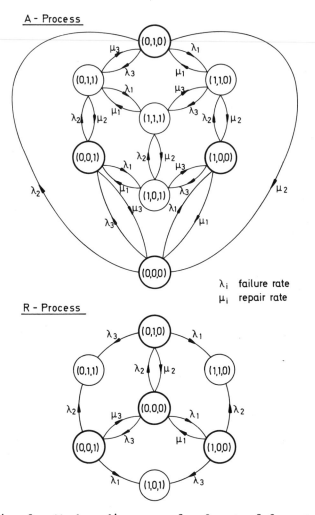

Fig. 3.   Markov diagrams of a 2-out-of-3 system

A (t) : = Probability that the system is working correctly
at time t (even though it may previously passed
through some failed states)

the expression

$$A (t) = P \left[X_t = (i,j,k), \ i+j+k \leq 1 \right],$$ (6)

and for the reliability at time t defined by

R (t) : = Probability that the system has been working
correctly during the whole operation time until t

the expression

$$R(t) = P\left[X_t = (i,j,k),\ i+j+k \leq 1 \,\middle|\, X_u \neq (i,j,k), \right.$$
$$\left. i+j+k \geq 2;\ u < t \right].\quad (7)$$

In the Markov diagram for the A-process there are from each state transitions to three other states. However, for the R-process the number of transitions is considerably reduced. There is even an absorbing state, i.e. (1,1,1), which will never be reached if the system starts in an operating state. This does not represent an exception. In larger systems (as e.g. in a 2-out-of-4 system) there may be many absorbing states which cannot be reached from any operating state. So it is allowed to cancel from an R-process states of this type.

3.3   Identifying in a formal way the failed states of a Markow model

As we have seen before, we must know the failed states of a system in order to be able to calculate both its availability and its reliability. In our example we can easily verify that the failed states of the Markov model may be found by the following A-rule:

A-rule
There corresponds to each minimal cut of a fault tree model at least one failed state of the A-Markov process. Wo obtain all failed states induced by a minimal cut if we set each of its cut variables equal to one and take for the remaining variables all combinations of zero and one.

These failed states have to be interpreted as absorbing states if we want to identify all absorbing states of the corresponding R-Markov process. Considering an arbitrary coherent fault tree there is, as far as we know, no R-rule for direct selection of the relevant absorbing states of the R-process which is as simple as the A-rule. In the special case of a k-out-of-n system, however, we may use the following simple rule if the Poisson assumption holds:

R-rule for a k-out-of-n system
There corresponds to each minimal cut of a fault tree model exactly one relevant absorbing state of the R-Markov process. We obtain this state if we set in the minimal cut each of its cut variables equal to one and the remaining variables equal to zero.

Now, applying to our example the A- and R-rule, respectively, we obtain for the A-process the failed states (i,j,k), $i+j+k \geq 2$ from (* means 0 or 1) :

$$x_2 \wedge x_3 = 1 \longrightarrow x_1 = *, \; x_2 = 1, \; x_3 = 1, \; \text{i.e.} \; (0,1,1), \; (1,1,1)$$

$$x_1 \wedge x_3 = 1 \longrightarrow x_1 = 1, \; x_2 = *, \; x_3 = 1, \; \text{i.e.} \; (1,0,1), \; (1,1,1)$$

$$x_1 \wedge x_2 = 1 \longrightarrow x_1 = 1, \; x_2 = 1, \; x_3 = *, \; \text{i.e.} \; (1,1,0), \; (1,1,1)$$

and for the R-process the relevant absorbing states from

$$x_2 \wedge x_3 = 1 \longrightarrow x_1 = 0, \; x_2 = 1, \; x_3 = 1, \; \text{i.e.} \quad (0,1,1)$$

$$x_1 \wedge x_3 = 1 \longrightarrow x_1 = 1, \; x_2 = 0, \; x_3 = 1, \; \text{i.e.} \quad (1,0,1)$$

$$x_1 \wedge x_2 = 1 \longrightarrow x_1 = 1, \; x_2 = 1, \; x_3 = 0, \; \text{i.e.} \quad (1,1,0).$$

References

1. H. Wenzelburger, "On generalizing a fault tree model of a binary system to a Markov model," KfK-Bericht (being published).
2. P. Sbarigia, R. Somma, "Introduction to computer aided reliability analysis program," Rivista Tecnica Selena, Vol. 4, No. 3 (1977) 37-42.
3. A. Blin, A. Carnino, J.P. Georgin, J.P. Signoret, "Use of Markov processes for reliability problems," NATO ASI (1978).
4. R.E. Barlow, F. Proschan, "Statistical theory of reliability and life testing," Holt, Rinehart and Winston, New York (1975).
5. W. Feller, "An introduction to probability theory and its applications," Wiley, New York (1965).
6. S. Karlin, "A first course in stochastic processes," Academic Press, New York (1969).

RESPONSE SURFACE METHODOLOGY IN RISK ANALYSIS

L. Olivi

Commission of the European Communities, Joint Research Centre, Ispra Establishment, 21020 Ispra (Varese) - Italy

ABSTRACT

The Response Surface Methodology as a general approach to the system identification is presented. The method organises several statistical techniques in order to provide an estimate of the p.d.f. of the output variable of the identified system as a function of the p.d.f.'s of the input variable, as the final result.
In particular the following techniques are dealt with:

- the sensitivity analysis;
- the choice of the approximating function;
- the experimental design;
- the parameter estimation.

A typical application is provided.

INTRODUCTION

The Response Surface Methodology is a general approach to the system identification, i.e. it approaches problems in which a yield variable Y varies in the same pattern according to the levels of one or more stimulus variables X. (Mead and Pike 1975 [27].) In general, the variation of Y cannot be expected to have a typical behaviour, due either to the complexity of the problem under examination, or to the lack of information.

This method unifies techniques already known in a rigorous discipline and establishes:
- the sensitivity analysis on the variables;
- the choice, if possible, among the families of surfaces, suitable for an easy study, of that surface which at best can be used for exploring the main characteristics of the system, as optimal points, relevance of certain variables, expected

313

asymptotic behaviour, etc.;
-      the choice of a proper experimental design [8];
-      the estimation of the model's parameter;
-      the probability distribution function of the output variable as the propagation
       of the uncertainties on the input variables;
-      the contrast between the observed behaviour of the system and the model
       response, not only as a statistical fitting to the observed data, but also as the
       representation of the main physical characteristics in the mathematical structure
       of the model;
-      analysis of the fitted model.

DEFINITION OF THE RESPONSE SURFACE

The obvious assumption which is behind this approach is that there exists a
regular law which governs the behaviour of the system:

$$Y = G \ (X/p) \tag{1}$$

where Y is the observed dependent stochastic variable, X is the set of the stimulus
independent variables, p an unknown parameter.

Both p and X are considered having a deterministic behaviour. The expected
value of Y defines in the X hyperspace a surface, around which the Y points are
distributed according to a probability distribution function, the function $f(x/p)$,
which approximates this surface is what is called the Response Surface:

$$Y = g(x/p) = f(x/p) + \xi + \in \tag{2}$$

The deviation of the response surface $f(x/p)$ from $g(x/p)$ is explained and
expressed in terms of a sum of a bias plus a stochastic error. ξ is the bias, $\in$ is the
error. The analysis of the equation (2) shows the significance of the already mentioned
performances of this methodology and the main questions to be dealt with.

In fact, the deviation of the response surface from $g(x/p)$ depends on several
circumstances, such as:
-      the mathematical fitting, which defines the extent of the bias;
-      the intrinsic stochasticity of the system, which determines the value of $|\in|^2$;
-      the number of observations, which have to be established in an optimal way,
       in order to perform a parameter estimation, which ensures the adequacy of the
       model together with a sufficiently low number of observation.

It follows that the choice of the response surface is a crucial point in this methodology because it influences both the estimation procedure and the experimental
design. It has to be also outlined that no sophisticated estimation procedure can
improve a bad choice of the surface and, on the opposite, the performances of
various estimation procedures are not so different, when the response surface fits well.
Unfortunately, the estimation techniques available cannot be applied to the parameter
estimation of every kind of surface; therefore, the study of families of surfaces is
restricted to those families for which it is possible to define appropriate estimators.

SENSITIVITY ANALYSIS

In general, the response surface methodology is a very efficient tool for exploring the system behaviour, one is limited in its use from the cost of running the codes. For this reason, a very simple use of the response surface methodology, which still offers some advantages for a preliminary sensitivity analysis, is the Box method [3,5]. Once identified the region of interest, the exploration is performed, by approximating this region, or a small part of it, with a linear model. The parameters of this model are, in a first approximation, the sensitivity coefficients in this region.

Other methods are available as the partial rank correlation methods [23], but they do not seem to lead to a more precise evaluation of the relative weight of the variables, except for very complex models where the Box approach also, could be too expensive.

The problem of establishing which variables play a major role and which could be negligible in building a model is quite hard to solve in general. Nevertheless, typical applications in single cases lead to satisfactory results [32], mainly when the a priori knowledge of the behaviour and of the influence of a sub-set of variables on the output may determine an empirical but efficient selection technique.

General references for the sensitivity analysis techniques in risk analysis in nuclear reactor safety applied to typical problems can be found in the proceedings of the ANS Topical Meeting on "Probabilistic Analysis of Nuclear Reactor Safety", Los Angeles, May 9-10, 1978.

CHOICE OF THE APPROXIMATION FUNCTIONS

The selection of the response surface is an heuristic process which needs the knowledge of the properties of basic families of linear and non-linear functions and some insight about the system, as the existence of optimal points, asymptotic behaviour and the relative weight of independent variables, which can be carried out by a preliminary sensitivity analysis. Up to now, two important families of functions have been studied, in a way that estimation procedures and experimental design techniques can be satisfactorily applied: the polynomials and the inverse polynomials.

Polynomials

$$Y(X/p) = P_m (X_1 \dots X_K) = \sum_{j=0}^{r} \beta_j Z_j \qquad (3)$$

where $P_m (X_1 \dots X_K)$ is the m-degree polynomial in the K variables $X_1 \dots X_K$ with the unknown coefficients β_j, $j = 1 \dots r$, where r is the number of terms in the polynomial and each term has the form:

$$Z_j = X_1^{j_1} X_2^{j_2} \dots X_K^{j_K} \text{ with } \sum_{i=1}^{K} j_i \leqslant m$$

The most commonly used form is the quadratic one; the opportunity of this choice is due to:

(i)   it involves only the squared and the crossed extra-terms to the straight
         hyperplane relationship;
(ii)   it is quite simple to identify the optimal point;
(iii)   the method of least squares produces estimates of parameters without com-
         plex calculations and with an acceptable correlation among the Z_j variables.

Advantages are:
(i)   in a sufficiently small region of the X space it can reproduce the system be-
         haviour, as a second approximation of a Taylor expansion around an inte-
         resting point;
(ii)   it is a simple and readily available smoothing surface;
(iii)   it can be used alternatively to the hyperplane form, as a pre-exploring surface
         around the main interesting points, in order to perform a more accurate pre-
         liminary sensitivity analysis [3].

Disadvantages are:
(i)   no physical justification;
(ii)   extrapolation virtually impossible, because the form of the polynomial can-
         not be constrained outside the range of the X set used;
(iii)   quadratic form may present undesirable symmetries around the optimal point;
(iv)   no asymptotic behaviour, which instead, is a pattern frequently found in
         physical data.

The polynomial fitting is always an ill posed problem from the least squares estimation point of view, because of the correlation among the Z_j variables for $m > 1$,
therefore the use of the polynomials with a degree higher than quadratic one is quite
rare and applied to typical cases.

Inverse polynomials

        The inverse polynomials (Nelder 1966 [29]) are a more flexible family of
functions as fitting surfaces, but could present some difficulties in the choice of an
optimal experimental design and an appropriate estimation. The general form is:

$$\prod_{i=1}^{k} X_i / Y (X/p) = P_m (X_1 \ldots X_k) \tag{4}$$

They have the following performances:
(i)   the first order relationship provides the inverse linear relationship, which of-
         ten occurs in some theories;
(ii)   asymptotic behaviour;
(iii)   extrapolation does not lead to absurdity;
(iv)   the surface is bounded;
(v)   the quadratic form is not built in symmetry.

EXPERIMENTAL DESIGN

        The experimental design problem is to choose the input variable in an experi-
mental region χ in order to satisfy some criterion of optimality in connection with

both the form of the model and the objective of the study.

Linear models can profit by the experimental design developed for multiple linear regression analysis. In this field the first contribution is due to Smith (1918) [33], who stated a criterion for polynomial regression in one variable in a region $\chi = (-1, 1)$, she proposed to minimize the maximum variance of $Y(X)$ where $Y(X)$ is the estimated output variable.

$$\min \max V(Y(X))$$

$$(X_i, i = 1 \dots n) \quad X \in \chi$$

This criterion is later studied by Kiefer and Wolfowitz (G-Optimality) (1959) [22], who further established the equivalence theorem (1960) [23]. This theorem shows that maximizing the $\text{Det}(X'X)$ over some region X (D-Optimality, Wald (1943) [36]) is equivalent to minimizing the maximum variance of $Y(X)$ for $X \in \chi$. In practice, algorithms are available for computing D-optimum designs (St. John and Draper (1975) [31]). The most relevant results are:

(i)   for model with p parameters, the design is supported at p distinct points;
(ii)   design measure has equal weight at these p points.

In non-linear model experimental design, the technique of the Taylor series expansion about the preliminary estimates is considered. The approximated linearized model can be dealt with several criteria:

-    Chernoff (1953) [10]: maximum $\text{tr}(X'X)$, $X \in \chi$;
-    Box and Lucas (1959) [7]: maximum $\text{Det}(X'X)$, $X \in \chi$ (D-optimality);
-    Box and Hunter (1965) [6]: maximum posterior probability of parameters at least squares solution.

It has to be pointed out that this topic is very wide and still under development, therefore, for typical application, ad hoc optimal criteria can successfully be introduced.

PARAMETERS ESTIMATION

The estimation methods cannot, in general, provide an appropriate estimator for every kind of functional relationship; the polynomials can be estimated through the multiple linear regression approach, which is linear in the parameters and in the Z_{ji}, for the inverse polynomials a weighted ordinary least squares estimation can be used. In both cases one can meet ill posed problems and some corrections have to be introduced. Techniques which provide the estimation of non-linear functions are possible by the use of the available algorithms for parameter estimation in non-linear multiple regression models. This area of study is still being developed and a complete global methodology for the response surfaces, which also takes into account the experimental design, is not ready yet. Nevertheless, some methods for non-linear parameter estimations are diffused in other applications and can usefully be applied for R.S.M. purposes [14,28].

Polynomial parameter estimation
<u>   </u>

The estimation of parameters can be performed under the following three norms:
- L 1 minimization of the sum of absolute errors (MSAE);
- L 2 ordinary least squares estimation (OLSE);
- L ∞ minimization of the maximum absolute value (Minimax).

These three norms refer, in a stochastic framework, to different structures of the $\in$ vector; in particular maximum likelihood estimators for β are provided under the norm L1, L2, L∞ if the $\in$'s are independent and follow respectively a Laplace distribution, a normal distribution and a uniform distribution.

In the following, we refer to the multiple linear regression model, where the values of the X's are substituted from the new variables Z's which contain the zero, the linear, the mixed, the quadratic and the upper order terms.

Estimation under L1 norm [35]

$$\underline{Y} = Z\underline{\beta} + \underline{r} \tag{5}$$

where $\underline{Y}$ is the nx1 vector of the observed response variable, Z in the $[nx\,(r+1)]$ matrix of the prediction variables, $\underline{\beta}$ is the $[(k+1) \times 1]$ vector of the unknown parameters, $\underline{r}$ represents the vector of an unabservable random error, n is the number of observations.

Under the norm L1, $\underline{\beta}$ must be determined so that the

$$\sum_{i=1}^{n} |e_i| \quad \text{is minimum.}$$

If e_i^+ and e_j^- denote the magnitude of the deviation of the jth observation, above and below the fitted line, the problem is stated as:

$$\text{minimize } \phi = \Sigma \, (e_i^+ + e_i^-)$$

Subject to:

$$\sum_{i=1}^{n} Z_{ji}\,\beta_j + e_j^+ + e_j^- = Y_j \qquad j = 0, 1 \ldots K$$

$$e_j^+ \, e_j^- > 0$$

The optimal ϕ value is the L1-MSAE value.

Estimation under the norm L2

The OLS estimator can be applied to the form (5) of multiple linear regression model, which minimize the expression:

$$\text{SSE } (\hat{\underline{\beta}}) = (Z\underline{\beta} - \underline{Y})\,'\,(Z\underline{\beta} - \underline{Y})$$

where

$$\hat{\underline{\beta}} = (Z'Z)^{-1} Z'\underline{Y} \tag{6}$$

is the estimated parameter vector.

The variance - covariance matrix of OLS estimate is:

$$\text{VAR } (\hat{\beta}) = \hat{\sigma}^2 (Z'Z)^{-1} \tag{7}$$

where

$$\hat{\sigma}^2 = \frac{\text{SSE } (\hat{\beta})}{n-r} \tag{8}$$

The MSE is given by

$$\text{MSE } (\hat{\beta}) = E \left[(\hat{\beta}-\beta)'(\hat{\beta}-\beta) \right] = \hat{\sigma}^2 \sum_{j=1}^{r} l_j^{-1}$$

where l_j's are the eigenvalues of the $Z'Z$ matrix.

In this study, under the norm L2, some interest has to be devoted to the biased estimators too, which have to be introduced if the correlation matrix is ill conditioned, as often it occurs in the polynomial representation of the response surface [13,15,16,17,18,19,20,21,25,26,37].

Three estimators as Principal Component (PC), Latent Root Regression (LRR), Ridge Regression (RR) can be used in order to correct the OLS estimate [2]. A main objection against the use of bias estimator consists in claiming that the quality of the estimation is measured by the SSE which is a quantity which increases with the bias. In reality the SSE measures only the quality of the mathematical fitting on Y, while the quality of the estimate is interpreted by the MSE, because the mathematical properties of the $g(X/p)$ are better recovered as well as the estimated $\hat{\beta}$ is close to β. Therefore, whenever in a bias estimate of an ill posed problem, the value of the SSE is not drastically different from the SSE in the OLS estimate and the eigenvalues of the $Z'Z$ matrix show a strong multicollinearity, biased estimate is an obliged choice because it can guarantee a better adequacy of the model.

Estimation under L∞ norm

For the L∞ norm estimation the Chebyshev criterion can be used; the β_j's values are estimated in order to minimize the maximum absolute error between the fitted relation and Y.

By linear programming one can solve:
minimize e
subject to:

$$-\sum_{j=0}^{r} Z_{ij}\, \beta_j + e \geqslant -Y_j$$

$$\sum_{j=0}^{r} Z_{ij}\, \beta_j + e \geqslant Y_j \qquad j = 1 \ldots n$$

Inverse polynomial estimation

The inverse polynomial can be rewritten in the form $\sum_{i=1}^{r} \beta_i u_i$, so that u_i may represent expressions such as x_1, $x_1^2 x_2$, $x_1^{-1} x_2$ etc. which appear in the inverse polynomial expression and r is the number of terms.

A method of estimation based on a weighted least squares estimation (Nelder) [29] can be used:

Suppose that $\qquad Y_j = E(y_j) = (\Sigma_i \beta_i u_{ij})^{-1}$

and $\quad$ var $(Y_j) = \sigma^2 Y_j \quad$ where $i = 1, 2 ... n \qquad i = 1, 2 ... k$

this is equivalent to assume that Y^{-1} is linearly related to the r known independent variables u_i with unknown coefficients β_i and the proportional standard deviation of Y is constant.

Taking a weighted least squares criterion, it has to be minimized.

$$\Sigma_j \frac{1}{Y_j^2} (y_j - Y_j)^2 = \Sigma_j [\frac{y_i}{Y_i} - 1]^2 = \Sigma_j [y_j (\Sigma \beta_i u_{ij}) - 1]^2$$

This leads to normal equation of the form $A\hat{\beta} = \underline{W}$, where $\underline{W}$ is a (kx1) vector with elements $w_i = \Sigma_j u_{ij} Y_j$, A is a (kxk) matrix with elements $a_{pq} = \Sigma_j u_{pj} u_{qj} Y_j^2$, and $\hat{\beta}$ denotes the vector of estimates of β.

Therefore, the estimator is

$$\hat{\beta} = A^{-1} \underline{W}$$

The weighted least squares estimation is of practical use because of its simplicity but cannot, in general, be considered the most appropriate. The estimate of β provided by this technique can be used for a more precise iterative solution [29]. The implementation of this method is being studied.

THE COMPUTATION OF THE OUTPUT VARIABLE PROBABILITY DENSITY FUNCTION AS PROPAGATION OF THE INPUT VARIABLES PROBABILITY DENSITY FUNCTIONS

An important problem in risk analysis is the evaluation of how the uncertainties in the input variables are propagated in the output variable's p.d.f. [1,32]. That is: once known the mechanism of a failure occurrency as a consequence of some possible levels taken from the variables governing the system; which is the probability of the failure occurring, given the p.d.f.'s of the input variables?

The response surface methodology recovers in a simple handable model the physical properties of the system under study. This model can also represent the failure mechanism and the relationship between the stimulus variables and the output variable may be used to compute the output p.d.f. as propagation of the uncertainties assigned to the stimulus variables. Two techniques can be applied: numerical convolution (COVAL) [1,4] and Monte Carlo Simulation [11,34].

Both the techniques provide the histogram of a function of some independent variables, given the histograms (or the p.d.f.'s) of the independent variables.

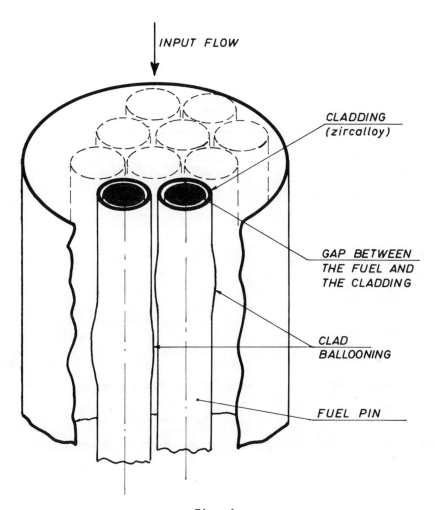

Fig. 1

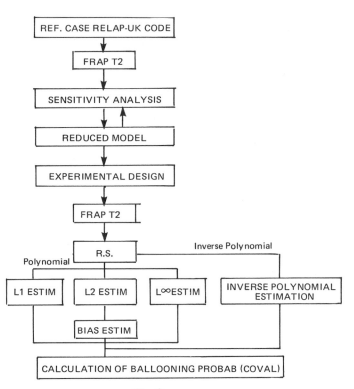

Fig. 2

The last application enlights the power of the response surface methodology applied to the risk analysis. In fact, only the use of very expensive simulation codes together with Monte Carlo simulation can provide an analogous result: in some cases this last approach is totally unpracticable.

A TYPICAL APPLICATION IN NUCLEAR REACTOR SAFETY AND CONCLUSIONS

A practical example of the response surface methodology, from a nuclear safety point of view, is the study of the problem of the structural integrity of the fuel rods during a "Loss of Coolant Accident" (LOCA) in a light water reactor [1]. The consequences of such accidents are prevented by the intervention of a subsidiary coolant circulation in an emergency circuit, to maintain the temperature below a defined guard level during the reactor shut-down. Nevertheless, some possibility exists that a sizeable blockage of the emergency coolant circulation in the bundle of fuel rods is provocated by the clad ballooning. Clad ballooning is a local enlargement at the rods clads due to an abnormal temperature increase which reduces even drastically the cross section of the coolant flow. In fact, if a wide ballooning occurs on the rods clads closely above and below the same plane, the resulting deformation constitutes a real plug against the emergency coolant flow (Fig.1). Small cladding temperature variations due to the uncertainties from manufacturing variables and from operational conditions seriously affect the ballooning during a "LOCA".

The study of this kind of problem is carried out by the use of codes, which reproduce the physical mechanisms by mathematical models and compute the values of the state variables of the system under examination. In this example, a reference case has been calculated on the basis of an experimental test section of 52 pins, 2 meter length, PWR geometry. The code RELAP-UK [9] has been used for calculating the thermohydraulic coolant conditions during the programmed blow-down sequence. The results of this test case have been input in the code FRAP T2 [12], that analyses the fuel rod behaviour for what concerns temperature and deformation history and produces as output the initial time of the ballooning occurrency. There are a great many parameters which interact in affecting the behaviour of the rods. Hence, there will be variations in behaviour from one rod to another, even at the same axial height. Because of this complexity, a great many runs would be necessary to estimate the probability distribution function of the ballooning time. Unfortunately, this procedure is so long-running and so costly to be totally impracticable. In the following, the response surfaces techniques applied to this problem will be briefly illustrated, as a typical approach, without considering the engineering details and the specific results (Fig.2).

(i)   Calculation of the input parameters by RELAP-UK code. 25 input parameters are obtained.

(ii)   Sensitivity analysis. Chosen a defined configuration of the input parameters for the FRAP T2 runs, each parameter is independently varied in order to measure its relative weight on to the output variable (ballooning time), in this input configuration. Five significant input parameters are chosen as the most determinant variables in the ballooning mechanisms: fuel thermal conductivity, cladding strength coefficient, cladding coolant heat transfer coefficient, gap thickness, specific heat of zircalloy.

(iii) Chosen the ranges for the five variables, an experimental design D-optimal under L2 norm estimation for a quadratic polynomial has been constructed, by the choice of an orthogonal central composite design. 27 observation points are obtained.

(iv) Observations. The FRAP T2 has run 27 times, producing the out-variable vector of the times at which the ballooning initiates.

(v) Response surface. On this design two response surface configurations have been fitted: quadratic polynomial and inverse quadratic polynomial. Once an optimal design for inverse polynomial was available, one could perform another series of observations appropriate for inverse polynomials. In this case the D-optimality should have been utilized only for the quadratic polynomial.

(vi) Parameter estimation. The parameter estimation has been performed by using a polyvalent algorithm under the three norms L1, L2, L∞ for quadratic polynomial and weighted L2 for inverse polynomial. A first test of bias estimation is also proved.

(vii) Convolution. Once defined the p.d.f.'s of the five input variables, the probability density function of the ballooning time has been calculated by a COVAL program for numerical convolutions.

This example shows how this statistical methodology can be applied in a problem of risk analysis and which future developments are necessary because of the specificity of this field. Particularly non-linear regression analysis and estimation as well as ad hoc experimental design techniques have to be studied. Multivariate regression models will have to be taken into consideration in order to study multiresponse problems [3,4] with correlated output variables.

Moreover, a theoretical effort is needed to focus the non negligible sensitivity analysis problems in studying large systems [32]. Some techniques already applied in other fields could be specifically implemented for risk analysis purposes, while other appropriate studies have to be developed ex novo.

Response surface methodology can be considered in a wide sense as a statistical filter; in risk analysis it filters all the pieces of information one cannot get directly and assumes to be not too determinant. In this sense it establishes an approximation threshold to the knowledge of the system under study.

Therefore, this methodology requires the certainty that the studied system does not offer atypical and unexpected behaviour, such that it could be cut from the response surface interpretation.

Two opposite aspects of its application have to be balanced; the chance to approach problems, whose solutions are otherwise precluded and the filter attenuation. Hence, an a priori evaluation and an appropriate analysis of the problem is preliminarily indispensable as well as a critical judgement of the result from the physical and engineering point of view.

ACKNOWLEDGEMENTS

The author wishes to thank Dr. F. Argentesi, Mr. M. Astolfi and Dr. Ing. G. Mancini for many helpful discussions and collaboration. Furthermore, he is indebted to Dr. J. Larisse and to Dr. Ing. G. Volta for the accurate proofreading of this work and to Dr. D.J. Pike for important suggestions.

MEANING OF THE MAIN SYMBOLS AND THEIR USE

$Y, \underline{Y}, \hat{Y}$: Output variable under the form of continuously observable function, of observable vector $(Y_1, \ldots Y_N)$, of estimated vector $(\hat{Y}_1, \ldots, \hat{Y}_N)$

X : Set of the observed input variables; in the regression model it takes the form of the $n \times k$ matrix of elements X_{ij}, where n is the number of observations and k the number of predictor variables.

$P_n(X_1, \ldots, X_k)$: Polynomial of m degree in the k variables $X_1, \ldots, X_k$. In the regression model $Y_i = P_m(X_{i1}, \ldots, X_{ik}) + \in_i$, each term is linear in the β's parameters. For simplicity each product

$$X_{i1}^{j_1} \cdot X_{i2}^{j_2} \cdot X_{i3}^{j_3} \cdots X_k^{j_k}$$

is substituted by the variable Z_{ij}.

$\beta, \hat{\beta}$: Parameter vector $(\beta_1 - \beta_k)$ and estimated parameter vector $(\beta_1 - \beta_k)$.

$V(\cdot)$: Variance.

$\text{tr}(X'X)$: Trace of the symmetric matrix $X'X$.

$\text{Det}(X'X)$: Determinant of the symmetric matrix $X'X$.

$\text{VAR}(\beta)$: Variance-covariance matrix.

$E(\cdot)$: Expected value.

REFERENCES

[1] Argentesi F., Astolfi M., Mancini G. and Olivi L., A Probabilistic Method of Calculating the Effect of Clad Ballooning in Large Bundle LOCA Experiment - A.N.S. Topical Meeting on "Probabilistic Analysis of Nuclear Reactor Safety", Los Angeles, May 8-10, 1978.

[2] Argentesi F., Astolfi M., Olivi L., Implementation and Analysis of a Polyvalent Algorithm for Multiple Linear Regression, SEAS 1978, Stresa Italy, 1978.

[3] Argentesi F., Olivi L., Statistical Analysis of Simulation Models. An RSM Approach. 1978 Summer Computer Simulation, New Port Beach, 1978.

[4] Astolfi M., Elbaz J., COVAL - A Computer Code for Random Variables Combination and Reliability Evaluation, EUR 58043, 1977.

[5] Box G.E.P., Multifactor Designs of First Order. Biometrika 39, 49-57, 1952.

[6] Box G.E.P. and Hunter W.G., Sequential Design of Experiments for Non-linear Models. IBM Scientific Computing Symposium in Statistics 113-137, 1965.

[7] Box G.E.P. and Lucas H.L., Designs of Experiments in Non-linear Situations. Biometrika, 46, 77-90, 1959.

[8] Box G.E.P. and Wilson K.B., On the Experimental Attainment of Optimum Conditions, J.R. Statistic. Soc. B13, 1-45, 1951.

[9] Brittain I. et al., The Status of RELAP-UK at July 1976, SGHW/HTWG/P(77) 322e (1076), 1976.

[10] Chernov H., Locally Optimum Designs for Estimating Parameters. Ann. Math.
      Statistics, 24, 586-602, 1953.

[11] Dahlgren D.A., Steck G.P., Easterling R.G. and Iman R.L., Uncertainty Propa-
      gation through Computer Codes. ANS Topical Meeting on "Probabilis-
      tic Analysis of Nuclear Reactor Safety", Los Angeles, May 9-10, 1978.

[12] Dearien J.A. et al., "FRAP T2". A Computer Code for the Transient Analysis of
      Oxide Fuel Rod, Aerojet Nuclear Company, 1975.

[13] Dempster A.P., Shatzoff M. and Wermuth N., A Simulation Study of Alterna-
      tives to Ordinary Least Squares. Journal of the American Statistical
      Association 72, 77-106, 1977.

[14] Elfring G.L., Metzler C.M., 3rd Symposium Compstat, Leiden, 1978.

[15] Gunst R.F. and Mason R.L., Advantages of Examining Multicollinearities in
      Regression Analysis. Biometrics 33, 249-260, 1977.

[16] Gunst R.F. and Mason R.L., Biased Estimation in Regression: An Evaluation
      Using Mean Squared Error. Journal of the American Statistical Asso-
      ciation, 72, 616-628, 1977.

[17] Gunst R.F., Webster J.T. and Mason R.L., A Comparison of Least Squares and
      Latent Root Regression Estimators. Technometrics, 18, 75-83, 1976.

[18] Hoerl A.E. and Kennard R.W., Ridge Regression: Biased Estimation to Non-
      orthogonal Problems. Technometrics 12, 55-67, 1970(a).

[19] Hoerl A.E. and Kennard R.W., Ridge Regression: Applications to Non-orthogo-
      nal Problems. Technometrics 12, 69-82, 1970(b).

[20] Hoerl A.E., Kennard R.W. and Baldwin K.F., Ridge Regression: Some Simula-
      tions. Communications in Statistics, 4, 105-123, 1975.

[21] Hoerl A.E. and Kennard R.W., Ridge Regression: Iterative Estimation of the
      Biasing Parameter. Communications in Statistics A5, 77-88, 1976.

[22] Kiefer J. and Wolfowitz J., Optimum Designs in Regression Problems. Ann. Math.
      Statistics. 30, 271-294, 1959.

[23] Kiefer J. and Wolfowitz J., The Equivalence of Two Extremum Problems.
      Canad. J. Math. 12, 363-366, 1960.

[24] McKay M.D., Bolstad J.W. and Whiteman D.E., An Application of Statistical
      Techniques to the Analysis of Reactor Safety Codes. ANS Topical
      Meeting on "Probabilistic Analysis of Nuclear Reactor Safety", Los
      Angeles, May 8-10, 1978.

[25] Marquardt D.W., Generalized Inverses Ridge Regression, Biased Linear Estima-
      tion and Non-linear Estimation. Technomatrics 12, 591-612, 1970.

[26] Marquardt D.W. and Snee D.D., Ridge Regression in Practice. The American
      Statistician 29, 3-20, 1975.

[27] Mead R. and Pike D.J., A Review of Response Surface Methodology from a
      Biometric Viewpoint. Biometrics 31, 813-851, 1975.

[28] Metzler C.M., Elfring G.L. and McEwen A.J., A User Normal for Non-linear and
      Associated Programs, Research Biostatistics, The Upjohn Company,
      Kalamazoo, Mich. 49001, 1974.

[29] Nelder J.A., Inverse Polynomials, A Useful Group of Multi-factor Response
      Functions. Biometrics 22, 128-41, 1966.

[30] Pike D.J., Private Communication - Applied Statistics Department, University
      of Reading, Reading, England, 1979.

[31] St. John R.C. and Draper N.R., D-Optimality for Regression Designs: A
      Review Technometrics, 17, 15-23, 1975.

[32] Sheron B.W., Bases and Criteria for the Selection of Response Surface Parameters for the Statistical Assessment of a LOCA - ANS Topical Meeting on "Probabilistic Analysis of Nuclear Reactor Safety", Los Angeles, May 8-10, 1978.

[33] Smith K., On the Standard Deviations of Adjusted and Interpolated Values of an Observed Polynomial Function and its Constants and the Guidance they give towards a Proper Choice of the Distribution of Observations. Biometrika, 12, 1-85, 1918.

[34] Vaurio J.K., Response Surface Techniques Developed for Probabilistic Analysis of Accident Consequences. ANS Topical Meeting on "Probabilistic Analysis of Nuclear Reactor Safety", Los Angeles, May 8-10, 1978.

[35] Wagner A.W., Linear Programming Techniques for Regression Analysis, Journal of American Statistical Association, 54, 206-212, 1959.

[36] Wald A., On the Efficient Design of Statistical Investigations. Ann. Math. Statistics 14, 134-140, 1943.

[37] Webster J.T., Gunst R.F., Mason R.L., Latent Root Regression Analysis. Technometrics 16, 513-522, 1974.

OPTIMIZATION PROBLEMS ON SYSTEM SUPERVISION

Toshiyuki Inagaki

Department of Precision Mechanics, Faculty of Engineering,
Kyoto University, Kyoto 606, Japan

This paper discusses optimization of system supervision for the following two situations: (A) States of some components are monitored all the time by supervisors and states of other components are not monitored at any time, (B) Every component is subject to a supervisor with active and inactive times. For the first situation, we give an optimum supervisors allocation problem together with a simple method of solution. The second situation is discussed for protective systems. We give an optimization problem which is useful in systematic construction of a non-synchronized supervision schedule. For both situations, illustrative examples are given.

INTRODUCTION

System maintenance is of great importance in attaining high reliability and safety of systems. Most of previous studies on system maintenance deal with probability models where repair starts immediately after any component fails. These models are valid when the following conditions are satisfied:

a)   complete information on states of all components is available;
b)   there is no queue for repair.

Putting aside considerations on condition (b), let us focus our attention on condition (a). This condition requires that the state of every component is monitored all the time and the states of all components are exactly known without any uncertainty. In some cases we cannot expect that this requirement is satisfied because monitoring every component all the time is expensive and might be inherently impossible.

We therefore consider the following two situations:

(A) States of some components are monitored all the time by supervisors and states of others are not monitored at any time.

(B) Every component is subject to a supervisor with active and inactive times. In active time of a supervisor, state of the component is monitored and exactly known. In inactive time of a supervisor, state of the component is not monitored and cannot be known at all.

For the first situation, it is of importance to determine to which components supervisors should be allocated. Part I of this paper gives a Markov availability model for a series system with suspended animation [1] and presents an optimum supervisors allocation problem together with a simple method of solution.

The second situation is discussed in Part II of this paper especially for protective systems of multiple components. Protective systems of plants are activated only when emergency occurs in the plants and are not activated in normal operation of the plants. For this kind of protective systems we can know the state of the protective system only when supervision is active. Availability of each component is represented by a Markov model which is the same as the model of Kontoleon et al. [2] presented for a one-component protective system. Our aim is to maximize the minimum of pointwise availability of the protective system. From the viewpoint of accomplishing this aim, non-synchronised supervision schedules are shown to be superior to synchronised supervision schedules. We give an optimization problem which is useful in systematic construction of a non-synchronised supervision schedule.

PART I : OPTIMIZATION OF SUPERVISORS ALLOCATION

Model Description

1) The system is series.
2) Failures of components are mutually s-independent.
3) While the system is failed, no component can fail.
4) System failure is self-announcing.
5) A supervisor knows the state of a component exactly. Thus, if a component has a supervisor, repair starts immediately after the component fails.
6) Failures of components which do not have supervisors are not announced at all. We need identification time, viz. time for identifying a failed component, and repair starts after completing the identification of the failed component.
7) The s-expected time for checking component state is the same for every component.
8) The identification time is exponentially distributed with constant rate ν. The identification rate ν is assumed to be a function of the total number of supervisors allocated in the system. The functional relation is assumed to be known.
9) The failure and repair rates are constant.

Notation

n	number of components in the system
λ_i, μ_i	constant failure and repair rates of component i
α_i	1 if a supervisor is allocated to component i 0 otherwise
α	$(\alpha_1, ..., \alpha_n)$, an allocation
k	number of supervisors allocated
$\alpha(k)$	an allocation satisfying $\Sigma_i \alpha_i = k$
ν	constant identification rate
$\nu(k)$	value of ν when $\Sigma_i \alpha_i = k$
β	system states: 0 operating iF component i is failed but is not announced iR component i is in repair
$P_\beta(t)$	probability that the system is in state β at time t
P_β	steady-state probability for $P_\beta(t)$
Q_0	$1 - P_0$
S	planning interval of system operation
C_i	cost of the supervisor allocated to component i
C_F	loss per unit time caused by system failure

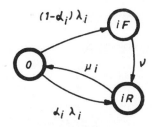

Fig. 1 : Transition Diagram

The state transition diagram is partially illustrated in Fig.1. For an arbitrary allocation α, balance equations are given in (1) — (5).

$$P_0'(t) = - \Sigma_i \lambda_i P_0(t) + \Sigma_i \mu_i P_{iR}(t) \tag{1}$$

$$P_{iF}'(t) = (1 - \alpha_i)\,[\lambda_i P_0(t) - \nu\, P_{iF}(t)] \tag{2}$$

$$P_{iR}'(t) = \alpha_i \lambda_i P_0(t) + (1 - \alpha_1)\,\nu\, P_{iF}(t) - \mu_i P_{iR}(t) \tag{3}$$

$$P_0(t) + \Sigma_i\,[P_{iR}(t) + (1 - \alpha_1)\, P_{iF}(t)] = 1 \tag{4}$$

$$P_0(0) = 1, \quad P_{iR}(0) = P_{iF}(0) = 0, \quad \text{for all i} \tag{5}$$

The steady-state unavailability is

$$Q_0 = \Sigma_i \lambda_i \, [1/\mu_i + \alpha_1)/\nu] \, / \, 1 + \Sigma_i \lambda_i \, [1/\mu_i + (1 - \alpha_i)/\nu] \tag{6}$$

We now assume that

10) $\lambda_i \ll \mu_i$ and $\lambda_i \ll \nu$

Then we get an approximate expression of Q_0 as

$$Q_0 \approx \Sigma_i \lambda_i \, [1/\mu_i + (1 - \alpha_i)/\nu] \tag{7}$$

Optimum allocation of supervisors

Let the objective function be the sum of two quantities: a) total cost of supervisors, b) s-expected loss caused by system.failure during the planning time interval S. Optimization problem is formulated as follows:

Problem   Select α to minimize

$$J \equiv \Sigma_i \alpha_i C_i + C_F S \Sigma_i \, [1/\mu_i + (1 - \alpha_i)] \tag{8}$$

This problem is a non-linear 0-1 integer programming (0-1 IP) problem because ν is a function of $\Sigma_i \alpha_i$.

We propose a two-phase solution method for the above problem.

Phase 1 :   Solve $n-1$ subproblems which are linear 0-1 IP problems.

Subproblem—k: For each k, $1 < k < n-1$, select $\alpha(k)$ which gives

$$J(\alpha(k)) \equiv \begin{cases} \min \ \Sigma_i \alpha_i C_i + C_F S \Sigma_i \lambda_i [1/\mu_i + (1-\alpha_i)/\nu(k)] \\ \qquad\qquad \text{for } 1 < k < n-2 \\ \min \ \Sigma_i \alpha_i C_i + C_F S \Sigma_i \lambda_i / \mu_i \quad \text{for } k = n-1 \end{cases} \tag{9}$$

subject to the constraint $\Sigma_i \alpha_i = k$.

The above subproblems are solved by hand calculation. In subproblem—k, for example, we only have to calculate coefficients of α_i's, i.e. $C_i - C_F S \lambda_i / \nu(k)$, and set $k \alpha_i$'s to be equal to 1 whose coefficients are smaller than those of the remaining $n-k \, \alpha_j$'s. The resulting $\alpha(k)$ is optimum for subproblem—k.

Remark 1.   The reduced form of the objective function for $k = n-1$ results from the property that $n-1$ supervisors are necessary and sufficient for immediate identification of the failed component under assumption 4).

Phase 2 :   Select $\alpha(k)$ which gives

$$J^* \equiv \min \ J(\alpha(0)), \ ..., \ J(\alpha(n-1)) \tag{10}$$

where $J(\alpha(0)) \equiv C_F S \Sigma_i \lambda_i \ [1/\mu_i + 1/\nu(0)]$ (11)

The minimizing $\alpha(k)$ is the optimum allocation for the original problem and J^* gives the minimum of J.

Numerical example

We will consider a five-component series system. Let $C_F = 10^5$ units of money per hour, $S = 10$ years. The other parameters are as follows:

component	1	2	3	4	5
λ_i (per 10^4 hr)	1.1	1.2	0.8	0.9	1.5
μ_i (per hr)	1.0	1.0	1.0	1.0	1.0
c_i (10^5 units money)	5.0	5.4	4.8	4.9	5.5

$\nu(0) = 0.5$/hr	$\nu(1) = 1.0$/hr	$\nu(2) = 1.5$/hr	$\nu(3) = 2.0$/hr

The optimum solutions of subproblems in Phase 1 and $j(\alpha(0))$ are:

k	$\alpha(k)$					$J(\alpha(k))$ (10^6)
0	(0,	0,	0,	0,	0)	14.45
1	(0,	0,	0,	0,	1)	8.87
2	(0,	1,	0,	0,	1)	7.54
3	(1,	1,	0,	0,	1)	7.15
4	(1,	1,	1,	1,	0)	7.37

The optimum allocation α^* is obtained in Phase 2 as $\alpha^* = \alpha(3) = (1,1,0,0,1)$ where $J^* = J(\alpha(3)) = 7.15 \times 10^6$.

Remark 2.   The presented Markov model is easily extended to the case where supervisors can fail in two modes: a) the supervisor looks over the occurrence of component failure, b) the supervisor regards a component as being failed even if it is actually normal. The Markov availability model and a method of solution for optimum supervisors allocation problem are given in [3].

PART II : OPTIMIZATION OF SUPERVISION SCHEDULES FOR PROTECTIVE SYSTEMS

Model description

1)   The protective system consists of n components whose performance processes [1] are mutually s-independent.

2)   Failure and repair rates are constant.
3)   Each component is subject to a supervisor with active and inactive times which appear alternately. While a supervisor is active, the component is perfectly monitored and repair starts immediately after the component failure is detected. While a supervisor is inactive, the component is not monitored and the occurrence of the component failure cannot be detected.
4)   Supervisors do not harm to the operation of components.

Notation

r, T	time lengths of active and inactive supervisions in one cycle of supervision
λ_i, μ_i	constant failure and repair rates of component i
$P_0(t)$	pointwise availability of the protective system at time t
$a_i(t)$	pointwise availability of component i at time t
a_i^*	minimum of $a_i(t)$

Markov availability model

A.   Component availability

Under assumptions 2) − 4), Kontoleon et al. presented an availability model for a one-component protective system subject to a supervisor with active and inactive times [2]. They showed that availability indicates periodic behaviour with period r + T after sufficient number of iterations of supervision cycle. In one cycle [0, r+T], the availability is given as:

$$a(\tau) = \begin{cases} \dfrac{\mu}{\lambda + \mu} + B_1 \exp\left[-(\lambda + \mu)\tau\right] & \text{for } 0 \leqslant \tau \leqslant r \\[2ex] B_2 \exp\left[-\mu(\tau - r)\right] + B_3 \exp\left[-\lambda(\tau - r)\right] \\[1ex] \qquad\qquad \text{for } r \leqslant \tau \leqslant r + T \end{cases} \tag{12}$$

where

$$B_1 = p/(1 - q)$$

$$B_2 = \frac{\mu}{\mu - \lambda} \; B_1 \exp\left[-(\lambda + \mu)r\right] - \frac{\lambda}{\lambda + \mu}$$

$$B_3 = 1 - \frac{\lambda}{\mu} B_2$$

$$p = \frac{\mu}{\mu^2 - \lambda^2} \; \lambda\left[1 - \exp(-\mu T)\right] - \mu\left[1 - \exp(-\lambda T)\right]$$

$$q = \frac{\exp\left[-(\lambda + \mu)r\right]}{\lambda - \mu} \; \left[\lambda \exp(-\lambda T) - \mu \exp(-\mu T)\right]$$

Availability $a(\tau)$ takes its minimum at $\tau = 0$, i.e. at the beginning of each supervision cycle. The minimum is

$$a^* = \frac{\mu}{\lambda + \mu} + B_1 \tag{13}$$

B.   System availability

Under assumption 1) the availability of the protective system is given by

$$P_0(t) = h(a_1(t), ..., a_n(t)) \tag{14}$$

where h is the reliability function of the protective system. In (14), $a_i(t)$ is given by $a_i(\tau_i)$ of (12) where τ_i is the time measured in a cycle $[0, r_i + T_i]$, $0 \leqslant \tau_i \leqslant r_i + T_i$.

Optimization of supervision schedule

The time lengths of active and inactive supervision can differ from component to component. From the practical point of view, however, supervision schedules of this type are not preferred because these schedules require the keeping of records of starting time of active supervision for every component.

In the following discussions we restrict our attention to the practical case where $r_i = T$ for every i. Let D be a class of all supervision schedules of this type. Let us assume that r and T are already given (determination of r and T is discussed in [4]).

The probability of preventing the plant from catastrophic events takes its minimum when the availability of the protective system is minimum. It is therefore important to maximize the minimum availability of the protective system by adopting the best supervision schedule.

Since reliability function h is component-wisely increasing, the pointwise availability of the protective system $P_0(t)$ subject to any supervision schedule in D satisfies the following inequality for any t:

$$P_0(t) \geqslant P_0^* \equiv h(a_1^*, ..., a_n^*) \tag{15}$$

In (15) the equality $P_0(t) = P_0^*$ holds at some t if and only if every $a_i(t)$ takes its minimum a_i^* simultaneously. Note that it is the case of a synchronized supervision schedule where active supervision starts at the same time for every component.

We can make the minimum of $P_0(t)$ greater than P_0^* when we stagger the starting times of active supervision. The extreme non-synchronized supervision schedule is obtained by staggering active supervisions of any pair of components. However, the practically interesting non-synchronized supervision schedule is the one which has the following properties:

a)   components are divided into several subgroups;
b)   components in the same subgroup are subject to synchronized supervision;
c)   active supervisions of different subgroups are staggered.

An important problem in constructing this kind of non-synchronized super-vision schedule is how we should divide components into subgroups. Our aim is to obtain a grouping scheme which is optimum in the sense that the schedule maximizes the minimum of $P_0(t)$. Previous studies on non-synchronized super-vision schedules [5,6] do not present methods for optimizing the component grouping. This paper gives a systematic way of grouping optimization.

The pointwise availability $P_0(t)$ has several local minima because active super-visions of subgroups are staggered. It is noted that $P_0(t)$ can have its local minima not in the periods where availabilities of all components are decreasing but in the periods where availability of at least one component is increasing. For simplicity of discussion we make the following assumption.

5) $P_0(t)$ can have its local minima when active supervisions of subgroups start, i.e. if we divide all components into M subgroups, all local minima of $P_0(t)$ are contained in the set $h(z_{1k}, ..., z_{nk})$, $k = 1, ..., M$ where

$$z_{ik} \equiv a_i^* y_{ik} + \sum_{\substack{j=1 \\ j \neq k}}^{M} a_j(s_{kj})\, y_{ij} \tag{16}$$

$y_{ik} \equiv$ $\begin{array}{l} 1 \text{ if component i is a member of subgroup k} \\ 0 \text{ otherwise} \end{array}$

$s_{kj} \equiv$ $r + T - d_{kj}$
$d_{kj} \equiv$ remaining time to start of next active supervision of subgroup j from the time point when active supervision starts for subgroup k.

We give an optimization problem which determines a grouping scheme dividing components into M subgroups so that the global minimum of $P_0(t)$, viz. min $h(z_{11}, ..., z_{n1}), ..., h(z_{1M}, ..., z_{nM})$, is maximized. The problem is formulated as follows:

Problem   maximize w subject to the constraints

$$h(z_{1k}, ..., z_{nk}) \geqslant w, \quad \text{for all } k \tag{17}$$

$$\sum_{k=1}^{M} y_{ik} = 1, \quad \text{for all } i \tag{18}$$

$$1 \leqslant \sum_{i=1}^{n} y_{ik} \leqslant n - k + 1, \quad \text{for all } k \tag{19}$$

$$y_{ik} = 0 \text{ or } 1, \quad \text{for all } i \text{ and } k \tag{20}$$

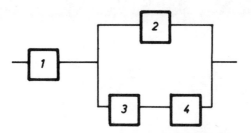

Figure 2.   System structure.

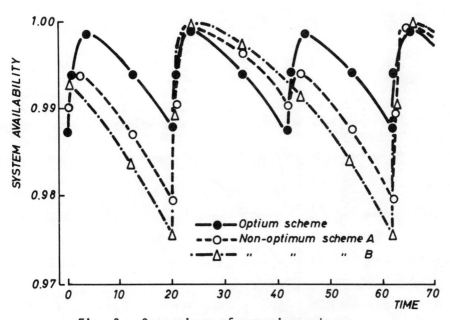

Fig. 3.   Comparison of grouping schemes.

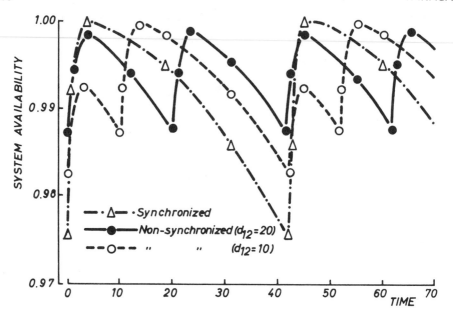

Figure 4.   Synchronized and non-synchronized supervision schedules.

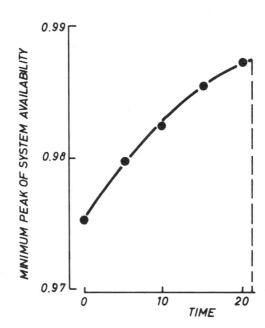

Fig. 5.   Effect of staggering.

Eq.(18) states that every component is a member of one of subgroups. Eq.(19) states that every subgroup has at least one component.

The above problem is a multilinear mixed-integer programming (MIP) problem because $h(z_{1k}, ..., z_{nk})$ is multilinear in Y_{ik} and has terms in the form of y_{ik}. By introducing some new 0—1 variables according to the technique of Watters [7], h can be represented as a linear function of y_{ik}'s and introduced 0—1 variables. Thus the problem is transformed into a linear MIP problem.

Remark 3.   Though some of $h(z_{ik}, ..., z_{nk})$'s may not be local minima of $P_0(t)$, it does not cause any inconvenience to the above problem formulation.

Remark 4.   In the case where maximum allowable number of components for sub-group k is specified as $m(k)$, $(n - k + 1)$ in (19) is replaced by $m(k)$.

Illustrative example

Consider a four-component protective system whose structure is as shown in Fig.2. Let parameters be as follows:

$\lambda_1 = 1.0 \times 10^{-5}$, $\lambda_2 = 3.0 \times 10^{-3}$, $\lambda_3 = 2.0 \times 10^{-3}$, $\lambda_4 = 4.0 \times 10^{-3}$, $\mu_1 = 1.0$ for all i.

Let consider the case where components are divided into two subgroups. Let $r = 1.49$, $T = 40.17$ and $d_{12} = 20$ where r and T are obtained in [4] by using the max—min decision rule for the same protective system. The optimum scheme of component grouping is obtained as shown in Table 1. Table 1 also lists other two grouping schemes which are chosen arbitrary and thus are non-optimum.

Table 1 : Component grouping schemes for $d_{12} = 20$

components in	Subgroup 1	Subgroup 2
Optimum scheme	3, 4	1, 3
Non-optimum Scheme A	1, 3	2, 4
Non-optimum Scheme B	1	2, 3, 4

For the above three grouping schemes we illustrate in Fig.3 time-dependent be-haviours of pointwise availability of the protective system under consideration. The minimum of $P_0(t)$ for each component grouping scheme is: 1) optimum scheme: 0.9872; 2) non-optimum scheme A: 0.9794; 3) non-optimum scheme B: 0.9755. Fig.3 shows the importance of the selection of component grouping scheme in constructing non-synchronized supervision schedules.

Fig.4 illustrates time-dependent behaviours of pointwise availability of the protective system for a) synchronized supervision schedule, b) optimum non-syn-chronized supervision schedule for $d_{12} = 20$ (presented above) and c) optimum non-synchronized supervision schedule for $d_{12} = 10$ where subgroup 1 has component

4 and subgroup 2 has components 1, 2 and 3 as members. The minimum of $P_0(t)$ for each supervision schedule is:

a) 0.9753,   b) 0.9872,   c) 0.9826.

The effect of supervision staggering d_{12} on minimum of $P_0(t)$ is also examined. The result is shown in Fig.5.

Remark 5.   Linear MIP problem is solved by use of an application program called FACOM M-190 MPS/X (Mathematical Programming System/eXtended) at the Data Processing Center of Kyoto University.

REFERENCES

[1] Barlow R.E., Proschan F., Statistical Theory of Reliability and Life Testing, Holt, Rinehart and Winston, New York, 1975.

[2] Kontoleon J.M., Kontoleon N., Chrysochoides N.G., Optimum Active-Inactive Times in Supervised Protective Systems for Nuclear Reactors, Nuclear Science and Engineering, Vol.55, pp. 219-224, 1974.

[3] Takami I., Inagaki T., Sakino E., Inoue K., Optimal Allocation of Fault Detectors, to appear in IEEE Trans. Reliability, Vol.R-27, Oct., 1978.

[4] Inagaki T., Inoue K., Akashi H., Optimization of Supervision Schedules for Protective Systems, submitted for publication to IEEE Trans. Reliability.

[5] Vesely W.E., Goldberg F.F., Time Dependent Unavailability Analysis for Nuclear Safety Systems, IEEE Trans. Reliability, Vol.R-26, Oct. 1977, pp. 257-260, 1977

[6] Bonhomme N.M., Evaluation and Optimization of Inspection and Repair Schedules with Application to Nuclear Power Generation Stations, PhD dissertation, Carnegie-Mellon University, May 1972.

[7] Watters L.J., Reduction of Integer Polynomial Programming Problem to 0—1 Linear Programming Problems, Operations Research, Vol.15, pp. 1171-1174, 1967.

ACKNOWLEDGEMENT

The author expresses his appreciation to Prof. Koichi Inoue of Kyoto University for his valuable comments and suggestions.

CALCULATION OF SYSTEM DOWNTIMES RESULTING FROM PARALLEL SUBSYSTEM REPAIR

Bernd Krogull

Shape Technical Centre, The Hague, Netherlands

ABSTRACT

This method was developed to convert "raw" maintainability data (as collected in the field or derived by the analyst) into system characteristics which can be used in subsequent effectiveness models or directly to compare the recoverability of alternate systems.

Maintainability characteristics of system elements can be described in terms of the probability of maintenance after an operating time interval and the mean and variance of its repair time. The report derives the equations to compute system downtime and repair time distribution from this data in a deterministic manner. The computation has been mechanized for use on direct access computing equipment.

1. INTRODUCTION

A key factor in the effectiveness evaluation of a system maintainability is its downtime, the time required for scheduled and unscheduled maintenance during a period of sustained operation. Scheduled maintenance in the form of preflight, postflight and phased inspections is done in preplanned time intervals based on the required flight schedule. Since each scheduled maintenance "package" is defined, the elapsed maintenance times can be found through time line analysis and the calculation of system downtimes due to scheduled maintenance poses no particular problem.

Unscheduled maintenance actions are repair tasks caused by degraded performance and malfunction or suspected malfunction of system elements (subsystems). The requirement for repair of subsystems arises in a random manner independently for each subsystem. After an operating time interval Δt, n subsystems can assume $(2)^n$ different repair states from "no subsystem needs repair" to "all subsystems require repair". In general two or more subsystems can be repaired simultaneously (parallel repair) if they fail during the same operating time interval and the elapsed repair time for any repair state is the largest subsystem repair time encountered in that state. However, repair times for individual subsystems are not a constant. They vary depending on the nature of the trouble, the experience and the skill of maintenance men, environmental conditions, e.g. weather, or just plain chance due to the varying success in trouble-shooting.

Due to the complexity of this problem, most analytical methods which deal with unscheduled maintenance downtimes are Monte Carlo computer programs. Simulation models are powerful tools for the treatment of interdependent probabilistic problems, however, the results are achieved at the cost of long computer running times which limits the use of such programs in early system development phases when input data are rapidly changing and many alternatives must be investigated in short time.

This report describes a deterministic calculation of system downtimes resulting from parallel subsystem repair. The following section 2 shows how a particular array of n subsystems reduces the number of repair states for which elapsed times must be computed from $(2)^n$ to n and interpretes system downtime as a weighted average of the elapsed state repair times. Two methods to calculate these elapsed times are explained in sections 3 and 4. Section 5 discusses some of the problems germane to the calculation of unscheduled downtimes.

2. GENERAL METHOD

A system S shall consist of n subsystems S_i which can be repaired at the same time if they fail during the same operating time interval (parallel maintenance). The maintainability characteristics of each subsystem S_i shall be described by its parameters

o $P_i (\Delta t)$, the probability that subsystem S_i will require repair after an operating time interval Δt, and

o $f (r_i)$, the frequency function of its repairtime r_i, where $r_1, r_2, ..., r_i, ..., r_n$ is a set of independent random variables.

All possible combinations of subsystems S requiring repair at the same time are shown in Fig. 1 for 3 subsystems. A grouping is introduced such that group i contains all repair/no repair combinations of S_1 through $(S_{(i-1)}, S_i$ requires repair and S_{i+1}, $S_{i+2}, ..., S_n$ require no repair. It is evident that there are $n+1$ groups (including group $i = 0$ with no repair action and resulting repairtime $r_0 = 0$) for n subsystems. The probability of encountering the general group i is

$$c_i = p_i \prod_{k}^{i+1,n} (1-p_k) \tag{1}$$

Since the n groups include all possible combinations, it is

$$\sum_{i}^{0,n} c_i = 1$$

Let the random variable x_i be the repairtime for group i. That is, for an operating interval at

$$x_i = \max (r_k), \quad k = 1, ..., i$$

Let $f(x_i)$ denote the frequency function of x_i. The determination of $f(x_i)$ is of course the major problem in this approach. Approximations to it will be discussed after deriving the characteristics of the repair time distribution for the entire system S.

The probability that x_i is the largest repair time encountered after an operating time interval Δt is

$$c_i = p \{\max (r_k) = x_i\}, \quad k = 1, n$$

and the repair time for the entire system, denoted by the random variable X is the weighted sum of the group variables x_i

$$X = \sum_i^{o,n} [p \ \max (r_k) = x_i \ * x_i], \quad k = 1, n$$

or

$$X = \sum_i^{o,n} [p_i \prod_k^{i+1,n} (1-p_k) * x_i]$$

with frequency function

$$f(X) = \sum_i^{o,n} [p_i \prod_k^{i+1,n} (1-p_k) * f(x_i)]$$

and moment generating function

$$M_X(\theta) = \sum_i^{o,n} [p_i \prod_k^{1+1,n} (1-p_k) * M_{X_i}(\theta)]$$

In particular, first and second moment are

$$E(X) = \sum_i^{o,n} [p_i \prod_k^{i+1,n} (1-p_k) * E(x_i)] \tag{2}$$

and

$$E(X)^2 = \sum_i^{o,n} [p_i \prod_k^{i+1,n} (1-p_k) * E(X_i^2)] \tag{3}$$

So far the total system downtime after an operating time interval Δt has been interpreted as a weighting of the repair times x_i of certain repair/no repair configurations of n subsystems. The key to this deterministic solution is to find a satisfactory approximation to the repair time functions $f(x_i)$. In the following pages two approaches will be discussed. The first one (referred to as a first order approximation) can be worked with a desk calculator and yields system downtime distributions where the computed mean is within 10% of the true mean in most cases. The second approach referred to as a second order approximation) is suitable for electronic computers and yields for the entire distribution results comparable to results from maintenance simulation programs (SAMSON II).

3. A FIRST ORDER APPROXIMATION TO x_i

Referring back to Fig. 1, it was defined that repair time x_i results from the combination of repair actions where subsystem S_i failed while subsystems S_{i+1} to S_n need no repair and subsystems S_1 to S_{i-1} assume all possible repair/no repair configurations.

GROUP	SUBSYSTEM						REPAIR
	1	2	3	——	i	—— n	
(0)	+	+	+		+	+	0
1	—	+	+		+	+	$f(x_1)$
2	+	—	+		+	+	$f(x_2)$
	—	—	+		+	+	
3	+	+	—		+	+	$f(x_3)$
	—	+	—		+	+	
	+	—	—		+	+	
	—	—	—		+	+	
i	All repair/no repair combinations S_1 through $S_{(i-1)}$			No repair $S_{(i+1)}$ through S_n			$f(x_i)$
n	All repair/no repair combinations S_1 through S_{n-1})						$f(x_n)$

+ Subsystem requires no repair
— Subsystem requires repair

Fig. 1 : Grouping of repair combinations for n subsystems

We assume now that the variance of all repair time distributions $f(r_i)$ is small compared to their means $E(x_i)$, and rank the subsystem in increasing order of their means

$$S_1, S_{21}, ..., S_n \quad \text{with} \quad E(r_1 < E(r_2) < ... < E(r_n)$$

The repair time r_i of subsystem S_i is now the dominant repair time of the group i repair action because (with a high probability) all repair actions on subsystems S_i to S_{i-1} will be finished before the one on S_i. Subsystems S_{i-1} to S_n with higher repair times were defined as not failed. Consequently, using the approximation $x_i = r_i$ the total system downtime frequency function is

$$f(X) = \overset{0,n}{\underset{i}{\Sigma}} [P_i \overset{i+1,n}{\underset{k}{\Pi}} (1-P_k) * f(r_i)]$$

Usually the repair time distribution for subsystem i is known to the analyst by its mean, $MTTR_i$, and its variance, VAR_i. It is convenient to compute mean and variance of the system downtime in these terms:

The mean downtime MDT is

$$MDT = \overset{l,n}{\underset{i}{\Sigma}} [P_i \overset{i+1,n}{\underset{k}{\Pi}} (1-P_k) * MTTR_i] \tag{4}$$

from equation (2). The second moments (about the origin) of subsystem repair times r_i,

$$E(r_i^2) = VAR_i + MTTR_i^2 {}^*) ,$$

yield the second moment of the entire system

$$E(X^2) = \overset{0,n}{\underset{i}{\Sigma}} [P_i \overset{i+1,n}{\underset{k}{\Pi}} (1-P_k) * (VAR_i + MTTR_i^2)] \tag{5}$$

from equation (3). Converting back to the moment about the system mean MDT results in the system downtime variance

$$VDT = \overset{1,n}{\underset{i}{\Sigma}} [P_i \overset{i+1,n}{\underset{k}{\Pi}} (1-P_k) * (VAR_i + MTTR_i^2)] - MDT^2 \tag{6}$$

The group $i = 0$ (the no repair case) was not included in equations (4) and (6) since $MTTR_0 = 0$ and $VAR_0 = 0$ do not yield a contribution to MDT and VDT.

If only the cumulative downtime, rather than the individual subsystem contributions are required, this can be computed in a time saving way. The mean downtime for one subsystem is

$$MDT_{S1} = P_1 * MTTR_1$$

adding a second system with a larger repair time yields

$$MDT_{S2} = P_1 (1-P_2) * MTTR_1 + P_2 * MTTR_2$$

from equation (4). This is equivalent to

---

*) from $VAR_i = E(r_i^2 - [E(r_i)]^2$

$$MDT_{S2} = P_2 * MTTR_2 + (1-P_2) * MDT_{S1}$$

Considering subsystems S_1 and S_2 as one unit and adding a third system with $MTTR_3 > MTTR_2$ ($> MTTR_1$ yields in the same way

$$MDT_{S3} = P_3 * MTTR_3 + (1-P_3) * MDT_{S2}$$

and for n subsystems

$$MDT_{Sn} = P_n * MTTR_n + (1-P_n) * MDT_{S(n-1)} \tag{7}$$

Note that the index Si indicates the cumulative downtime of i subsystems, not the downtime of the individual subsystem i, such that MDT_{Sn} is equal to the mean downtime for n subsystems, MDT, in equation (4).

The second moments about the origin, $E(r_i^2)$, can be accumulated in the same manner.

$$G_{S1} = P_1 * E(r_1^2) = P_1 * (MTTR_1^2 + VAR_1)$$

$$G_{S2} = P_2 * (MTTR_2^2 + VAR_2) + (1-P_2) * G_{S1}$$

$$G_{Si} = P_i * (MTTR_i^2 + VAR_i) + (1-P_i) * G_{S(i-1)}$$

The final value, G_{Sn}, is converted back to the moment about the system mean:

$$VDT_{Sn} = P_n * (MTTR_n^2 + VAR_n) + (1-P_n) * G_{S(n-1)} - (MDT_{Sn})^2 \tag{8}$$

The above equations describe the system downtime per time interval Δt. They include the probability c_0 that no repair is required after the operating time Δt. In same cases the repair time density function, given that at least one repair action has to be performed, is of interest. Mean and variance of this distribution, which is generally assumed to be log normal, can be computed readily from system downtime mean and variance. It is mean repairtime, given repair is required:

$$MR = MDT/P_R \tag{9}$$

where

$$P_R = 1 - \overset{1,n}{\underset{i}{\Pi}} (1-P_i)$$

is the probability that at least one repair action is required. The variance about the mean repairtime, VR, can be derived from the second moment about the origin (equation (5)) for the downtime,

$$E(X^2) = \overset{0,n}{\underset{i}{\Sigma}} [P_i \overset{i+1,n}{\underset{k}{\Pi}} (1-P_k) * (VAR_i + MTTR_i^2)].$$

The repair time variance excludes the no-repair case, consequently

$$i = 1, n$$

and P_i must be replaced by P_i/P_R to fulfill the condition

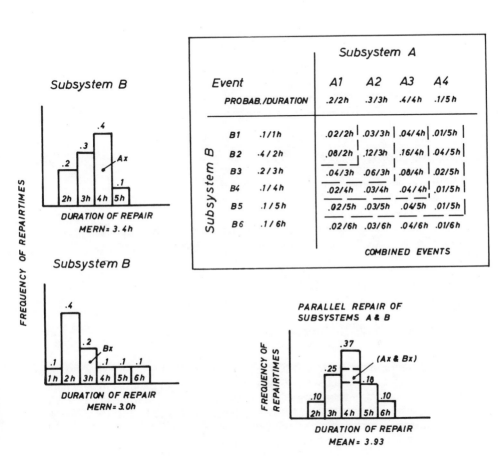

Fig. 2: Combination of discrete repair events.

$$\sum_{i}^{1,n}[P_i/P_R * \prod_{k}^{i+1,n}(1-P_n)] = 1$$

Converting to the moment about the repair time mean yields

$$VR = \sum_{i}^{1,n}[P_i/P_R \prod_{k}^{i+1,n}(1-P_k) * (VAR_i + MTTR_i^2)] - MR^2$$

The sum in the above equation is equivalent to the sum in equation (6), thus

$$\sum_{i}^{1,n}[P_i \prod_{k}^{i+1,n}(1-P_k) * (VAR_i + MTTR_i^2)] = VTD + MDT^2$$

and

$$VR = \frac{VDT + MDT^2}{P_R} - (\frac{MDT}{P_R})^2 \tag{10}$$

4. SECOND ORDER APPROXIMATIONS

In the previous chapter the equations for mean system downtime (equation (4)) and its variance (equation (6)) were derived under the assumption that the mean and variance of group i repair actions are approximately those of the dominant subsystem i, namely $MTTR_i$ and VAR_i. Replacing these values by the true mean and variance of group i repair actions, X_i and VX_i, equations (4) and (6) can be written in their exact form:

$$MDT = \sum_{i}^{1,n}[P_i \prod_{k}^{i+1,n}(1-P_k) * X_i] \tag{11}$$

$$VDT = \sum_{i}^{1,n}[P_i \prod_{k}^{i+1,n}(1-P_k) * (VX_i + X_i^2)] - MDT^2 \tag{12}$$

The second order approximation to X_i and VX_i takes into account, that the mean repairtime of two or more subsystems which are repaired in parallel, in general is larger than the mean of either repairtime distribution. Fig. 2 demonstrates a way to compute the resulting distribution for two subsystems A and B with discrete repair time distributions. The principle of the computation is to compute for all possible combinations of repair events their probability of occurrence and the resulting repair time which is the maximum of all repair times related to the events. For example, events A3 and B3 have a probability of occurring simultaneously of

$$P (A3, B3) = P (A3) * P (B3) = (.4) (.2) = .08$$

and a resulting repair time

$$X (A3, B3) = max (X(A3)X(B3)) = max (4h, 3h) = 4h$$

Adding all combined event probabilities of the same repair time class yields the combined distribution shown in the lower right hand corner of Fig. 2. By approximating

GROUP		SUBSYSTEM						$f(x)$
		1	2	3	4	-----	n	
0		+	+	+	+	+	+	
1		−	+	+	+	+	+	$f(x_1) = f(r_1)$
2	0	+	−	+	+	+	+	$f(x_2) = f(x_1, r_2)$
	1	−	−	+	+	+	+	
3	0	+	+	−	+	+	+	$f(x_3) = f(x_1, x_2, r_3)$
	1	−	+	−	+	+	+	
	2	+	−	−	+	+	+	
		−	−	−	+	+	+	
4	0	+	+	+	−	+	+	$f(x_4) = f(x_1, x_2, x_3, r_4)$
	1	−	+	+	−	+	+	
	2	+	−	+	−	+	+	
		−	−	+	−	+	+	
		+	+	−	−	+	+	
		−	+	−	−	+	+	
	3	+	−	−	−	+	+	
		−	−	−	−	+	+	

Fig. 3 : Repair/no repair combinations relevant to f(x)

continuous functions through step functions they can be treated in the same way.

The procedure described above can be used readily in an electronic computer. However, even a modest number of subsystems yields such a large number of possible combinations, that a systematic computation of all combinations would offer no computer time advantage over a simulation model. It is possible, however, to take advantage of the grouping of subsystems shown in Fig. 1 and compute mean X_i and Variance VX_i for each group of repair actions from the results obtained for the previous group. Thus only $(n-1)$ of the described combining procedures are required for a system with n subsystems.

Fig. 3 shows the grouping of repair actions introduced in Fig. 1. The solid boxes indicate the combinations of repair/no repair actions resulting in a repair time distribution $f(x_i)$ for each group. Note that the repair actions of group 1 are included in group 2 actions, group 3 includes the repair actions of group 1 & 2, etc. In general, group i includes all previous repair actions of groups 1 through $(i-1)$. The computation of mean and variance of group i repairtimes, X_i & VX_i, takes advantage of this fact by combining the (previously calculated) repairtime density function of systems 1 through $(i-1)$ with the repair time function $f(r_i)$ of system i. This yields $f(x_i)$ for group i. The result in turn can be used to compute $f(x_{i+1})$ etc.

5. CONCLUSIONS

The method derived in the previous sections is based on the following assumptions:

- All subsystems of a system can be repaired simultaneously if they fail in the same operating time interval.
- Individual and combined repair times are lognormally distributed.
- Mean and variance of individual repair times are known.

The first assumption is obviously an idealization of the true situation. There will always be a certain number of system elements which must be repaired in sequence. For instance, if two subsystems which are located in the same equipment bay fail, only one maintenance crew may be able to work in that bay at one time due to space limitations. Other subsystems might not be maintained simultaneously due to safety reasons, e.g. fuel system/engine or landing gear/radar, etc. To a certain extent these maintenance conflicts can be handled by a proper selection of the input level. Two incompatible subsystems can be treated as one system element, using the equations for serial maintenance to compute the maintenance characteristics of the new "subsystem". If a subsystem is maintenance incompatible with all other elements of the subsystem, it can be excluded from the computation of parallel maintenance and added later as a serial element. In practice, it was found that the majority of maintenance conflicts has little impact on the resulting system repair time and that only conflicting subsystems with a high maintenance frequency (MTBUMA < 10) need to be manipulated in this way.

The assumption that individual system elements repair times are lognormally distributed is widely accepted in the maintenance literature. No mathematical proof that the repairtime of n subsystems is lognormally distributed (given lognormal elements) can be offered here; however, system repair time distributions generated by a maintenance simulation model (SAMSON II) compare very closely with the lognormal distribution computed deterministically (Fig. 4).

Probability that repair time does not exceed T

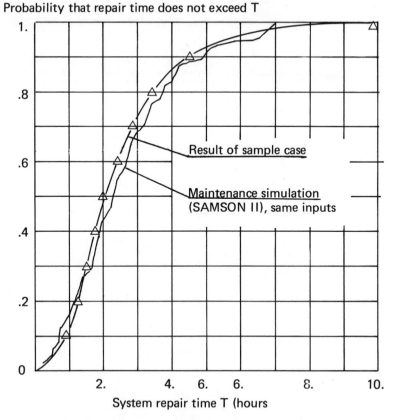

Fig. 4 : Comparison of repair time distribution functions

For the second order approximation the variance of individual repair times is required as an input. In early phases of a system development this information may not be available. In this case the first order approximation will yield estimates of the mean system down and repair time compatible with the accuracy of the sub-system mean repairtime estimates. Though equations (8) and (10) will yield a result for the repairtime variance based on the spread of the subsystem means, it should be realized that the value is lower than the true variance and not a close estimate of the latter.

SECTION 4

MAN-SYSTEM INTERACTIONS

Introduction by the Editors

This section considers certain problems that arise when dealing with relations and reciprocal influences of man and physical systems. The interest is in the entire life cycle of the system and all its phases or stages [1]. Phases that should be accounted for include design, construction or installation, testing and evaluation, commissioning and operation, maintenance, decommissioning, disassembling and ultimate disposal of the system. Therefore, in consideration of this sequence and of other possible environmental factors and constraints, there is a variety of ways and modes by which men relate and interfere with physical systems or machines to produce some desired system output. Two somewhat contrasting goals may be of importance to the analyst, to maximize the human's contribution to the effectiveness of the system of which he is a part and to reduce possible negative impacts or risks which may stem from that overall system on him. The interaction between man and his system creates a closed-loop relationship. For instance, in machine operation practice the operator manipulates the machine and the machine responds; this response stimulates the operator who then responds by a further machine manipulation, and so on.

The general concern is to organize the equipment, environment, tasks and personnel variables in such a way that the whole meets system goals in a manner which is satisfactory both to the system and man, whatever they are, e.g. operators, designers, population, etc.

In this context, it is of importance to point out aspects that are distinctive of man-system interaction, when comparing with system-system or machine-machine interactions. Some aspects of primary concern are as follows:

(i)   Man is an adaptive and learning system element, who might respecify a function or a task.
(ii) Human operator is a multipurpose element. He may be occupied by another task and omissions of specified functions may be due to other events in the system rather than human failure mechanisms.
(iii) Man is in many respects a "holistic data processor" responding to total situations rather than to individual events or system states.

(iv) Man has the ability of selfmonitoring and error correction.

These distinctive aspects of human behaviour lead to a number of difficulties in the search for general models, representations and solutions. Man indeed does not obey the deterministic system or machine specification. We say that a system or machine is state determined, if having specified a time interval, a configuration of internal states and any input function, we can also specify a state transition map which determines next state and then an output function [2]. Engineers are constantly designing deterministic systems as a part of computing, communications, power and other equipment. Yet, at the present time, no practical way appears to model deterministically aspects of human operators and man-system interfaces. Imprecision arises from the unexactness (or inherent approximation) which characterizes the definition of the basic space of events. Therefore, no matter how fully we specify subsequent inputs, we cannot determine exactly what the subsequent states and outputs will be. This line of thought may naturally lead us to the concept of a fuzzy (relational) system, where the fuzziness arises when assigning descriptions and states. Viewed in this perspective, the traditional techniques of system analysis would not be well suited for dealing with situations of interaction of man with physical systems, because these techniques fail to embrace the fuzziness of human behaviour and thinking [3]. Thus, to deal with such systems realistically, one would not look for approaches which make a fetish out of precision, mathematical formalism and models. Rather, interest would lie in a methodological framework which is tolerant of unexactness and partial truths.

Another problem which we would like to be able to treat in man-system interaction is that of completeness of a given model and formal representation. It can be remarked that this problem bears important implications in mathematical logic, where it relates with the concepts of representability and undecidability [4]. Now, in the case of man-system interactions, can we give a reason why we adopt a description of tasks and subtasks and we stop with just these? Might we with advantage attempt to discover other tasks or other important characteristics or attributes which could be added to give more adequate models? To be able to answer these questions, which embrace also other systems beyond man, we must first provide some criterion as to what we want to be able to model and represent. We are therefore led to the idea of completeness and validity relative to a representation of man-system interaction. These notions of completeness and validity may be impossible to prove for most types of systems, however. The inherent variability of humans, their idiosyncrasy and creativity make the attempt of earning complete descriptions of their behaviour unrealistic. Instead, we shall have to consider from case to case the necessary conditions for the use of methods to predict the probability that a specified mission involving man and his interaction with the system is performed satisfactorily.

In this respect, it can be said that man and system interactions are situation-specific in the sense that must be afforded through the consideration of each situation or case in itself. The study of cases would serve to point out and reveal structures and patterns which are testimony of some sort of a global nature of the problem under consideration. In other words, in the search for a representation, there is little to be gained by developing separate and different approximations for each subtask which regards man-system interaction might be isolated. We must admit our inability in finding some standard technique for decomposing the man-system interface into component parts as it is commonly done for physical systems. Rather, in reporting and describing situations where man is involved one has to obey some criteria. These criteria ought to precede the analysis and recognition of common structures and patterns found in different situations. The criteria refer to a certain need of repeatability and reproducibility in any specific man-system interaction. Under practical circumstances the need of allowing for repeatability and reproducibility entails a group of attributes and sentences which must be used to describe the situation. Particularly, if the nature of the system and of the reciprocal interactions between man and system satisfies some general necessary conditions, one could envisage kinds of systematic or general analysis and quantification [5]. Obviously, no assurance can ever provide that any model or representation really works.

In examining man-system interface, therefore, we are faced with a number of possible situations. Errors, failures which affect this interface may be classified in various ways, e.g. in terms of what caused the error, in terms of what the consequences are, in terms of the stage of system development and deployment in which errors may occur. In this section of the book we found useful to provide not only the logical argument, but the evidence, for the inclusion of man-system interactions in the various stages of the life of real systems.

In essence, the scope is to present a number of specific cases from which the reader may gain at least partial information on three types of recurrent problems. First, is the state of the art. Particularly, the procedures which can be followed in a probabilistic approach and the developments which are deemed necessary. Next, is the influence that probabilistic methods of analysis may have in understanding the relationships between man and machine systems. Third, is the problem of evaluating the relative weight of man-system interactions during the phases of system life cycle.

Thus, the contributed papers have been arranged in an order in which we believe the novice will find it most profitable to read them. The paper by Rasmussen, "Notes on Human Error Analysis and Prediction", is a good introduction to the problem. It explores the various ways in which human errors and behaviours can be defined, describes the assumptions under which human factors analysts perform, introduces the man-system interaction and interface concept and the effect of error on system safety. Some questions where answers can be provided are listed. Attention is generally focused on the immediate man-machine interface which may turn out to be a control panel or console. This is not to say that during system operation there are no other man-machine interfaces. For example, calibration and test points, test equipment, are all interfaces for the maintenance man and deserve consideration.

The paper by Rzevski, "Improving System Reliability by the Elimination of a Class of Design Errors", should prove valuable to the reader with a background in engineering or logical design, in helping him to get a feel for those design errors which may undermine the reliability of the system and are most amenable to a treatment and corrective action. Particularly, Rzevski makes explicit the basic relationship between the concept of perceivable system and principles which can be used in the management of the project.

Philipson in dealing with "LNG Operations Risk Analyses: Evaluation and Comparison of Techniques and Results", considers the phase of the evaluation of a design and project. This subject seems - so to speak - parallel to the one considered by Rzevski. Major public hazards may result from many man-made systems. As a result, efforts are made to estimate the risk and to evaluate if it can be accepted. Once risk concept has been defined, it is impossible, however, to place a precise number on it. The evaluation process is then faced with a situation of incomplete information.

Andow and Lees in their paper "Real Time Analysis of Process Plant Alarms", provide a diagrammatic approach to the search for causal links and data structures related with alarm signals. Since this approach is in real time, it should also prove valuable for the correct operation of the system through the discovery of failures and disturbances that caused the problem.

"Material Control Study: A Directed Graph and Fault-Tree Procedure for Adversary Event Set Generation", a paper by Lambert et al. covers the case of system or plant protection against improper use or operation, i.e. diversion of special nuclear material. A quantitative and qualitative analysis of the event sets and simulation allow one to determine the effectiveness of material controls. A key tool in the identification of adversary actions and conditions of controls is the diagraph-fault-tree methodology.

The paper by Daniels, "The Availability of a Computer System Communications Network as Perceived by a User and Viewed Centrally" closes the section. The author discusses the way in which the needs of customers and users of a system are met. It is admitted that effective operation of the system must rely upon some optimization in view of contrasting objectives. State transition model and short cut techniques would offer a basis for judging the relative merits of particular designs.

REFERENCES

[1] D. Meister, "Human factors: Theory and practice", Wiley-Interscience, New York, N.Y. (1971).

[2] L. Padulo, M.A. Arbib, "System theory - A unified state-space approach to continuous and discrete systems", W.B. Saunders Co., Philadelphia, Pa.(1974).

[3] L.A. Zadeh, Outline of a new approach to the analysis of complex systems and decision processes, IEEE Trans. on Systems, Man, and Cybernetics, SNC-3: 28 (1973).

[4] S.C. Kleene, "Introduction to metamathematics", North-Holland Publ. Co., Amsterdam, The Netherlands (1952).

[5] "Human error analysis and quantification", Task Force on Problems of Rare Events in the Reliability Analysis of Nuclear Power Plants, Committee on Safety of Nuclear Installations, SINDOC (78) 84, OECD-NEA, Paris, France (1978).

NOTES ON HUMAN ERROR ANALYSIS

AND PREDICTION

Jens Rasmussen

Risø National Laboratory
Electronics Department
DK-4000 Roskilde, Denmark

INTRODUCTION

An increasing effort is being put into the study of
human error analysis and quantification. Unfortunately,
the need for results has been growing more rapidly than
the research needed to supply the basic knowledge on
human functions in industrial installations and the related human failure mechanisms. Accordingly, the following review will be as much a review of problems as a
survey of possible solutions. However, if the conditions
under which present methods are applicable can be stated
explicitly, then these conditions can be used as design
criteria for systems by serving as "criteria of analysability". Those criteria can then be modified or released
as more efficient methods of analysis and better data
become available.

RISK ANALYSIS, THEORY, AND PRACTICE

When discussing the role of the human element in
industrial reliability and safety analysis, it is worth-
while to consider the relation between risk analysis and
the actual, real life risk of losses due to accidental
events.

The outcome of an analysis of the risk imposed by
an industrial plant or system is a theoretical construct
which relates empirical data describing functional and
failure properties of components and parts of a system

to a quantitative or qualitative statement of the overall risk to be expected from the operation of the system.
This relation is derived from a definition of the boundaries of the system considered; a model describing the
structure of the system and its functional properties in
the relevant normal and accidental states; together with
a number of assumptions made to facilitate the mathematical modelling. These assumptions, the model, and the
source of the empirical data, are equally as important
parts of the result of the risk analysis as the statement
of risk level found. Therefore, in the overall judgement
of the risk potential of the system, it is necessary to
consider different categories of risk:

Accepted Risks

These are the risks related to the states of accidental maloperation and to the causes and effects considered in the analysis. It goes without saying that any
risk of unacceptable magnitude uncovered during an analysis will result in a change of the design. The functions
of the operating staff in the operation and maintenance
of the system will be an important part of this analysis.

Oversights and Design Errors

The quality of a risk analysis depends upon the completeness of the analysis. In modern complex industrial
installations based on very large production units, an
important contribution to the overall risk is due to
"major loss" situations of very low probability, often
resulting from a complex chain of events including coincidence of errors and from a priori improbable failure
modes. Therefore, sources of risk hidden behind an incomplete analysis become a major problem. Whether such
discrepancies between the analytical model and the actual
plant are considered to be design errors or errors of
analysis depends upon what is taken for given. The general problem of verifying the completeness of an analysis
and thus insuring that a safety-related design target has
been met, can very probably lead to the need for criteria
related to "design for risk analysability".

Errors of Management

The value of a risk analysis largely depends upon
the degree to which the actual, operating plant will
satisfy the conditions and assumptions underlying the
analysis. Again, this largely depends upon the managerial
organization within the plant. This type of risk is re-

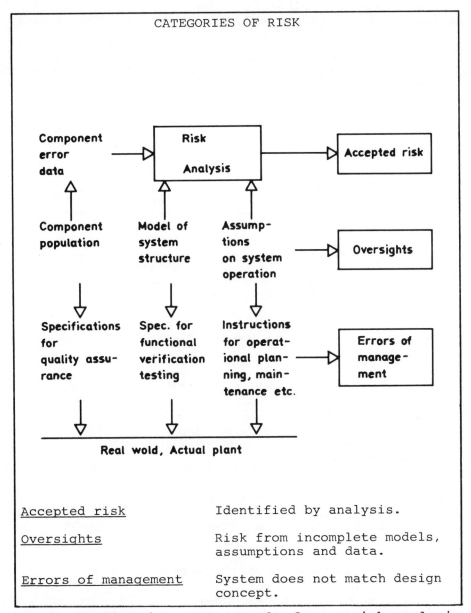

Fig.1. The most important result from a risk analysis
is <u>not</u> the accepted risk figure, but the
mode<u>ls</u>, data, and assumptions which should
serve as instructions for management.

lated to such activities as planning of quality control, inspection, and testing which serve to ensure that the components and parts of the plant do match the populations forming the base for the empirical fault data, and that the plant is built according to the design specification and will not be subject to modifications and changes without proper risk evaluations. This relates to the technical equipment as well as to selection, training, and organization of operating staff and to the design of work procedures and operating instructions.

It lies in the nature of oversights and errors of management that they are tied to human errors, but it also lies in the variety and complexity of organizations and design activities that quantitative risk modelling in these areas is practically impossible at present. However, a comprehensive qualitative analysis has been made by Johnson (1973).

The following discussion of the systematic analysis of the human role in system reliability and safety will be concerned with the analysis behind the first category of risk discussed in the previous section (i.e. accepted risks). It follows from the nature of things that oversights are not included. "Errors of management" are violating the basic assumptions of the systematic methods, and they are therefore not considered explicitly in the discussion.

However, what is meant by "systematic analysis" is not always evident and invites some discussion. In the present paper, systematic method will be synonymous to engineering analysis when viewed as the alternative to expert judgement, which is taken to be more akin to the performance of a professional _art_. In general, engineering analysis is based on quantitative data and invariate relations applied to systems and structure which are accessible to inspection or control. Practically speaking, the opposite is often the case for the behavioural sciences which depend upon personal, professional skills. It is a "well-known fact that the aim of a skilful performance is achieved by the observance of a set of rules which are not known as such to the person following them" (Polanyi 1958). Clearly, great care should be taken when including human behaviour in engineering models. In addition, a drastic limitation in the cases which can be handled must be expected, if the analysis is to be based on formalized, systematic methods rather than on expert judgement.

Of course the importance of this aspect depends upon the application of the reliability and safety analysis. If the analysis is used for a relative ranking of different alternative solutions during system design, a number of conditions can be considered equal, and the criteria for analysability will lead to less tight constraints compared with the situation where the analysis aims at a verification or documentation of the design target in terms of quantitative risk level.

A special problem is caused by current developments of large computer codes for overall system reliability and safety analysis. This development is ahead of the formulation of acceptable models of human functions and error mechanisms in the systems under consideration.

Consequently, the only solution for the time being is to include simplistic models of human performance. To be compatible, such models are depending on the mathematical or logical structure of the program rather than on psychological properties. This is acceptable as long as such human error models are used only for sensitivity analysis, to determine the range of uncertainty due to human influences. If quantitative risk figures are derived, these should be qualified by the assumptions underlying the human error models used, and by a verification of the correspondence of the assumptions to the system which is analysed.

"HUMAN ERROR" - DEFINITION AND CLASSIFICATION

The term "human error" is loaded and very ambiguous. Basically, a human error is committed if the effect of human behaviour exceeds a limit of acceptability. Of course, the classification of a specific behaviour as an error depends as much upon the limits of acceptability as it depends upon the behaviour itself. In practise, the limits are sometimes defined after the fact, by someone who can base his judgements on a careful, rational evaluation of the function of the system, while the specific behaviour possibly was a quick response in a stressed dynamic situation. Therefore, as it has been argued by Rook (1965) and Swain (1969), it is necessary to distinguish clearly between errors induced by inappropriate limits of acceptability; i.e., by the design of the work situation, and errors caused by inappropriate human behaviour. Furthermore, as discussed by Rigby (1969), errors can be classified as random errors, due to random variability of human performance such as variations in manual

precision or force; differences in timing; simple mistakes; and slips of memory; as <u>systematic errors</u> which
can be caused by personal abnormalities or inappropriate
system design; and, finally, <u>sporadic errors</u>, occasional
"faux pas" which are infrequent and often unexplainable
erroneous actions. From this definition it follows that
it is difficult to give general characteristics of sporadic errors.

The influence from <u>random errors</u> largely depends
upon the extent to which the limits of acceptability can
be arranged to span the range of natural variability of
performance of the people selected to the task, and the
opportunity given the operator to monitor his performance
and correct the errors he commits.

<u>Systematic errors</u> can be related deterministically
to specific properties of the work situation and can be
eliminated if the causal relations can be identified and
changed. It is a very important category of errors within
the context of monitoring and supervisory task in automated systems where the operators typically have to respond to changes in system operation by corrective actions.

In the present general discussion, two types of
systematic errors seem to be important and should be
considered:

First, human responses to changes in a system will
be systematically wrong if task demands exceed the limits
of capability. Demands and capability may conflict at
several aspects of a task such as time required, availability of state information, background knowledge on
system functioning, etc. The operator must be able to
trade off demands and limitations by choice of a proper
strategy. An example would be for the operator to remove
time constraints by first bringing the system to a safe,
stationary state.

Secondly, systematic human errors may be caused by
several kinds of procedural traps. During normal work
condition human operators are extremely efficient due
to a very effective adaptation to convenient, representative signs and signals. On the other hand, these will
very probably lead the man into difficulties when the
behaviour of the system changes. An operator will only
make conscious observations if his attention is alerted
by an interrupt from the subconscious processes. This
means that he will only deal with the environment con-

sciously when his subconscious, automated, or habitual responses no longer will control the environment adequately. Likewise, he cannot be expected to cope with a new unique change or event in the system in the problem oriented way of thinking if the interrupt is caused by information, which immediately associates to a familiar task or action. It is very likely that familiar associations based on representative, but insufficient information will prevent the operator from realizing the need to analyse a complex, unique situation. He may more readily accept the improbable coincidence of several familiar faults in the system rather than the need to investigate one new and complex fault of low probability. In this way, the efficiency of man's internal world model allows him to be selective and therefore to cope effectively with complex systems in familiar situations, and, at the same time, may lead him into traps which are easily seen after the fact. Davis concludes from an analysis of traffic accidents (Davis, 1958):

> "It is usual for a person to have expectations, or to hold to what may be called an hypothesis about every situation he meets, even when information is notably incomplete. This hypothesis, which is in some degree the product of his previous experience of similar situations, governs the way in which he perceives the situation and the way in which he organizes the perceptual material available to him. As he receives further information, his hypothesis tends to be modified or amended or abandoned and replaced. Sometimes, however, an hypothesis and the expectations which go with it, appear to be unduly resistant to change."

The importance of the different categories of errors depends upon the task conditions. In repetitive tasks which are preplanned, errors due to demands exceeding resource limits and errors due to procedural traps, etc., will be of minor importance since when experienced they are readily removed by redesign of the task. Therefore, random errors related to human variability would typically be more prevalent.

On the other hand, systematic errors are significant contributors when operators have to respond to abnormal plant condition during monitoring and supervisory tasks. Reviews indicate that failure of human operators to identify abnormal states of a plant or system plays an important role in accidents and incidents in complex systems (Rasmussen 1969, Cornell 1968). However, even if

the state of the system is correctly identified, the
operator may still be caught in a procedural trap. A familiar, stereotyped sequence of actions may be initiated
from a single conscious decision or association from the
system state. If the corresponding procedure takes some
time; e.g., it is necessary to move to another place to
perform it, the mind may return to other matters, and
the subconscious actions will become vulnerable to interference, particularly if part of the sequence is identical to other heavily automated sequences. Systematic
human errors in unfamiliar tasks are typically caused by
interference from other more stereotyped situations and,
therefore, the potential for systematic errors depends
very much upon the level of the operator's skill. The
fact that operators can control a system successfully
during a commissioning and test period is no proof that
operators will continue to do so during the plant life-
time.

A basic problem when dealing with systematic erroneous responses to unfamiliar situation is the very
low probability of such complex situations. In a properly designed system there should be a reverse relation
between the probability of occurrence of an abnormal
situation and its potential effect in terms of losses
and damage. In modern large centralized systems, the
consequence of faults can be very serious and consequently the effect of human errors in situations of extremely low probability must be considered. In such cases,
the potential for systematic errors cannot be identified
from experience, but only by a systematic functional
analysis of realistic scenarios modelling the relevant
situations.

Sporadic errors are, by definition, infrequent errors which are not caused by excessive variation in the
normal pattern of behaviour, but rather are extraneous
acts with peculiar effects. They must be considered in
risk analysis even though they are insignificant contributors to error rates because they are likely to
escape the designer's attention. Therefore, they may not
be covered by the automatic protective systems and can
cause chains of event with large consequences.

RELIABILITY AND SAFETY ANALYSIS

In discussing the methodological problems of including the human element of a system in a systematic analysis, it appears to be practical to consider the problems

related to reliability analysis and safety analysis separately. The terms, safety and reliability, are not too
well defined. In the following discussion, they are used
to characterize two different aspects of the sensitivity
of a process plant to accidental maloperation.

Reliability is a measure of the ability of a system
to maintain the specified function. Classical reliability
analysis leads to figures describing the probability that
a system will perform the specified function during a
given period or at a given time (M.T.B.F., Availability
etc.). Reliability analysis is related to the effects
caused by absence of specified function. In case of a
process plant reliability, figures are used to judge the
expected average loss of production; in case of a safety
system to judge the expected average loss of protection.

System safety is related to. the risk, i.e., the
expected average losses, caused directly by the presence
of a state of accidental maloperation, in terms of human
injuries, loss of equipment etc. To judge the safety of
a system, it is, therefore, necessary to study the probability of specific courses of events initiated by the
primary fault, and to relate the probability to the effects of the maloperation, i.e., judgement of system
safety is based upon an extensive accident analysis.

In the following discussion a very clearcut distinction between the methods used for reliability and
safety analyses is drawn, and very simplistic descriptions of the methods are used. This is tolerable since
the purpose of the discussion is to reach some general
conclusions regarding the conditions which should be
met by a system in order to make a systematic risk analysis possible.

HUMAN FACTORS PROBLEMS IN RELIABILITY ANALYSIS

The definition of the reliability of a system or
system component is generally stated in terms of the
probability of a specified function versus time, such
as: "Reliability is defined as that characteristic of
an item expressed by the probability that it will perform its required function in the desired manner under
all relevant conditions and on the occasion or during
the time intervals when it is required so to perform"
(Green and Bourne 1972).

Reliability analysis is concerned with the departure from the specified function of the plant and its parts and components. "Specified function" is rather stable during plant operation and is unambiguous related to the functional design intention. Therefore, the frame of reference of reliability analysis is generally well established. The basic method of reliability analysis is to decompose a complex system into parts or components, to a level at which component properties are recognized from widespread use, so that empirical fault data can be collected. In principle, this break-down must be carried through to a level where component function is invariate with application. This is possible for many standard components, which are designed for a specific function and used according to specifications in system design, e.g., resistors, pumps. In some cases, however, alternative "specified functions" are possible at the level of breakdown at which data collection can be arranged. For example, in practice relays and valves can serve to close or break a circuit. Fault data must then be classified according to the function performed, as the related probabilities of failure may be very different for different functions.

Overall reliability characteristics of the system are derived by means of models representing the relations between component and system failures. The degree of sophistication of the probabilistic system models used to derive reliability figures characterizing the total system depend upon the quality of the component fault data available. If only bulk data on component failure rates are available, as is typically the case for process plant components, simple probabilistic models are used which represent system structure only as far as to specify whether components functionally are connected in series or parallel during specified system function (reliability block diagrams, simple fault trees). If more detailed descriptions of failure mechanisms are available, and if good data are available for failure and repair rates, then much more complete failure modelling becomes worthwhile.

In the methods of human reliability prediction in practical use (Meister 1971, Swain 1973), this technique has been transferred to human performance. The complex and often very system-specific human functions are broken down into typical, recurrent functions for which reliability data can be collected. Such elementary functions are in practice only distinguishable by their external effects, and are therefore generally charactierized as "subtasks". This technique must, however, be used with caution, since the human element within a technical system has properties which cause difficulties with respect to the basic aspects of reliability analysis:

Man is an <u>adaptive and learning system element</u>, and may very probably respecify a function or a task. Consider for example a monitoring task from a power plant. The specified task: "If the frequency meter indicates below 58 C/S, disconnect load to save the generator". If an operator has only met readings below 58 C/S due to poor meter performance, he may very reasonably respecify his task: "If ...., then calibrate meter" - and lose a generator (as happened at one stage in the US power black out in 1965). Unless such respecifications are known, reliability prediction will be systematically wrong.

Furthermore, a human operator is a <u>multipurpose element</u>. He may be occupied by another task, and omission of specified function may be due to other events in the system rather than human failure mechanisms.

Man is in many respects a <u>holistic data processor</u> responding to total situations rather than to individual events or system states. Complex functions may be performed by skilled operators as one integrated and automated response. In this case fault data can only be obtained by a realistic simulation of the total function (Regulinski 1973). Break-down of complex functions is only acceptable if the performance is paced by the system, i.e., cues from the system serve to initiate elementary skilled subroutines individually and to control their sequence. This is the case in many manual tasks, e.g., mechanical assembly tasks, but can probably also be arranged by more complex mental tasks by properly designed interface systems.

The failure properties of a specific function depend upon the operating conditions, and for technical components weighting functions are generally used to modify fault data according to load and environmental effects. The <u>great variability</u> of human performance makes a similar weighting of fault data by "performance shaping factors" mandatory (Swain 1973), but the application is difficult as "operating conditions", such as motivation, stress, fatigue, etc., are badly defined and difficult to quantify; "expert judgements" are generally the only method available.

New problems arise if <u>several internal mechanisms</u>

TYPICAL TASK STRUCTURES

Stereotyped Sequence

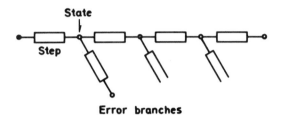

Activity made up by a sequence of steps, controlled by
a set of rules - a procedure - which relates specific
actions with the state of work. Error detection typically occurs when the subsequent steps turn out more
difficult. Task context must be considered when collecting error rate data.

Sequence of Goal-Oriented Steps

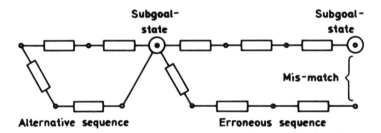

Goal-oriented performance facilitates error detection
at the subgoal states. If error correction is possible
then feed-back effects control overall reliability.
Performance between goal states is flexible and collection of error data for its elements is irrelevant.

Fig. 2. Simplified illustration of typical task
         structures.

with very different failure probabilities can serve the
same external component function. The more flexible a
component is, the more difficult will these problems be,
especially if the internal organization has autonomous
features such as optimization, adaptation, learning. These
are the prominent features of the human elements in a system. The internal process used to perform a specific external task by a man depends strongly upon his training
and skill, his prior experiences of system behaviour, his
subjective performance criteria etc. Failure data collected from a system in which an operator meets a specific task frequently and performs it by a sensory-motor
response will have no relation to the failure probability
in a system where the demand for the task is infrequent,
e.g., as part of an emergency action. The response will
then probably be performed by a sequence of cognitive
functions. The resulting problem can only be solved by
classifying fault data according to the internal functions
used to perform a task. In this situation, weighting of
fault data collected from standard, frequently initiated
tasks, by means of "performance shaping factors" is not
acceptable. At present, this means that human reliability
prediction is only feasible, if "specified function" of
human operators is synonymous with a familiar task performed by a skill maintained through frequent use or ex-
ercise.

A human trait having great influence upon the reliability of human performance is the <u>ability of self-
monitoring and error correction</u>. The mechanism of error
detection depends upon the task situation and the intention of the operator. If the intention is to perform a
given sequence of actions, as will be the case in most
familiar and stereotyped tasks, error detection will
typically be due to difficulties in the sequence caused
by errors in the preceding steps. It is obvious that
this kind of error detection has drastic effects on reliability. The probability of selecting the wrong key in
your key-ring is high; however, the probability that you
should not succeed in entering your house of this reason
is nil.

In more open and flexible situations, the human
intentions will typically be related to attainment of a
specific goal, and the reliability in reaching the goal
will be related to the persistence in the intention and
the care with which a discrepancy is observed or detected,
rather than error probability during the striving towards
the goal. If you intend to spend a comfortable night reading a good book, the probability of success is not related

to the error rate in operating the lamp switch nor to the
reliability of the power system, but rather to the probability of having a supply of candles and matches or the
proximity of a good restaurant.

Clearly, the error correction features of a task
depend upon the structure of the sequence, and not on
the individual steps. The potential for error correction
influences the reliability of the task drastically and
determines which parts of the task should be considered
in detail as well as the data needed in an analysis.

Monitoring and error correction act as a feed-back
loop around the task performance, and the overall quality of the basic performance itself. In addition to the
use of this feed-back feature to improve the reliability
of a task design, a proper design of the error detection
and correction function can be used as the means for making a reliability analysis of the total task practical,
since the lower limit of the overall reliability can be
determined independently of the error rate by the reliability of the monitoring function alone together with
the frequency of error opportunities. This may be the
only way to assess the reliability of poorly structured
complex human performance - e.g. in response to unfamiliar
situations. It should also be noted that the influence of
error correction features of a task will lead to a strong
dependence of the error rates collected for human actions
upon the context from which they are collected.

To sum up, systematic analysis and quantification
of system reliability is not feasible unless the design
of the system and the work situation of its operators
satisfy some general conditions. Necessary conditions for
the use of decomposition methods to predict the probability that a specified task is performed satisfactorily
by human operators are:

- there is no significant contribution from systematic
  errors due to redefinition of task, interference from
  other tasks or activities, etc.;
and
- the task can be broken down to a sequence of separate
  subtasks at a level where failure data can be obtained
  from similar work situations;
and
- these subtasks are cued individually by the system or
  by other external means, so that systematic modification of procedure does not take place;

<u>or</u>
- if these conditions are not satisfied, e.g., because
  the task is performed as one integrated whole, or it
  is performed by complex and variable human functions
  such as higher level cognitive functions, then the effect of the task must be reversible and subject to an
  error detection and correction function, which in turn
  satisfies the above-mentioned conditions for predictability.

      In this discussion it has been assumed that empiri-
cal data on human error rates in industrial process plants
are available. Unfortunately, such data are very scarce.
Most of the data discussed in the literature seem to be
derived from the original work done at the American Institute of Research (Payne et al. 1962, Munger et al.
1962) or to be very general estimates. Systematic data
collection in industrial plants has not been reported
apart from the Licensee Event Reports published by US-NRC
(see later). Error rates are difficult to derive from
these reports because the denominators, the number of error opportunities, are not known. An attempt to estimate
the denominators to be used with the Licensee Event Reports has been made by Fullwood et al. 1976.

HUMAN FACTORS PROBLEMS IN SAFETY ANALYSIS

      System safety is related to the risk, i.e. the ex-
pected average loss, in terms of human injuries or damage to equipment or environment, caused by transitions
from specified function into a state of accidental maloperation.

      System safety has to be judged from an extensive
accident analysis. To identify the course of events following the initiating fault, and to determine the ultimate effect, and its probability, it is necessary to use
a detailed functional description of the system including
functional properties both within and outside the normal
operating régimes of the plant. Different systematic
techniques have been developed for this purpose, based on
fault tree analysis (Fussel 1973, Powers 1973) and cause-
-consequence analysis (Nielsen 1971, Taylor 1977).

      To evaluate the effects of accidental maloperation,
statistical data differentiating the different modes of
failure of the components must be available. Furthermore,
severe effects are generally results of course of events
of extremely low probability, and may be related to com-

ponent modes of failure which are a priori improbable
and insignificant contributors to component bulk data.

In the analysis of accidents, the human element is
the imp of the system. The human reliability, i.e., the
probability that operators perform the "specified functions" is of course an important factor in system safety,
e.g. when operators are assigned special monitoring and
protective functions. In safety analysis, however, a more
difficult problem is the analysis of the effect of
specific, erroneous human acts. The variability and flexibility of human performance together with human inventive-
ness make it practically impossible to predict the effects
of an operator's actions when he makes errors, and it is
impossible to predict his reaction in a sequence of accidental events, as he very probably misinterprets an unfamiliar situation.

These cases indicate that search strategies used to
identify accidental chains of events in the technical
system will not be adequate to identify the human potential for creating hazardous situations. In general, search
strategies related to fault tree analysis and cause-consequence analysis are sufficient to identify the effects
on one part of a system from errors which an operator
commits during work on that part due to mistakes etc. However, contrary to reliability analysis, a safety analysis
cannot solely be based on search strategies which use the
specified task as a guide or structure. Effective search
strategies have to take into account the fact that operators are multipurpose components moving freely around in
the system. Rare, but risky events in one part of the
system can be caused by erroneous acts by operators working on quite different parts of the system; such as dis-
connection of cables to facilitate vacuum cleaning;
interference from manipulation of electric welding gear;
short circuits from dropped tools. These types of errors
must be found by a search guided by a topographical proximity criterion - analysis of all activity close to the
part of the system in question. Furthermore, psychological
proximity should be considered. It happens that features
of an unfamiliar situation demanding a special procedure
instead release an automated routine belonging to other
task conditions, especially if parts of the two task sequences psychologically speaking are very similar.
Examples are given in the case stories in the appendix.

However, a heuristic search based on these criteria
may not be sufficient to identify the potential for high
consequence, low probability situations which typically

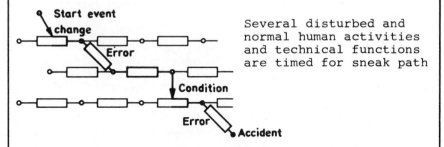

TYPICAL STRUCTURES OF ANALYSES

Reliability Analysis

Structure of reliability analysis is tied to the
structure of the specified or normal task sequence.

Risk Analysis

Structure of risk analysis depends on the total set
of accidental chains of events. Completeness problem
can be circumvented by feed-back techniques, if collec-
tive critical events can be defined and monitored.

Sneak Path Analysis

Several disturbed and
normal human activities
and technical functions
are timed for sneak path

Low probability, dramatic consequence chains of events
can be identified morphologically. Find potential
sources and targets for accident, "design" the necessary route and find errors and changes which will open
it up.

Fig.3. Simplified illustration of typical structures
of analysis.

are related to complex situations caused by <u>several</u> coincident abnormal conditions and events. A heuristic
strategy to identify such situations resembles a design
algorithm: First, potential for accidents such as high
energy accumulations, toxic material concentrations etc.
are identified together with potential targets for accidental release such as people, environment etc. Then possible accidents are <u>designed</u>, i.e., the technical (mal)-
functions and human actions which are necessary to form
the route from source to target are determined. Finally,
it is determined how changes in the normal system together
with coincident normal and abnormal human activities will
meet the designed accident pattern. Such accidents are
sometimes due to "sneak paths" which are formed by minor
mishaps or malfunctions in simultaneous human activities
which only become risky in case of very specific combinations and timing.

In practice therefore, human variability makes a
quantitative safety analysis unrealistic, unless the system design satisfies a number of conditions. Like other
problems in system design caused by component performance
variability, the problems in accident analysis can be
circumvented if feed-back functions are introduced, i.e.,
if feed-back links are introduced in accidental courses
of events by means of monitoring and correction functions,
as it has also been discussed in the previous section.
Major losses or human injuries caused by accidental maloperation are typically related to uncontrolled release
of stored energy in the system. Apart from accidents
caused by spontaneous fractures of energy barriers and
explosions, accidents are typically the effects of disturbances of mass or energy balances. There is, therefore,
a time delay between the primary cause and the release
due to the integrating effect of a disturbed balance. This
time delay makes correcting actions possible.

Furthermore, critical variables related to the energy
level of the balance can be found which can indicate potentially risky maloperation irrespectively of the preceding course of events. If a safe state of the system can be
defined, and it can be reached through the action of a
monitoring and protection function which does not in itself introduce potential risks, an upper bound of the
probability of a large class of event sequences leading
to the effect which is monitored can be found by a <u>re-
liability</u> analysis of the protecting function together
with the frequence of error opportunities. Such protective
functions can be performed by human operators if the task
is designed so as to be accessible to human operator re-

liability analysis, or can be performed by automatic safety systems.

A properly designed protective function enables the derivation of the probability figures needed in accident analysis by means of a reliability analysis of the protective function. Together with data on the frequency of error opportunities, this analysis leads directly to upper bounds on probability of courses of events leading to the effect which is monitored. It is the extensive use of automatic, protective systems in nuclear power plants that has made it possible to perform a quantitative analysis - including human performance - of the safety level of such installations (Norman Rasmussen et al. 1975).

The difficulty to get the empirical data from real life situations needed to predict the probability of specific erroneous human acts which are possible contributors to rare chains of events leading to accidents, results in the following conditions for quantification of system safety:

The probability of specific consequences of accidental events in a system can only be derived by a decomposition analysis:

- it can be demonstrated that the effect of erroneous human acts are not significant contributers to the probability; if necessary by introduction of interlocks or barriers which prevent human interaction;
or
- the effects of erroneous human acts are reversible and detectable by a monitoring or safety function which can be performed by operators or automatically.

If the <u>reliability</u> of such barriers and safety functions can be quantified then an upper bound of the probability of the event in question can be derived from the frequency of error opportunities.

THE TASK OF CALIBRATION AND TESTING

As a basis of a more specific discussion, the task of calibration and testing has been chosen since it has a great influence upon the reliability of automatic safety systems. The following data are based on a review of "Licensee Event Reports" as they are edited and compiled by "Nuclear Power Experience". The reports reviewed

are from the January 1978 state of the collection and
include those in the category of operator/technician errors: <u>calibration, setting and testing</u>.

In general, reliable statistical information on human
error rates related to different types of human errors is
difficult to gather from this kind of event reporting.
While the denominator problem of obtaining the actual frequency of error opportunities can be solved in principle,
the reports do not actually give information on the total
frequency of errors committed, but rather the frequency
of errors which are not immediately corrected by the operator himself. This means that the frequencies of different
categories of errors found in the reports are heavily
biased by factors depending upon the specific work situations. Clearly, human errors which lead to latent system
faults or to effects which are not reversible by immediately counteraction will typically find their way to the
reports.

To judge the effect of error recovery and to relate
the errors found in the reports to task content in general, a description of the task in rather general terms
is useful. Generally, the task of calibration is a well
defined, proceduralized task. The system states, goals and
procedures implied in the task are familiar to the operator and subject to formal instruction and training. The
errors to be expected are typically omission of steps in
the procedure and faults/mistakes related to rather elementary acts. Problems related to conflicts of goals and
misinterpretation of system states, which are typical of
responses to unfamiliar situations, are of minor importance in the present context.

The task of calibration consists of subtasks of different content, and a preliminary review of the case
stories indicates that the following phases should be
treated separately:

1. <u>Establishment of the test circuit</u>. The component or
   subsystem to be tested is isolated from the plant and
   connected to the test equipment.
2. <u>The calibration act</u>. The test equipment and/or the subsystem to be tested is manipulated or adjusted according to a specified procedure, and the response is com-
   pared/judged according to the specified standard in
   order to obtain agreement.
3. <u>Restoration of normal operating condition of the sys-
   tem</u>. The test equipment is removed, and the normal
   "line-up" of valves and switches in the system is restored.

The principal observation is the high contribution from omissions of steps in the procedure. It should be noted that nearly all these steps are functionally unrelated to the calibration itself and include such things as return of switches or valves to operating position after test; check of standby channels before disconnecting a channel for test; or purely administrative steps (table 1). It should also be noted that most of the omitted steps are found in the last phase of the task. One explanation of the large contribution from such omissions could be that the effect of these omissions is not directly apparent which therefore prevents any immediate recovery. However, this may not be the only cause. The fact that the steps omitted are unrelated to the prime goal of the task - the calibration - may in itself lead to a high probability of omission. In an analogous context, Whorf (1956) in analysing causes of industrial fires observes that "the name of a situation affects behaviour" - which can lead to similar effects. It is also noteworthy that this type of error to some extent is repeated in several redundant channels (see table 2).

Another significant class of errors are "faults and mistakes" which mainly include two types: One is mistakes such as replacement of sample size with that of another task; use of positive correction factor instead of negative; calibration with increasing pressure instead of decreasing, etc. Another type is the faults concerned with incorrect or inaccurate set points. This class of error is most significant within the calibration act itself, which is the only part of the task subject to quantitative specifications and which may lead to mistakes without immediate detectable functional effects. Broadly speaking, we here have two related kinds of error: Variability and inaccuracy in a quantitatively specified adjustment and mistaken interchange of two or more possibilities.

During the first phase of the task, the establishment of the test circuit, the different types of errors all contribute. This might be expected a priori, since this phase gives the operator most freedom for action, and there will be large differences in task conditions between different types of circuits or components to be tested or calibrated. Again the largest group is omission of functionally isolated - including administrative - acts. Extraneous acts are found only in this phase, and two types are noted - effects on other systems can be caused by inappropriate spatial orientation such as misplacement of jumpers, or by simple "clumsiness".

TABLE 1

HUMAN ERRORS IN TEST AND CALIBRATION
111 CASES FROM U.S. LICENSEE EVENT REPORTS

Type of error / Phase of task		Test circuit set-up	Calibration Adjustment	Restoration of normal operation
Omissions	Functionally isolated acts omitted	7	–	(50)
	Administrative acts omitted	5	–	–
	Other	1	2	1
Errors in task	Improvisation insuff. knowledge	2	–	–
	Secondary condition not considered	3	3	1
	Misinterpretation	2	2	–
	Faults and mistakes	4	(13)	3
	Manual "clumsiness"	1	2	–
Extr. acts	Topographic misorientation	3	–	–
	"Clumsiness"	1	–	–

Table 2 COMMON MODE ERRORS IN TEST AND CALIBRATION

Number of channels	Number of cases
1	95
2	11
3	2
4	2
17	1

One type of error affecting all three phases is due to change of procedures in a way that secondary features affect the calibration, i.e. influence of properties of the system which are not effective or obvious when the prescribed procedure is used. They may have the character of procedure "improvements": Adding recorders (which load signal sources); too rapid adjustments (not considering time constants); use of another available size of filter paper (which changes calibration) etc.

The following comments can be made regarding the predictability of the reliability of this specific task:

- Systematic errors play a minor role in the cases considered.

- The task of calibration can be broken down into rather independent subtasks which are frequently performed and for which empirical fault data therefore can be collected. Error rates of the following categories of error are relevant:

  . Omission of acts which are functionally isolated from the task sequence.

  . Using the wrong alternative of two possible, when the choice has no functional effect upon the subsequent steps.

  . Spread in accuracy when adjusting variables to reference values.

  . Operational "improvement" of procedures by exclusion of secondary conditions which have no immediate influence upon the task.

There is no indication in the cases reviewed that extraneous acts committed during work on other systems or during other activities play any role in the availability of the systems. In some cases miscalibration or defeat of system function is explained in the event report by such extraneous, inadvertent acts, but the number is insignificant.

Special problems are found in redundant safety systems in attempting to predict the probability of repetition of errors in subsequent calibration tasks. The cases reviewed indicate that repetition of "omission of functionally isolated acts" in subsequent tasks plays an important role, but, as could be expected, there is also an indication that systematic errors caused by misinterpretations and operational "procedure improvements"

play a much more significant role in the overall reliability of redundant systems. Therefore, to make probabilistic prediction meaningful, strict control of the
task sequence and its content by constraints from equipment design is necessary to limit effectively the possibility of improvisation and "improvement". This also
places a need for hard constraints upon the <u>managerial
system, which can be the source of changes leading to
common mode errors</u>.

In passing it should be mentioned that the causes
behind the dominant types of human errors can very probably be removed through a proper design of equipment and
work content. For instance, equipment can be designed so
as to link necessary, but functionally isolated acts,
tightly to other acts which lead to immediate apparent
functional effects if they are omitted. From the present
review of event reports it appears that even a simple reliability analysis of the task sequence, based on human
reliability data presently available, can support a redesign of the calibration task.

In conclusion, the features of the task of calibration and testing are such that the reliability of the
task can be estimated if empirical error rates can be obtained.

The Licensee Event Reports supply valuable information on human errors in this task, but further in-plant
investigations are needed to supply denominator figures
or error rates. Furthermore, analysis of operator's opportunities of self-monitoring and error correction in the
specific work situations will be needed to facilitate
general use of the data.

CONCLUSION

In principle, a process plant design, which is not
based on extensive experience from similar concepts, is
only acceptable if performance design targets can be verified by systematic analysis including a quantitative reliability and safety analysis.

A quantitative safety analysis is only possible if
the plant design is performed according to guidelines
derived from the limitations of the available methods.

The design must be based upon a qualitative accident
analysis. Accident potentials cannot be identified by an

evaluation of the effects of all possible courses of accidental events. They must be identified directly by a
systematic search. Heuristic search strategies related
to energy and poisonous matter concentrations have been
developed to serve this purpose (Johnson 1973, Powers
1973).

When accident potentials are identified in this way,
the sequences of accidental events, which are capable of
triggering an accident, must be identified by a systematic, qualitative cause-consequence or fault tree analysis. If a quantitative probabilistic evaluation of the
sequences so identified indicates unacceptable risk - or
if a quantitative analysis is not possible due to lack of
statistical data, monitoring and protection functions
must be introduced in the design.

Such functions must be designed so as to be accessible to a quantitative reliability analysis. During the
reliability analysis of complex protective systems, it is
generally important to keep track of the temporal relations of events, and simple reliability block diagram
analysis must be replaced by more sophisticated methods,
such as Markov models, renewal theory etc., compatible
with an analysis of causal chains of events.

A protective function can be performed by an automatic system or a human operator.

Reliability analysis of human performance is only
feasible if the tasks are performed by sequences of
skilled subroutines which are separated and initiated by
proper cues from the system. The reliability of more complex and freerunning tasks cannot be predicted directly;
an acceptable prediction of results can only be made in
this situation if the effects of the actions are reversible and subject to verification by an operator, following
a predictable check procedure, or covered by an automatic
protective function.

Automation in this way does not remove man from a
system, neither does it force him into the role of a
trained robot. Automation serves to replace unexpected
tasks at unpredictable moments by tasks which can be
planned and trained and which can be based upon qualified
decisions, such as supervision, test, and maintenance.

A proper design policy will decrease ·the influence of
unpredictable performance shaping factors, such as stress
and motivation. When introducing automatic safety systems,

the designer takes responsibility of plant safety and thus relieves the operator from stress. The actions of safety systems are related to rather general criteria concerning the initiating plant states and complex, safe protective systems will decrease plant reliability. The operator thus has a supervisory task to protect the plant from unnecessary automatic safety actions. The responsibility of the operators is related to the reliability of plant operation.

The motivation of plant operators can be maintained in automatic systems if they are allowed to use their abilities and take responsibility in the tasks they are allocated. There is no reason not to permit this as long as the system is designed in a way which allows them to verify the effects of their decisions and actions in a predictable way.

REFERENCES

Cornell, C.E., 1968. "Minimizing Human Errors". Space Aeronavtics 1968, Vol. 49, March, pp. 72-81.

Davis, D. Russel, 1958. "Human Errors and Transport Accidents". Ergonomics 2, pp. 24-33.

Fullwood, R.R., and Gilbert, K.J., 1976. "An Assessment of the Impact of Human Factors on the Operations of the CRBR SCRS". Science Applications Incorporated Report SAI-010-76-PA.

Fussell, J.B., 1973. "Fault Tree Analysis - Concepts and Techniques". NATO Conference Liverpool 1973. In: Generic Techniques in Systems Reliability Assessment. Edited by E.J. Henley and J.W. Lynn. NATO Advanced Study Institute. (Nordhoff, Leiden, 1976).

Green, A.E., and Bourne, A.J., 1972. "Reliability Technology". Wiley-Interscience, 1972.

Johnson, W.G., 1973. "MORT - The Management Oversight and Risk Tree". Prepared for the U.S. Atomic Energy Commission. SAN 821-2. Submitted to AEC. February 12, 1973.

Meister, D., 1971. "Comparative Analysis of Human Reliability Models". AD-734 432, 1971.

Munger, S.J., Smith, R.W., and Payne, D., 1962. "An Index of Electronic Equipment Operability: Data Store". American Institute for Research Report AIR-C-43-1/62--RPL. Contract DA-36-039-SC-80555.

Nielsen, D.S., 1971. "The Cause-Consequence Diagram Method as a Basis for Quantitative Reliability Analysis". Risø-M-1374. ENEA CREST, May 26-28, 1971.

Nielsen, D.S., 1974. "Use of Cause-Consequence Charts in Practical Systems Analysis". In: Reliability and

Fault Tree Analysis. Theoretical and Applied Aspects of Systems Reliability and Safety Assessment. Papers of the Conference on Reliability and Fault Tree Analysis. Berkeley, September 3-7, 1974. Society for Industrial and Applied Mathematics. Philadelphia, 1975, pp. 849-880.

Nuclear Power Experience. Edited by Nuclear Power Experience Inc., P.O. Box 544, Encino, California.

Payne, D., and Altman, J.W., 1962. "An Index of Electronic Equipment Operability; Report of Development". AIR-C-1/62 FR.

Polanyi, M., 1958. "Personal Knowledge". Routledge and Kegan Paul. London 1958.

Powers, G.J., and Tomkins, I.C., 1973. "Fault Tree Synthesis for Chemical Processes". AICHE Journal Vol. 20 No. 2, pp. 376-387.

Powers, G.J,, and Lapp, S.A., 1977. "The Synthesis of Fault Trees". In: J.B. Fussel and G.R. Burdick (Eds.): Nuclear Systems Reliability Engineering and Risk Assessment. SIAM, Philadelphia, 1977.

Rasmussen, J., 1969. "Man-Machine Communication in the Light of Accident Records". IEEE-GMMS, ERS International Symposium on Man-Machine Systems. Cambridge, 1969. IEEE Conf. Records No. 69 (58-MMS. Vol. 3).

Rasmussen, N. et al., 1976. "Reactor Safety Study, Appendix 2". WASH-1400.

Regulinski, T.L., 1973. "Human Performance Reliability Modelling in Time Continuous Domain". NATO Conference, Liverpool, 1973. Also in Henley and Lynn (Ed.): Generic Techniques in System Reliability Assessment, Nordhoff, 1976.

Rigby, L.V., 1969. "The Nature of Human Error". Sandia Laboratories, SC-DC-69-2062, October 1969.

Rook, L.W., 1965. "Motivation and Human Error". Sandia Laboratories, SC-TM-65-135, September 1965.

Swain, A.D., 1973. "Improving Human Performance in Production". Industrial and Commercial Techniques Ltd. 30-32 Fleet Street, London EC4.

Swain, A.D., 1969. "Human Reliability Assessment in Nuclear Reactor Plants". Sandia Laboratories. SC-R-69-1236.

Taylor, J.R., and Hollo, E., 1977. "Experience with Algorithms for Automatic Failure Analysis". In: J.B. Fussel and G.R. Burdick (Eds.): Nuclear Systems Reliability Engineering and Risk Assessment. SIAM, Philadelphia, 1977.

Whorf, B.L., 1956. "The Relation of Habitual Thought and Behaviour to Language". In: Language, Thought and Reality. Selected Writings of Whorf. Ed. John B. Carroll, MIT Press, 1956.

APPENDIX

CASE STORIES

The following case stories illustrate some of the phenomena which make reliability and safety prediction difficult. Unless otherwise indicated, they have been obtained from private communications with process plant operators. In such cases details have been deleted and the information generalized to avoid reference to the source.

Case

During normal operation of a process plant the power supply to the instrumentation and the control console slowly disappears.

Investigation

The manual main circuit breaker in a motor-generator supply is found to be in the off position. The conclusion of an investigation was that a roving operator, inadvertently had switched from a routine check-round to the Friday afternoon shut down check-round and turned off the supply. The routes of the two check-rounds are the same, except that he is supposed to pass by the door of the generator room on the routine check, but to enter and turn off the supply on the shut down check. Something "en route" obviously has conditioned him for shut down check (sunshine and day dreams?). The operator was not aware of his action, but did not reject the explanation.

Comments

Human operators move around in the plant, and it can be difficult to predict where in the causal structure of the plant he interferes. His actions may not be initiated by an event in the system or specified by a program, but by subconscious mechanisms, i.e. it is difficult to predict when he interferes and how.

Case

During start up of a process plant the plant is automatically shut down during manual adjustment of a cooling system.

Investigation

During start-up the operator monitored the temperature of a primary cooling system and controlled it by switching off and on a secondary cooling pump to avoid water condensation in the primary system due to the cold cooling water. On this occasion he observed the temperature to reach below the low limit, signalling a demand to switch off the secondary pump, while he was talking to a co-operator over the phone. He then switched off the primary pumps and the plant immediately shut down automatically. He did not recognize the cause immediately, but had to diagnose the situation from the warning signals.

The control keys for the two sets of pumps are positioned far apart on the console. A special routine exists during which the operator switches the primary pumps on and off to allow an operator in the basement to adjust pump valves after pump overhaul while they communicate by phone. Is the cause of the event subconscious switching of procedures due to the phone call?

Comment

The case illustrates some features of operator behaviour:

- Change in procedures by secondary, unpredictable events or conditions.

- The operator introduces couplings in the system by coincident omission of one task and performance of an inappropriate action.

- The risk may be related to the inappropriate and unpredictable act rather than to the omission.

Case

An experimental plant shuts down automatically during normal operation due to inadvertent manual operation of cooling system shut off valve.

Investigation

A safety shut-off valve in the cooling system which is routinely closed during post-shut-down check procedures, was closed manually. The valve control switch is placed behind the operating console, and so is the switch of a flood lighting system used for special operations

monitored through closed circuit television. The switches
are neither similar nor closely positioned. The operator
has to pass the valve switch on his way to the flood
light switch.

In this case the operator went behind the console to
switch off the flood light, but operated the shut off
valves which caused plant shut down through the interlock
system.

Comments

Strongly automated and stereotyped action sequences
are frequently initiated by a single conscious decision.
If the action takes some time, e.g., you have to move to
another place to perform the action, the mind may return
to other matters, and the sequence is vulnerable to unpredictable conditions, particularly if the sequence intended in some of the steps overlap other familiar and
automated sequences.

Case

Butadiene explosion at Texas City. (Loss Prevention,
Vol. 5, Am. Inst. Chem. Eng. 1971).

Investigation

"Loss of butadiene from the system through the leak-
ing overhead line motor valve resulted in substantial
changes in tray composition ...". ..."The loss of liquid
in the base of the column uncovered the calandria tubes,
allowing the tube wall temperature to approach the temperature of the heat supply. The increased vinylacetylene
concentration and high tube wall temperature set the stage
for the explosion which followed". ..."The make flow meter
showed a continuous flow: however, the operator assumed
that the meter was off calibration since the make motor
valve was closed and the tracing on the chart was a
straight line near the base of the chart. The column base
level indicator showed a low level in the base of the
column, but ample kettle vapor was being generated".

Comment

Wisdom after the event tells that closed valve
together with continuous flow signals possible leak, and
the risk implied calls for investigation. The skilled
operator, however, conforms his observations individually

with his expectations and process-feel. If abnormal observation refers to a familiar situation, he sees no problem
and does not investigate the matter. You cannot predict
his response without knowing his daily experiences. It
can be difficult to predict the probability that an operator performs a specified function because he may have
respecified his function - sometimes with good reason.

This can happen, even if there is a clear prewarning:

Case

Melt down of fuel element in nuclear reactor. "Nuclear Safety", September 1962.

Investigation

Certain tests required several hundred process coolant tubes to be blocked by neoprene disks. Seven disks
were left in the system after the test, but were located
by a test of the gauge system that monitors water pressure on each individual process tube. For some reason the
gauge on one tube was overlooked, and it did not appear
in a list of abnormal gauge readings prepared during the
test. There was an additional opportunity to spot the
blocked tybe when a later test was performed on the system. This time the pressure for the tube definitely indicated a blocked tube. The shift supervisor failed, however, to recognize this indication of trouble. The gauge
was adjusted at that time by an instrument mechanic to
give a midscale reading which for that particular tube was
false. This adjustment made it virtually certain that the
no flow condition would exist until serious damage resulted.

Case

Docket 50219-167: Two diesel generators set out of
service simultaneously.

Event Sequence

8.10 permission to perform surveillance test on containment spray system No. 1 including electrical and mechanical inspection of diesel generator No. 1.

8.20 permission to take diesel No. 2 out of service
for oil addition.

Both systems out of service for 45 min. Foreman overlooked test of No. 1 system when permitting diesel No. 2
operation.

Comment

Coincident unavailability of redundant systems
caused by improper timing of routine tasks. Difficult to
predict due to dependence on station "software" vulnerable
for changes and oversight due to absence of cues from the
system supporting attention.

IMPROVING SYSTEM RELIABILITY BY THE ELIMINATION OF A CLASS OF

DESIGN ERRORS

George Rzevski, Dipl.Ing.

School of Electronic Engineering and Computer Science,
Kingston Polytechnic
Kingston upon Thames, U.K.

ABSTRACT

This paper considers a hypothesis on the relationship between system design methods and system reliability. It sets out to discuss a class of human errors which affect system reliability and are committed, or indirectly caused, by system designers.

It defines the concept of 'perceivable' systems and illustrates how perceivability reduces the frequency of occurrence of human errors. A method for the design of perceivable systems is then described. The method is based on a set of principles, which are summarised in the paper, and on a set of detailed guidelines, which are referenced. The same principles can be applied to the design of hardware, software and management systems; different guidelines are required for different classes of systems.

Finally, comments are made on experience gained in using the method by members of staff and postgraduate students in the School of Electronic Engineering and Computer Science at Kingston Polytechnic.

A CLASS OF DESIGN ERRORS WHICH MAY SERIOUSLY AFFECT SYSTEM RELIABILITY

There exists considerable evidence that a significant number of system failures is caused by human error.

It is perhaps less widely known that the majority of these

errors are committed by system designers rather than system operators (1).

Many errors which occur during the system design stage and cause system unreliability may be classified as oversights and omissions rather than errors of judgment.

The following example may serve to illustrate this type of error: in a large and very well known electronics company, with which the author was associated some years back, the design office produced large overlapping sheets of diagrams containing hundreds of logic gates and interconnecting wires. The complexity of the diagrams was such that in spite of careful checking some design omissions and mistakes regularly passed unnoticed and later caused system failures.

The most common design error which passed undetected through various stages of design checking and prototype testing was the incorrect wire connection on logic diagrams.

It is important to note that design oversights of this kind may cause system failures many years after the commissioning of the system. Large systems often have many different modes of operation and the particular mode which contains a 'bug', that is, a design error, may occur very rarely, perhaps only in exceptional circumstances.

However, large, cluttered and poorly organized design drawings, diagrams, specifications and descriptions may cause system unreliability even if they are correct. Since they are difficult to comprehend and interpret, they could be said to impair communication between system designers and others. Production and testing engineers, maintenance personnel, operators and even reliability analysts are known to have made mistakes attributable to incorrect interpretation of badly devised system descriptions and instructions.

These mistakes, which may be said to have been caused indirectly by bad design practices, are often responsible for serious system failures.

Omissions, oversights and inadequate design documentation are, however, only a small part of the problem.

Far more important for system reliability is the fact that many large systems are designed primarily to meet specified performance requirements while not much attention is paid by designers to the processes of testing, maintaining, repairing and operating the system.

Could such bad design practice itself be classified as a human error? Arguably yes — an error of judgment potentially as dangerous for system reliability and safety as, say, overstressing of important system components.

Examples of such design errors may be found in almost every field of engineering activity. A collection of most drastic examples of this kind exists in the software industry. Software engineers know that many expensive large computer programs have been designed with almost total disregard for functions of testing, maintenance and updating.

THE NOTION OF 'PERCEIVABLE' SYSTEMS

All human errors discussed in the preceding section have a common cause: the complexity of the system in relation to which a person is expected to undertake a task, i.e. the complexity of the diagram one is expected to check for correctness, the complexity of design documentation one is expected to interpret, the complexity of circuitry one is expected to repair, etc.

It is important to note that what matters here is the complexity of the system _as perceived_ by the person who is expected to carry out the task rather than the complexity in some absolute sense.

The 'perceivability' of a system plays an important part in system reliability and needs defining.

A system is considered _perceivable_ if all system elements and their interconnections can be "held in mind" at one and the same time (2).

Although the ability to perceive a system (in the above sense) varies from one person to another, there seems to be a reasonable agreement amongst researchers on the factors which make a system perceivable:

(a)   the number of system elements and their interconnections must not be excessive. For example, systems are considered imperceivable if they consist of more than 10–12 elements,

(b)   the purpose and function of each element must be clearly defined; multi-functional elements reduce perceivability,

(c)   the format of the system, i.e., its physical layout, layout of diagrams, etc., must be simple. For example, one functional block on a single printed circuit board,

one flowchart on a single page, etc., make for
perceivable systems,

(d)   the variety of types of elements and of types of
       patterns formed by element interconnections must be
       limited;   that is, a considerable degree of standardi-
       sation of elements and interconnection patterns is
       required to make a structure perceivable.

A question which presents itself immediately upon reading these
conditions is how to make an exceedingly complex system perceivable.
Is it conceivable that a large chemical plant, or a large digital
computer, or a large software system can be designed so that a
person can 'hold in mind all system elements and their interconnections at one and the same time'?

The answer is a tentative 'yes'. By designing a system as a
hierarchy it appears to be possible to achieve that at each hierarchical level all conditions which are required for perceivability
are satisfied.

The importance of the notion of perceivable systems cannot be
over-emphasised. It is well known that people tend to neglect or
to underestimate the importance of things they cannot perceive and
understand. All available evidence seems to show that perceivable
systems, because of their ease of checking, testing, maintaining,
modifying and operating, are much more reliable and safe.

A METHOD FOR THE DESIGN OF PERCEIVABLE SYSTEMS

In order to improve system reliability by reducing the
occurrence of human error it is necessary to develop a method of
making the system itself, as well as the system documentation,
perceivable to all those who are expected to perform tasks related
to the system. In other words, there is a need for the development of a method for the design of perceivable systems.

Research with the aim of developing such a method has been
undertaken at Kingston Polytechnic. Some results have been
reported in (3), (4), (5).

The method which has emerged appears to be applicable to a
very wide range of engineering hardware and software systems and
has a potential use in design of management systems.

Although developed independently, the method has many similar-
ities with the structured programming as reported in (6), (7).

The design method is based on a number of principles, some of which are stated and discussed briefly below.

1.   Principle of trial-and-error

The design is, basically, a trial-and-error process which consists of three distinctly different activities carried out iteratively at every stage of the design. These activities are as follows:

(a)   the creation of a number of tentative design solutions,
(b)   the testing of each tentative solution against the design specification,
(c)   the selection of the best solution.

The process of creation of tentative design solutions cannot be logically explained (8), (9). However, a number of techniques which may help to generate original solutions exist and are described, for example, in (10),(11). A classical work on creativity is (12). The technique incorporated in the Kingston methodology, which appears to be helpful in carrying out the activity (a) is to create as many alternatives as practical before converging on the definitive design solution.

The activity (b), that is, the testing of tentative solutions, can be undertaken only if the design specification clearly states the desired performance parameters. This activity consists of: testing for correctness, for realisability and for feasibility.

The testing for correctness consists of evaluating tentative design solution behaviour under specified input conditions and comparing this behaviour with that specified.

The evaluation can be carried out by experimentation (with a prototype), by analysis, or by simulation. This activity is deterministic and can be, at least in principle, computerised. In some cases correctness of a solution can be proved using formal methods.

Testing for realisability means determining whether the proposed solution can be, in toto, implemented by an existing real system, for example whether a proposed data transformation can be realised by an existing subroutine. Those solutions which are not realisable must be tested for feasibility - that is, whether a real system which would implement the solution under consideration may be constructed.

For the activity (c) to be performed consistently throughout
the design process it is important that the design specification contains the criterion for selection of optimal solutions.

2.   Principle of decomposition

The creation of tentative design solutions consists of:

(a)   decomposing future system, as described by the design
      specification, into constituent elements,
(b)   devising a specification for each element, and
(c)   interconnecting the elements.

These three activities amount to creating a new structure.

In general, design can be usefully categorized as inventive
design, which offers radically new solutions to design
problems, or evolutionary design, which offers some improvement to existing solutions.

The principle of decomposition is applicable only to inventive design. In an evolutionary design the creation of
tentative solutions, that is, of new structures, consists
simply of modifying elements and/or element interconnections
of existing structures.

3.   Principle of minimizing connectivity

Decomposition of a system into subsystems must be performed
in such a way that the transfer of information/energy/
materials between subsystems is minimized.

Adhering to this principle ensures that interfaces between
newly created subsystems are simplified and that their interconnections are reduced to a minimum.

4.   Principle of top-down approach

The preferred sequence of design is top-down. Commencing
with the specification the highest level in the hierarchical
structure is first created then the subsequent lower levels
are established through to the design details.

This principle accords with a general 'wholistic' strategy
for problem solving as described by Pask, and is in complete
contrast with the popular approach, practised by many

designers who commit themselves early on to a set of components and then attempt to interconnect them into the system.

5.   Principle of optimal life-cycle

The best design solution must take into account the requirements and constraints imposed by each stage of the system
life-cycle.

A typical system has the following life-cycle: conception,
design, design testing, design modifications, production,
assembling, quality control, packaging, storing, marketing,
distribution, installing and commissioning, operation, maintenance and repairs, up-dating, replacement.

This principle must not be overlooked when the design
specification is being devised. For example, the convenience
of usage, the ease of testing and maintenance, etc. must be
included in the specification together with more conventional
requirements, such as (computational) efficiency.

6.   Principle of continuity

The design process has no natural end; it often continues
throughout the system life-cycle.

As design progresses both the client and designer learn and
consequently tend to modify system requirements. According
to Popper (8), this is inevitable - the solution of a problem
always generates new problems. Implications are that:

(a)   the planning of the design must allow for modification
      contingencies, and,
(b)   design solutions must be such that they can be easily
      modified.

7.   Principle of universality

A very large number of real systems can be designed using
only a small selection of classes of abstract models and
design techniques.

This is, perhaps, the most important principle of General
Systems Theory (13). It provides a basis for the development
of a design methodology which may be applicable across conventional subject disciplines.

Based on these principles detailed guidelines for the design of software systems have been formulated.

Guidelines for the design of hardware systems, based on the same set of principles, are in preparation.

EXPERIMENTAL TESTING OF THE PROPOSED DESIGN METHOD

An extensive method of testing of the proposed design principles and guidelines has been undertaken.

The testing has been organized in the following manner: post-graduate students attending our Master's Course in the Computer-Aided Design of Engineering Systems are divided into two groups and each student from the first group undertakes to design a software system of reasonable complexity according to a slightly different set of design guidelines; students from the second group are then given to test, modify or translate programs designed by the first group. Difficulties in understanding computer programs designed by somebody else are observed and conclusions drawn about the effectiveness of proposed design guidelines.

Such a method of testing the design methodology requires a great deal of time, students' cooperation and patience. It is, nevertheless, a practical method, and its main advantage is that it gives fast feedback.

Preliminary results fully confirm the hypothesis that in order to improve system reliability by reducing the frequency of occurrence of human error, it is necessary to design the system to be perceivable to all those who are expected to perform tasks related to the system.

It is perhaps worth noting that on a number of occasions the same set of principles has been used as a basis for the design of educational systems, as reported, for example, in (14) and (15).

REFERENCES

(1) J. Rassmussen, Human Reliability, Nato ASI, Sogesta, July 1978.
(2) Börje Langfors, Theoretical Analysis of Information Systems, Auerbach 1973.
(3) M. Renton, G. Rzevski, POLYMARK – A Suite of Programs for the Computer-Aided Solution of Stochastic Problems, Proc. CAD 78 Conference, Brighton 1978.
(4) G. Rzevski (editor), Notes on Computer-Aided Design Methodology, Kingston Polytechnic 1978.

(5)   L.M. Popovic, An Algorithmic Approach to Large Scale Problem
      Solving, Ph.D. Thesis, Kingston Polytechnic, January 1978.
(6)   O.J. Dahl, E.W. Dijkstra, C.A.R. Hoare, Structured Programm-
      ing, Academic Press 1972.
(7)   Infotech State of Art Report − Structured Analysis and Design,
      Infotech International 1978.
(8)   Karl Popper, The Logic of Scientific Discovery.   Hutchinson
      1972.
(9)   Karl Popper, Objective Knowledge, Oxford University Press.
(10) Christopher Jones, Design Methods, Seeds of Human Futures,
      Wiley 1971.
(11) Edward de Bono, Lateral Thinking − A Textbook of Creativity,
      Ward Lock Educational 1970.
(12) A Koestler, The Act of Creation, Pan Books 1964.
(13) Ludwig von Bertalanffy, General System Theory, George
      Braziller 1968.
(14) A.A. Kaposi, G. Rzevski, An Approach to the Design of CAD
      Courses, Proc. CADED International Conference, Middlesbrough,
      July 1977.
(15) G. Rzevski, A Systems−Oriented Degree Course in Electrical
      and Electronic Engineering, Proc. Conference on Teaching of
      Electronic Engineering in Degree Courses, University of Hull,
      April 1976.

LNG OPERATIONS RISK ANALYSES: EVALUATION AND COMPARISON OF TECHNIQUES AND RESULTS

Lloyd L. Philipson

Institute of Safety and Systems Management, University of Southern California, Los Angeles, California 90007

ABSTRACT

This paper surveys the results and compares the techniques that have been employed in LNG risk analysis for three prospective sites of large scale LNG import terminals. Risks may arise from LNG vessel operations near populated areas and from operations at the terminal. The probability of an accident occurring in LNG operations, that would be a significant threat to the public, is very small. Should such an accident occur, nevertheless, its consequences could be great. Moreover, it has to be recognised that, with a view to the differences in the models and hypotheses on which computations are based, significant uncertainties may affect final estimates.

1. INTRODUCTION

The analysis of public safety risks in liquefied natural gas (LNG) importation is comparable in bredth and depth with that of the risks of nuclear power. Many of the same issues have arisen with regard to the analytical methods which are adopted and the completeness, accuracy and overall credibility of the results (1). Still, not all hazards are entirely understood and some analysis processes require data and assumptions that are not completely satisfactory. Readers will perhaps also be aided in recognising the generality of application of the same kinds of techniques to other large scale hazardous systems as well.

LNG, consisting primarily of methane, is produced at a liquefaction plant where natural gas is cooled to a temperature of about $-162°C$ and is thereby reduced to a liquid with about 1/600 of the original volume. In this form it is efficiently carried by specially constructed ships, nominally carrying five 25,000-cubic meters, insulated tankloads of the LNG, to an import terminal. There it is piped ashore through an insulated pipeline and stored in several large insulated tanks, each containing for example 88,000 cubic meters. A vaporisation plant draws liquid from these tanks, heats it to its original gaseous form and pumps the gas into a distribution network. The public risks of LNG derive from its great concentration of energy, able to be released in an accident by a spill and large fire; or by a spill and formation of a neutrally buoyant cloud of flammable vapour that might drift to a nearby populated area and there ignite.

The problem of estimating the probability of an accident occurring in LNG operations seems to be eased somewhat because consequential accidents can occur only at points in the LNG system where large amounts of LNG are present and that are located sufficiently near a populated area. These points are the ship near the shore or in harbour, underway or docked; the land storage tanks; and, perhaps, the cryogenic pipeline carrying the LNG from the ship to the tanks. Given this situation, this paper deals with the problem of risks in LNG vessel operations near populated areas and then in the operations of the fixed storage and processing systems of a large scale LNG import terminal. Examples considered are the once proposed Los Angeles and Oxnard, California, terminals, located in populated coastal areas and the present-ly proposed terminal at Point Conception, located in a remote area of the California coast.

2. RISK ANALYSIS FOR VESSEL OPERATIONS

Fig. 1 exhibits the principal steps in a vessel spill risk analysis. As applied to LNG ships, the inputs define the characteristics that are relevant to modeling the pro-

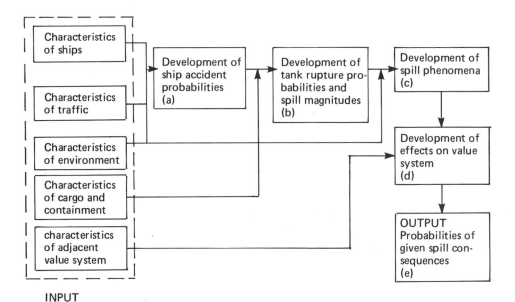

INPUT

Fig. 1: Procedure for vessel spill risk analysis. Input data and principal steps.

bability of (a) having an accident near a populated area on shore that (b) results in a major spill. The vapour from the spill (c) either immediately burns, or develops a vapour cloud that ultimately extends to a populated area. Here, it ignites and burns, (d) resulting in certain number of fatalities, injuries and dollars of property loss. (e) The probabilities of all the events leading to these consequences are then combined with the magnitudes of the consequences to provide the estimated public risks, in terms of expected fatalities, or expected fatalities per exposed individual, per year, from the nearby population. The approach to these steps is outlined below, together with the specific models adopted in its conduct.

Probability of vessel accidents and spills (Steps (a) and (b)).
Essentially this problem has been treated in two ways: statistical inference or simulation. The first approach has been employed both by the Federal Power Commission (FPC), based on work of the Oceanographic Institute of Washington (2) and by Socio-Economic Systems, Inc. (SES) in developing ship accident estimates for the Oxnard LNG Project Environmental Impact Report (EIR) (3). The estimates for the probabilities of the occurrence of collisions, groundings and rammings (the kind of accidents that can lead to ship tank ruptures and spills) for a given LNG vessel are established starting from vessel accident report data and statistical data on vessel transits in ports and harbours similar to those of interest. Data are developed first for a larger class of ships for which reasonable accident statistics exist, such as oil tankers, and then successively modified to account for the anticipated differences in LNG ships and their operations. This has been done primarily by employing judgement to assess the proportion of past accidents that would not have occurred if various capabilities of the system had been in place.

Similarly, in the analysis of tank rupture probabilities and spill magnitudes, past general tanker statistics are again modified to reflect the special design characteristics of the LNG ship and the geometry of its transit. Here, naval architectural considerations of hull strength and tank location versus penetration forces are involved, as well as the potential striking angles presented by the particular movements of the LNG ship and its tugs as they move through a port scenario.

The second method for the first two steps of the risk analysis is exemplified by the work of Science Applications, Inc. (SAI) in its studies in support of the California terminal applications (4) and by the work of A.D. Little, Inc. (ADL) for the proposed Point Conception, California, LNG terminal (5). SAI and ADL employ a similar procedure, although differing in the details. In particular, SAI analyses ship collisions by assuming that ship motions are entirely random in a zone of interest corresponding to the short interval of time preceeding an accident. A simulative approach allows one to obtain the expected number of collisions per year under this assumption for a port area with specific configurational and traffic characteristics. A calibration to the actual average conditions of seven representative vessel operating areas is then made by scaling the model to fit actual past collision frequencies in these harbours. Rammings and groundings can also be considered in the model. SAI assumes, however, that rammings and groundings have negligible probabilities of occurrence and of causing tank ruptures for LNG ships operating in the three proposed ports.

Finally, the probability of a tank rupture and spill following an accident is then developed in sub-models of energy exchange and hull rupture dynamics. The former sub-model computes the collision energy lost in vessel motion after impact and the amount remaining to rupture the hull of the struck ship. The hull rupture model determines the likelihood the cargo containment will fail due to the application of the net energy.

Consequences estimation

All LNG risk assessments conduct steps (c), (d) and (e) in conceptually the same way. A given size and rate of spill leads to specific consequences from an immediate fire or the formation, propagation and ignition of a vapour cloud. Casualties in a specified target value (population and property) structure are then computed. This is done, for example, by describing the value distribution in a grid overlaid on the populated area and assessing the portion of the grid covered by the range of a given effect, such as thermal radiation above a fatal level. The total value, or a specified fraction of the value in this portion, is then accounted as lost due to the given effect.

The total probability per vessel transit of the sequence of events leading to a specific consequence, times the number of transits per year, is the risk of that consequence. The sum of all the products of all possible consequences (e.g. number of fatalities) and their probabilities, is a measure of the overall risk from vessel operation, the expected (or average) number of fatalities from the exposed population, per year. The risk can also be expressed in terms of expected fatalities per exposed individual per year, by dividing by the size of the total exposed population.

The most controversial element in LNG spill consequence modeling is the vapour cloud model, of concern because of the assumed possibility that the vapour might not ignite immediately following an accident. The vapour then forms a cold cloud of gas which is heavier than the warm air around it. The cold gas mixes with air, gaining some heat and cooling some air. While mixing with air the cloud spreads out laterally. If there is a wind blowing, the cloud drifts downwind. The spreading and drifting continue until the cloud dissipates completely or until it reaches a source of ignition and burns.

Several factors affect the maximum cloud size, how far it drifts and when it might ignite. These include wind speed, atmospheric stability and spill rate - instantaneous versus the same amount spilling over a period of many minutes to hours. The volume of the cloud that may ignite depends on both average and peak gas concentrations. Experimental data on LNG spills are available so far only for spills of up to 100 cubic meters. For risk assessments, calculations of spill effects start with spills of 1,000 cubic meters and may go up to over 300,000 cubic meters. Experimental data then have to be scaled up by two to three orders of magnitude. Part of the controversy in vapour cloud modeling arises in how to accomplish this.

Methane gas will burn when it is mixed with air and the gas concentration lies between about five and fifteen percent by volume. In some experiments with LNG vapour clouds, it has been observed that average mixtures of as low as 0.5% gas in air have ignited. This is attributed to fluctuations in the concentration ratio of the mixture. In effect, is says that although the average concentration may be well below the five percent lower flammable limit, there can be peak concentrations high enough to allow ignition.

The general formulation for the vapour dispersion process involves several simultaneous partial differential equations for the gas concentration as a function of the spatial and time coordinates. These equations express various physical balance conditions. SAI has solved a somewhat simplified set of these equations by numerical integration, for different input factors. Analysis suggest that, for large spills, the peak concentration is very close to the average. Other organisations (e.g. ADL), have developed and applied very much simpler models, based on stronger a priori assumptions on the structure of the solution fractions. No one model has yet been accepted as "best" by the scientific community.

Distances of travel of a vapour cloud from a 25,000 m^3 spill onto the water under roughly worst-case wind and atmospheric conditions very from less than a mile to as much as 50 miles. A maximum range of 11 − 17 miles is most accepted but, this could be very overstated due to the conditions assumed. ADL's most recent estimates range from 4 to 7 miles, for instance (5).

The probabilities of an accident, a spill and then a pool fire or cloud (it is usually assumed "conservatively" that a pool fire will occur in 90% of the spills), then combine to produce the risks from LNG vessel operations. Table 1 summarises the orders of magnitude of the overall results, derived after some interpretations to establish a common basis for comparison, for the three proposed California terminals.

Table 1 : Estimates of probability per year of significant accident (at least one tank spill). 565 ship arrivals per year are assumed.

Site	SAI	SES	ADL
Los Angeles	$10^{-6}-10^{-3}$ (a)	−	−
Oxnard	10^{-6}	10^{-3}	
Pt. Conception	10^{-6}	−	10^{-4} (b)

(a)   Depends on specific harbour area

(b)   ADL also estimates 5×10^{-5} for a less significant, but still felt to be a public hazard, LNG pipeline accident

3. RISK ANALYSIS FOR TERMINAL OPERATIONS

The modeling of component failures from internal causes has been accomplished primarily with fault-tree models supported by engineering analyses of such specific areas as responses to stresses. The work that has been performed for LNG facilities has been analogous to that conducted in the Reactor Safety Study (6) for nuclear plant facilities. The techniques employed are generally accepted for comparative design evaluations but are highly controversial in their ability to provide meaningful absolute risk quantifications.

On the other hand, statistical modeling combined with engineering analyses has been applied to the responses to external forces by the LNG terminal facilities, including the docked ship, transfer systems and storage tanks. For example, the predicted probability of occurrence of an earthquake that would establish acceleration forces greater than those designed for is the risk of the spill and the consequences from it that would then result. The development of the inferred probability of such an earthquake is not a settled procedure.

Similarly, the effects of the other external events (i.e. storms and tsunamis, aircraft, missile fragment and meteorite strikes)* have been analyzed in a fashion like that employed for nuclear plants by developing statistical estimates of the probabilities of occurrence of these events and the responses of key facility components to them. The predicted resulting spills take into account the possible locations on the

---

*The consequences, but not the probability of occurrence of another significant external event, sabotage, have also been analysed.

components of the impacts, the spill magnitudes being lower, for example, for the relatively more likely impacts near the top of a tank.

The modeling for land spills of the consequences of a fire or of a vapour cloud's formation, travel and delayed ignition, proceeds in the same way as for water spills, taking into account an analytical representation of the distribution of population in the area potentially affected. The primary differences arise from the facts that firstly a major land spill will be confined in all but the most extreme cataclysms by a dike built for the purpose; and secondly, the rate of vaporisation of the spill and so fire magnitude or vapour cloud size and potential travel distance will be much less than for a spill on water. This is because the freezing of the ground tends to insulate it so as to diminish the rate of thermal transfer from it to the LNG. The confinement of the spill by a dike onto a limited area of ground enhances this property (as do also dike insulating materials, sometimes provided). Nevertheless, for instance, ADL estimates a maximum cloud dispersion distance of 1.6 to 9 miles for a full 88,000 cubic meters tank spill into the wide dike area planned for Point Conception (5).

Some propabilities may therefore exist for spills to occur whose effects can reach nearby population. These probabilities combine with the consequences of these effects to add to the estimated risks of the facility.

4. OVERALL RISK ESTIMATES

The risks arising in the vessel and terminal operations phases of LNG's operations have been quantified according to the results of the different risk assessment studies. Analyses by ADL and SAI seem to be the most comprehensive. That of the FPC less so, but more conservative. SES's is a comparative integration of the work of several organisations.

The results for the various terminals as shown in Table 2 expressed in terms of the expected number of fatalities per exposed person per year, or approximately, the chance of death per exposed person per year, differ by about a factor of 10 to 1,000.

Table 2 : Order of magnitude of probability of fatality per exposed person per year

	SAI	FPC	SAI	FPC	SES	SAI	FPC	ADL
	Los Angeles		Oxnard			Point Conception		
Vessel operations	10^{-7}	10^{-4}	10^{-8}	10^{-5}	10^{-4}	10^{-9}	10^{-4}	(c)
Terminal operations	10^{-7}	–	10^{-7}	–	10^{-6}	10^{-7}	–	(c)
Total chance of fatality per exposed person per year	10^{-7}	10^{-4}	10^{-7}	10^{-5}	10^{-4}	10^{-7}	10^{-4} (d)	10^{-7}

(c) Not separately given
(d) A new estimate is 10^{-6}

The main cause of the differences in the results is in the calculated probability of a ship accident. As has been described, fundamentally different approaches have been followed in this calculation in the various studies. For example, for Oxnard, SAI's estimate (4) is some 2,800 times smaller than that established by Socio-Economic Systems, Inc. (SES) in the Oxnard EIR (3), which estimates a chance of a ship accident capable of a spill of 1/75 per year. SES notes, however, that the introduction by the Coast Guard of an automated VTS System would decrease the estimate to 1/300.

ADL does not always give adequate detail on the derivation of its results for Point Conception (5). The estimate nevertheless developed from these results and given in Table 2 is seen to be of the same order as SAI's, despite the different models that were employed by the two organisations.

The report for the California Energy Commission (1) and the EIR prepared by SES for the City of Oxnard (3) argue that the SAI analysis provides a good basis for the estimates of the risks, but that in view of the differences in the results of other studies, significant uncertainties must nevertheless be recognised to exist. An uncertainty factor of about 100 is recommended to be considered. A reasonable upper limit on the risk for Oxnard, for example, is then between 10^{-4} and 10^{-5}. It may be noted that this is in the moderate or marginal range of acceptable involuntary risks, in terms of Chauncey Starr's risk evaluation procedure based on historic risk acceptance behaviour (7).

REFERENCES

1. L.L. Philipson, "The systems approach to the safety of liquefied natural gas import terminals," A report prepared for the California Energy Resources Conservation and Development Commission, Calif., (May 1977).

2. "Pacific-Indonesia Project. Draft and final environmental impact statements", U.S. Federal Power Commission, Washington D.C. (May 1976 and Dec. 1976).

3. "Environmental impact report for the proposed Oxnard LNG facilities", Socio-Economic Systems Inc., Calif. (July 1977).

4. "LNG terminal risk assessment studies for Los Angeles, Oxnard and Point Conception, California and for Nikiski, Alaska", a report prepared by Sciences Applications Inc., for Western LNG Terminal Co., Calif. (Dec. 1975 - Jan. 1976).

5. "Draft environmental impact report for proposed Point Conception LNG project", a report prepared by A.D. Little for California Public Utilities Commission, Calif. (Feb. 28, 1978).

6. "Reactor safety study", WASH-1400, U.S. Nuclear Regulatory Commission, Washington D.C. (Oct. 1975).

7. C. Starr, "Benefit-cost studies in Socio-Technical Systems", in: "Proceedings of Conference on Hazard Evaluation and Risk Analysis", Houston, Texas (Aug. 1971).

REAL TIME ANALYSIS OF PROCESS PLANT ALARMS

P. K. Andow and F. P. Lees

Loughborough University of Technology,

Loughborough, Leics., U.K.

HISTORICAL BACKGROUND

The human operator has received little attention in the design of process monitoring and control systems. His tasks are not usually clearly defined. The instruments and controls that he is provided with might be considered as a collection of individual components rather than as a properly-engineered system.[1] In the case of alarms in a nuclear power station there may be several thousand alarms. Each alarm in a conventional system consists of a fascia panel mounted in grids on the control room walls. When an alarm occurs the fascia panel is illuminated and made to flash until the alarm is "accepted" by the operator. In the United Kingdom during the 1960's it was decided that this type of system was not suitable for the 3000 alarms in use. The systems specification called for an "alarm analysis" to be made available to the operator that would incorporate the following features:

1. Alarms that were related to the same basic cause should be displayed in a group that was logically separate from all other groups.
    This contrasted with conventional systems where alarms related to the same basic cause may be spread over a number of panels and be mixed with other groups.

2. Where possible the system should direct the operator to the mechanical failure or disturbance that caused the problem. This contrasts with most conventional systems in which the operator is left to deduce this information from the pattern of alarms and their time-sequence

Computer-based systems were devised and reported in the literature in the late 1960's.[2,3] These systems were based on the definition of a set of cause-effect links between alarms. Cathode ray tubes were used as display media. On modern large process plants there are similar problems but the use of an alarm analysis system is expensive because of the high cost of data preparation.

It was decided to investigate the possibility of producing the data automatically from plant models. It had also been observed that list-processing techniques provided a natural means of carrying out this task.

OUTLINE OF METHOD

Two independent off-line computer programs have been written to perform the task of data structure generation. These programs require three types of data:

1.   Unit models of plant items in simple form. These are not full dynamic models but they do define how different variables affect each other in a qualitative way (e.g. "If A is HI then B may be LO in about 5 minutes").

2.   Process topology data to define the links between plant items.

3.   A list of the variables that are measured.

The first of the two off-line programs[4,5] was written in ALGOL-68. This program produces a network representing the casual links between all the variables in the system and then reduces the network so that it eventually only contains links between the measured variables. The program output may then be transported to a process control computer for use in real-time.

The second of the two off-line programs[6,7] uses an approach based on the conventional fault-tree representation. This program generates trees which contain formal AND gates (which were lacking in the first program). The program may be used to generate trees for design or real-time purposes. This second program and the real-time programs which use the data structures are written in the high-level process control language RTL/2 which allows the representation of list-structures. The real time program then continually updates the data to reflect the current analysis of the alarms as they occur and the results displayed via a V.D.U. using a separate display program. All of the programs are independent of the plant being considered.

EXAMPLE

Consider the header tank system shown in Figure 1. The system is designed to give a constant reactor feed flow. This is

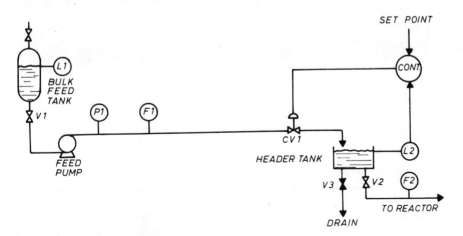

Fig. 1 Reactor feed system

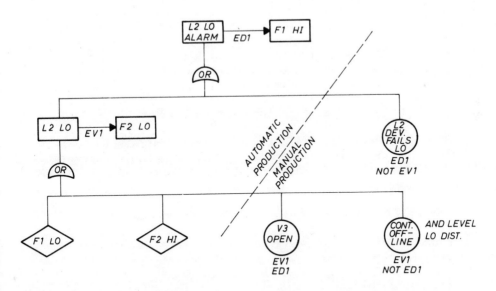

Fig. 2 Augmented fault tree for L2 LO alarm

preferred to a flow control system because the tank capacity gives a built-in time delay for operator action in the event of a feed fault. The most hazardous condition is F2 LO. The alarm L2 LO is provided to give advance warning of F2 LO. If a fault tree were to be drawn for the alarm L2 LO it might look as shown in Figure 2. Notice that the alarm of interest is the top event in the tree and that the alarm L2 LO is treated as being quite distinct, but related, to the event L2 LO. Notice also that the effects of the alarm and the event are quite different and are shown as such on the diagram by the effect links EV1 and ED1. The diagram also shows the normal propagation paths for information flow through the system in that F1 LO and F2 HI are shown as possible causes of L2 LO.

The three basic events L2 DEVICE FAILS LO, V3 OPEN and CONT OFF-LINE AND LEVEL LO DISTURBANCE are also related to the alarm and event L2 LO. Each of the basic events is marked with the effects that are/are not consistent with it. In the current example the three basic events all have unique sets of consistent events but this will not always be the case.

Consider the sequence of events that take place following inadvertant opening of valve V3 (unknown to the control room operator). The tank drains quickly, because the flow is large compared to the maximum make-up flow, and hence alarm L2 LO occurs and this is rapidly followed by F1 H1. The alarm analysis would then display the result shown in Figure 3, indicating that L2 LO is most important and has given rise to F1 HI. If the operator does not find the fault then F2 LO will also occur but now a set of conditions that are consistent with the event V3 OPEN exists and therefore the analysis displays the complete result shown in Figure 4. This indicates that the basic cause is V3 OPEN and that this has led to the 3 simple alarms shown below.

This example is simple but serves to illustrate the basic principles. Note also that displays will frequently occur in which all the alarms are not related to the same basic cause. This is handled quite easily by the analysis program.

PROBLEMS ENCOUNTERED

A number of problems have been encountered during the project:

1. Process models are not generally binary in nature. The data can become very complex and is time-dependent.

2. Realistic process models must reflect a two-way flow of

DISPLAY AT 9:24:09 ON 2/06/78 ANALYSIS AT 9:24:07 ON 2/06/78

*	TANK LEVEL L2	LO	9:24:07
	INPUT FLOW F1	H1	9:24:08

FIGURE 3

DISPLAY AT 9:26:30 ON 2/06/78 ANALYSIS AT 9:26:29 ON 2/06/78

*	DRAIN VALVE V3	OPEN	9:26:29
	TANK LEVEL L2	LO	9:24:07
	INPUT FLOW F1	H1	9:24:08
	OUTPUT FLOW F2	LO	9:26:27

FIGURE 4

information. The vast majority of models in the literature only transmit information in the direction of process flow.

3.   The problem of instrument failure. A large proportion of failures on plants are in this category. Detection of failed instruments is very useful but adds further complexity to the analysis.

4.   Alarm threshold definition must be carefully considered or alarms can occur in misleading sequences.

5.   Definition of deduced alarm data. This has been carried out manually. Work is now in progress on automatic production of this data.

6.   The alarm analysis program must be efficient since the whole process is carried out in real-time.

7.   The data must be compact because process computers generally have relatively small memories.

CURRENT STATUS

The programs are being tested with a small computer-controlled pilot plant in the University Laboratories. Tests have also been carried out using simulations of incidents provided by two companies The overall method worked but improvements are still being made.

ACKNOWLEDGEMENTS

The authors wish to acknowledge the support of the Science Research Council via the grant "Alarm analysis using a process computer".

REFERENCES

1.   Andow, P.K. and Lees, F.P. "Process Plant Alarm Systems: General Considerations" in "Loss Prevention and Safety Promotion in the Process Industries", C.H.Buschmann (Ed) Amsterdam (1974).
2.   Patterson, D., "Application of a computerised alarm-analysis system to a nuclear power station", Proc IEE, 115 (12), December (1968).
3.   Welbourne, D., "Alarm Analysis and Display at Wylfa nuclear power station", Proc. IEE, 115 (11), November, (1968).
4.   Andow, P.K. "A method for Process Computer Alarm Analysis", Ph.D. Thesis, Loughborough University, (1973).
5.   Andow P.K. and Lees, F.P., "A Method for Process Computer Alarm Analysis using List-Processing", Trans. I.Chem.E., 53, 195, (1975).
6.   Martin-Solis, G.A., Andow P.K., and Lees, F.P. "An Approach to Fault Tree Synthesis for Process Plants" in "Loss Prevention and Safety Promotion in the Process Industries", Heidelberg, (1977).

7.   Martin-Solis, G.A., "Fault Tree Synthesis for Real Time and Design Applications on Process Plant", Ph.D. Thesis, Loughborough University of Technology, (1978).

MATERIAL CONTROL STUDY: A DIRECTED GRAPH AND FAULT-TREE PROCEDURE
FOR ADVERSARY EVENT SET GENERATION†

H.E. Lambert*, J.J. Lim** and F.M. Gilman**

*TERA Corp., Berkeley, CA 94704
**Lawrence Livermore Laboratory,
Livermore, CA 94550

ABSTRACT

Lawrence Livermore Laboratory is developing an assessment procedure to evaluate the effectiveness of a potential nuclear facility
licensee's material control (MC) system. The purpose of an MC system
is to prevent the theft of special nuclear material such as plutonium
and highly enriched uranium. The key in the assessment procedure is
the generation and analysis of the adversary event sets by a directed
graph and fault-tree methodology. The methodology is described step-
by-step and its application illustrated by an example.

1. INTRODUCTION

The Lawrence Livermore Laboratory is conducting a Material
Control and Accounting Study for the Nuclear Regulatory Commission
(NRC), Office of Nuclear Regulatory Research. As part of their duties,
the NRC is responsible for the licensing of new nuclear facilities.
Since the safeguarding of nuclear materials has become increasingly
important in recent years, the NRC must be able to systematically
evaluate the material control systems of proposed nuclear facilities
and to guarantee their effectiveness to the public. Each facility
has a material control system to protect against the theft of special

†This report was prepared for the U.S. Nuclear Regulatory Commission,
Office of Nuclear Regulatory Research under research order No. 66-
77-012 and under the auspices of the U.S. DOE, Contract No. W-7405-
ENG-48.

nuclear material, SNM, such as plutonium and uranium 235. In the
three year-old study the Laboratory has been developing an assessment procedure to evaluate the effectiveness of a potential nuclear
licensee's material control system.[1]

The assessment procedure, shown in the block diagram in Figure
1, needs two types of data: license applicant information and the
NRC/LLL data base. Applicant data include the plan of the facility
physical plant, operational procedures, descriptions of special
nuclear material processing, and the details of the material control
and accounting system. The NRC/LLL data base will contain the
mathematical models (such as models of the performance of the SNM
detection monitors) necessary to evaluate an applicant's submittal.

The first step in the assessment procedure is to identify targets within the facility that contain theft-attractive SNM. The
second step is to determine the adversary actions and conditions of
the material control system that could allow successful diversion of
special nuclear material, that is, generate the adversary event sets.
Simulation of the events is required for those adversary event sets
where timeliness and ordering of events is important for successful
diversion. The qualitative and quantitative analysis of the event
sets and the simulation results allow the effectiveness of the
material control system to be determined.

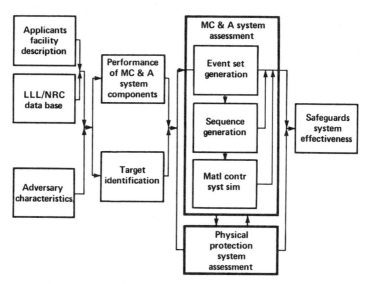

Figure 1.   The LLL Assessment Procedure

2.0 ADVERSARY EVENT SET GENERATION PROCEDURE

The key in the LLL assessment procedure for evaluating the effectiveness of a material control system is the generation and analysis of adversary event sets. We have developed a procedure based on a directed graph (digraph) and fault-tree methodology by which the event sets can be generated and analyzed. This methodology has been used by Lapp and Powers[2] to assess the safety of chemical processing systems. As described by Lambert and Lim[3], this methodology was extended to model intentional diversionary or malevolent acts by an adversary so that these acts appear in the event sets.

The procedure for the generation and analysis of the event sets is next described, in detail, as delineated by the block diagram in Figure 2.

2.1 General System Schematic

The first step in the procedure (Figure 2) is the formulation of a general schematic for system modeling. Information from piping and instrumentation diagrams, the physical plant layout, and material control related procedures is used to formulate the schematic for

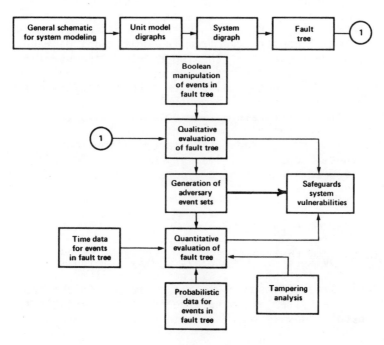

Figure 2. Procedure for Generation and Analysis of Adversary Event Sets.

system modeling. The general schematic delineates the unit model
digraphs needed to model the system and the overall system interactions. The unit models include models of adversary movement in the
facility, monitors, process equipment, and procedures.

2.2 Unit Model Digraphs

In step 2 (Figure 2), unit model digraphs, the basic building
blocks of the procedure, are generated. Digraphs are functional
cause-and-effect network models that describe the relationship between various system variables and the conditions that are necessary
for these relationships to exist.[2,3] In addition, digraphs can show
events such as adversary actions that may nullify or change the
relationships between variables. Digraphs are useful since they are
multivalued network models and they can readily model the dynamics
of the relationships between variables. The advantage of generating
unit model digraphs is that a separate analysis can be performed on
system components without performing an entire system analysis.
These unit models are analogous to mini-fault trees described by
Fussell, et al[4] and decision tables described by Salem, et al.[5]

2.3 System Digraph

The third step in Figure 2 is the generation of the system
digraph, which is constructed from the unit model digraphs for a
selected top event variable (the top event is the event being modeled
The system digraph is obtained by deductively following the information flow given in the general system schematic. The material
control system is modeled as a control system designed to counter
the actions of the adversary. The potential ways the material
control system may respond to prevent special nuclear material theft
are modeled in terms of "adversary cancellation loops" of the system
digraph. These loops are similar in concept to the negative feedback
and negative feedforward control loops designed to cancel disturbance
in process variables.

2.4 System-Fault Tree

In the fourth step (Figure 2), the system-fault tree is generated
from the system digraph via a synthesis algorithm. The top event
in the fault tree corresponds to a disturbance in the top event
variable of the system digraph. The top event variable for the material control study is M_{DIV}, defined by

$$M_{DIV} = \begin{cases} +1 \text{ if sucessful diversion of} \\ \text{special nuclear material occurs} \\ 0 \text{ otherwise} \end{cases}$$

A zero value for a variable on the system digraph corresponds to a true or expected value. Any other value, hence, corresponds to a deviation or disturbance. The top event in the system fault tree for the material control study is $M_{DIV} = +1$. All loops in the system digraph that model the corrective actions of the material control system must fail for a disturbance in the top event variable to exist.

For successful diversion of SNM to occur, all adversary cancellation loops must fail. These loops fail as the result of:

● random monitor failure

● inadequate monitor measurement sensitivity

● human error, including slow guard response

● adversary activity, including equipment tampering and collusion

The synthesis algorithm creates an AND logic gate in the fault tree each time a cancellation loop in the system digraph fails.

Once generated, the fault tree can be evaluated qualitatively and quantitatively to assess the vulnerabilities of the safeguard system.

2.5 Qualitative Analysis

The qualitative analysis of the fault tree provides much valuable information without using numerical data. It includes performing Boolean manipulations of the basic events, generating the adversary event sets, structurally ranking the basic events, determining the collusion requirements, and evaluating the effect of power loss on the material control system.

A structural ranking of the basic events in the event sets helps to identify important basic events for further analysis. This type of ranking is a function of the number of event sets in which a basic event appears in and the relative length of those event sets.

Common cause analysis is used to determine the collusion requirements (the number and identity of plant personnel) and the effects of power loss of key components of the material control system for successful special nuclear material theft. In addition, a vital location analysis can be performed to determine the locations which must be visited for successful tampering.

The computer codes Fault-Tree Analysis Program (FTAP)[6] and the Set Equation Transformation System (SETS)[7], designed to generate and handle numerous, high-ordered minimal cut sets, are used to perform the qualitative analysis.

2.6 Quantitative Analysis

To further identify the weaknesses of the material control system, a quantitative analysis is performed. This analysis assesses the impact of material control system components with various failure rates and detection probabilities, the effect of maintenance policies, and the ease with which component tampering can occur. The IMPORTANCE computer code[8] is used to perform the quantitative assessment.

Inputs required for the quantitative analysis are a listing of the event sets, probability data for the basic events, and the assumption of statistical independence of the basic events.

The probability of successful theft of special nuclear material can be calculated for four specific cases:

(1) No material control system tampering, no alarm signal generated.

(2) No material control system tampering, slow safeguards response.

(3) Material control system tampering, no alarm signal generated.

(4) Material control system tampering, slow safeguards response.

A sensitivity analysis of the probability of successful theft for the above cases as a function of the amount of special nuclear material stolen is also done. Quantities of SNM investigated are 0.5 g, 200 g, and 5 kg. The maximum expected performance of the material control system occurs when there is no system tampering. However, clever adversaries may tamper with the material control system to render it ineffective. In the tampering analysis, the following adversary attributes and material control system charac-teristics are considered:

● Type of tools and resources required for tampering

● Accessibility of components to potential adversaries

● Monitoring of equipment for tampering

● Availability of tools and resources required for
  tampering

● Personnel required for tampering

The probability of successful tampering is then a function of
the probability that each of the above can occur with either no or
slow material control system response.

3.   DEMONSTRATION OF THE EVENT SET GENERATION PROCEDURE

The event set generation and analysis procedure has been
applied in the assessment of the material control system[9] in a
prototype nuclear facility, the Test Bed.[10]

3.1 Test Bed Assessment

The Test Bed is based upon the plutonium nitrate storage area
of the Allied-General Nuclear Services, AGNS, facility in Barnwell,
S.C., but with substantial modifications. These modifications are
added to further develop and test the assessment procedure and are
not criticisms or "fixes" to the AGNS current design. The modifications include the addition of check valves, limit switches on
valves, a computer controlled access system, computerized material
control and accounting and procedure monitoring logic, and other
safeguards components.

The general form of the system digraph for the Test Bed is
shown in Figure 3. The arrows represent information flow with
regard to (1) movement of special nuclear material and people, and
(2) the material control system response which acts to prevent the
theft of special nuclear material. The initial conditions for the
Test Bed assessment are shown on the left of Figure 3.

The fault tree generated from the system digraph by the
synthesis algorithm contained 125 gate events and 113 basic events.
The qualitative analysis of the fault tree generated 814,042 event
sets for the case of no safeguards response. These adversary event
sets ranged in length from 18 basic events to 28 basic events.
These event sets were very descriptive and contained all the adversary
acts necessary for successful diversion, including the route for
adversary movement in and out of the facility.

The collusion analysis established that successful diversion
can occur only if three particular plant personnel are in collusion
or if two persons are in collusion when random failures occur.

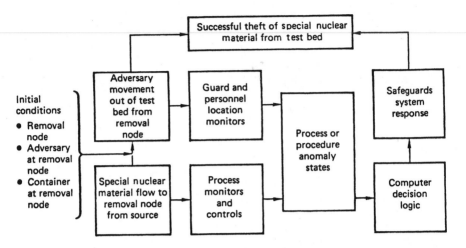

Figure 3. General Form of System Digraph for Test Bed

The IMPORTANCE computer code[8] determined the probability of each basic event contributing to the probability of successful diversion. The ranking of these basic events determined the following vulnerable points in the Test Bed:

computer hardware and software

remote control panel

crash door alarms

maintenance policies

Although the Test Bed is a facility with an automated and sophisticated material control system, the assessment has found several basic weaknesses. A similar assessment can determine the effect of strengthening the afore-mentioned areas. Thus, the Test Bed demonstration has shown the directed graph-fault tree procedure (Figure 3) to be an effective assessment tool. The procedure can also be used for safety and reliability analysis.

3.2 Storage Tank Example

An application of the directed graph-fault tree methodology is illustrated by an example in the Appendix. The example consists of a storge tank of plutonium nitrate with a differential pressure cell used to measure the solution mass. The tank is located in a protected area called a material access area, MAA. The MAA is protected by a roving guard and a guard stationed outside the MAA.

4.   CURRENT ACTIVITIES

Alternative and complementary material control assessment procedures have been developed and tested at Lawrence Livermore Laboratory.

One alternative approach is the <u>Logic Diagram Model</u> as
described by Lim and Huebel.[11] The logic diagram models the information flow in a way similar to that of the digraph. The logic
diagram is a Boolean logic model and Boolean equations are defined
directly on the logic model. On the other hand, the digraph is a
multi-valued logic model and a synthesis algorithm is needed to
generate a fault tree. Both approaches have advantages and disadvantages. The digraph-fault tree approach is more complex to
use. It requires that the loops in the system digraph be found and
a synthesis algorithm be used. The logic model approach is simpler
to generate, however, the logic model contains in general many
Inhibit gates which generate NOT gates and efficient prime implicant algorithms must be used.[12,13]   Current computer codes do not
easily handle a large number of equations with complemented events.

Another approach, the <u>Structured Assessment Approach</u>, models
the movement of SNM and the flow of information in the material
control system by adjacency matrices. One output of the approach
are target sets, the sets of conditions and monitor failures that
permit successful theft of SNM to occur. The approach is described
in detail by Sacks et al.[14]

APPENDIX A: EXAMPLE OF THE USE OF THE DIGRAPH-FAULT TREE
              METHODOLOGY

The objective of the digraph-fault tree methodology is to systematically produce a fault tree for qualitative and quantitative
evaluation. A fault tree is deductive Boolean logic model of a Top
Event, an undesired event or system state.

The Top Events are events such as "fire", "explosion", or
"system shutdown" for safety and reliability analyses. For material control assessment, the Top Event can be an event such as "Successful theft of SNM from the facility." The Top Event is defined in
terms of basic events which provide the limit of resolution for the
fault tree.

The basic events in safety and reliability analysis include
human error, equipment failure, and environmental conditions. For
material control assessment, the basic events include adversary
activity, such as equipment destruction and records falsification,
in addition to those given above.

A brief description of the digraph-fault tree terminology and
notation is now presented.

A.1 NOTATION AND TERMINOLOGY

A digraph is a set of nodes and connecting edges. Nodes in the
digraph represent variables. If one variable effects another variable
or event, a directed arrow or edge connects the independent variable
to the dependent one. The directed edge may either be a normal edge
which indicates the relationship is normally true, or a conditional
edge which indicates the relationship is true only when another event
(or condition) exists. Edges connecting any pair of nodes are mutually exclusive; only one edge relationship is true at a given time.

Numbers may be placed on the directed edge to represent the
gains between the two events. These gains are based on the mathematical definition of gain, $\partial Y/\partial X$, where X and Y denote the independent and dependent variables or events respectively. The magnitudes
of the gains used in the digraphs for the assessment are quantized
into three discrete values of -1, 0, +1. Gains of +1 represent
normal disturbances which a negative feedback loop is able to cancel.
Gains of 0 indicate the nullification of any relationship existing
between the two events.

Events are represented by alphanumeric labels on the nodes. For
instance "P2", M3", FIRE at HX" represent pressure at location 2,
mass flow rate at location 3, and fire at heat exchanger, respectively. The direction of the deviations in the values of variables are

denoted by "+" and "-". These deviations have magnitudes of "0" and "1". Magnitude of 1 indicates a range of values that is considered moderate. A magnitude of 0 represents a true or expected range of values of the event. The same scheme of -1, 0, +1, is also used to represent the deviations in the values of events. For instance P2(0) represents the true or expected value of pressure at location two, and M3(+1) represents a moderate mass flow rate at location 3.

Some events may be univariant; that is, they deviate only in the positive direction or only in the negative direction. For instance, "FIRE at HX" is a univariant variable.

A.2 UNIT MODEL DIGRAPHS

An example to illustrate unit model digraph generation is now given.

Fig. A.1 shows a storage tank containing plutonium nitrate with a differential pressure cell. The solution mass in the tank is determined by measurement of the difference between pressures P_1 and P_2 given by the following relationship:

$$\text{STATIC PRESSURE} = \rho g(L-L_1) = p_1 - p_2$$

where ρ is the solution density, g is the acceleration constant due to gravity, L is the level of solution in the tank and L_1 is the level at which air enters the tank at line 1. An air supply (not shown) provides air to lines 1 and 2.

The glove box shown in Fig. A.1 is used to sample plutonium nitrate from the storage tank via the sample line. A technician transfers the sample through a pneumatic sample line to the laboratory for chemical analysis.

In order to safeguard the plutonium nitrate solution, the material control system will notify security when the following stimuli are received:

● Loss of vacuum detected by a pressure sensor on the glove box

● Change in solution mass determined by a differential pressure cell measurement

Then MC procedure requires a security guard to be sent to the MAA entrance in the event an anomolous signal is received and apprehend anyone stealing SNM. Also, a roving guard is required to inspect the glove box and apprehend anyone stealing SNM.

Figures A.2, A.3, A.4 and A.5 show respectively unit model digraphs of the following:

- Glove box with pressure sensor
- Storage tank with differential pressure cell
- MC computer decision logic
- Roving guard

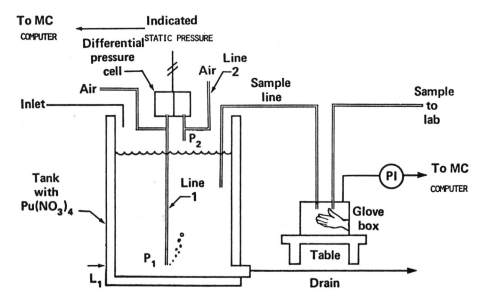

Fig. A.1.   Storage Tank with Differential Pressure Cell

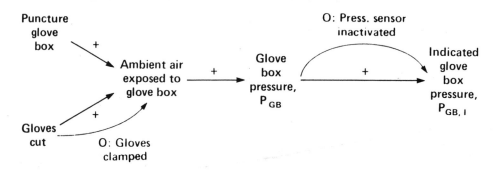

Fig. A.2.   Unit Model Digraph of Glove Box with Pressure Sensor

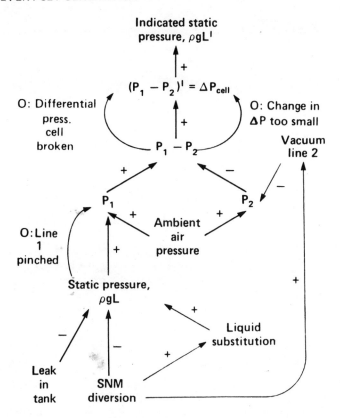

Fig. A.3. Unit Model Digraph of Storage Tank with Differential Pressure Cell

By definition successful theft of SNM occurs when SNM crosses the boundary ot the MAA. For this to occur, the adversary must perform a minimum necessary and sufficient set of acts to get SNM out of the MAA. These acts include:

- Movement within MAA
- Penetration of the glove box
- Removal of SNM from sampler

As the result of attempting these acts, signals will be generated and an MC response generated. If successful theft is to occur, the information flow associated with these signals must be nullified. As shown in the unit model digraphs, there are two ways that the information flow can be nullified:

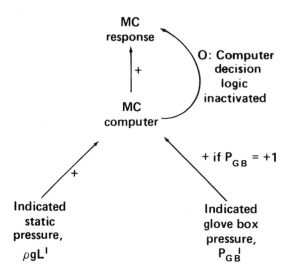

Fig. A.4. Unit Model Digraph of MC Computer Decision Logic

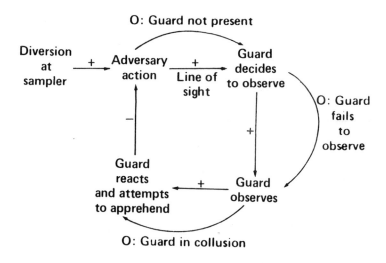

Fig. A.5. Unit Model Digraph of Roving Guard

- Zero gain events (events following the zero on the edges of the digraphs) that cause an MC component to be inactive such as human errors, equipment failure and measurement insensitivity

- Stimulus variable cancellation resulting in no signal when an adversary activity is committed. Stimulus refers to a disturbance in an MC variable that occurs as the result of adversary activity. As an example, refer to Fig. A.3. If an adversary steals SNM at the glove box and simultaneously adds liquid to the tank or applies a vacuum on line 2, then the indicated solution mass will <u>not</u> change and a signal will not be generated

A.3 SYSTEM DIGRAPH GENERATION

The unit model digraphs described previously are linked together to form the system digraph by starting at the node, $M_{DIV,MAA}$ defined by:

$$M_{DIV,MAA} = \begin{cases} +1 \text{ successful theft of SNM from the MAA} \\ 0 \cdot \text{otherwise} \end{cases}$$

Digraphs are generated in a similar manner as fault trees are constructed. One starts from the Top Event variable, works strictly backwards (i.e., deductively) and determines variables that can directly cause a disturbance in the variable under development. This causal information is obtained from either the unit model digraph or from the connectivity information in the system schematic. The limit of resolution is reached when variables are encountered which have no inputs. These variables are called primal variables (similar in scope to basic events in fault trees).

Using the process described above, we generate the system digraph as shown in Fig. A.6. The corrective actions of the material control system are modeled as negative feedforward loops (NFFL's) and negative feedback loops (NFBL's).

A NFFL consists of two or more paths which start at the same node and merge together at a different node. NFFL's have the property that the sign of the normal gains on one path (i.e., without failures) is different from the other paths. In contrast, a NFBL is path which starts and ends at the same node. NFBL's have the property that the product of the normal gains around the NFBL is negative.

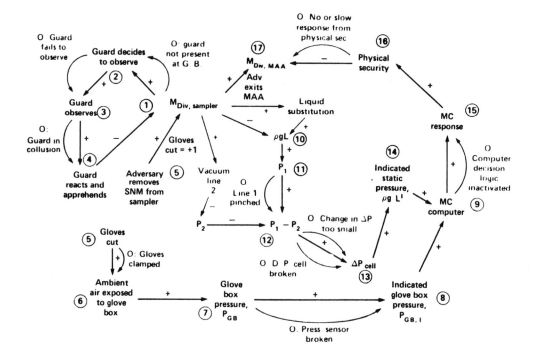

Fig. A.6. System Digraph

There is one NFBL in the system digraph in Fig. A.6

● Response from roving guard (nodes 1,2,3 and 4)

and two NFFL's

● Response from security to change in static pressure
  path 1 - (nodes 1 and 17)
  path 2 - (nodes 1,10,11,12,13,14,9,15,16 and 17)
● Response from security to change in golve box pressure
  path 1 - (nodes 5,1 and 17)
  path 2 - (nodes 5,6,7,8,9,15,16 and 17)

Path 1 for the two NFFL's describes the conditions necessary for SNM movement out of the MAA. Path 2 represents the corrective action of the MC system in preventing SNM theft.

A.4 FAULT TREE GENERATION

The fault tree is constructed from the system digraph via a synthesis algorithm,[9,14] starting from the top event node, $M_{DIV,MAA}$. For MC assessment, the algorithm generates AND gates in two basic ways:

● The adversary attempts to steal SNM <u>and</u> conditions must be satisfied for removal of SNM
● The adversary commits an act which generates a signal <u>and</u> the MC system fails to respond to the signal because the corrective action of the NFBL or NFFL fails

The fault tree constructed using the synthesis algorithm is shown in Fig. A.7. Examination of the fault tree shows that all three loops must fail for successful theft to occur.

A.5 QUALITATIVE ANALYSIS

The minimal cut sets of the fault tree in Fig. A.7 are the adversary event sets. There are 36 event sets as shown in factored form in Fig. A.8: 33 event sets generate no MC response and three event sets generate an inadequate response.

The first line in Fig. A.8 represents the conditions necessary for removal of SNM, (See system digraph in Fig. A.6.). The second line in Fig. A.8 represents the basic events necessary to fail the roving guard, i.e., the NFBL. The third line represents the "common mode" events that can simultaneously fail both NFFL's. The

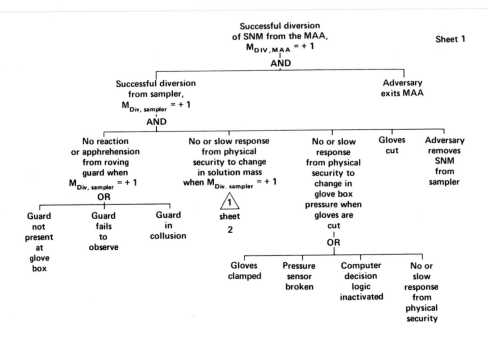

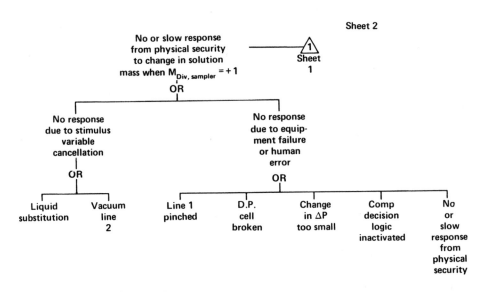

Fig. A.7.   Fault Tree for Successful Diversion from Storage Tank

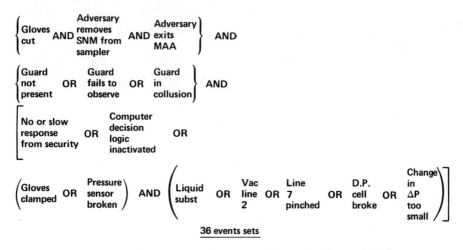

Fig. A.8.   Event Set Representation in Factored Form

fourth line represents 10 combinations of basic events taken two-at-a-time that fail both NFFL's.

By performing a Boolean substitution for the basic events in terms of plant personnel who can perform the events, the collusion requirements for the event sets are determined:

● 22 event sets can be accomplished solely by the technician or the roving guard

● 11 event sets can be accomplished by two people --
   the technician and the roving guard in collusion

● 3 event sets can be accomplished by three people --
   the technician, the roving guard and the guard at
   the security station in collusion

Much useful information can be obtained without quantitative information. We see the usefulness of the system digraph in displaying system topology and information flow.

A.6   OTHER CONSIDERATIONS

The authors[9] and Sacks et al.[14] discuss in detail the reliability assessments of MC systems. The assessments must consider tampering, records falsification and equipment destruction. The importance of a reliability analysis is not so much the absolute numbers that result but the sensitivity analysis which indicates

the relative strengths and weaknesses of the MC system in quantitative terms.

The example in this appendix did not discuss the incorporation
of consistency checks in the fault tree analysis. Consistency checks
are important in considering the interaction of time periods, i.e.,
an adversary can take advantage of monitors that are inactive during
various modes of operation. In addition, the example did not consider the incorporation of dynamics in the analysis, i.e., given
that anomolous signals are generated, is the MC response fast
enough? These matters are considered in detail by the authors.[9]

REFERENCES

1. A. Maimoni, "Safeguards Research: Assessing Material Control
    and Accounting System," Energy and Technology Review,
    Lawrence Livermore Laboratory, Rept. UCRL-52000-77-11/12
    (1977).*
2. S. A. Lapp and G. J. Powers, "Computer Aided Synthesis of
    Fault Trees" in IEEE Trans on Rel. R-26 (1)(1977).
3. H. E. Lambert and J. J. Lim, The Modeling of Adversary Action
    for Safeguards Effectiveness Assessment, Lawrence Liver-
    more Laboratory, Rept. UCRL-79217, Rev. 1 (1977).*
4. J. B. Fussell et al., A Collection of Methods for Reliability
    and Safety Engineering, Idaho National Engineering Labora-
    tory, Idaho Falls, Rept. ANCR-1273 (1976).*
5. S. L. Salem, G. E. Apostolakis, and D. Okrent, "A New Method-
    ology for the Computer-Aided Construction of Fault Trees,"
    Annals of Nuclear Energy, 4 (1977) 417-433.
6. R. Willie, Fault Tree Analysis Program, Operations Research
    Center Report No. ORC 78-14, University of California,
    Berkeley (1978); Rept. UCRL-13981, Lawrence Livermore
    Laboratory.*
7. R. B. Worrell, Set Equation Transforation System (SETS), San-
    dia Laboratories, Albuquerque, New Mexico, Rept. SLA-73-
    0028A (1974).*
8. H. E. Lambert and F. M. Gilman, The IMPORTANCE Computer Code,
    Lawrence Livermore Laboratory, Rept. UCRL-79269 (1977).*
9. H. E. Lambert, J. J. Lim and F. M. Gilman, A Digraph-Fault
    Tree Methodology for the Assessment of Material Control
    Systems, Lawrence Livermore Laboratory, Rept. UCRL-52170
    (1979).*
10. I. J. Sacks, et al., Material Control System Design: Test
    Bed Nitrate Storage Area (TBNSA), Lawrence Livermore
    Laboratory, Rept. UCID-17525-77-3 (1978).*
11. J. J. Lim and J. G. Huebel, Modeling Adversary Actions Against
    a Nuclear Material Accounting System, Proceedings of the
    1st annual ESARDA Symposium on Safeguards and Nuclear
    Material Management, Palais des Congres, Brussels (1979).

12.   B. L. Hulme and R. B. Worrell, "A Prime Implicant Algorithm
      with Factoring," IEEE Trans. on Computers, (November,
      1979).
13.   R. R. Willie, Computer Oriented Methods for Assessing Complex
      System Reliability, Ph.D. Thesis, Dept. of Operations
      Research, U.C. Berkeley, (1979).
14.   I. J. Sacks, A. A. Parziale, T. R. Rice, S. L. Derby, The
      Structured Assessment Analysis of Facility X, Volume 1 -
      Executive Summary, MC 79-12-D, Lawrence Livermore Labora-
      tory, to be published as a NUREG Report (1979).*

---

*   Available from National Technical Information Service, Spring-
    field, VA 22151, USA.

NOTICE

"This report was prepared as an account of work sponsored by the
United States Government. Neither the United States nor the United
States Department of Energy, nor any of their employess, nor any of
their contractors, subcontractors, or their employees, makes any
warranty, express or implied, or assumes any legal liability or
responsibility for the accuracy, completeness or usefulness of any
information, apparatus, product or process disclosed, or represents
that its use would not infringe privately-owned rights."

Reference to a company or product names does not imply approval or
recommendation of the product by the University of California or
the U.S. Department of Energy to the exclusion of others that may
be suitable.

THE AVAILABILITY OF A COMPUTER SYSTEM COMMUNICATIONS NETWORK
AS PERCEIVED BY A USER AND VIEWED CENTRALLY

B.K. Daniels

National Centre of Systems Reliability
United Kingdom Atomic Energy Authority
Culcheth
Warrington, UK

ABSTRACT

A communications network has been assessed for availability as perceived by a user of the system and also as seen from the centralised computer. The user view analysis uses a state transition model to demonstrate that high availability is attainable for individual services at remote locations. There is a penalty that might be incurred in achieving this level of service which is revealed in a simulation model of the distribution of availability of the complete system. The second analysis based on the central view of the system confirmed the need for a centrally located operators console to control the interconnection and fault diagnosis of the communications equipment. The paper describes the communications network, gives a summary of the user view analyses and the results of the simulation.

INTRODUCTION

A centrally sited computer system is to provide a service to local and remote users via a communications network. Each user may have a high speed service for Remote Job Entry via card reader, terminal or local computer and for return of output a line printer may well be provided. A high speed service may also be used for a single or clustered video terminal. Also, one or more low speed services may be provided for time sharing terminals. Each service will use the facilities of a Communications Processor at the central site which buffers and interfaces all communications equipment to the main processor.

Each user of the system requires a service to be provided with

437

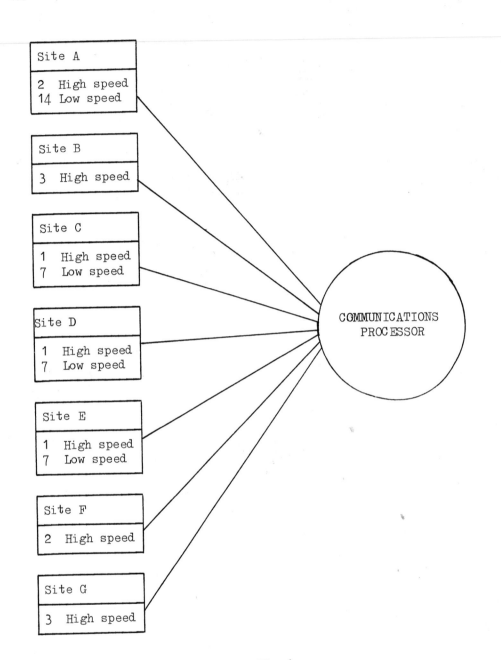

Fig 1

Remote Site Service Provision

the minimum of interruptions, and at the maximum service speed which
is available at any instant in time. To maximise the availability of
each service, the system design includes a number of redundant and
diverse features. To demonstrate the various features of the design
to the user groups, a quantitative assessment of the service availability has been carried out.

It was found possible to use approximations in the analysis of
the system which provided a degree of accuracy commensurate with the
needs of the users. These approximations are detailed in the later
sections. Where calculations are to be carried out at an early
stage in design, as in this case, similar approximations are frequently used. What is important is to demonstrate that the system
is capable of meeting the design aims, and an accuracy of the order
of two significant digits is more than adequate.

Two analyses are described. The first, the 'User view' quan-
tifies the service to be expected at each site. A state transition
modelling technique is used with manual calculation of the results.
The aim is to provide a prediction of the service which will be
supplied to each user — the 'subjective' user measure of the service
provided by the computer system.

The second analysis, the 'Central view' uses a simulation model
to provide a prediction of the complete system behaviour as perceived
by the system operators at the central computer site. The two
analyses are distinct and cannot be combined in any way.

THE SYSTEM

A summary of the user services is given in figure 1.

For the high speed services the remote sites have a modem,
either 9600 bits per second (bps) or 4800 bps, which is linked to the
terminal equipment and via a Post Office telephone line to an equivalent modem at the central site. The central modem is then connected
via switching circuits into one of two Communications Processors.
The central operators have spare 4800 and 9600 bps modems which can
be switched into any service to replace a faulty modem. In general
there will be more than one telephone line to each remote site and
this will be installed over geographically different routes to avoid
common cause outages in this area of the network.

Where low speed service is required then similar modem pairs and
telephone circuits are utilised but the modems are dual ported to give,
for example, a 4800 bps high speed service and a 4800 bps multiplexed
low speed service from a single 9600 bps modem. To provide the multiplexed low speed services an additional piece of hardware, a multiplexor, is required at each end of the telephone line. At the Central
Site this multiplexor will be connected via several interfaces into

one or other of the Communications processors, each interface offering
a choice of operating speeds. At the remote site the multiplexor can
be hard-wired direct to terminal equipment, or alternatively into a
local dial-up terminal service.

For reference figure 2 shows the complete layout of the communications equipment included in an availability assessment on which
this paper is based. The aim of the communications network is to
provide the computer service each user requires for as much of the
time period it is required. A measure of the success in providing
this service can be obtained from the two metrics Availability and
Throughput. For completeness, the usage of these terms is now
defined.

$$\text{Availability} = \frac{\text{Total Time Computer Service on in Time Period}}{\text{Time Period Service Required}}$$

$$\text{Throughput} = \frac{\text{Actual data that could be passed by system}}{\text{Maximum data passable by system in the time period}}$$

Very loosely, Availability is the measure of some service being
present at any instant in the time period, or the probability of
getting a service. Throughput is the measure of how much work can
be done in a period of time. The maximum data possible is obtained
from the fastest service rate multiplied by the time period. The
actual data is calculated from the summation of time period – service
rate products, for all service rates.

The computer system and communications network will be nominally
switched on and working 24 hours each day of the year. However
because of differences in manning and usage at the different locations
three time periods were defined for the purpose of the analyses which
closely correspond with the pattern of the normal working week.
Slight changes in this pattern due to public holidays were not
included.

Daytime   Monday through Friday, 08.00 to 18.00 or 50 hours
                        per week

Silent Hours   Monday 18.00 – Tuesday 08.00
                        Tuesday 18.00 – Wednesday 08.00
                        Wednesday 18.00 – Thursday 08.00
                        Thursday 18.00 – Friday 08.00
                        or 56 hours per week

Weekend   Friday 18.00 – Monday 08.00
                        or 62 hours per week.

The assumptions used in the analysis on manning were that the
central site had operators present at all times, and remote sites
were manned only during Daytime. This means that when a fault occurs

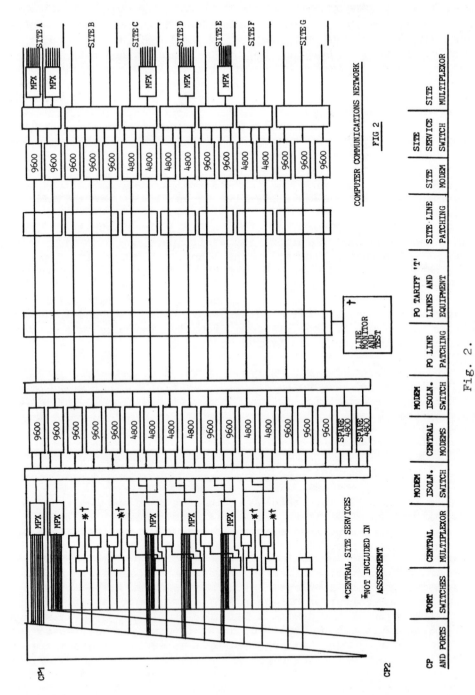

Fig. 2.
Computer communications network.

during Daytime hours then repair of the fault can be started immediately following a 'Diagnosis Time' during which the location of the
faulty equipment is confirmed. In parallel with the repair of faulty
equipment, alternative equipment may be switched in to prov de a
rapid return to full service, or perhaps some reduced high speed
service or smaller number of low speed services might be provided.
There are a number of these operating rules which apply to the system
and all have been included in the analyses. In particular a fault
occurring outside Daytime, and diagnosed to be outside the Central
Site, will be subject to a waiting time before repair commences,
which has the effect of starting repair the next Daytime morning at
08.00 hours. Whenever a repair starts it is assumed it will be completed in the same working session.

Throughout the analysis negative exponential times to failure,
times to diagnose, times to repair, times to reconfigure and waiting
times have been assumed. The table in Fig 3 gives details of these
mean times which were obtained from user experience of similar equipment. For the Post Office telephone lines, the sites were classified
as being of below, average or higher than average failure rates, and
the user average experience was modified by a factor of 2 in each
direction. This adjustment is based on qualitative rather than
quantified information. It might, for example, be argued that the
greater the length of the telephone circuits, the more equipment is
used, and so the higher the failure rate.

The overall system was analysed in two distinct ways, firstly
the "User view" of the system and secondly the "Central view" of the
system. For the user view it was found that simple calculations
could be used based on the approximation to be found in reference 3,

Availability $= 1 - \lambda T$

where $\qquad \lambda T \ll 1$

and λ is the mean failure rate and T is some mean outage time, both
being parameters of negative exponential distributions (T is used
variously to represent mean diagnose time, mean repair time, etc).
Also it was found possible to limit the calculations to a single
component faulty at any instant of time within each user service. A
state transition model was derived for each user service, and some of
these models will be developed in the next section of the paper.
More complete information can be found in reference 1. For
the central view of the system a computer simulation program was used,
PADS (Plant Availability Distribution Synthesis), the derivation of
data from figure 3 for this program and the results obtained are given
in the third section of the paper.

COMPONENT	MTTF HOURS	$\lambda = \dfrac{1}{MTTF}$	DIAG/ RECON HOURS	REPAIR HOURS	RECON HOURS
CP	750	1.3×10^{-3}	0.5	6	0.5
MODEM	22000	4.6×10^{-5}	0.5	8	0.25
MPX	10000	10^{-4}	0.5	8	0.5
PO SITE A	1000	10^{-3}	0.75	12	0.25
SITE G	1000	10^{-3}	0.75	12	0.25
SITE B	2000	5×10^{-4}	0.75	12	0.25
SITE C, D	4000	2.5×10^{-4}	0.75	12	0.25
SITE E	4000	2.5×10^{-4}	0.75	12	0.25
SITE F	4000	2.5×10^{-4}	0.75	12	0.25
PORT SWITCH	100000	10^{-5}	0.5	12	0.5

FIG 3

Table of user derived data used in the
Availability Analysis

THE USER VIEW OF THE COMMUNICATIONS SYSTEM

Each user on the computer system "sees" only a small part of the
overall system in both practical and availability senses. A site B
user is not directly concerned if a site G user has lost a service.
However, the loss of a service to another site might possibly improve
the service to all the remaining users by reducing service overheads
and job queue lengths. Primarily for the purpose of this analysis it
is assumed that whatever happens to all the other site services, the
communications network service to the site of interest will not be
directly affected. This does not exclude the probability that
services to several sites might be lost at the same time due to a
single common event, for example a fault in a Communications Processor.
However, when this type of event has been included in the analysis for
a site, it means that all events on other sites are of no further concern.

The analysis is based on events, and an event will lead to a
change of state of the user service. For example, if a central site
modem were to fail then the spare modem could, and would, be switched
in and the full service restored after the diagnosis time. When the
repair to the faulty modem is complete then the system would be
returned to its normal configuration during a reconfigure time. This
event sequence is represented in figure 4, and forms the minimal outage
sequence. Two further basic event sequences need to be developed and

these are given in figure 5 which represents the substitution of a
smaller service for the regular service whilst repair is completed.
This affects availability in the same way as the full standby service
but will result in a lower throughput for that service. The final
sequence is the no-standby service given in figure 6. Here the service is unavailable for the whole of the diagnose and repair times,
but no reconfigure time is necessary since the service can be restore
to the user as soon as the repair is completed.

    These three basic event sequences and state transition diagrams
are sufficient for daytime working, but the added factor of waiting
time needs to be included to each of the basic diagrams and these are
shown in figs 7-9.

    Using the six state transition models thus developed, and pro-
ducing a list of the models which can apply to each service, it is
now possible to assign availability to particular features of that
service.

    In later tables and diagrams an abbreviated nomenclature will be
used to describe the state diagrams. The initiating event will be
indicated by a downward pointing triangle, thus

Modem ∇

will indicate a modem going faulty. To this will be appended the
service transitions which immediately follow that event, thus

Modem ∇ H-O-H

will indicate that before the transition a (H) high speed service was
being provided, the event causes a total (O) loss of this service,
which is restored by a full standby situation (H) following diagnosis.
This service will remain until the faulty modem is repaired when there
will be an event

Modem ΔH-O-H

which indicates the modem has been repaired, before reinstating the
modem a High Speed service was being provided (H), then during a
reconfiguration time no service is provided (O), then the normal
high speed service is restored.

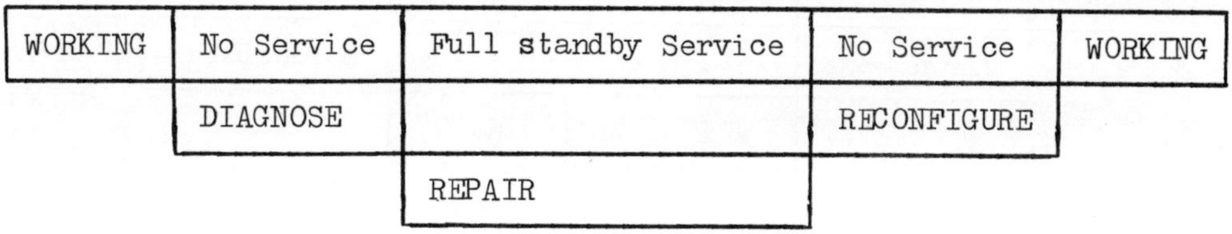

WORKING	No Service	Full standby Service	No Service	WORKING
	DIAGNOSE		RECONFIGURE	
		REPAIR		

Fig 4

Full standby service, no waiting time penalty

WORKING	No Service	Alternative Service	No Service	WORKING
	DIAGNOSE		RECONFIGURE	
		REPAIR		

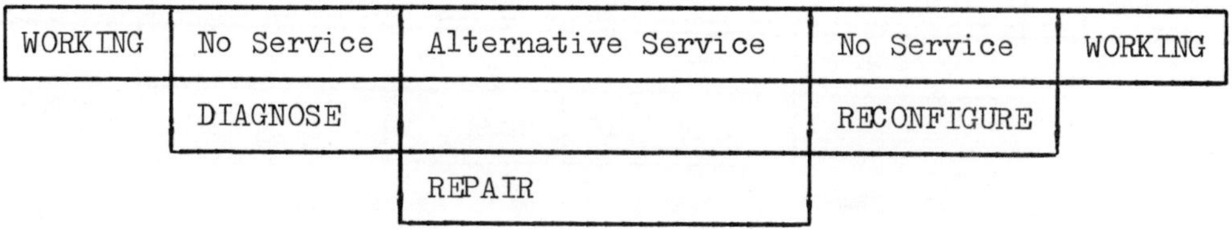

Fig 5

Alternative standby service, no waiting time penalty

WORKING		No Service		WORKING
	DIAGNOSE			
		REPAIR		

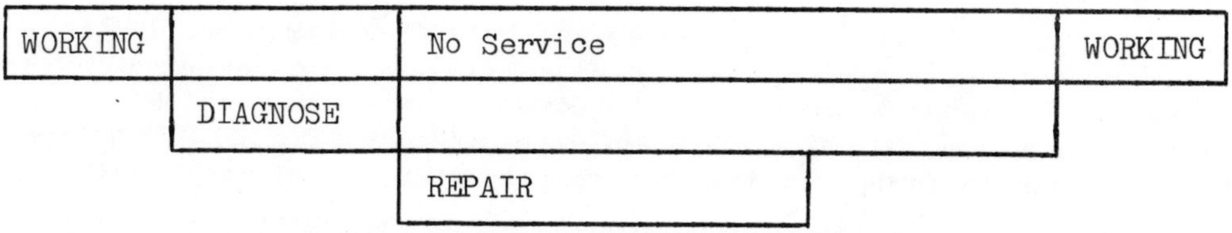

Fig 6

No standby service, no waiting time penalty

WORKING	No Service	Full Standby Service	No Service	WORKING
	DIAGNOSE		RECONFIGURE	
		WAIT TIME | REPAIR		

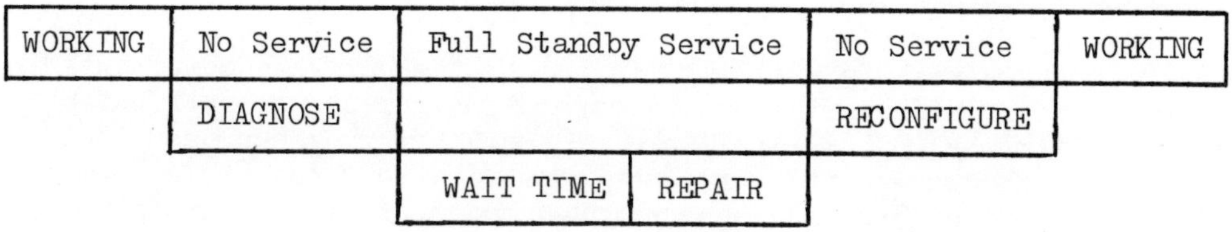

Fig 7

Full standby service with waiting time penalty

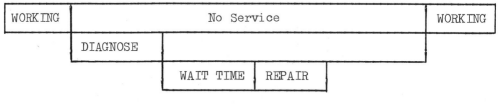

WORKING	No Service	Alternative Service	No Service	WORKING
	DIAGNOSE		RECONFIGURE	
		WAIT TIME	REPAIR		

Fig 8

Alternative standby service with waiting time penalty

WORKING	No Service		WORKING
	DIAGNOSE		
	WAIT TIME	REPAIR	

Fig 9

No standby service with waiting time penalty

To take a particular example, sites C, D and E have identical communications equipment and are classified as below average failure rate for telephone circuits. The normal service to these sites is given in figure 10 which has been extracted from figure 2. However, during single fault periods, the operating rules and equipment redundancies make it possible to arrange for different levels of alternative service. For example the normal low speed multiplexed service is for 7 terminals, using the switching features at the central site, and with the co-operation of the local operators this service may be changed to 6, or 3 or zero terminals for certain faults. Thus the redundant features of the communications system allow for a degree of graceful degradation.

The analysis is strictly limited to the hardware components in the network, and apart from the "operating rules" no contribution to outage time by computer software or operator error has been included. Also the hardware covers only the communications network equipment, from Communications Processor through modem, telephone lines and modem, but specifically excludes any terminal equipment on the user site. Of course, faults in any of these excluded areas will degrade the availability of the system as perceived by a user.

Figure 11 lists the events which might affect the high speed service to one of the sites in this example. The abbreviated form of

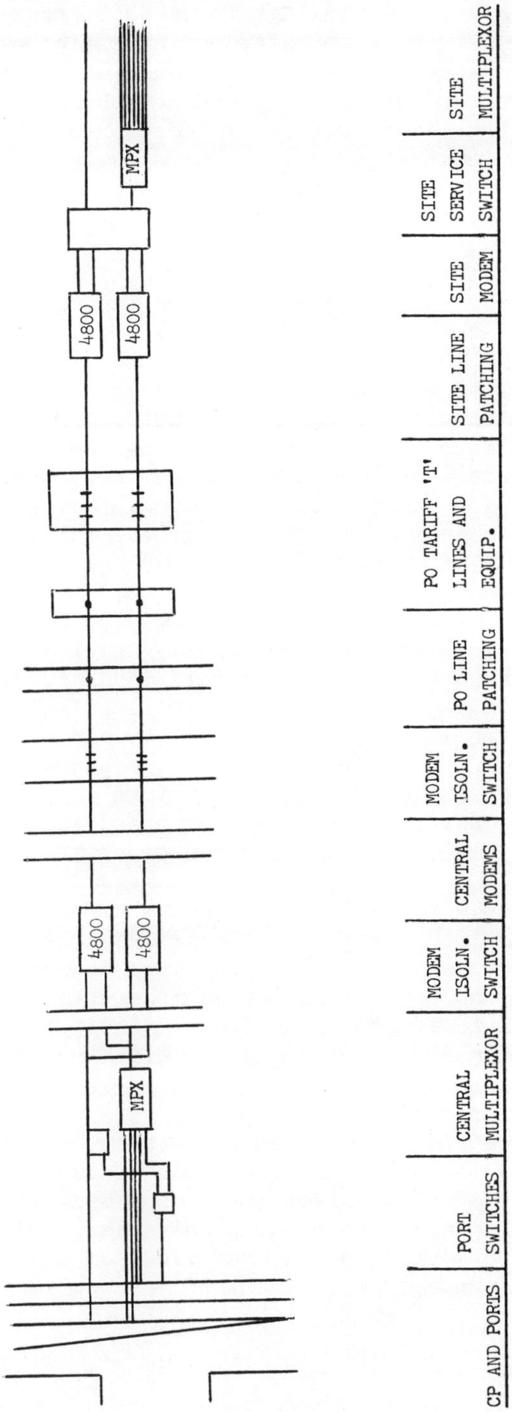
MPX
4800
4800
4800
4800
MPX
CP AND PORTS
PORT SWITCHES
CENTRAL MULTIPLEXOR
MODEM ISOLN. SWITCH
CENTRAL MODEMS
MODEM ISOLN. SWITCH
PO LINE PATCHING
PO TARIFF 'T' LINES AND EQUIP.
SITE LINE PATCHING
SITE MODEM
SITE SERVICE SWITCH
SITE MULTIPLEXOR

Fig 10
NORMAL SERVICES TO SITES C, D AND E

service transition is used. Note that for events occurring at the
central location the switching and standby facilities give good
coverage for the high speed service. For equipment faults outside
the control of the central operators, then some high speed service
can be provided with the co-operation of the remote site operators,
but this may be at a reduced (L) rate. During silent hours and at
weekends a wait time (W) will be incurred if the remote site operator is not available to carry out switching.

By using the service transitions it is possible to calculate
the availability of the various services from the data presented
earlier in fig 3, and this is done in fig 12. Here the daytime
service has been spiit into a "some service" and "low rate service"
columns. Because of the working rules of the system, and the
assumption that repairs will be completed inside a Daytime period,
then any low rate working can only occur during daytime. Since each
of these events is independent of the other events, the Availabilities
may be combined by the product rule to produce an overall service
availability. This is done at the bottom of the table.

For daytime these figures can be interpreted as in fig 13 to
obtain a full rate service availability of 0.9840, no service probability of .0024, and low rate service 0.013. Combining the daytime,
silent hours and weekend availabilities this leads to a 0.992
throughput figure on a yearly basis, with availabilities as given in
figure 14.

Similar tables of service state transitions and calculations of
availability can be constructed for the low speed services, and full
details of these and all other services can be obtained in reference
1.

Figure 15 gives the results of the analysis for low speed terminal services and again demonstrates the gradual reduction in service which can be achieved with the degree of redundancy and flexibility of switching incorporated in the communications network. The
very low contribution to availability from 6 lines as compared to 7
lines shows the low dependency on the port switching equipment.

The general features of the results for all services were in the
same direction of high availability of prime service, with reduced
services being available during those periods of equipment fault
which prevented full service. Also, throughput measured on a yearly
basis was high. These calculations were sufficient validation of the
basic design of the network from the user view for the customer to
continue with the design and procurement of the equipment.

Events	Daytime	Silent Hours	Weekend
CP1 ▽	H-O-H	H-O-H	H-O-H
CP1 △	H-O-H	H-O-H	H-O-H
PS1 ▽	H-O	H-O	H-O
PS1 △	O-H	O-H	O-H
C Modem 1▽	H-O-H	H-O-H	H-O-H
C Modem 1△	H-O-H	H-O-H	H-O-H
C Modem 2▽	H-H-H	H-H-H	H-H-H
C Modem 2△	H-H-H	H-H-H	H-H-H
PO1 ▽	H-O-L	H-O-W-L	H-O-W-L
PO1 △	L-O-H	L-O-H	L-O-H
Modem 1▽	H-O-L	H-O-W-L	H-O-W-L
Modem 1△	L-O-H	L-O-H	L-O-H
Modem 2▽	H-H-L	–	–
Modem 2△	L-L-H	–	–
PO2 ▽	H-H-L	–	–
PO2 △	L-L-H	–	–

Fig 11

Service transitions for sites C, D, E high speed
services — User view

	Daytime		Silent Hours	Weekend
	Some Service	Low Rate		
CP1 ▽	0.9993	–	0.9993	0.9993
CP1 △	0.9993	–	0.9993	0.9993
PS1 ▽	0.9999	–	0.9999	0.9999
PS1 △	–	–	–	–
C Modem 1▽	–	–	–	–
C Modem 1△	–	–	–	–
C Modem 2▽	–	–	–	–
C Modem 2△	–	–	–	–
PO1 ▽	0.9992	0.9970^3	0.9980	0.9921
PO1 △	0.9999	–	–	–
Modem 1▽	–	0.9996^3	0.9996	0.9986
Modem 1△	–	–	–	–
Modem 2▽	–	0.9996	–	–
Modem 2△	–	–	–	–
PO2 ▽	–	0.9970	–	–
PO2 △	–	0.9999	–	–
π gives	0.9976	0.9864	0.9961	0.9892

Fig 12

Availabilities calculated for sites C, D, E high speed
services – User view

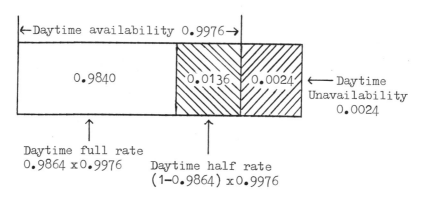

Fig 13

Apportionment of daytime availabilities

	Availability				Throughput
	Daytime	Silent Houts	Weekend	Yearly	
No Service	0.0024	0.0029	0.0108	0.0060	)
Low rate service	0.0136	−	−	0.0040	) 0.9920
Full rate service	0.9840	0.9961	0.9892	0.9892	)

Fig 14

Availability and throughput results for sites C, D, E
high speed service — User view

	Availability				Throughput
	Daytime	Silent Hours	Weekend	Year	
No service	0.0027	0.0079	0.0311	0.0140	)
3 lines	0.0185	0.0320	0.0955	0.0520	) 0.9560
6 lines	0.0001	0.0001	0.0001	−	)
7 lines	0.9787	0.9600	0.8733	0.9340	)

Fig 15

Availability and throughput results for sites C, D, E
low speed service — User view

Component	No in System	Mean time out hours	Failure Rate per hour
CP	2	7	1.33×10^{-3}
Central Modem	18	0.5	4.6×10^{-5}
Site Modem	16	20.7	4.6×10^{-5}
Multiplexer	10	15.9	10^{-4}
PO site A, G	5	26.3	10^{-3}
PO site B	3	26.3	5×10^{-4}
PO other sites	8	26.3	2.5×10^{-4}
PS	15	13.0	10^{-5}

Fig 16

Data for simulation model of system — Central view

THE CENTRAL VIEW OF THE SYSTEM

The calculation and analysis methods chosen for the user view
were not suitable for the analysis of the complete system. The prime
reason being the large number of common areas of equipment to be
accounted for. Other methods could have been used, but the time and
cost restraints placed on the work precluded Reliability Network,
Fault Tree or Full Simulation techniques. However, a computer program
PADS (Plant Availability Distribution Synthesis) was available which
could in certain circumstances be applied to a problem of this nature,
reference 2. An analytic model based on the PADS algorithms has been
proposed by Platz in reference 4.

PADS is a simulation programme that will represent a series or
logical 'and' reliability network. That is, a network where any one
component failing will cause the whole system to fail. The programme
calculates the probabilistic distribution of availability for the
system given an exponential distribution for time to failure and a
repair distribution chosen from normal, lognormal, exponential,
weibull, or rectangular distributions. The problem in using PADS for
this view of the system was to obtain an interpretation of the
availability distribution.

If the communications network was to be seen as a maintenance

problem, then any component going faulty would require some maintenance effort to be used in restoring the system to its full working
condition. In this way the complete communications network can be
seen to be a logical 'and' type of network, and the distribution of
availability obtained from a PADS run using suitable data would be a
measure of the probability that something somewhere in the communications system would be faulty for a certain proportion of time.
Using PADS in this way gave the computer operators some idea of the
amount of work involved in providing the highly available service to
the remote users.

To be able to use PADS, some modification to the basic user data
in fig 3 was required, and fig 16 shows the data used in the computer
run.

Mean time out was calculated in the following way

$$\text{Mean time out} = \text{Daytime outage} \times \frac{\text{Daytime hours in year}}{8760}$$

$$+ \left[\text{Weekend hours outage} + \text{Daytime low rate hour} \times \frac{\text{Low Rate}}{\text{Full Rate}} \right]$$

$$* \frac{\text{Weekend hours in year}}{8760}$$

$$+ \left[\text{Silent hours outage} + \text{Daytime low rate hours} \times \frac{\text{Low Rate}}{\text{Full Rate}} \right]$$

$$* \frac{\text{Silent hours in year}}{8760}$$

which includes allowances for outages weighted to proportions of daytime, silent hours and weekend hours in a year, and those outages on
which repair work cannot start until the next daytime period weighted
by the time period which caused the daytime repair work. A negative
exponential repair distribution was assumed with a repair rate based
on the reciprocal of the mean time out as calculated for each system
component.

The PADS simulation was run 1000 times for a system full life of
10 years, but looking at the distribution of availability on a yearly
basis. The resulting distribution is given in fig 17. Here it can be
seen that the mean unavailability to be expected is 0.22 on a yearly
basis. Taking the symmetric 0.9 probability levels, it can be seen
that unavailability can be expected to lie between 0.18 and 0.27, and
there is a possibility that unavailability could exceed 0.30.

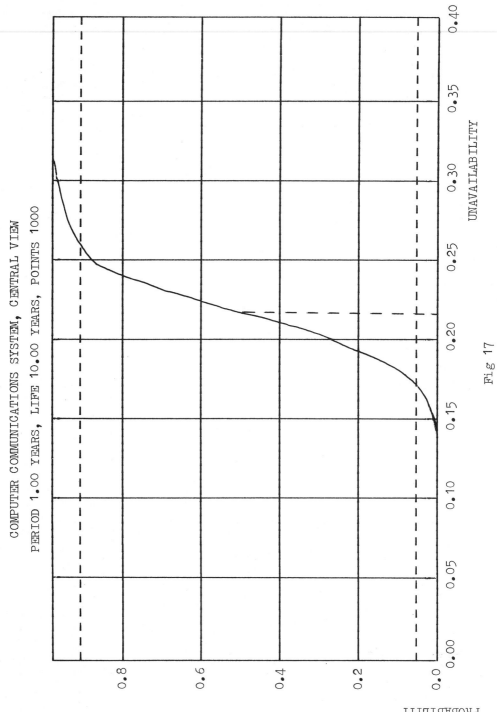

COMPUTER COMMUNICATIONS SYSTEM, CENTRAL VIEW

PERIOD 1.00 YEARS, LIFE 10.00 YEARS, POINTS 1000

Fig 17

This analysis provided the customer with the second justification for the design of the communications system. With a system of that size the management of signal connections, equipment location and repair and maintenance access becomes such that positive design decisions need to be taken. From this work the customer was able to quantify some of his suspicions and to justify the design and manufacture of a centrally located operators control console to control the interconnection and fault diagnosis of the communications equipment.

CONCLUSIONS

This paper is based on an assessment carried out for a customer of the National Centre of Systems Reliability. The project cost and duration were strictly limited, and the needs of the customer imprecisely defined. The choice of two entirely separate analysis techniques was based on the interpretation of the customer's needs, together with an estimate of the degree of accuracy really necessary or possible in this type of work.

The state transition models and the techniques developed within the project timescale for this particular application will have uses elsewhere, and the calculation of availability using short cut techniques is a fairly widely established practice where the degree of sophistication only calls for manual one-off calculation. The massaging of system logic to allow specialised computer programs to be used is not new, however it is important to obtain the right interpretation of the computer output in relation to the changed system logic.

The provision of redundancy both on-line and in standby mode has a price. If the justification for the redundancy is in providing a high level of availability in a user orientated service environment, then the cost of providing such a service will be borne by the customers. It is desirable that simple techniques should be available for the supplier, and also for the customer, to allow each to judge the relative merits of particular designs. It is preferable that this should be done in quantified terms.

REFERENCES

1. NCSR 15 "Analysis of the Availability of a Computer System Communications Network", B K Daniels (available from National Centry of Systems Reliability, Wigshaw Lane, Culcheth, Warrington WA3 4NE, UK).
2. "PADS User Guide", B K Daniels (available as in 1).
3. Reliability Technology. A E Green, A J Bourne, Wiley, London, 1972.
4. Methods for calculating down time distributions. O Platz, National Rel Conf, September 1977, Nottingham, UK.

ORGANIZING COMMITTEE

L. Caldarola
Kernforschungszentrum Karlsruhe
Karlsruhe, Germany

Mme. A. Carnino
Centre d'Etudes Nucléaires, Saclay
91190 GIF s/Yvette, France

J. Fussell
University of Tennessee
Knoxville, Tennessee, U.S.A.

Eric Green
System Reliability Service
UKAEA-Culcheth, U.K.

Arthur Liewlyn
Computer Aided Design Centre
Cambridge, U.K.

J. Lynn
University of Liverpool
Liverpool, U.K.

R. Taylor
RISO
Rotskilde, Denmark

W. Vinck
CEC
Brussels, Belgium

LIST OF PARTICIPANTS

Anibal Traga Almeida
University of Coimbra, Coimbra
Portugal

A. Amendola
CEC, Joint Research Centre
21020 Ispra (Va), Italy

P. Andow
Chem. Eng. Dept.
Loughboro University, Loughboro
Leichestshire, U.K.

G. Apostolakis
University of California
5532 Boelter Hall
Los Angeles CA 90024, USA

M. Astolfi
CEC, Joint Research Centre
Ispra (Va), Italy

A. Bottomley
School of Social Sciences
University of Bradford
Bradford 7 W. Yorks, U.K.

L. Caldarola
IRE, Kernforschungszentrum
Karlsruhe
7500 Karlsruhe, Germany

Jerome L. Caldwell
2067 Burus Ave
St. Paul, MN 55119, U.S.A.

R. Castello
Università di Genova
Viale F. Gausa 13
Genova, Italy

C. Clarotti
CNEN, C.S.N.
Casaccia, S.P. Anguillarese
Roma, Italy

A.G. Colombo
CEC, Joint Research Centre
Ispra Establishment
21020 Ispra (Va), Italy

S. Contini
SIGEN
Viale Europa 46
Cologno Monzese (Mi), Italy

B.K. Daniels
NCRS UKAEA
Wigshaw Lane, Culcheth,
Warrington, WA3 7JR, England

Elio De Agostino
CNEN
Casaccia S.P. Anguillarese
Roma, Italy

Bernard Duchemin
Serma/Lep. CEN/Saclay
B.P. 2, 91190 Gif sur Yvette, France

Kent Ekberg
Swedish State Power Board
Jamtlandsgatan 99
S - 16287 Vallingby, Sweden

Ralph A. Evans,
Product Assurance Consultant
804 Vickers Avenue
Durham, North Carolina 17701, USA

Gunnar Fredrikson
Central Institute for Ind. Research
Postbok 350, Bunder, Oslo 3, Norway

Sergio Famagalli
Corso Garibaldi 72
20030 Seveso, Italy

J. Fussel
University of Tennessee
Knoxville, Tennessee 37916, USA

S. Garribba
CESNEF - Politecnico di Milano
Via G. Ponzio 34/3, 20133 Milano, Italy

Torkell Gjerstad
SINTEF
Avd. 18, 7034 Trondheim - NTH
Norway

Steen Krenk
RISO National Laboratory
4000 Roskilde, Denmark

Bernd Krogull
Supreme Headquarters Allied Powers
Europe - Technical Centre
P.O.Box 174, The Hague, Netherlands

Vinod Kumar
Ecole Nationale Sup. des Télécommuni-
cations B - 222
46 Rue Barrault, 75634 Paris, France

Howard Lambert
TERA Corp.
Berkeley, CA, 94704
USA

Marie Langeveld
Shell Research N.V.
P.O.Box 3003, Amsterdam,
Netherlands

F.P. Lees
University of Technology
Loughboro, Leichestshire LE 11 3 TU
England

F. Lomazzi
AGIP Nucleare
Corso di Porta Romana 68
20100 Milano, Italy

Jose Carlos Lopes
Centre Engenhara Quimici
Facoltade de Engenhara
Oporto, Portugal

Enrico Guagnini
Via Orelli 4
20035 Lissone (Mi), Italy

Erik Heldor
DET Norske Veritas
P.O.Box 300 N-1322 Hovik, Norway

E.J. Henley
College of Engineering
University of Houston
Houston, Texas 77004, USA

T. Inagaki
Kyoto Universit
Dept. of Precision Mechanics
Kyoto 606, Japan

O. Jakobsen
RISO National Laboratory
4000 Roskilde, Denmark

P.K. Jensen
Technical University of Denmark
2800 Lyngby, Denmark

T. Johanssen
Dept. of Electrophysics
Technical University of Denmark
DK 2800 Lyngby, Denmark

H. Kalli
Serma/Lep CEN/Saclay
B.P. 2, 91190 Gif sur Yvette, France

Bernard Magnon
NERSA
177 Rue Garibaldi
Lyon, France

G. Mancini
CEC, Joint Research Centre
Ispra Establishment
21020 Ispra (Va), Italy

Myron J. Miller
Factory Mutual Research
1151 Boston Providence
Turnpike Norwood
Massachusetts 02062, USA

P. Mussio
C.N.R., Laboratorio di Fisica
Cosmica e Tecnologie Relative
Via Celoria 16, 20133 Milano, Italy

F. Naldi
C.N.R., laboratorio di Fisica
Cosmica e Tecnologie Relative
Via Celoria 16, 20133 Milano, Italy

D. Nudds
School of Social Sciences
University of Bradford
Bradford 7 X. Yorks. , U.K.

L. Olivi
CEC, Joint Research Centre
Ispra Establishment
21020 Ispra (Va), Italy

G.W. Parry
UKAEA SDR
Wigsham Lane, Culcheth
Warrington, WA3 4NE, U.K.

Lloyd Philipson
Institute Safety & Systems Mgt.
University of Southern California
Los Angeles, CA 90403, USA

André Poucet
Katholieke Universiteit Leuven
Dept. Metaalkunde de Croylaan
3030 Helverlee, Belgium

H. Procaccia
E.D.F.
25 Allée Privée Carrefour Pleyel
93206 Saint Denis Cedex, France

Jen Rassmussen
RISO National Laboratory
4000 Roskilde, Denmark

G. Reina
Dept. of Biomathematics
Inst. of Pharmacology
University of Milan
Via Vanvitelli 32, Milano, Italy

George Rzevski
Kingston Polytechnic
School of Electrical & Electronics Eng.
Penrhyn Road, Kingston upon Thames
Surrey, KT 12 EE, England

Jean Signoret
CEN
Fontenay aux Roses, B.P. 6
92260 Fontenay aux Roses, France

R. Somma
Selenia S.p.A.
Via Tiburtina, 00131 Roma, Italy

G. Squellati
ARS
Viale Majno 35, 20122 Milano, Italy

Berg Steinar
Sintef
N - 7031 Trondheim NTH, Norway

Robert Taylor
RISO National Laboratory
4000 Roskilde, Denmark

Haward Toresen
DET Norske Veritas
P.O.Box 300
N-1322 Hovik, Norway

Odd Tveit
DET Norske Veritas
P.O.Box 300
N-1322 Hovik, Norway

Alain Villemeur
E.D.F.
1 Av. du Général de Gaulle
92141 Clamart Cedex, France

G. Volta
CEC, Joint Reserach Centre
Ispra Establishment
21020 Ispra (Va), Italy

M. Weber
Nuken G.m.b.H.
P.O.B. 110080, Dr 6450
Hanau 11, Germany

Heinz Wenzelburger
I.R.E.
Kernforschungszentrum
Postfach 3640
D - 7500 Karlsruhe, Germany

Paul Morten Wiencke
DET Norske Veritas
P.O.Box 300
N - 1322 Hovik, Norway

Eva Windebank
British Gas Corporation
London Research Station
Michael Road, London SW6 2AD
England

E.M.W. Windridge
Dep. of Nuclear Science & Techno-
logy, Royal Navy College
Greenwich, London SET 0, U.K.

Lars Wrendenberg
Swedish State Power Board
Jamtlandsgatan 99
S - 16287 Vallingby, Sweden